Ford Cortina III Owners Workshop Manual

by J H Haynes
Member of the Guild of Motoring Writers

P G Strasman
and B L Chalmers-Hunt
TEng (CEI), AMIMI, AMIRTE, AMVBRA

Models covered

Covers all models fitted with 1298 cc and 1599 cc
ohv engine. Manual and automatic.

ISBN 0 900550 70 8

HAYNES PUBLISHING GROUP
SPARKFORD YEOVIL SOMERS
distributed in the USA by
HAYNES PUBLICATIONS INC
861 LAWRENCE DRIVE
NEWBURY PARK
CALIFORNIA 91320
USA

D1349100

Acknowledgments

Thanks are due to the Ford Motor Company for their permission to reproduce certain illustrations and for their supply of technical information. Castrol Limited supplied lubrication details and the Champion Sparking Plug Company supplied the illustrations showing the various spark plug conditions. The bodywork repair photographs used in this manual were provided by Lloyds Industries Limited who supply 'Turtle Wax', 'Dupli-color Holts', and other Holts range products.

Lastly, thanks are due to all of those people at Sparkford who assisted in the production of this manual, particularly Stanley Randolph, Trevor Hosie, Ian Robson and John Rose.

About this manual

Its aims

This is a manual by a practical owner/maintainer for practical owner/maintainers. The author, and those assisting him, learned about this range of models the only thorough way, by studying all available information and then going ahead and doing the work, under typical domestic conditions and with a typical range of tools, backed only by their experience as keen car men over a number of years.

Unlike other books of this nature, therefore, the hands in most of the photographs are those of the author, and the instructions cover every step in full detail, assuming no special knowledge on the part of the reader except how to use tools and equipment in a proper manner, firmly and positively but with due respect for precise control where this is required.

Its arrangement

The manual is divided into thirteen chapters. The chapters are each divided into sections, numbered with single figures, e.g. 5; and the sections into paragraphs (or sub-sections), with decimal numbers following on from the section they are in, e.g. 5.1, 5.2, 5.3, etc.

It is freely illustrated, especially in those parts where there is a detailed sequence of operations to be carried out. There are two forms of illustration: figures and photographs. The figures are numbered in sequence with decimal numbers, according to their position in the Chapter: e.g. 6.4 is the 4th drawing/illustration in Chapter 6. Photographs are numbered (either individually or in related groups) the same as the Section or sub-section of the text where the operation they show is described.

There is an alphabetical index at the back of the manual as well as a content list at the front.

Reference to the 'left' or 'right' of the vehicle are in the sense of a person in a seat facing fowards towards the engine.

Points for the reader

The accumulation of good tools normally must take place over a period of time and this is the one expense which the do-it-yourself owner must face. Cheap tools are never worth having, as they are not cheap in the long run. They rarely last, often make the work more difficult, and may even cause accidental damage which could cost more to put right than the cost of a good tool in the first place.

Certain jobs requiring special tools and where these are essential, the manual points this out. Otherwise, alternative methods are given.

Be discreet about borrowing tools; even with great care, accidents still happen, and the replacement of a lost or damaged tool can be costly. Do not be offended, if refused: the person approached may have had an unhappy experience already!

Where appropriate, fault finding instructions are given at the end of Chapters. Accurate diagnosis of troubles depends on a careful, and, above all, systematic approach, so avoid the attitude "if all else fails, read the handbook." It is better, and almost always quicker, to say: "This could be one of several things, so let's have a look at the Haynes manual before trying anything."

Modifications

The policy of the manufacturer of these vehicles is one of continuous development, and designs and specifications are frequently being changed as a result. It follows naturally that spares may sometimes be purchased which differ both from the original part removed and from the part referred to in this manual. However, suppliers of genuine Ford spare parts can usually settle queries about interchangeability by reference to the latest information issued by the manufacturer. (Read the section **Ordering Spare Parts**).

Every care has been taken to ensure the accuracy of this manual but no liability can be accepted by the authors and publishers for any loss, damage or injury caused by any errors in or omissions from the information given.

MARK THREE CORTINA 1600 XL

MARK THREE CORTINA 1600 ESTATE

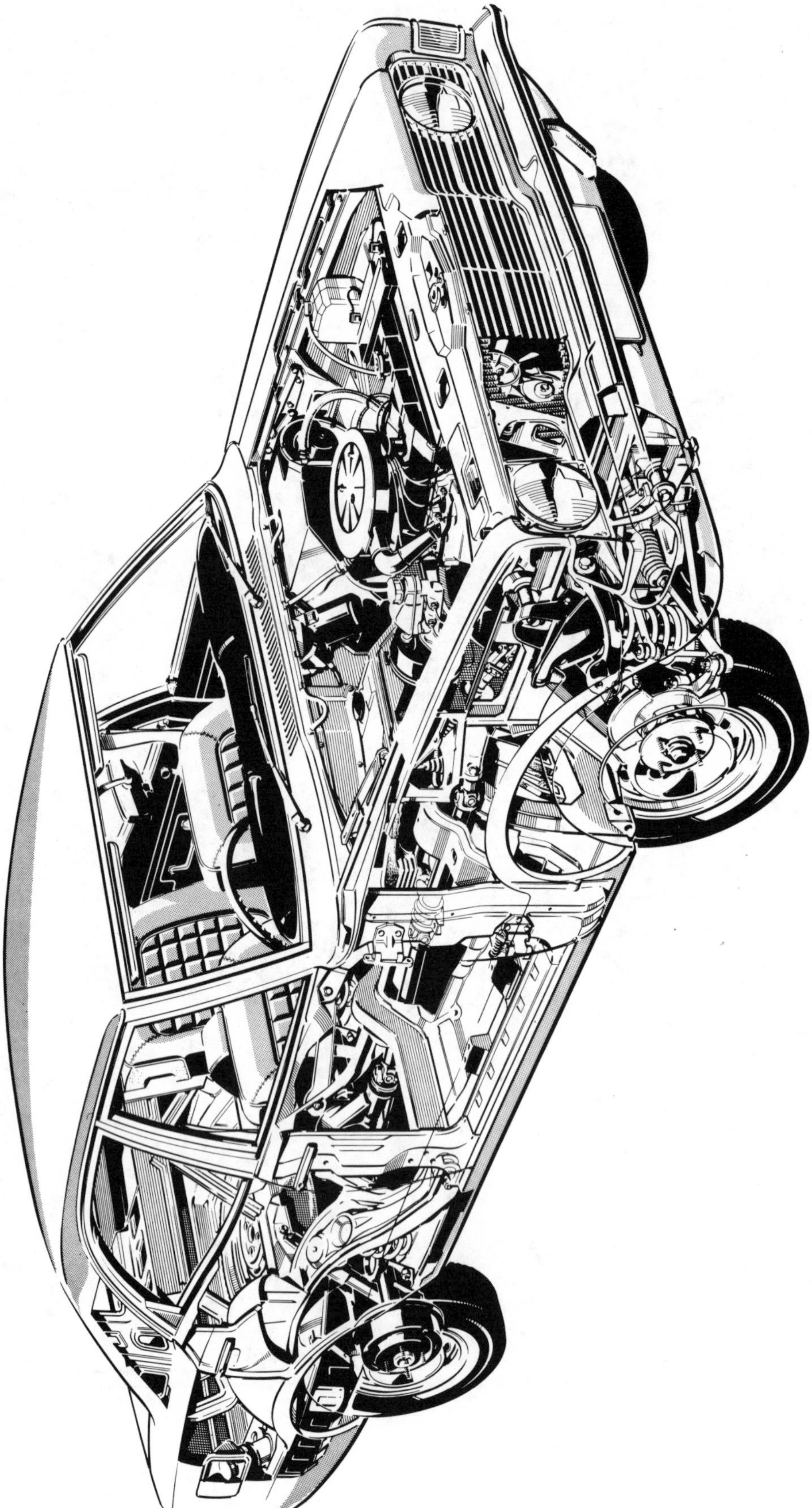

Contents

Routine maintenance

The maintenance instructions listed are basically those recommended by the manufacturer. They are supplemented by additional maintenance tasks proven to be necessary.

The additional tasks are indicated by an asterisk and are primarily of a preventative nature in that they will assist in eliminating the unexpected failure of a component due to fair wear and tear.

Fig 1 Brake master cylinder reservoir

Weekly, before a long journey or every 250 miles (400 Km)

1 Remove the dipstick and check the engine oil level which should be up to the MAX mark. Top up with Castrol GTX. On no account allow the oil to fall below the MIN mark on the dipstick.

2 Check the tyre pressures with an accurate gauge and adjust as necessary. Make sure that the tyre walls and treads are free of damage. Remember that the tyre tread should have a minimum of 1 millimetre depth across three quarters of the total tread width.

3 Check the battery electrolyte level and top up as necessary with distilled water. Make sure that the top of the battery is always kept clean and free of moisture.

4 Refill the windscreen washer bottle with soft water. Add a special anti-freeze satchet or methylated spirits in cold weather to prevent freezing (Do not use ordinary anti-freeze). Check that the jets operate correctly.

5 Remove the wheel trims and check all wheel nuts for tightness but take care not to overtighten.

Every 3000 miles (5000 km) or 3 months

Complete the service items in the weekly service check plus:

1 Check the level of coolant in the engine cooling system when cold. Remove the radiator pressure cap and check the level of coolant which should be 0.5 inch (12.7 mm) below the filler orifice. Overfilling will merely result in wastage. In winter an anti-freeze solution must be used.

2 Wipe the top of the brake master cylinder reservoir, unscrew the cap and top up with Castrol Girling Brake Fluid as necessary. Take care not to spill any hydraulic fluid on the paintwork as it acts as a solvent (See Fig 1).

3 Run the engine until it is hot and then place a container of 8 pints (4.55 litres) under the engine sump drain plug. Unscrew and remove the drain plug and allow the oil to drain out for 10 minutes. Whilst this is being done change the oil filter as described in the next service operation. Clean the oil filter cap in petrol and shake dry. Refill the engine with 6.25 pints (3.5 litres) of Castrol GTX and clean off any oil which may have been spilt over the engine or its components. Run the engine and check the oil level. The interval between oil changes should be reduced in very hot or dusty conditions or during cool weather with much slow or stop start driving.

4 Unscrew the oil filter canister and discard it. Wipe the area around the filter location on the side of the cylinder block. Smear a little engine oil on the rubber 'O' ring located on the face of the new oil filter canister and screw on until it is hand tight. Do not overtighten. (See Fig 2).

5 Remove the spark plugs and inspect and clean them as described in Chapter 4.

6 Clean and adjust the distributor contact breaker points as

Fig 2 Engine oil filter
Arrow shoes direction of rotation for refitting

Fig 3 Emission control valve components

described in chapter 4.

7 Spring back the two clips and remove the distributor cap. Lift off the rotor arm. Apply a few drops of thin oil to the felt pad in the centre of the cam spindle and on the moving contact breaker pivot. Apply a smear of grease to the cam surface. Remove any excess oil or grease with a clean rag. Apply a few drops of oil through the hole in the contact breaker base plate to lubricate the automatic timing control.

8 Check the ignition timing as described in Chapter 4. Wipe the distributor cap HT leads and top of the coil with a clean rag to remove traces of dust or oil.

9 Refer to Chapter 3 and check the carburettor idling and mixture settings.

10 Detach the emission control valve hose located at the rear of the carburettor and pull the valve out of its grommet. Dismantle the valve by removing the circlip and withdrawing the valve seal, valve and spring from the valve body. Thoroughly wash the components in petrol to remove any sludge. Reassemble the valve and refit the circlip. Push the valve back into its grommet and reconnect the hose. (See Fig 3).

11 Refer to Chapter 1, check the valve clearances and adjust if necessary.

12 The fan belt adjustment must be tight enough to drive the dynamo or alternator without overloading the bearings, including the water pump bearings. The method of adjusting the fan belt is described in Chapter 2. It is considered to be correct when it can be pressed in 0.5 inch (13 mm) at the mid point between the dynamo or alternator and water pump pulleys. (See Fig 4)

13 Tighten the dynamo or alternator mountings to the correct torque wrench setting of 15 - 18 lb ft (2.07 - 2.49 kg m) and the mounting bracket to a torque wrench setting of 20 - 25 lb ft (2.76 - 3.46 kg m).

14 Refer to Chapter 10, and check the specific gravity of the electrolyte.

15 Wipe the top of the battery free of dust and moisture. Clean off any corrosion round battery terminals and clamps, and lightly smear such areas with a trace of petroleum jelly such as vaseline. Check earth connection is firm.

16 Generally inspect radiator and heater hoses for signs of perishing and if evident, fit new hoses. Check tightness of the hose clips.

17 Lubricate accelerator pedal pivot and linkage with a little Castrol GTX. Check for correct adjustment and if necessary adjust as described in Chapter 3.

18 Refer to Chapter 3 and clean the fuel pump filter.

19 Generally check the engine for signs of oil and water leaks and rectify as necessary.

20 Wipe the area around the manual gearbox combined filler and level plug. Undo and remove the plug and check the oil level which, when correct, should be up to the bottom of the threaded hole. Top up if necessary with Castrol Hypoy Light (See Fig 5).

21 Automatic transmission only: With the car on a level surface and the transmission unit at normal operating temperature, move the selector to the 'P' position and allow the engine to idle for two minutes. With the engine still idling in the 'P' position withdraw the dipstick, wipe it clean and replace it. Quickly withdraw it again and if necessary top up with Castrol TQF Automatic Transmission Fluid. The difference between the LOW and FULL marks on the dipstick is 1 pint (0.59 litres). (See Fig 6).

22 Wipe the area around the rear axle combined filler and level plug. Undo and remove the plug and check the oil level which, when correct, should be up to the bottom of the threaded hole. Top up if necessary with Castrol Hypoy. (See Fig 7).

23 Refer to Chapter 9 and check the thickness of the front disc brake pads and rear drum brake shoe linings. Make sure that the adjusting mechanism is functioning correctly. Remove traces of dust from each brake unit.

24 Generally check all brake lines and flexible hoses for signs of leaks. Also inspect the calipers and wheel cylinders for signs of leaks. Rectify as necessary.

25 Inspect the exhaust system for signs of blowing or excessive rusting. Replace defective components as necessary. Check tightness of exhaust manifold to downpipe securing bolts.

Fig 4 Fan belt adjustment

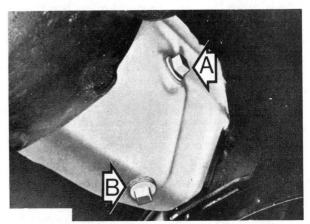

Fig 5 Manual gearbox:
A - filler and level plug
B - drain plug

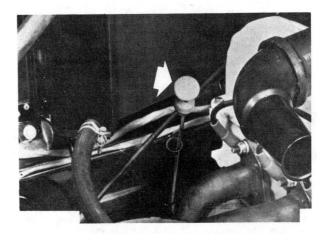

Fig 6 Automatic transmission oil level dipstick

26 Generally check all suspension and steering linkages for signs of wear. Rectify if necessary as described in Chapter 11.
27 Refer to Chapter 5 and check the clutch cable adjustment.
28 Check the operation of all controls, lights and instruments and rectify any fault found.
29 Lubricate all door locks, lock cylinders, bonnet safety catch pivot, door striker wedges, door check straps hinges and all other oil can points.
30 Refer to Chapter 9 and check the handbrake adjustment. Lubricate the handbrake linkage.
31 Check the seat belts for signs of wear and the fixing points for security.
32 Lubricate the dynamo rear bearing with a few drops of Castrol GTX.
33 Check the valve rocker clearances as described in Chapter 1 and adjust as necessary.

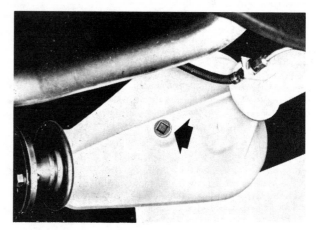

Fig 7 Rear axle combined filler and level plug

Every 12000 miles (20000 km) or 12 months

Complete the service items in the 3,000 mile service check plus:
1* Wash the bodywork and chromium fittings and clean out the interior of the car. Wax polish the bodywork including chromium and bright metal trim. Force wax polish into any joints in the bodywork to prevent rust formation.
2* Check all fuel lines and union joints for leaks. Rectify any leaks found.
3* Balance the wheels to eliminate any vibration, especially from the steering. This should be done at a Ford garage.
4* If it is wished, change over the tyres to equalise wear.
5* Lubricate the washer around the wiper spindles with several drops of glycerine. Fit new windscreen wiper blades.
6* Have the underside of the body steam cleaned and clean the engine and gearbox exterior as well as the whole of the front compartment.

Every 15,000 miles (25,000 km) or 15 months

Complete the service items in the 3000 miles service check plus:
1 Remove the air cleaner top cover and lift away the element. Wipe the inside of the container and fit a new element. (See Fig. 8).
2* Examine the hub bearings for wear and replace as necessary. Full information will be found in Chapter 11.
3* Check tightness of the battery earth lead on the bodywork.
4* Renew the condenser in the distributor, See Chapter 4.
5* Remove the starter motor, examine the brushes and replace as necessary. Clean the commutator and starter drive as described in Chapter 10.
6* Test the cylinder compressions, and if necessary remove the cylinder head, decarbonise, grind in the valves and fit new valve springs. Full information will be found in Chapter 1.
7 Lubricate the front suspension ball joints. Slacken the wheel nuts, jack up the front of the car and support on firmly based stands. Remove the wheel, withdraw the blanking plug from its location in the upper arm, and using a grease gun with a suitable pointed adaptor fill the joint with grease. Refit the blanking plug and wheel. (See Fig 9).
8* Remove the dynamo, examine the brushes and replace as necessary.

Every 39,000 miles (65,000 km) or 3 years

Completely drain the brake hydraulic fluid from the system. All seals and flexible hoses throughout the braking system should be examined and preferably renewed. The working surfaces of the master cylinder, wheel cylinders and caliper pistons should be inspected for signs of wear or scoring and new parts fitted as considered necessary. Refill the hydraulic system with Castrol Girling Brake Fluid.

Fig 8 Air cleaner element renewal

Fig 9 Front suspension balljoint lubrication

BODY IDENTIFICATION PLATE

VEHICLE IDENTIFICATION PLATE

Ordering spare parts

Buy genuine Ford or Motorcraft spare parts from a Ford dealer direct or through any garage. Ford authorised dealers carry a comprehensive stock of GENUINE PARTS and can supply most items 'over the counter'.

When ordering spare parts it is essential to give full details of your car to the storeman. He will want to know the commission, car, and engine numbers. When ordering parts for the gearbox, rear axle, or body, it is also necessary to quote the casing or body numbers. If you can take along the old part to be renewed as well, it is helpful. Modifications are a continuing and often unpublicised process in car manufacture, apart from all variations of model types. If a member of the Parts Department says he cannot guarantee that the part he supplies is correct because the

engine or vehicle number is not known, he is perfectly justified. (Variations can even occur from month to month).

The vehicle identification plate is mounted on the left hand side of the front body panel and may be seen once the bonnet is open.

When obtaining new parts remember that many assemblies can be exchanged. This is very much cheaper than buying them outright and throwing the old part away. Normally the Factory Exchange Unit Scheme covers practically every major assembly on any Ford car marketed in the last ten years.

Before handing back an item in exchange, always clean it to remove dirt and oil.

Recommended lubricants and fluids

COMPONENT	TYPE OF LUBRICANT OR FLUID	CASTROL PRODUCT
ENGINE SUMP	Multigrade engine oil	GTX
GEARBOX	SAE 80 EP	Castrol Hypoy Light
AUTOMATIC TRANSMISSION	Fluid meeting Ford specification M2C33F	Castrol TQF
REAR AXLE	SAE 90 EP	Castrol Hypoy
STEERING BOX	SAE 90 EP	Castrol Hypoy
FRONT WHEEL HUB BEARINGS	Lithium based grease	Castrol LM Grease
DISTRIBUTOR, STARTER & DYNAMO BUSHES	Light engine oil	GTX
DISTRIBUTOR CONTACT BREAKER CAM & BATTERY TERMINALS	Petroleum jelly	
HYDRAULIC PISTONS	Rubber grease	
BRAKE MECHANISMS (ADJUSTER CAM & SHOES TO BACKPLATES)	High melting point white grease	Castrol PH Grease
HYDRAULIC SYSTEM	Hydraulic fluid (SAEJ1703C) to Ford... specification ESEA-1001A	Castrol Girling Brake Fluid
ANTI-FREEZE	Fluid meeting Ford specification M97B18-C	Castrol Anti-freeze

Additionally Castrol Everyman oil can be used to lubricate door, boot and bonnet hinges, and locks, pivots, etc.

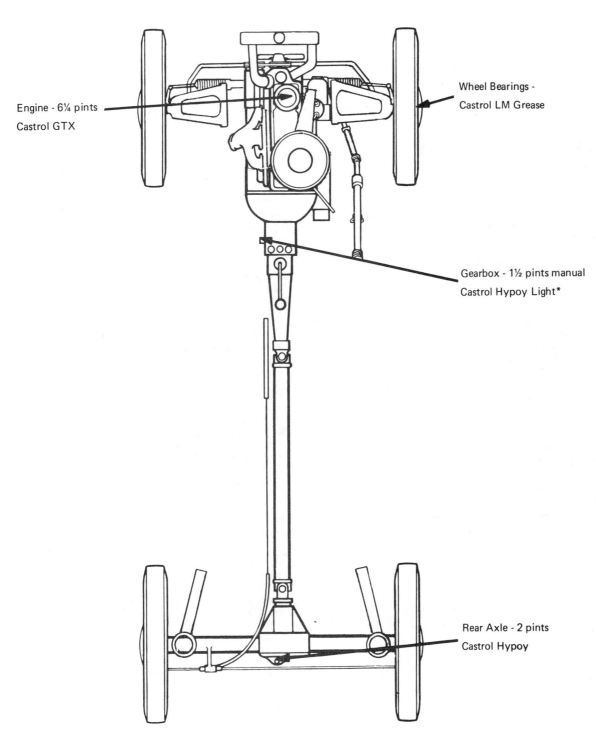

Engine - 6¼ pints
Castrol GTX

Wheel Bearings -
Castrol LM Grease

Gearbox - 1½ pints manual
Castrol Hypoy Light*

Rear Axle - 2 pints
Castrol Hypoy

* See Automatic gearbox section for automatic cars.

LUBRICATION CHART

Chapter 1 Engine

Contents

Specifications

Engine:

Identification symbol	1300 LC	JIA
	1300 HC	J2A
	1600 LC	L1A
	1600 HC	L2A
Bore (all models)	3.1882 in (80.98 mm)	
Stroke	(1300)	2.4799 in (62.99 mm)
	(1600)	3.0559 in (77.62 mm)
Cubic capacity	(1300)	1298 cc
	(1600)	1599 cc
Compression ratios	(1300)	8.0 : 1
	(1300) HC	9.0 : 1
	(1600) LC	8.0 : 1
	(1600) HC	9.0 : 1
Compression pressure at starter speed	(1300) LC	128 - 156 lb in^2
	(1300) HC	140 - 170 lb in^2
	(1600) LC	140 - 170 lb in^2
	(1600) HC	156 - 184 lb in^2
Firing order	1 - 2 - 4 - 3	
Idling speed	680/720 rev/min	
Maximum engine speed	(1300 cc)	5800
	(1600 cc)	5580

Engine hp (Din-ps)	(1300) LC 54
	(1300) HC 57
	(1600) LC 65
	(1600) HC 68
Number of main bearings	5

Cylinder block:

Cylinder bore dia grades (all models)	
Grade 0	3.1869 - 3.1872 in (80.947 - 80.955 mm)
Grade 1	3.1872 - 3.1875 in (80.955 - 80.962 mm)
Grade 2	3.1875 - 3.1877 in (80.962 - 80.970 mm)
Grade 3	3.1877 - 3.1881 in (80.970 - 80.978 mm)
Grade 4	3.1881 - 3.1884 in (80.978 - 80.985 mm)
Grade 5	3.1884 - 3.1887 in (80.985 - 80.993 mm)
Grade 6	3.1887 - 3.1890 in (80.993 - 81.001 mm)
Grade 7	3.1890 - 3.1893 in (81.001 - 81.008 mm)
Spigot bearing length	1.0560 - 1.0580 in (26.822 - 26.873 mm)
Main bearing liners fitted, vertical inner diameter	
Standard RED	2.1268 - 2.1281 in (54.021 - 54.054 mm)
BLUE	2.1269 - 2.1273 in (54.023 - 54.033 mm)
Undersize 0.254 mm (0.01 in)	2.1169 - 2.1173 in (53.769 - 53.779 mm)
0.508 mm (0.02 in)	2.1069 - 2.1073 in (53.515 - 53.525 mm)
0.762 mm (0.03 in)	2.0969 - 2.0973 in (53.261 - 53.271 mm)
Main bearing parent bore	2.2710 - 2.2715 in (57.683 - 57.696 mm)
Oversize 0.381 mm (0.015 in)	2.2860 - 2.2865 in (58.064 - 58.077 mm)
Bore for camshaft	1.6885 - 1.6895 in (42.888 - 42.913 mm)
Oversize mm	+0.020 in (+0.508 mm)

Crankshaft

End float mm	0.0030 - 0.01102 in (0.075 - 0.28 mm)
Main bearing journal diameters	
Standard RED	2.1257 - 2.1261 in (53.993 - 54.003 mm)
BLUE	2.1253 - 2.1257 in (53.983 - 53.993 mm)
Undersize 0.254 mm (0.01 in)	2.1152 - 2.1157 in (53.726 - 53.739 mm)
0.508 mm (0.02 in)	2.1055 - 2.1060 in (53.480 - 53.492 mm)
0.762 mm (0.03 in)	2.0955 - 2.0960 in (53.226 - 53.238 mm)
Centre (serviced) - YELLOW	2.1157 - 2.1161 in (53.739 - 53.749 mm)
GREEN	2.1153 - 2.1157 in (53.729 - 53.739 mm)
Length, spigot bearing bush	0.9950 - 1.0050 in (25.273 - 25.527 mm)
Main bearing clearance	
BLUE standard	0.0005 - 0.0019 in (0.013 - 0.048 mm)
RED undersize	0.0004 - 0.0018 in (0.010 - 0.046 mm)
Crankpin journal diameter	1.9368 - 1.9376 in (49.195 - 49.215 mm)
Undersize 0.254 mm (0.01 in)	1.9268 - 1.9276 in (48.940 - 48.961 mm)
0.508 mm (0.02 in)	1.9168 - 1.9176 in (48.687 - 48.707 mm)
0.762 mm (0.03 in)	1.9068 - 1.9076 in (48.433 - 48.453 mm)
1.016 mm (0.04 in)	1.8968 - 1.8976 in (48.179 - 48.199 mm)

Camshaft

Drive	chain.
Thrust plate thickness	0.176 - 0.178 in (4.46 - 4.51 mm)
Cam lift (all models) inlet	0.2356 in (5.985 mm)
exhaust	0.2424 in (6.158 mm)
Journal diameter	1.5605 − 1.5596 in (39.637 − 39.616 mm)
Bearing (inside diameter)	1.5615 - 1.5620 in (39.662 - 39.675 mm)
End float	0.0024 - 0.0079 in (0.06 - 0.2 mm)

Pistons (fitted as standard)

	1300 cc	1600 cc
Grade 0	3.1847 - 3.1850 in (80.891 - 80.900 mm)	3.1850 - 3.1853 in (80.899 - 80.907 mm)
1	3.1850 - 3.1853 in (80.899 - 80.907 mm)	3.1853 - 3.1856 in (80.907 - 80.914 mm)
2	3.1853 - 3.1856 in (80.907 - 80.914 mm)	3.1856 - 3.1860 in (80.914 - 80.922 mm)
3	3.1856 - 3.1860 in (80.914 - 80.922 mm)	3.1860 - 3.1862 in (80.922 - 80.929 mm)
4	3.1860 - 3.1862 in (80.922 - 80.929 mm)	3.1862 - 3.1865 in (80.929 - 80.937 mm)
5	3.1862 - 3.1865 in (80.929 - 80.937 mm)	3.1865 - 3.1868 in (80.937 - 80.945 mm)
6	3.1865 - 3.1868 in (80.937 - 80.945 mm)	3.1868 - 3.1871 in (80.945 - 80.952 mm)
7	3.1868 - 3.1871 in (80.945 - 80.952 mm)	3.1871 - 3.1874 in (80.952 - 80.960 mm)

Oversizes available ... ... 0.0025/0.0015/0.0030 in (0.064/0.38/0.76 mm)

	1300 cc	1600 cc
Piston clearance in cylinder bore	0.0019 - 0.0025 in (0.048 - 0.064 mm)	0.0016 - 0.0022 in (0.041 - 0.056 mm)

Piston ring gaps (all types) ... ... 0.0091 - 0.0142 in (0.23 - 0.36 mm)

Gudgeon pins
Length ... ... 2.780 - 2.810 in (71.12 - 71.37 mm)
Diameter (Grade) 1 ... ... 0.8119 - 0.8120 in (20.622 - 20.625 mm)
              2 ... ... 0.8120 - 0.8121 in (20.625 - 20.627 mm)
              3 ... ... 0.8121 - 0.8122 in (20.627 - 20.630 mm)
              4 ... ... 0.8122 - 0.8123 in (20.630 - 20.632 mm)
Interference fit in piston ... ... 0.0001 - 0.0003 in (0.003 - 0.008 mm)
Clearance in small end bush ... ... 0.0001 - 0.0003 in (0.003 - 0.008 mm)

Connecting rods
Big end bore mm ... ... 2.0827 - 2.0831 in (52.90 - 52.91 mm)
Small end bush inside diameter - Grade
  White ... ... 0.8121 - 0.8122 in (20.627 - 20.630 mm)
  Red ... ... 0.8122 - 0.8123 in (20.630 - 20.632 mm)
  Yellow ... ... 0.8123 - 0.8124 in (20.632 - 20.635 mm)
  Blue ... ... 0.8124 - 0.8125 in (20.635 - 20.638 mm)
Inside diameter standard ... ... 1.9385 - 1.9397 in (49.238 - 49.268 mm)
Undersize 0.051 mm (0.002 in) ... ... 1.9405 - 1.9417 in (49.289 - 49.319 mm)
         0.254 mm (0.010 in) ... ... 1.9485 - 1.9497 in (49.492 - 49.522 mm)
         0.508 mm (0.020 in) ... ... 1.9585 - 1.9597 in (40.746 - 49.776 mm)
         0.762 mm (0.030 in) ... ... 1.9685 - 1.9697 in (50.000 - 50.030 mm)
         1.016 mm (0.040 in) ... ... 1.9785 - 1.9797 in (50.254 - 50.284 mm)
Crankpin to bearing liner clearance ... ... 0.0004 - 0.0024 in (0.01 - 0.06 mm)

Cylinder head
Valve seat angle ... ... 44° 30' - 45°
Valve guide inside diameter inlet and exhaust ... ... 0.3113 - 0.3125 in (7.907 - 7.937 mm)
Bore for guide bushes ... ... 0.4383 - 0.4390 in (11.133 - 11.153 mm)

Valves
Valve clearance (hot), inlet ... ... 0.010 in (0.25 mm)
              exhaust ... ... 0.021 in (0.53 mm)
Inlet opens ... ... 23° BTDC
Inlet closes ... ... 53° ABDC
Exhaust opens ... ... 53° BBDC
Exhaust closes ... ... 23° ATDC
Valve spring, number of coils ... ... 4 or 6
Tappet stem diameter ... ... 0.4359 - 0.4364 in (11.072 - 11.085 mm)
Tappet clearance in block ... ... 0.0005 - 0.0020 in (0.013 - 0.05 mm)

Inlet valve
Length ... ... 4.173 ±0.008 in (106 ±0.2 mm)
Valve head diameter ... ... 1.507 - 1.497 in (38.28 - 38.02 mm)
Valve stem diameter standard ... ... 0.3098 - 0.3105 in (7.868 - 7.886 mm)
Oversize 0.076 mm (0.003 in) ... ... 0.3128 - 0.3135 in (7.945 - 7.962 mm)
Oversize 0.381 mm (0.0005 in) ... ... 0.3248 - 0.3255 in (8.249 - 8.267 mm)
Valve guide bore in cylinder head
standard ... ... 0.3113 - 0.3125 in (7.907 - 7.938 mm)
Valve stem to guide clearance ... ... 0.0008 - 0.0027 in (0.02 - 0.068 mm)
Valve lift ... ... 0.3630 in (9.219 mm)

Exhaust valve

Length	4.17 - 4.165 in (106 - 105.8 mm)
Valve head diameter	1.244 - 1.232 in (31.6 - 31.3 mm)
Valve stem diameter (standard)	0.3096 - 0.3089 in (7.863 - 7.846 mm)
Oversize 0.076 mm (0.003 in)	0.3126 - 0.3119 in (7.939 - 7.922 mm)
Oversize 0.381 mm (0.005 in)	0.3245 - 0.3239 in (8.243 - 8.227 mm)
Valve stem to guide clearance	0.0017 - 0.0036 in (0.043 - 0.091 mm)

Sump capacity	7.5 pts (4.25 litres)

Minimum oil pressure	700 rev/min	5 - 7 lb in^2
	1500 rev/min	35 - 40 lb in^2

Oil pump outer rotor and housing clearance (max)	0.010 in (0.25 mm)
Oil pump drive shaft to body clearance	0.006 in (0.15 mm)
Inner and outer rotor clearance	0.006 in (0.15 mm)
Inner and outer rotor end float	0.005 in (0.13 mm)

Tightening torque:

	lb ft	kg m
Main bearing caps	65 - 70	8.970 - 9.660
Connecting rod big ends	20 - 25	2.760 - 3.450
Flywheel bolts	50 - 55	6.900 - 7.590
Oil pump body bolts	13 - 15	1.794 - 2.070
Oil pump cover bolts	5 - 7	0.690 - 0.966
Rocker shaft pillar bolts	17 - 22	2.346 - 3.036
Cylinder head bolts (HOT)	65 - 70	8.970 - 9.660
Sump retaining bolts...	7 - 9	0.966 - 1.242
Manifold nuts and bolts	15 - 18	1.66 - 2.07
Camshaft thrust plate	5 - 7	0.69 - 0.97
Camshaft sprocket	12 - 15	1.66 - 2.07
Crankshaft pulley bolt	24 - 28	3.32 - 3.87

1 General description

1 The engine fitted to the **Cortina Mark 3 base, L and XL** models is of four cylinders, four stroke, in-line type. The bore in both the **1300** and **1600** models is identical, the difference in capacity being achieved by varying the engine stroke.

2 The engine is known as a Type 'A' and has overhead valves operated by tappets and pushrods from a roller chain driven camshaft.

3 The cylinder head is of Crossflow design with bowl-in-piston combustion chambers and having inlet ports on the right hand side and exhaust ports on the left hand side.

4 Two valves per cylinder are mounted vertically in the cast iron cylinder head and run in integral valve guides. They are operated by rocker arms, pushrods and tappets from the camshaft which is located at the base of the cylinder bores in the right-hand side of the engine. The correct valve stem to rocker arm pad clearance can be obtained by the adjusting screws in the ends of the rocker arms.

5 The cylinder block and the upper half of the crankcase are cast together. The height of the block varies depending on the stroke of the crankshaft fitted. The open half of the crankcase is closed by a pressed steel sump.

6 The pistons are made from anodised aluminium alloy with solid skirts. Two compression rings and a slotted oil control ring are fitted. The gudgeon pin is retained in the little end of the connecting rod by circlips. On cross-flow engines the combustion chamber is machined in the piston crown and a different piston is used for each engine capacity and compression ratio. The bearings are all steel backed and may be of copper/lead, lead/bronze, or aluminium/tin.

7 At the front of the engine a single chain drives the camshaft and crankshaft chain wheels which are enclosed in cast alloy cover. The chain is tensioned automatically by a snail cam which bears against a pivoted tensioner arm. This presses against the non driving side of the chain so avoiding any lash or rattle.

8 The camshaft is supported by three renewable bearings located directly in the cylinder block. End float is controlled by a plate bolted to the front of the cylinder block and positioned between the front bearing journal and the chain wheel flange.

9 The statically and dynamically balanced forged steel crankshaft is supported by five renewable thinwall shell main bearings which are in turn supported by substantial webs which form part of the crankcase. Crankshaft end float is controlled by semi-circular thrust washers located on each side of the centre main bearing. The main bearings fitted are of the white metal type.

10 The centrifugal water pump and radiator cooling fan are driven, together with the dynamo, from the crankshaft pulley wheel by a rubber/fabric belt. The distributor is mounted towards the front of the right-hand side of the cylinder block and advances and retards the ignition timing by mechanical and vacuum means. The distributor is driven at half crankshaft speed from a skew gear on the camshaft.

11 The oil pump is mounted externally on the right-hand side of the engine under the distributor and is driven by a short shaft from the same skew gear on the camshaft as for the distributor and is of the eccentric bi-rotor type.

12 Bolted to the flange on the end of the crankshaft is the flywheel to which in turn is bolted the clutch. Attached to the rear of the engine is the gearbox bellhousing.

13 Engines are available in high or low compression ratio types and the major components are shown in Fig 1 : 1.

2 Major operations possible with engine in vehicle

The following major operations can be carried out to the engine with it in place in the bodyframe. Removal and replacement of the:

1 *Cylinder head assembly*
2 *Oil pump*
3 *Engine front mountings*
4 *Engine/gearbox rear mounting*

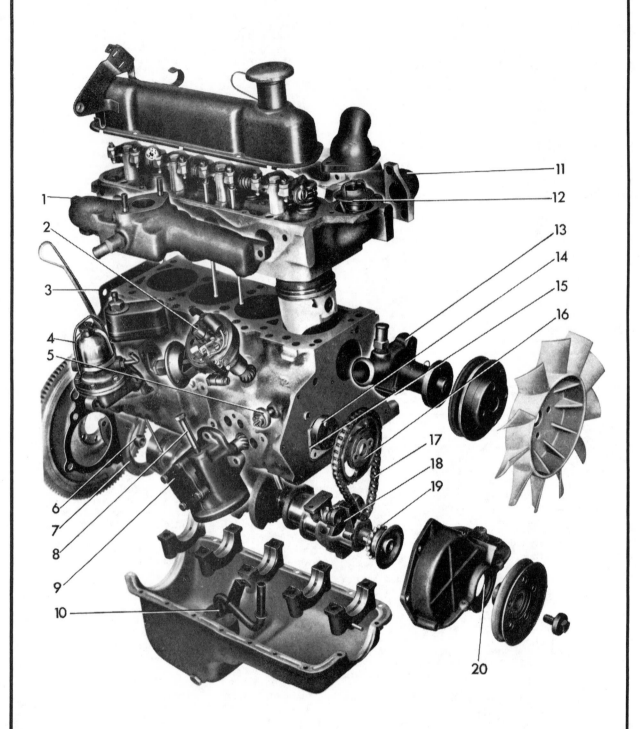

FIG 1 : 1 ENGINE COMPONENTS

1 Inlet manifold	6 Primary shaft bearing	11 Exhaust manifold	16 Camshaft sprocket
2 Distributor	7 Crankshaft oil seal carrier	12 Thermostat	17 Timing chain
3 Engine rear shield	8 Bolt, securing oil filter	13 Water pump	18 Chain tensioner
4 Fuel pump	9 Oil pump	14 Camshaft	19 Crankshaft sprocket
5 Oil pressure switch	10 Oil pump strainer with intake tube	15 Camshaft thrust plate	20 Oil seal, timing cover

3 Major operations with engine removed

The following major operations can be carried out with the engine out of the bodyframe and on the bench or floor. Removal and replacement of the:
1 *Main bearings*
2 *Crankshaft*
3 *Flywheel*
4 *Crankshaft rear bearing oil seal*
5 *Camshaft*
6 *Sump*
7 *Big-end bearings*
8 *Pistons and connecting rods*
9 *Timing chain and gears*

4 Method of engine removal

The engine complete with gearbox can be lifted as a unit from the engine compartment. Alternatively the engine and gearbox can be split at the front of the bellhousing, a stand or jack placed under the gearbox to provide additional support, and the engine lifted out. The easiest method of engine removal is to remove it leaving the gearbox in place in the car. If the engine and gearbox are removed as a unit they have to be lifted out at a very steep angle which can be difficult.

5 Engine removal without gearbox

1 The average do-it-yourself owner should be able to remove the engine fairly easily in about 3½ hours. It is essential to have a good hoist, and two strong axle stands if an inspection pit is not available. Engine removal will be much easier if you have an assistant.

2 Open the bonnet and undo and remove the two bolts and washers from the bonnet side of each of the two hinges. (photo) Lift the bonnet off and place it somewhere it will not fall over or be bumped into.

3 Open the water drain plug on the left-hand side of the underside of the radiator and with a spanner turn on the water drain plug in the left-hand rear side of the block. (photo)
Do not drain the water in your garage or the place where the engine is going to be removed unless receptacles are at hand to catch the water. Re-use the water if it is full of anti-freeze. Drain the engine oil by removing the drain plug on the bottom of the sump and drain the oil from the gearbox if the latter is being removed with the engine.

4 It is best to remove the battery from the engine compartment. Undo the winged nut which secures the clamp to the ledge on the base of the battery (photo).

5 Disconnect the main lead and then the earth lead from the top of the battery, lift the battery out of the car and store it in the boot for safe keeping.

6 To remove the air cleaner undo the screws in the air cleaner cover and take off the bolt from the cleaner support strap on the rear of the inlet manifold (photos). Lift away the air cleaner.

7 Unscrew the H.T. lead from the centre of the coil. NOTE - On some models the lead is a simple push fit.

8 Pull the small wire and connector off the CB tag on the coil (photo).

9 Remove the connections from the dynamo (1300 engine) or the alternator (1600 engine) (photo).

10 Disconnect the lead from the oil pressure sender switch (5) Fig 1 : 1 (photo).

11 Detach the choke and carburettor controls at the carburettor

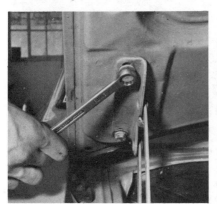
5.2 Releasing the bonnet hinges

5.3 Removing the cylinder block drain plug

5.4 Removing a battery clamp bolt

5.6a Lifting the air cleaner lid

5.6b Removing the air cleaner and support straps

5.8 Pulling the CB connector from the coil.

and, if automatic transmission is fitted, disconnect the 'kick-down' cable (photos).

12 Undo the clip from the thermostat end of the top hose (photo) and pull the hose off the thermostat outlet pipe leaving the other end connected to the radiator.

13 Loosen the clip on the hose leading to the water pump and pull the hose off (photo).

14 Then pull the rubber overflow pipe off the outlet on the neck of the radiator filler pipe (photo). Disconnect the distributor advance and retard pipe.

15 Undo the two bolts on each side of the radiator which hold it in place. The photo shows the removal of the top right-hand bolt.

16 Carefully lift the radiator out of the car complete with top and bottom hoses.

17 Disconnect the water temperature wire from the sender unit (photo).

18 Turning to the heater hoses, undo the clips which hold them to the inlet manifold and pull them away,

19 Pull the heater hose off the water pump (photo) after loosening the clip which holds the hose in place.

20 Disconnect the hoses from the clips on the side of the engine (photo).

21 Pull the fuel pipe from the inlet nozzle on the fuel pump and plug the pipe.

22 Undo the exhaust pipe clamp bolts and free the exhaust pipe from the manifold (Fig 1 : 2).

23 Undo the nut holding the starter cable to the starter motor. (photo) Take off the engine earth lead next. It will be attached to one of the top bellhousing bolts.

24 Undo the bolts holding the starter motor in place and remove the motor.

25 Undo the lower clutch bellhousing bolts and take off the cover. Note that on cars fitted with automatic transmission this operation also disconnects the reinforcing bracket. On cars using automatic transmission turn the engine as required to gain access to the drive plate to torque converter bolts which must be undone.

26 Undo the bolts which hold the engine endplate to the bell-housing.

27 Support the gearbox adequately with a jack or blocks.

28 Attach a lifting chain or strong rope round the engine, and take the weight on suitable lifting tackle. (Fig 1 : 3) Undo the bolt on each side which holds the front engine mountings in place (photo). These bolts are not very accessible and may take some time to remove.

29 Slightly raise the engine, and pull it forwards and up until the clutch is free from the first motion shaft in the gearbox. It is important that no excess load is placed on the clutch so take great care at this stage. Once clear of the bellhousing pull the engine forwards tilting the front further upwards to clear the front of the car and wind the engine out of the car (photo).

6 Engine removal with gearbox

1 Carry out the procedure described in paragraphs 1 - 24 inclusive.

2 Drain the oil from the gearbox and retain for further use.

3 Depress the gear lever gaiter, loosen the locknut and unscrew the knob (Fig 1 : 4).

4 Where fitted, remove the centre console and parcel tray. To do this, push the front seats fully forward and remove the tray and console securing screws. Remove the handbrake centre bolt (Fig 1 : 5).

5 Push the seats fully back and remove the console and instrument panel. Disconnect all leads as the instruments are withdrawn but mark them first for correct replacement.

6 Lift out the carpet and release the rubber gaiter securing ring.

7 Remove the circlip at the base of the gear lever and then bend back the locking tab from the plastic dome nut. Unscrew the nut and withdraw the gearchange lever.

8 Mark the edges of the propeller shaft and rear axle pinion

5.9 Disconnecting the dynamo leads

5.10 Disconnecting the lead from the oil pressure switch

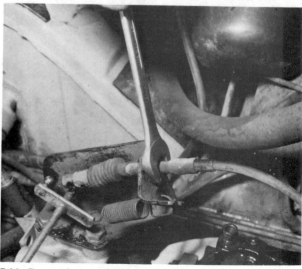
5.11a Removing the accelerator cable from its bracket

5.11b Unscrewing the choke cable pinch screw

5.11c Disconnecting throttle cable to shaft clip

5.12 Removing the top hose from the thermostat elbow

5.13 Pulling the lower hose from the water pump

5.14 Removing the radiator overflow pipe

5.15 Removing a radiator securing bolt

5.17 Disconnecting the water temperature transmitter lead

5.19 Removing a heater hose clip

5.20 Removing the heater hoses from their clips

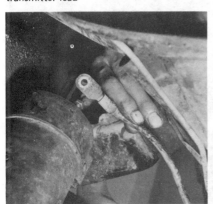
5.23 Disconnecting the starter cable

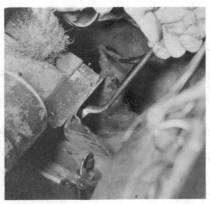
5.28 Unscrewing an engine mounting bolt

5.29 Hoisting the engine from the car

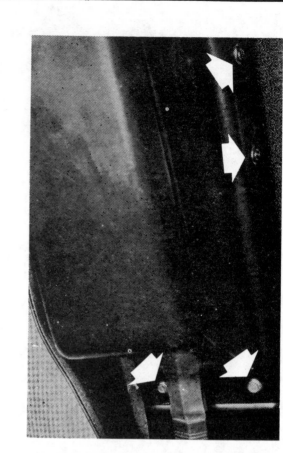

FIG 1 : 3 ENGINE LIFTING HOIST IN POSITION

FIG.1.5. CONSOLE SECURING SCREWS

FIG 1 : 2 MANIFOLD TO EXHAUST DOWNPIPE FLANGE
AND COMPONENTS

FIG 1 : 4 GEAR LEVER KNOB AND LOCK COLLAR

driving flanges for correct replacement and unscrew the flange connecting bolts and nuts (photo). If a split (two section) type of propeller shaft is fitted, remove the centre bearing.

9 Withdraw the propeller shaft from its engagement with the gearbox rear extension housing (photo).

10 Remove the rear engine cover plate and bracket assembly from the clutch bellhousing (Fig 1 : 6). Detach the bracket from its connection with the cylinder block and swing it clear.

11 Unscrew the clutch cable locknut and adjusting screw sufficiently far to permit the rubber gaiter to be peeled back and the inner and outer cables to be released (photos).

12 Unscrew the front exhaust mounting bracket at its connection with the exhaust down pipe (Fig 1 : 7).

13 Disconnect the speedometer drive cable at its entry to the gearbox. To do this, remove the circlip as shown in Fig 1 : 8.

14 Support the gearbox on a jack or block and unscrew and remove the sunken bolt which secures the gearbox to the crossmember (Fig 1 : 9) and then detach the crossmember (photos).

15 Attach a lifting chain or rope to the engine (Fig 1 : 3) and remove the engine front mounting bolts (photo).

16 Hoist the engine/gearbox unit up and out of the engine compartment. This operation will necessitate inclining the unit at a steep angle and the help of an assistant to remove the gearbox support jack and to guide, will be useful. Unscrew the clutch housing bolts and separate the engine and gearbox.

7 Dismantling the engine - general

1 It is best to mount the engine on a dismantling stand but if one is not available, then stand the engine on a strong bench so as to be at a comfortable working height. Failing this, the engine can be stripped down on the floor.

2 During the dismantling process the greatest care should be taken to keep the exposed parts free from dirt. As an aid to achieving this, it is a sound scheme to thoroughly clean down the outside of the engine, removing all traces of oil and congealed dirt.

3 Use paraffin or a good grease solvent such as 'Gunk'. The latter compound will make the job much easier, as, after the solvent has been applied and allowed to stand for a time, a vigorous jet of water will wash off the solvent and all the grease and filth. If the dirt is thick and deeply embedded, work the solvent into it with a wire brush.

4 Finally wipe down the exterior of the engine with a rag and only then, when it is quite clean should the dismantling process begin. As the engine is stripped, clean each part in a bath of paraffin or petrol.

5 Never immerse parts with oilways in paraffin, i.e. the crankshaft, but to clean, wipe down carefully with a petrol dampened rag. Oilways can be cleaned out with pipe cleaners. If an air line is present all parts can be blown dry and the oilways blown through as an added precaution.

6 Re-use of old engine gaskets is false economy and can give rise to oil and water leaks, if nothing worse. To avoid the possibility of trouble after the engine has been reassembled ALWAYS use new gaskets throughout.

7 Do not throw the old gaskets away as it sometimes happens that an immediate replacement cannot be found and the old gasket is then very useful as a template. Hang up the old gaskets as they are removed on a suitable hook or nail.

8 To strip the engine it is best to work from the top down. The sump provides a firm base on which the engine can be supported in an upright position. When this stage where the sump must be removed is reached, the engine can be turned on its side and all other work carried out with it in this position.

9 Wherever possible, replace nuts, bolts and washers fingertight from wherever they were removed. This helps avoid later loss and muddle. If they cannot be replaced then lay them out in such a fashion that it is clear from where they came.

6.8 Removing the propeller shaft/pinion flange bolts

6.9 Withdrawing the propeller shaft from the gearbox

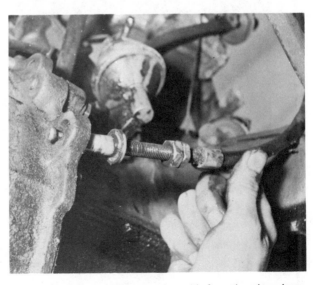

6.11a Disconnecting clutch operating cable from the release lever

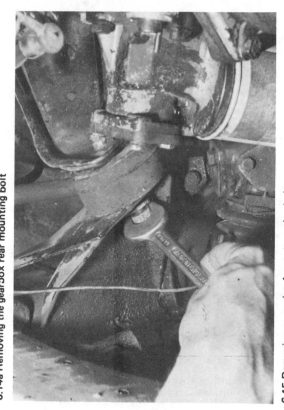

6.14a Removing the gearbox rear mounting bolt

6.15 Removing an engine front mounting bolt

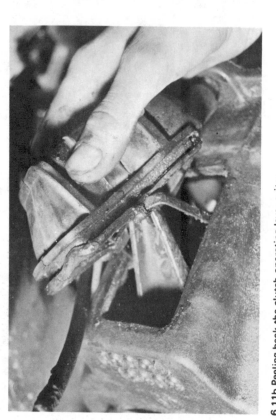

6.11b Peeling back the clutch operating lever gaiter

6.14b Removing a rear cross member securing bolt

FIG 1 : 7 EXHAUST DOWNPIPE BRACKET

FIG 1 : 9 THE GEARBOX REAR MOUNTING BOLT AND CROSSMEMBER

FIG 1 : 6 CLUTCH CABLE AND SUPPORT BRACKET

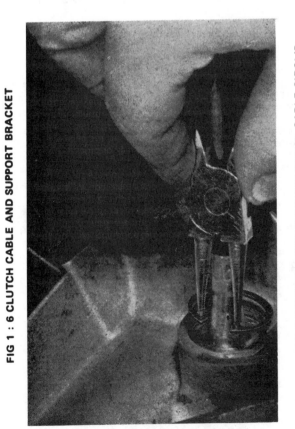

FIG 1 : 8 RELEASING THE SPEEDOMETER DRIVE CABLE CIRCLIP

8 Removing ancillary engine components

1 Before basic engine dismantling begins the engine should be stripped of all its ancillary components. These items should also be removed if a factory exchange reconditioned unit is being purchased.

2 Loosen the dynamo or alternator mounting bolts and adjustment strap bolt and push the unit in towards the engine in order to release and remove the fan belt (Fig 1 : 10).

3 Detach the electrical leads from the dynamo or alternator and then remove the unit from its mounting.

4 Unscrew the bolts from the fan and remove it together with the pulley.

5 Unscrew and remove the water pump securing bolts and withdraw the pump and fan belt adjustment strap (Fig 1 : 11).

6 Unscrew the single bolt which secures the distributor clamp plate to the cylinder block. Do not disturb the clamp plate pinch bolt.

7 Detach the H.T. leads from their connections with the spark-plugs and the coil. Detach the L.T. lead from the distributor. Lift the distributor from its location on the right hand side of the cylinder block.

8 Unscrew and remove the four screws and their plain washers which secure the rocker box and lift the rocker box away taking care not to break the cork gasket (photo).

9 Unscrew and remove the inlet (1) and exhaust (11) manifold securing bolts (Fig 1:1) (photo). Remove the manifolds and gaskets. The carburettor need not be unbolted from the inlet manifold flange. Unbolt the engine earth strap (photo).

10 Unscrew and remove the fuel pump securing bolts and lift the pump away, noting the thick insulating and sealing washers, (Fig 1 : 12).

11 Unscrew the securing bolts from the thermostat top housing, pull off the top housing and lift out the thermostat (12) (Fig 1 : 1). If the thermostat is difficult to remove, do not prise it out but cut round its joint with the housing recess, using a sharp pointed knife to release it.

12 Pull the regulator from its location in the oil separator and then lever the oil separator box from the crankcase (Fig 1 : 13) in which it is a push fit.

13 Unscrew the rocker shaft pillar bolts (evenly and a few turns at a time) and lift the rocker shaft assembly away (Fig 1 : 14).

14 Withdraw the push rods, keeping them in strict sequence for exact replacement.

15 Unscrew and remove the crankshaft pulley retaining bolt. A 'slogger' type ring spanner is most suitable for this operation and in any event any spanner used must be knocked in an anti-clockwise direction, turning the spanner will only rotate the crankshaft without loosening the bolt.

16 Remove the crankshaft pulley. If it is tight on the crankshaft, use a puller similar to the one shown in Fig 1 : 15.

17 Mark the position of the clutch pressure plate cover in relation to its location on the flywheel and unscrew the securing bolts evenly a few turns each at a time until the diaphragm spring pressure is released and the cover and driven plate can be removed, (Fig 1 : 17).

18 Withdraw the engine oil dipstick and then unscrew and remove the oil filter case and element. If the unit is tight to remove, use a strap type lever to unscrew it similar to that shown in Fig. 1·16

19 Unscrew and remove the oil pressure sender unit switch or the oil gauge pipe union, whichever is fitted, from its location in the cylinder block (Fig. 1 : 18).

20 The engine is now stripped of ancillary components and major dismantling may begin as described in the following sections.

9 Cylinder head removal - engine on bench

1 Having removed the rocker cover, rocker shaft and push rods as described in the preceding section, unscrew the cylinder head bolts, a turn or two at a time in the sequence shown in Fig. 1:19

8.8 Removing the rocker box

8.9a Unscrewing the manifold securing nuts

8.9b Engine earth strap removal

FIG 1 : 10 ALTERNATOR AND ADJUSTMENT STRAP

FIG 1 : 11 REMOVING THE WATER PUMP

FIG 1 : 12 LIFTING THE FUEL PUMP FROM THE BLOCK

FIG 1 : 13 PRISING THE OIL SEPARATOR FROM ITS LOCATION

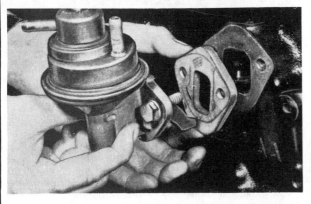
FIG 1 : 14 REMOVING THE ROCKER SHAFT ASSEMBLY

FIG 1 : 15 REMOVING THE CRANKSHAFT PULLEY-

FIG 1 : 16 UNSCREWING THE OIL FILTER BODY

FIG 1 : 17 REMOVAL OF THE CLUTCH PRESSURE PLATE AND DRIVEN PLATE

FIG 1 : 18 OIL PRESSURE SWITCH AND (ALTERNATIVE) PRESSURE GAUGE PIPE LOCATIONS

FIG 1 : 19 CYLINDER HEAD BOLT LOOSENING AND TIGHTENING SEQUENCE

FIG 1 : 20 COMPRESSING A VALVE SPRING TO RELEASE THE COLLETS

to avoid distortion of the head.

2 Remove the head. Should it be stuck, do not prise it off by placing levers in the joint but tap the sides of the head all round using a hammer on a hardwood block until it is freed. With the spark plugs in position and rotating the engine by turning the flywheel, it is possible to utilise the compression generated to release the head. Remove the gasket.

10 Cylinder head removal - engine in vehicle

1 The following operations are described in greater detail and illustrated in Section 5 to which additional reference should be made.

2 Disconnect the battery and remove it.

3 Drain the cooling system, retaining the coolant if anti-freeze solution is used.

4 Remove the air cleaner.

5 Detach the clips which secure the heater hoses.

6 Pull off the vacuum hose from the inlet manifold.

7 Unscrew and remove the manifold to exhaust down pipe bolts.

8 Detach the lead from the temperature gauge sender unit.

9 If automatic transmission is fitted, disconnect the kick-down cable at the carburettor.

10 Disconnect the throttle and choke controls, the fuel feed pipe to the carburettor and the rocker cover vent pipe.

11 Remove the H.T. leads from the spark plugs, slip aside the distributor cover clips and swing the distributor cover complete with   leads to one side.

12 Carry out the procedure described in the preceding Section, noting that the engine may be rotated by means of the crankshaft pulley wheel securing bolts.

11 Valve-removal

1 The valves can be removed from the cylinder head by the following method. Compress each spring in turn with a valve spring compressor until the two halves of the collets can be removed. Release the compressor and remove the spring and spring retainer (Fig 1 : 20).

2 If, when the valve spring compressor is screwed down, the valve spring retaining cap refuses to free to expose the split collet, do not continue to screw down on the compressor as there is a likelihood of damaging it.

3 Gently tap the top of the tool directly over the cap with a light hammer. This will free the cap. To avoid the compressor jumping off the valve spring retaining cap when it is tapped, hold the compressor firmly in position with one hand.

4 Slide the rubber oil control seal off the top of each inlet valve stem and then drop out each valve through the combustion chamber.

5 It is essential that the valves are kept in their correct sequence unless they are so badly worn that they are to be renewed. If they are going to be kept and used again, place them in a sheet of card having eight holes numbered 1 to 8 corresponding with the relative positions the valves were in when fitted. Also keep the valve springs, washers etc., in the correct order. Make No.1 hole the one at the front of the cylinder head.

12 Dismantling the rocker assembly

1 Pull out the split pin from either end of the rocker shaft and remove the flat washer, crimped spring washer and the remaining flat washer.

2 The rocker arms, rocker pedestals, and distance springs can now be slid off the end of the shaft.

13 Timing cover, gearwheel and chain - removal

1 The timing cover, gear wheels, and chain can be removed with the engine in the car provided the radiator, fan, and water pump are first removed. See Sections 6 and 8 for details.

2 Undo the bolt from the centre of the crankshaft fan belt pulley wheel noting the spring and large flat washer under the bolt's head.

3 The crankshaft pulley wheel may pull off quite easily. If not place two large screwdrivers behind the wheel at 180° to each other, and carefully lever off the wheel. It is preferable to use a proper pulley extractor if this is available but large screwdrivers or tyre levers are quite suitable, providing care is taken not to damage the pulley flange.

4 Undo the bolts which hold the timing cover in place noting that four sump bolts must also be removed before the cover can be taken off.

5 Check the chain for wear by measuring how much it can be depressed with the tensioner removed. More than ½ in. means a new chain must be fitted on reassembly. See Section 18 for details of tensioner removal.

6 With the timing cover off, take off the oil thrower. NOTE: The concave side faces outwards (Fig 1 : 21).

7 With a drift or screwdriver tap back the tabs on the lockwasher under the two camshaft gearwheel retaining bolts and undo the bolts (Fig 1 : 22).

8 To remove the camshaft and crankshaft timing wheels complete with chain, ease each wheel forward a little at a time levering behind each gear wheel in turn with two large screwdrivers at 180° to each other. If the gearwheels are locked solid then it will be necessary to use a proper gearwheel and pulley extractor, and if one is available this should be used anyway in preference to screwdrivers. With both gearwheels safely off, remove the woodruff key from the crankshaft with a pair of pliers and place it in a jam jar for safe keeping.

14 Sump - removal

1 The removal of the sump is not considered to be a practicable proposition whilst the engine is in the car, because of the necessity to detach steering, suspension and chassis components. If the engine has been removed from the car, detaching it from the gearbox, the procedure is as follows.

2 Ensure that the starter motor is detached from the engine.

3 Unscrew the sump securing bolts and remove the sump. Use a penknife to cut around the joint if it is stuck.

4 Remove the cork strips from the timing cover and rear oil seal carrier, then thoroughly clean all the mating surfaces of the sump flange and engine crankcase.

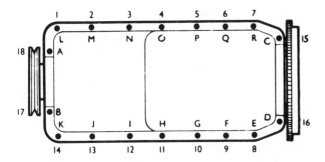

FIG 1:24 SUMP BOLT REMOVAL (NUMBERS) AND TIGHTENING (LETTERS) SEQUENCES

15 Oil pump - removal

1 The oil pump is mounted externally and reference should be made to Fig 1 : 25.

2 Unscrew and remove the retaining bolts and withdraw the pump and drive shaft from its engagement with the camshaft.

FIG 1 : 21 REMOVING TIMING COVER AND OIL THROWER

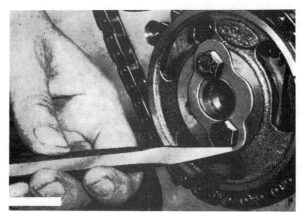

FIG 1 : 22 BENDING BACK THE CAMSHAFT SPROCKET BOLT TABS

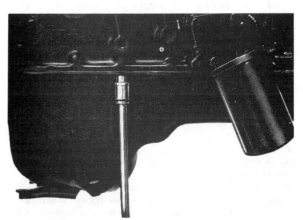

FIG 1 : 23 UNSCREWING THE SUMP RETAINING BOLTS

16 Camshaft - removal

1 The camshaft cannot be removed with the engine in place in the car primarily because of the restriction imposed by the inverted umbrella shaped tappets which can only be removed downwards, i.e. towards the camshaft.
2 With the engine inverted and sump, rocker gear, pushrods, timing cover, oil pump, gearwheels and timing chain removed take off the chain tensioner and arm.
3 Knock back the lockwasher tabs from the two bolts which hold the horseshoe shaped camshaft retainer in place behind the camshaft flange and slide out the retainer (Fig 1 : 26).
4 Rotate the camshaft so that the tappets are fully home and then withdraw the camshaft from the block. Take great care that the cam lobe peaks do not damage the camshaft bearings as the shaft is pulled forward.

17 Tappets - removal

1 With the engine inverted and the camshaft withdrawn as described in the preceding Section, the tappets may be withdrawn The operation will be facilitated if the crankshaft is first rotated into its TDC alignment as shown in Fig 1 : 27.
2 Keep the tappets in the sequence as removed for correct replacement.

18 Timing chain tensioner - removal

1 Undo the two bolts and washers which hold the timing chain tensioner in place. Lift off the tensioner (Fig 1 : 28).
2 Pull the timing chain tensioner arm off its hinge pin on the front of the block.

19 Piston, connecting rod and big end bearing - removal

1 The pistons and connecting rods can be removed with the engine still in the car or with the engine on the bench.
2 With the cylinder head and sump removed undo the big end retaining bolts.
3 The connecting rods and pistons are lifted out from the top of the cylinder block, after the carbon or 'wear' ring at the top of the bore has been scraped away.
4 Remove the big end caps one at a time, taking care to keep them in the right order and the correct way round. Also ensure that the shell bearings are kept with their correct connecting rods and caps unless they are to be renewed. Normally, the numbers 1 to 4 are stamped on adjacent sides of the big end caps and connecting rods, indicating which cap fits on which rod and which way round the cap fits (Fig 1 : 29). If no numbers or lines can be found then, with a sharp screwdriver or file, scratch mating marks across the joint from the rod to the cap. One line for connecting rod No. 1, two for connecting rod No. 2 and so on. This will ensure there is no confusion later as it is most important that the caps go back in the correct position on the connecting rods from which they were removed.
5 If the big end caps are difficult to remove they may be gently tapped with a soft hammer.
6 To remove the shell bearings, press the bearing opposite the groove in both the connecting rod, and the connecting rod caps and the bearings will slide out easily.
7 Withdraw the pistons and connecting rods upwards and ensure they are kept in the correct order for replacement in the same bore. Refit the connecting rod, caps and bearings to the rods if the bearings do not require renewal, to minimise the risk of getting the caps and rods muddled.

20 Gudgeon pin - removal

1 To remove the gudgeon pin to free the piston from the connecting rod remove one of the circlips at either end of the pin with a pair of circlip pliers.
2 Press out the pin from the rod and piston with your finger.
3 If the pin shows reluctance to move, then on no account force it out, as this could damage the piston. Immerse the piston in a pan of boiling water for three minutes. On removal the expansion of the aluminium should allow the gudgeon pin to slide out easily.
4 Make sure the pins are kept with the same piston for ease of refitting.

21 Piston ring - removal

1 Each ring should be sprung open only just sufficiently to permit it to ride over the hands of the piston body.
2 Once a ring is out of its groove, it is helpful to cut three ¼ in. wide strips of tin and slip them under the ring at equidistant points.
3 Using a twisting motion this method of removal will prevent the ring dropping into an empty groove as it is being removed from the piston.

22 Flywheel - removal

1 Remove the clutch as described in Section 8 : 19.
2 No lock tabs are fitted under the six bolts which hold the flywheel to the flywheel flange on the rear of the crankshaft.
3 Unscrew the bolts and remove them.
4 Lift the flywheel away from the crankshaft flange.
NOTE: Some difficulty may be experienced in removing the bolts by the rotation of the crankshaft every time pressure is put on the spanner. To lock the crankshaft in position while the bolts are removed, wedge a block of wood between the crankshaft and the side of the block inside the crankcase.

23 Main bearing and crankshaft - removal

1 With the engine removed from the car and the timing gears, flywheel, connecting rods and pistons and sump removed as described in the previous Sections, remove the oil pump intake pipe by pulling it with a to and fro motion.
2 Remove the rear oil seal carrier (Fig 1 : 30).
3 Unscrew the ten bolts which retain the five main bearing caps in position.
4 Lift out the bolts and lock washers and remove the main bearing caps together with the bottom halves of each shell bearing. Take great care to keep the caps the correct way round and in their right order, and the shells in the right caps. Mark No. 1 cap as such.
5 Remove the semi-circular thrust washer fitted to the centre main bearing.
6 Remove the crankshaft by lifting it out from the crankcase.

24 Lubrication system - description

1 The camshaft driven oil pump is of eccentric rotor type and mounted externally on the right hand side of the crankcase.
2 The pump draws oil from the sump through a mesh strainer and then forces it through a full-flow filter. The filtered oil passes through the centre of the filter element and via a passage to the oil pressure switch thence to the main oil gallery on the left side of the engine block.
3 Oil from the main gallery lubricates the five main bearings and provides a linked supply to the camshaft bearings.
4 Big end journals are supplied with oil via diagonal passages

FIG.1.25. REMOVING THE EXTERNAL MOUNTED OIL PUMP

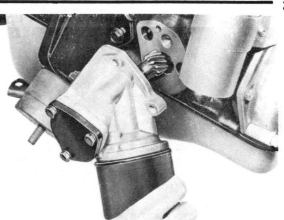

FIG.1.26. REMOVING THE CAMSHAFT RETAINER BOLTS

FIG.1.27. CRANKSHAFT POSITIONED TO FACILITATE TAPPET REMOVAL

FIG 1 : 28 THE TIMING CHAIN TENSIONER

FIG 1 : 29 BIG END BEARING CAP IDENTIFICATION AND MATING MARKS

FIG 1 : 30 REMOVING THE CRANKSHAFT REAR OIL SEAL CARRIER

from the adjacent main bearing.

5   Gudgeon pins and cylinder walls are splash lubricated, as are the timing chain and gears, from a drilling.

6   A machined pad on the front camshaft bearing forces oil through an oil passage to the rocker shaft assembly.

7   Fig 1 : 31 shows the engine lubrication flow circuit.

25 Crankcase ventilation system - description

1   A semi-closed positive ventilation system is fitted as standard (Fig 1 : 32). This consists of a breather in the oil filler cap; an oil separator mounted on top of the fuel pump attachment lug; an emission control valve fitted into a grommet on the top of the oil separator; and a pipe leading from the valve to the inlet manifold.

2   With some models an emission control valve is fitted to the rear of the carburettor.

3   The valve (Fig 1 : 33) should be removed and serviced regularly by disconnecting the hose and pulling it from its grommet.

4   Dismantle the valve by removing the circlip. Extract the seal, valve and spring. Wash all components in clean fuel and reassemble. Do not run the engine with the hose removed from the valve nozzle or the mixture strength will be excessively weak.

26 Oil filter - removal and replacement

1   The full flow oil filter is attached to the oil pump on the right-hand side of the engine towards the front. The element is removed by unscrewing the filter bowl from the body (Fig 1 : 17).

Now carefully lift away the filter bowl which contains the filter and will also be full of oil. It is helpful to have a large basin under the filter body to catch the oil which is bound to spill.

2   Throw the old filter element away and thoroughly clean down the filter bowl and associated parts with petrol, and when perfectly clean, wipe dry with a non-fluffy rag.

3   A rubber sealing ring is located in a groove round the head of the oil filter and forms an effective leak-proof joint between the filter head and the filter bowl. A new rubber sealing ring is supplied with each new filter element.

4   Carefully prise out the old sealing ring from the locating groove. If the ring has become hard and is difficult to move take great care not to damage the sides of the sealing ring groove.

5   With the old ring removed, fit the new ring (photo) in the groove at four equidistant points and press it home a segment at a time. Do not insert the ring at just one point and work round the groove pressing it home as, using this method, it is easy to stretch the ring and be left with a small loop of rubber which will not fit into the locating groove. Grease the exposed surface of the seal.

6   Offer up the bowl to the rubber sealing ring (photo) and check that the lip of the filter bowl is resting squarely on the rubber sealing ring.

7   Tighten the filter bowl by hand only until it just impinges on the sealing ring, then tighten by not more than a further half turn. Check for leaks after the engine has reached normal working temperature.

27 Oil pump - overhaul

1   If the oil pump is worn it is best to purchase an exchange reconditioned unit as a good oil pump is at the very heart of long engine life. Generally speaking an exchange or overhauled pump should be fitted at a major engine reconditioning. If it is wished to overhaul the oil pump, detach the pump and filter unit from the cylinder block, and remove the filter body and element.

2   Remove the bolts and lockwashers securing the end plate and remove the plate. Lift away the 'O' ring from the sealing groove in the body.

FIG 1 : 31 ENGINE LUBRICATION FLOW CIRCUIT

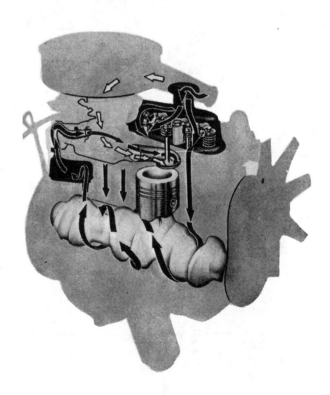

FIG 1 : 32 THE CRANKCASE VENTILATION SYSTEM
(DIAGRAMMATIC)

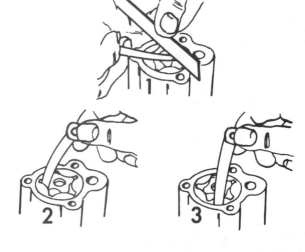

FIG 1 : 33 EXPLODED VIEW OF THE EMISSION CONTROL VALVE

FIG 1 : 34 METHODS OF MEASURING FOR OIL PUMP WEAR

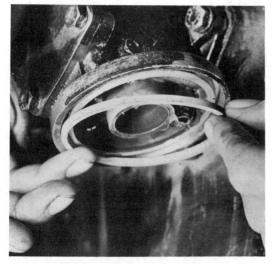

26.5 Fitting an oil filter body sealing ring

FIG 1 : 35 COMPONENTS OF THE OIL PUMP

26.6 Locating the oil filter bowl

28.5 Removing the crankcase engine mounting brackets

3 Check the clearance between the lobes of the inner and outer rotors in the positions shown in Fig 1 : 34 parts 2 and 3. The clearance must not exceed 0.010 in (0.25 mm).
4 Replacement rotors are supplied only as a matched pair so that, if the clearance is excessive, a new rotor assembly must be fitted.
5 Lay a straight edge across the face of the pump in order to check the clearance between the faces of the rotors and the bottom of the straight edge. This clearance should not exceed 0.005 in (0.13 mm). If the clearance is excessive the face of the pump body can be carefully lapped on a flat surface.
6 When it is necessary to renew the rotors, drive out the pin securing the skew gear and pull the gear from the shaft. Remove the inner rotor and drive shaft and withdraw the outer rotor. Install the outer rotor with the chamfered end towards the pump body.
7 Fit the inner rotor and drive shaft assembly, position the skew gear and install the pin. Tap over each end of the pin to prevent it loosening in service. Position a new 'O' ring in the groove in the pump body, fit the end plate in position and secure with the four bolts and lockwashers, tightening to a torque of 5 - 7 lb/ft (.690 - .966 lb ft kg m)
8 Refit the oil pump assembly together with a new gasket and secure in place with the bolts and lockwashers, tightening to a torque of 13 - 15 lb ft (1.794 - 2.070 kg m).
9 Components of the oil pump are shown in Fig 1 : 35.

28 Engine front mountings - removal and replacement

1 With time the bonded rubber insulators, one on each of the front mountings, will perish causing undue vibration and noise from the engine. Severe juddering when reversing or when moving off from rest is also likely and is a further sign of worn mounting rubbers.
2 The front mounting rubber insulators can be changed with the engine in the car.
3 Apply the handbrake firmly, jack up the front of the car, and place stands under the front of the car.
4 Lower the jack, take off the engine sump shield (where fitted) and place the jack under the sump to take the weight of the engine.
5 Undo the large bolt which holds each of the engine mountings to the body crossmember. Then knock back the locking tabs and undo the four bolts holding each of the engine mountings in place (photo).
6 Fit new mountings using new tab washers, tighten the four bolts down firmly and turn up the tabs on the washers. Refit the large crossmember to mounting bolt on each side, remove the stands and lower the car to the ground.

29 Examination and renovation - general

With the engine stripped down and all parts thoroughly cleaned, it is now time to examine everything for wear. The following items should be checked and where necessary renewed or renovated as described in the following Sections.

30 Crankshaft - examination and renovation

1 Examine the crankpin and main journal surfaces for signs of scoring or scratches. Check the ovality of the crankpins at different positions with a micrometer. If more than 0.001 in. out of round, the crankpin will have to be reground. It will also have to be reground if there are any scores or scratches present. Also check the journals in the same fashion.
2 If it is necessary to regrind the crankshaft and fit new bearings your local Ford garage or engineering works will be able to decide how much metal to grind off and the size of new bearing shells.

31 Big end and main bearings - examination and renovation

1 Big end bearing failure is accompanied by a noisy knocking from the crankcase, and a slight drop in oil pressure. Main bearing failure is accompanied by vibration which can be quite severe as the engine speed rises and falls, and a drop in oil pressure.
2 Bearings which have not broken up, but are badly worn will give rise to low oil pressure and some vibration. Inspect the big ends, main bearings, and thrust washers for signs of general wear, scoring, pitting and scratches. The bearings should be matt grey in colour. With lead-indium bearings should a trace of copper colour be noticed the bearings are badly worn as the lead bearing material has worn away to expose the indium underlay. Renew the bearings if they are in this condition or if there is any sign of scoring or pitting.
3 The undersizes available are designed to correspond with the regrind sizes, i.e. - .010 in (0.25 mm), bearings are correct for a crankshaft reground - .010 in (0.25 mm) undersize. The bearings are in fact, slightly more than the stated undersize as running clearances have been allowed for during their manufacture.
4 Very long engine life can be achieved by changing big end bearings at intervals of 30,000 miles (48000 Km) and main bearings at intervals of 50,000 miles (80000 Km), irrespective of bearing wear. Normally, crankshaft wear is infinitesimal and a change of bearings will ensure mileages of between 80,000 to 100,000 miles (128000 to 160000 Km) before crankshaft regrinding becomes necessary. Crankshafts normally have to be reground because of scoring due to bearing failure. Refer to Specifications for full information regarding regrinding tolerances.

32 Cylinder bores - examination and renovation

1 The cylinder bores must be examined for taper, ovality, scoring and scratches. Start by carefully examining the top of the cylinder bores. If they are at all worn a very slight ridge will be found on the thrust side. This marks the top of the piston ring travel. The owner will have a good indication of the bore wear prior to dismantling the engine, or removing the cylinder head. Excessive oil consumption accompanied by blue smoke from the exhaust is a sure sign of worn cylinder bores and piston rings.
2 Measure the bore diameter just under the ridge with a micrometer and compare it with the diameter at the bottom of the bore, which is not subject to wear. If the difference between the two measurements is more than .006 in (0.1524 mm) then it will be necessary to fit special pistons and rings or to have the cylinders rebored and fit oversize pistons. If no micrometer is available remove the rings from a piston and place the piston in each bore in turn about ¾ in. below the top of the bore. If an 0.010 in (0.25 mm) feeler gauge can be slid between the piston and the cylinder wall on the thrust side of the bore then remedial action must be taken. Oversize pistons are available as listed in Specifications.
3 These are accurately machined to just below the indicated measurements so as to provide correct running clearances in bores bored out to the exact oversize dimensions.
4 If the bores are slightly worn but not so badly worn as to justify reboring them, then special oil control rings and pistons can be fitted which will restore compression and stop the engine burning oil. Several different types are available and the manufacturer's instructions concerning their fitting must be followed closely.
5 If new pistons are being fitted and the bores have not been reground, it is essential to slightly roughen the hard glaze on the sides of the bores with fine glass paper so the new piston rings will have a chance to bed in properly.

33 Pistons and piston rings - examination and renovation

1 If the old pistons are to be refitted, carefully remove the piston rings and then thoroughly clean them. Take particular

care to clean out the piston ring grooves. At the same time do not scratch the aluminium in any way. If new rings are to be fitted to the old pistons then the top ring should be stepped so as to clear the ridge left in the cylinder bore, above the previous top ring. If a normal but oversize new ring is fitted, it will hit the ridge and break, because the new ring will not have worn in the same way as the old, which will have worn in unison with the ridge.

2   Before fitting the rings on the pistons each should be inserted approximately 2 in (50.8 mm) down the cylinder bore and the gap measured with a feeler gauge. This should be between 0.009 in and 0.014 in (0.23 mm and 0.36 mm). It is essential that the gap should be measured at the bottom of the ring travel, as if it is measured at the top of a worn bore and gives a perfect fit, it could easily seize at the bottom. If the ring gap is too small rub down the ends of the ring with a very fine file until the gap, when fitted, is correct. To keep the rings square in the bore for measurement, line each up in turn by inserting an old piston in the bore upside down, and use the piston to push the ring down about 2 in (50.8 mm). Remove the piston and measure the piston ring gap.

3   When fitting new pistons and rings to a rebored engine the piston ring gap can be measured at the top of the bore as the bore will not now taper (photo). It is not necessary to measure the side clearance in the piston ring grooves with the rings fitted as the groove dimensions are accurately machined during manufacture. When fitting new oil control rings to old pistons it may be necessary to have the grooves widened by machining to accept the new wider rings. In this instance the manufacturer's representative will make this quite clear and will supply the address to which the pistons must be sent for machining.

34 Camshaft and camshaft bearings - examination and renovation

1   Carefully examine the camshaft bearings for wear. If the bearings are obviously worn or pitted then they must be renewed. This is an operation for your local Ford dealer or local engineering works as it demands the use of specialized equipment. The bearings are removed with a special drift after which new bearings are pressed in, care being taken to ensure the oil holes in the bearings line up with those in the block.

2   The camshaft itself should show no signs of wear, but, if very slight scoring on the cams is noticed, the score marks can be removed by very gentle rubbing down with a very fine emery cloth. The greatest care should be taken to keep the cam profiles smooth.

3   Examine the skew gear for wear, chipped teeth or other damage.

4   Carefully examine the camshaft thrust plate. Excessive wear will be visually self evident and will require the fitting of a new plate.

35 Valves and valve seats - examination and renovation

1   Examine the heads of the valves for pitting and burning, especially the heads of the exhaust valves. The valve seatings should be examined at the same time. If the pitting on valve and seat is very slight the marks can be removed by grinding the seats and valves together with coarse, and then fine, valve grinding paste.

2   Where bad pitting has occured to the valve seats it will be necessary to recut them and fit new valves. If the valve seats are so worn that they cannot be recut, then it will be necessary to fit new valve seat inserts. These latter two jobs should be entrusted to the local Ford agent or engineering works. In practice it is very seldom that the seats are so badly worn that they require renewal. Normally, it is the valve that is too badly worn for replacement, and the owner can easily purchase a new set of valves and match them to the seats by valve grinding.

3   Valve grinding is carried out as follows:-
Smear a trace of coarse carborundum paste on the seat face and apply a suction grinder tool to the valve head. With a semi-rotary motion, grind the valve head to its seat, lifting the valve occasionally (photo) to redistribute the grinding paste. When a dull matt even surface finish is produced on both the valve seat and the valve, wipe off the paste and repeat the process with fine carborundum paste, lifting and turning the valve to redistribute the paste as before. A light spring placed under the valve head will greatly ease this operation. When a smooth unbroken ring of light grey matt finish is produced, on both valve and valve seat faces, the grinding operation is completed.

4   Scrape away all carbon from the valve head and the valve stem. Carefully clean away every trace of grinding compound, taking great care to leave none in the ports or in the valve guides. Clean the valves and valve seats with a paraffin soaked rag then with a clean rag, and finally, if an air line is available, blow the valves, valve guides and valve ports clean.

36 Valve guides - examination and renovation

1   Test each valve in its guide for wear. After a considerable mileage, the valve guide bore may wear elliptically and can be tested by rocking the valve in the direction of the arrows shown in Fig 1 : 36.

2   The remedy for wear is to ream the valve guide bores by the minimum amount to accommodate the smallest oversize valves as listed in Specifications.

3   It is preferable to leave this operation to a Ford dealer but where the home mechanic is competent then the reaming should be carried out from the valve seat end using paraffin as a cutting lubricant (Fig 1 : 37).

37 Timing gears and chain - examination and renovation

1   Examine the teeth on both the crankshaft gear wheel and the camshaft gear wheel for wear. Each tooth forms an inverted 'V' with the gearwheel periphery, and if worn the side of each tooth under tension will be slightly concave in shape when compared with the other side of the tooth, i.e. one side of the inverted 'V' will be concave when compared with the other. If any sign of wear is present the gearwheels must be renewed.

2   Examine the links of the chain for side slackness and renew the chain if any slackness is noticeable when compared with a new chain. It is a sensible precaution to renew the chain at about 30,000 miles (48000 km) and at a lesser mileage if the engine is stripped down for a major overhaul. The actual rollers on a very badly worn chain may be slightly grooved.

38 Rockers and rocker shaft - examination and renovation

1   Thoroughly clean the rocker shaft and then check the shaft for straightness by rolling it on the bench. It is most unlikely that it will deviate from normal, but, if it does, then a judicious attempt must be made to straighten it. If this is not successful purchase a new shaft. The surface of the shaft should be free from any worn ridges caused by the rocker arms. If any wear is present, renew the shaft.

Check the rocker arms for wear of the rocker bushes, for wear at the rocker arm face which bears on the valve stem, and for wear of the adjusting ball ended screws. Wear in the rocker arm bush can be checked by gripping the rocker arm tip and holding the rocker arm in place on the shaft, noting if there is any lateral rocker arm shake. If shake is present, and the arm is very loose on the shaft, a new bush or rocker arm must be fitted.

Check the tip of the rocker arm where it bears on the valve head for cracking or serious wear on the case hardening. If none is present reuse the rocker arm. Check the lower half of the ball on the end of the rocker arm adjusting screw. Check the pushrods for straightness by rolling them on the bench. Renew any that are bent.

33.3 Testing a piston ring gap

35.3 Grinding in a valve

FIG 1 : 36 TESTING FOR VALVE GUIDE WEAR

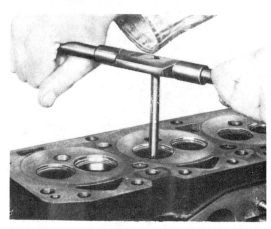

FIG 1 : 37 REAMING A VALVE GUIDE

42.1 Removing carbon from the cylinder head
combustion surfaces

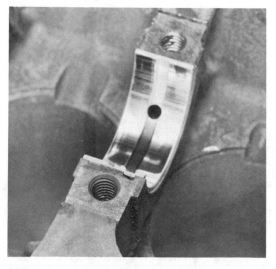

44.2 Correctly fitted main shell bearings

39 Tappets - examination and renovation

Examine the bearing surface of the mushroom tappets which lie on the camshaft. Any indentation in this surface or any cracks indicate serious wear and the tappets should be renewed. Thoroughly clean them out, removing all traces of sludge. It is most unlikely that the sides of the tappets will prove worn, but, if they are a very loose fit in their bores and can readily be rocked, they should be exchanged for new units. It is very unusual to find any wear in the tappets, and any wear is likely to occur only at very high mileages.

40 Connecting rods - examination and renovation

1 Examine the mating faces of the big end caps to see if they have ever been filed in a mistaken attempt to take up wear. If so the offending rods must be renewed.
2 Insert the gudgeon pin into the little end of the connecting rod. It should go in fairly easily, but if any slackness is present then take the rod to your local Ford dealer or engineering works and exchange it for a rod of identical weight.

41 Flywheel starter ring - examination and renovation

1 If the teeth on the flywheel starter ring are badly worn, or if some are missing then it will be necessary to remove the ring and fit a new one, or preferably exchange the flywheel for a reconditioned unit.
2 The number of teeth on the ring varies depending on the type of starter motor fitted. With the more usual inertia type starter (3 bolt fixing) the ring gear has 110 teeth. With the pre-engaged starter (2 bolt fixing) the ring gear has 132 teeth.
3 Either split the ring with a cold chisel after making a cut with a hacksaw blade between two teeth, or use a soft headed hammer (not steel) to knock the ring off, striking it evenly and alternately   at equally spaced points. Take great care not to damage the flywheel during this process.
4 Heat the new ring in either an electric oven to about 400°C or immerse in a pan of boiling oil.
5 Hold the ring at this temperature for five minutes and then quickly fit it to the flywheel so the chamfered portion of the teeth faces the gearbox side of the flywheel.
6 The ring should be tapped gently down onto its register and left to cool naturally when the contraction of the metal on cooling will ensure that it is a secure and permanent fit. Great care must be taken not to overheat the ring, indicated by it turning light metallic blue, as if this happens the temper of the ring will be lost.
7 It does not matter which way round the 132 toothed ring is fitted as it has no chamfers on its teeth. This also makes for quick identification between the two rings.

42 Cylinder head - decarbonisation

1 This can be carried out with the engine either in or out of the car. With the cylinder head off carefully remove with a wire brush mounted in an electric drill (photo) and blunt scraper, all traces of carbon deposits from the combustion spaces and the ports. The valve head stems and valve guides should also be freed from any carbon deposits. Wash the combustion spaces and ports down with petrol and scrape the cylinder head surface free of any foreign matter with the side of a steel rule, or a similar article.
2 Clean the pistons and top of the cylinder bores. If the pistons are still in the block then it is essential that great care is taken to ensure that no carbon gets into the cylinder bores as this could scratch the cylinder walls or cause damage to the piston and

rings. To ensure this does not happen, first turn the crankshaft so that two of the pistons are at the top of their bores. Stuff rag into the other two bores or seal them off with paper and masking tape. The waterways should also be covered with small pieces of masking tape to prevent particles of carbon entering the cooling system and damaging the water pump.
3 There are two schools of thought as to how much carbon should be removed from the piston crown. One school recommends that a ring of carbon should be left round the edge of the piston and on the cylinder bore wall as an aid to low oil consumption. Although this is probably true for early engines with worn bores, on later engines the thought of the second school can be applied; which is that for effective decarbonisation all traces of carbon should be removed.
4 If all traces of carbon are to be removed, press a little grease into the gap between the cylinder walls and the two pistons which are to be worked on. With a blunt scraper carefully scrape away the carbon from the piston crown, taking great care not to scratch the aluminium. Also scrape away the carbon from the surrounding lip of the cylinder wall. When all carbon has been removed, scrape away the grease which will now be contaminated with carbon particles, taking care not to press any into the bores. To assist prevention of carbon build-up the piston crown can be polished with a metal polish such as Brasso. Remove the rags or masking tape from the other two cylinders and turn the crankshaft so that the two pistons which were at the bottom are now at the top. Place rag or masking tape in the cylinders which have been decarbonised and proceed as just described.
5 If a ring of carbon is going to be left round the piston then this can be helped by inserting an old piston ring into the top of the bore to rest on the piston and ensure that the carbon is not accidentally removed. Check that there are no particles of carbon in the cylinder bores. Decarbonising is now complete.

43 Engine reassembly - general

1 To ensure maximum life with minimum trouble from a rebuilt engine, not only must everything be correctly assembled, but everything must be spotlessly clean, all the oilways must be clear, locking washers and spring washers must always be fitted where indicated and all bearing and other working surfaces must be thoroughly lubricated during assembly.
2 Before assembly begins renew any bolts or studs the threads of which are in any way damaged, and whenever possible use new spring washers.
3 Apart from your normal tools, a supply of clean rag; an oil can filled with engine oil (an empty plastic detergent bottle thoroughly cleaned and washed out, will invariably do just as well); a new supply of assorted spring washers; a set of new gaskets; and a torque spanner, should be collected together.

44 Assembling the engine

1 Thoroughly clean the engine block and remove all traces of old gaskets and jointing compound.
2 Position the upper halves of the main shell bearings in their locations so that the tabs engage in the machined keyways (photo).
3 Oil the main bearing shells after they have been fitted in position (photo).
4 Thoroughly clean out the oilways in the crankshaft with the aid of a thin wire brush or pipe cleaners (photo).
5 To check for the possibility of an error in the grinding of the crankshaft journal (presuming the crankshaft has been reground) smear engineer's blue evenly over each big end journal in turn (photo) with the crankshaft end flange held firmly in position in a vice.
6 With new shell bearings fitted to the connecting rods fit the correct rod to each journal in turn (photo) fully tightening down the securing bolts.
7 Spin the rod on the crankshaft a few times and then remove

44.3 Oiling the main shell bearings prior to fitting crankshaft

44.4 Cleaning crankshaft oilways

44.5 Checking crankshaft regrinding by first applying engineer's blue

the big end cap. A fine unbroken layer of engineer's blue should cover the whole of the journal. If the blue is much darker on one side than the other or if the blue has disappeared from a certain area (ignore the very edge of the journal) then something is wrong and the journal will have to be checked with a micrometer.

8   The main journals should also be checked in similar fashion with the crankshaft in the crankcase. On completion of these tests remove all traces of the engineer's blue.

9   The crankshaft can now be lowered carefully into place (photo).

10   Fit new end float thrust washers. These locate in recesses on either side of the centre main bearing in the cylinder block and must be fitted with the oil grooves facing the crankshaft flange. With the crankshaft in position check for float which should be between 0.003 and 0.011 in. (0.076 to 0.279 mm). If the end float is incorrect remove the thrust washers and select suitable washers to give the correct end float (photo).

11   Place the lower halves of the main bearing shells in their caps making sure that the locking tabs fit into the machined grooves. Refit the main bearing caps ensuring that they are the correct way round and that the correct cap is on the correct journal. The two front caps are marked 'F' (photo), the centre cap 'CENTRE' and the two rear caps 'R'. Tighten the cap bolts to a torque of 65 to 70 lb ft (8.280 to 9.660 kg m). Spin the crankshaft to make certain it is turning freely.

12   Check that the piston ring grooves and oilways are thoroughly clean and unblocked. Piston rings must always be fitted over the head of the piston and never from the bottom. The easiest method to use when fitting rings is to wrap a 0.020 in (0.5080 mm) feeler gauge round the top of the piston and place the rings one at a time, starting with the bottom oil control ring, over the feeler gauge.

13   The feeler gauge, complete with ring, can then be slid down the piston over the other piston ring grooves until the correct groove is reached. The piston ring is then slid gently off the feeler gauge into the groove.

14   An alternative method is to fit the rings by holding them slightly open with the thumbs and both index fingers (photo). This method requires a steady hand and great care as it is easy to open the ring too much and break it.

15   When assembling the rings note that the compression rings are marked 'top' (photo) and that the upper ring is chromium plated. The ring gaps should be spaced equally round the piston.

16   If the same pistons are being used, they must be mated to the same connecting rod with the same gudgeon pin. If new pistons are being fitted it does not matter which connecting rod they are used with. Note that the word FRONT is stamped on one side of each of the rods (photo). On reassembly the side marked FRONT must be towards the front of the engine.

17   Fit a gudgeon pin circlip in position at one end of the gudgeon pin hole in the piston and fit the piston to the connecting rod by sliding in the gudgeon pin (photo). The arrow on the crown of each piston must be on the same side as the word FRONT on the connecting rod. Should the gudgeon pin be tight to push in, do not force it but heat the piston in hot oil to expand it.

18   Fit the second circlip in position (photo). Repeat this procedure for the remaining three pistons and connecting rods.

19   Fit the connecting rod in position and check that the oil hole (arrowed in photo) in the upper half of each bearing aligns with the oil squirt hole in the connecting rod.

20   With a wad of clean rag wipe the cylinder bores clean, and then oil them generously. The pistons complete with connecting rods, are fitted to their bores from above (photo). As each piston is inserted into its bore ensure that it is the correct piston/connecting rod assembly for that particular bore, that the connecting rod is the right way round, and that the front of the piston is towards the front of the bore, i.e. towards the front of the engine.

21   The piston will only slide into the bore as far as the oil control ring. It is then necessary to compress the piston rings in a clamp (photo).

22   Gently tap the piston into the cylinder bore with a wooden

44.6 Checking the fit of connecting rods on the crankshaft

44.9 Lowering the crankshaft into position

44.10 Fitting crankshaft end float thrust washers

44.11 Correct location of crankshaft main bearing cap

44.14 Fitting piston rings

44.15 Piston ring fitting mark

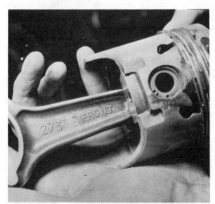

44.16 Piston/connecting rod orientation mark

44.17 Fitting a gudgeon pin

44.18 Fitting the final gudgeon pin circlip

44.19 Correct location of a connecting rod upper shell bearing

44.20 Fitting a piston/connecting rod assembly

44.21 Compressing the piston rings prior to entering the bore

or plastic hammer (photo). If a proper piston ring clamp is not available then a suitable jubilee clip does the job very well.

23 Note that the directional arrow may be on the side of the piston (photo).

24 Fit the shell bearings to the big end caps so the tongue on the back of each bearing lies in the machined recess (photo).

25 Generously oil the crankshaft connecting rod journals and then replace each big end cap on the same connecting rod from which it was removed. Fit the locking plates under the head of the big end bolts, tap the caps right home on the dowels and then tighten the bolts to a torque of 20 to 25 lb ft (2.760 to 3.450 kg m). Lock the bolts in position by knocking up the tabs on the locking washer (photo).

26 The semi rebuilt engine will now appear as in the photo and is ready for the cam followers (tappets) and cam to be fitted.

27 Fit the eight cam followers into the same hole in the block from which each was removed (photo). The cam followers can only be fitted with the block upside down.

28 Fit the woodruff key in its slot on the front of the crankshaft and then press the timing sprocket into place so the timing mark faces forward. Oil the camshaft shell bearings and insert the camshaft into the block (which should still be upside down). (photo).

29 Make sure the camshaft turns freely and then fit the thrust plate behind the camshaft flange as shown in photo. Measure the end float with a feeler gauge - it should be between 0.0025 and 0.0075 in (0.0635 and 0.2032 mm). If this is not so then renew the plate.

30 Fit the two camshaft flange bolts into their joint washer, and screw down the bolts securely (photo).

31 Turn up the tap (arrowed in photo) under the head of each bolt to lock it in place.

32 When refitting the timing chain round the gearwheels and to the engine, the two timing lines (arrowed in photo) must be adjacent to each other on an imaginary line passing through each gearwheel centre.

33 With the timing marks correctly aligned turn the camshaft until the protruding dowel locates in the hole (arrowed in photo) in the camshaft sprocket wheel.

34 Tighten the two retaining bolts and bend up the tabs on the lockwasher (photo).

35 Fit the oil slinger to the nose of the crankshaft, concave side facing outwards. The cut out (arrowed in photo) locates over the woodruff key.

36 Then slide the timing chain tensioner arm over its hinge pin on the front of the block (photo).

37 Turn the tensioner back from its free position so it will apply pressure to the tensioner arm and replace the tensioner on the block sump flange (photo).

38 Bolt the tensioner to the block using spring washers under the heads of the two bolts (arrowed in photo).

39 Remove the front oil seal from the timing chain cover and with the aid of a vice carefully press a new seal into position (photo). Lightly lubricate the face of the seal which will bear against the crankshaft.

40 Use jointing compound on the mating faces of the timing cover and block, and locate the timing cover on the front face of the block.

41 Screw in and tighten the two dowel bolts first. These fit in the holes nearest the sump flange and serve to align the timing cover. Use new lockwashers and tighten the bolts evenly.

42 Refit the tube or oil breather device to its recess in the top of the petrol pump housing on the block tapping it gently into place (photo). Replace the oil pump suction pipe using a new tab washer and position the gauze head so it clears the crankshaft throw and the oil return pipe (where fitted). Tighten the nut and bend back the tab of the lockwasher.

43 Drift out the old and press the new oil seal into the rear main bearing oil retainer.

44 Coat the mating faces of the retainer and the cylinder block and then slide the oil seal retainer over the flywheel mounting flange of the crankshaft.

44.22 Tapping the piston assembly into a cylinder bore

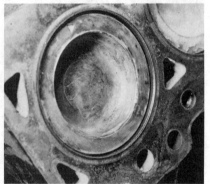
44.23 Piston directional fitting arrow

44.24 Correct fitting of big end cap shell bearing

44.25 Bending the locking tabs on the big end bolts

44.26 Partly rebuilt engine

44.27 Fitting the cam followers (tappets)

44.28 Inserting the camshaft into the engine block

44.29 Fitting the camshaft thrust plate

44.30 Tightening the camshaft flange bolts

44.31 Camshaft lock plates (arrowed)

44.32 Timing gear marks (arrowed)

44.33 Camshaft locating dowel (arrowed)

44.34 Camshaft gear bolt locking tabs

44.35 Correct fitting of the crankshaft oil slinger

44.36 Fitting the timing chain tensioner arm

44.37 Fitting the timing chain tensioner block

44.38 Timing chain tensioner block bolts and lockwashers (arrowed)

44.39 Pressing in a new oil seal to the timing cover

44.42 Tapping the oil breather into position in the block

FIG 1 : 38 CENTRALIZING THE CRANKSHAFT REAR
OIL SEAL CARRIER

FIG 1 : 39 METHOD OF FITTING SUMP GASKET AND
RUBBER SEALS

44.50 Coating the oil pump flange with jointing compound

45 Enter the retainer securing bolts but before tightening move the retainer to obtain perfect concentricity with the flywheel mounting flange. The use of a ring similar to the one shown in Fig 1 : 38 will assist the alignment. Tighten the bolts fully.

46 Fit a rubber sealing piece to both the grooves in the rear oil seal retainer (Fig 1 : 39) and the timing cover. Locate the sump side gaskets ensuring that their ends are tucked under the rubber sealing pieces.

47 Fit the sump and tighten the securing bolts to a torque of 7 to 9 lb ft (.966 to 1.11 kg m). Note that the two longer bolts are located at the rear. See Fig. 1.24.

48 Clean the mating faces of the flywheel flange and the flywheel and locate the flywheel on the flange so that the dowels engage correctly.

49 Screw in the flywheel retaining bolts to a torque of between 50 and 55 lb ft (6.9 and 7.590 kg m).

50 The engine can now be turned over so it is the right way up. Coat the oil pump flanges with jointing compound (photo).

51 Fit a new gasket in place on the oil pump (photo).

52 Position the oil pump against the block ensuring the skew gear teeth on the drive shaft mate with those on the camshaft (photo).

53 Replace the three securing bolts and spring washers and tighten them down evenly (photo).

54 Moving to the front of the engine align the slot in the crank-shaft pulley wheel with the key on the crankshaft and gently tap the pulley wheel home (photo).

55 Secure the pulley wheel by fitting the large flat washer, the spring washer and then the bolt which should be tightened securely (photo).

56 The next step is to thoroughly clean the faces of the block and cylinder head. Then fit a new cylinder head gasket (photo).

57 With the cylinder head on its side lubricate the valve stems and refit the valves to their correct guides (photo). The valves should previously have been ground in (see Section 35).

58 Then fit the valve stem umbrella oil seals open ends down (photo).

59 Next slide the valve spring into place (photo).

60 Slide the valve spring retainer over the valve stem (photo).

61 Compress the valve spring with a compressor as shown in the photograph.

62 Then refit the split collets (photo). A trace of grease will help to hold them to the valve stem recess until the spring compressor is slackened off and the collets are wedged in place by the spring.

63 Carefully lower the cylinder head onto the block.

64 Replace the cylinder head bolts and screw them down finger tight. Note that two of the bolts are of a different length and should be fitted to the holes indicated in the photograph.

65 With a torque wrench tighten the bolts to 65 to 70 lb ft (8.970 to 9.660 kg m) (photo) in the order shown in Fig 1 : 19.

66 Fit the pushrods into the same holes in the block from which they were removed. Make sure the pushrods seat properly in the cam followers (photo).

67 Reassemble the rocker gear into the rocker shaft and fit the shaft to the cylinder head (photo). Ensure that the oil holes are clear and that the cut-outs for the securing bolts lie facing the holes in the brackets.

68 Tighten down the four rocker bracket washers and bolts to a torque of 17 - 22 lb ft (2.346 - 3.036 kg m) (photo).

69 The valve adjustments should be made with the engine hot (except during the assembly stage following dismantling). The importance of correct rocker arm/valve stem clearances cannot be overstressed as they vitally affect the performance of the engine. If the clearances are set too open, the efficiency of the engine is reduced as the valves open late and close earlier than was intended. If, on the other hand the clearances are set too close there is a danger that the stems will expand upon heating and not allow the valves to close properly which will cause burning of the valve head and seat and possible warping. If the engine is in the car, access to the rockers is by removing the holding down screws from the rocker cover, and then lifting the rocker cover and gasket away.

70 It is important that the clearance is set when the tappet of the valve being adjusted is on the heel of the cam, (i.e. opposite

44.51 Fitting a new oil pump gasket

44.52 Meshing the oil pump drive gear

44.53 Tightening an oil pump securing bolt

44.54 Fitting the crankshaft pulley

44.55 Fitting the crankshaft pulley securing bolt

44.56 Fitting a new cylinder head gasket

44.57 Fitting a valve into its guide

44.58 Fitting an oil seal to a valve stem

44.59 Sliding a valve spring into place

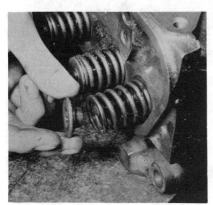
44.60 Fitting a valve spring retainer

44.61 Compressing a valve spring

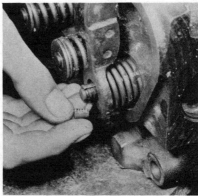
44.62 Fitting the split collets to the valve stem

44.64 Fitting the cylinder head bolts

44.65 Tightening the cylinder head bolts, using a torque wrench

44.66 Inserting the pushrods

44.67 Fitting the rocker shaft to the cylinder head

44.68 Tightening the rocker shaft pillars

44.71 Self locking rocker arm adjuster bolt

the peak). This can be ensured by carrying out the adjustments in the following order (which also avoids turning the crankshaft more than necessary):-

Valve fully open	Check & Adjust
Valve No. 8	Valve No. 1
Valve No. 6	Valve No. 3
Valve No. 4	Valve No. 5
Valve No. 7	Valve No. 2
Valve No. 1	Valve No. 8
Valve No. 3	Valve No. 6
Valve No. 5	Valve No. 4
Valve No. 2	Valve No. 7

71 The correct valve clearances between the valve stem and the rocker arm pad are given in the specifications. Working from the timing chain end of the engine, slacken each self-locking rocker arm adjuster bolt (photo), using a ring spanner and at the same time exerting a downward pressure. Insert a feeler gauge appropriate to the type of valve gap being measured and turn the bolt until the feeler gauge will just move in or out without being nipped and held stationary (Fig 1 : 40). Remove the feeler gauge and ring spanner. No locknuts are used with this type of rocker adjuster bolt which has self-locking tapered threads (photo). Alternative methods of valve clearance adjustment may be employed, using a proprietary tool or adjusting the clearances with the engine running.

72 Do not refit the rocker cover before replacing the distributor and setting the ignition timing. It is important to set the distributor drive correctly as otherwise the ignition timing will be totally incorrect. It is possible to set the distributor drive in apparently the right position, but, in fact, 180° out, by omitting to select the correct cylinder which must not only be at TDC but also must be on its firing stroke with both valves closed. The distributor drive should therefore not be fitted until the cylinder head is in position and the valves can be observed. Alternatively, if the timing cover has not been replaced, the distributor drive can be replaced when the lines on the timing wheels are adjacent to each other.

73 Rotate the crankshaft so that No. 1 piston is at TDC and on its firing stroke (the lines in the timing gears will be adjacent to each other). When No. 1 piston is at TDC both valves will be closed and both rocker arms will 'rock' slightly because of the stem to arm pad clearance.

74 Note the timing index on the timing case and the notch on the crankshaft pulley wheel periphery (Fig 1 : 41). When the pulley wheel notch is mid way between the 4° and 8° marks at TDC on its compression stroke, then this is the static initial advance as specified of 6° BTDC and is applicable to both 1300 and 1600 cc engines.

75 Hold the distributor in place so the vacuum unit is towards the rear of the engine and at an angle of about 30° to the block. Do not yet engage the distributor drive gear with the skew gear on the camshaft.

76 Turn the rotor arm so that it points towards number 2 inlet port (photo).

77 Push the distributor shaft into its bore and note, as the distributor drive gear and skew gear on the camshaft mate, that the rotor arm turns so that it assumes a position of approximately 90° to the engine (photo). Fit the bolt and washer which holds the distributor clamp plate to the block.

78 Loosen the pinch bolt on the distributor clamp plate and turn the distributor body until the points are just opening, whilst holding the rotor arm against the direction of rotation to take up any slackness in the drive. The use of a test lamp will help to establish the moment of points opening. Connect one wire from the test lamp to the distributor LT lead and the other wire to earth. Switch on the ignition and rotate the distributor body until the test lamp just lights, this indicates that the points are just open.

79 Fit a new gasket to the water pump and attach it to the front

FIG 1 : 40 ADJUSTING A VALVE CLEARANCE

FIG 1 : 41 TIMING CHAIN CASE AND CRANKSHAFT PULLEY TIMING MARKS

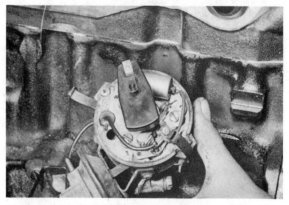

44.76 Location of rotor prior to meshing distributor drive gear

44.77 Location of rotor after meshing distributor drive gear

of the cylinder block (photo).

80 Note that the dynamo support strap fits under the head of the lower bolt on the water pump as shown in the photo. The bolt should not be tightened at this stage.

81 Replace the fuel pump using a new gasket and tighten up the two securing bolts (Fig 1 : 42).

82 Fit the thermostat, noting carefully its correct orientation as shown in Fig 1 : 43. Use a new gasket and then fit the top housing water outlet.

83 Fit the rocker cover and if the old gasket has broken or deteriorated, use a new one making sure to engage the lugs of the cork in the rocker cover recesses.

84 Fit the dynamo (or alternator) to its mountings and after fitting the fan belt, adjust the belt tension to permit not more than ½ in (12.5 mm) free movement between the water pump and generating unit pulleys (Fig 1 : 44). Tighten the strap bolts fully.

85 Refit the vacuum advance pipe between the distributor and the carburettor and refit the oil and water temperature sender units.

86 Replace the engine ancillary components such as the oil filter, oil breather separator, engine mountings and inlet and exhaust manifolds, using new gaskets for the latter (photo).

87 Refit the carburettor but at this stage do not fit the spark plugs. The engine is now ready for refitting to the vehicle.

45 Engine replacement - general

1 Although the engine can be replaced with one man and a suitable winch, it is easier if two are present, one to lower the engine into the engine compartment and the other to guide the engine into position and to ensure it does not foul anything.

2 At this stage one or two tips may come in useful. Ensure all the loose leads, cables, etc. are tucked out of the way. If not it is easy to trap one and so cause much additional work after the engine is replaced. Smear grease on the tip of the gearbox input shaft before fitting the gearbox.

3 Always fit a new fan belt and new cooling hoses and jubilee clips as this will help eliminate the possibility of failure while on the road. An exchange rebuilt carburettor also helps!

4 Two pairs of hands are better than one when refitting the bonnet. Do not tighten the bonnet securing bolts fully until it is ascertained that the bonnet is on straight.

46 Engine replacement without gearbox

1 Position a sling around the engine and support its weight on suitable lifting tackle. If using a fixed hoist raise the engine and then roll the car under it. Place a jack under the gearbox.

2 Lower the engine into the engine compartment ensuring that nothing is fouling. Line up the engine and gearbox raising the height of the gearbox if necessary with the jack until the splines on the gearbox input shaft mate with the splined grooves in the clutch disc centre. As the spark plugs have not yet been fitted, the crankshaft pulley may be easily turned by hand to facilitate engagement of the splined components. Do not allow the weight of the engine to hang upon the gearbox input shaft, even momentarily.

3 To line up the mounting bracket holes it may be necessary to move the engine about slightly and this will be found to be much easier if the lifting slings are still in position and taking most of the weight.

4 Replace the bolts and washers - one on each side - which hold the engine mountings to the bodyframe (photo).

5 Do up those engine to clutch housing bolts which are accessible from above. The earth strap for the engine is secured by the top left hand bolt. If automatic transmission is fitted turn the engine as required so that the drive plate to torque converter bolts can be fitted. Remove the slings from the engine, and jack up the front of the car securely so it can be worked on from underneath.

FIG 1 : 42 THE FUEL PUMP SECURING BOLTS

FIG 1 : 43 THERMOSTAT LOCATION AND GASKET

FIG 1 : 44 FAN BELT ADJUSTMENT DIAGRAM

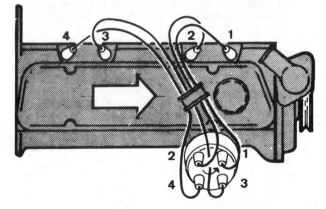
FIG 1 : 45 SPARK PLUG HT LEAD CONNECTIONS

44.79 Fitting water pump and gasket

44.80 Location of dynamo adjustment strap

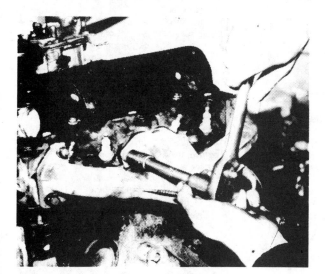

44.86 Tightening exhaust manifold nuts

46.4 Engine mounting to frame securing bolts

6 Working underneath the car, replace the lower clutch housing cover and all the lower clutch housing bolts. Do up the bolts holding the clutch housing to the rear of the engine.

7 Refit the starter motor, replace the retaining bolts, and the starter cable which is held in place with a nut and washer.

8 Reconnect the fuel lines to the pump.

9 Reconnect the HT lead to the coil centre terminal and the LT lead to the distributor.

10 Screw in the spark plugs, cleaned and set to the correct gap of 0.23 in (0.58 mm) and connect the leads from the distributor cap. Fig 1 : 45 shows the correct sequence for fitting the plug leads.

11 Connect the exhaust downpipe and the throttle and choke controls; connect the temperature gauge lead.

12 Replace the radiator and reconnect the top and bottom hoses and the heater hoses.

13 Replace the engine splash shield (where fitted); the air cleaner; the bonnet; and reconnect the two leads to the rear of the dynamo or alternator.

14 Reconnect the battery.

15 Check that the drain taps are closed and refill the cooling system with water and the engine with the correct grade of oil. Start the engine and carefully check for oil or water leaks. There should be no oil or water leaks if the engine has been reassembled carefully, all nuts and bolts tightened down correctly, and new gaskets and joints used throughout.

16 Run the engine up to normal operating temperature, then, whilst still hot, re-torque the cylinder head bolts to that specified and recheck the valve clearances.

47 Engine replacement with gearbox

1 Refitting the engine and gearbox as one unit will be similar to those operations described in the preceding Section with the following additions:

2 Tighten the rear mounting bolt of the gearbox to the crossmember and refit the crossmember.

3 Refit the propeller shaft, ensuring that the rear drive flanges have their mating marks aligned.

4 Refit the gear lever, gaiter and central console.

5 Refit the clutch slave cylinder and bracket assembly.

6 Reconnect the speedometer drive cable to the gearbox.

7 Fill the gearbox with the correct grade and quantity of lubricant.

8 Refit the handbrake lever centre bolt.

Symptom	Reason/s	Remedy
No current at starter motor	Flat or defective battery	Charge or replace battery. Push-start car.
	Loose battery leads	Tighten both terminals and earth ends of earth lead.
	Defective starter solenoid or switch or broken wiring	Run a wire direct from the battery to the starter motor or by-pass the solenoid.
	Engine earth strap disconnected	Check and retighten strap.
Current at starter motor	Jammed starter motor drive pinion	Place car in gear and rock from side to side. Alternatively, free exposed square end of shaft with spanner.
	Defective starter motor	Remove and recondition.
No spark at spark plug	Ignition damp or wet	Wipe dry the distributor cap and ignition leads.
	Ignition leads to spark plugs loose	Check and tighten at both spark plug and distributor cap ends.
	Shorted or disconnected low tension leads	Check the wiring on the CB and SW terminals of the coil and to the distributor.
	Dirty, incorrectly set, or pitted contact breaker points	Clean, file smooth, and adjust.
	Faulty condenser	Check contact breaker points for arcing, remove and fit new.
	Defective ignition switch	By-pass switch with wire.
	Ignition leads connected wrong way round	Remove and replace leads to spark plugs in correct order.
	Faulty coil	Remove and fit new coil.
	Contact breaker point spring earthed or broken	Check spring is not touching metal part of distributor. Check insulator washers are correctly placed. Renew points if the spring is broken.
No fuel at carburettor float chamber or at jets	No petrol in petrol tank	Refill tank!
	Vapour lock in fuel line (In hot conditions or at high altitude)	Blow into petrol tank, allow engine to cool, or apply a cold wet rag to the fuel line.
	Blocked float chamber needle valve	Remove, clean, and replace.
	Fuel pump filter blocked	Remove, clean, and replace.
	Choked or blocked carburettor jets	Dismantle and clean.
	Faulty fuel pump	Remove, overhaul, and replace.
Excess of petrol in cylinder or carburettor flooding	Too much choke allowing too rich a mixture to wet plugs	Remove and dry spark plugs or with wide open throttle, push-start the car.
	Float damaged or leaking or needle not seating	Remove, examine, clean and replace float and needle valve as necessary.
	Float lever incorrectly adjusted	Remove and adjust correctly.
No spark at spark plug	Ignition failure - Sudden	Check over low and high tension circuits for breaks in wiring.
	Ignition failure - Misfiring precludes total stoppage	Check contact breaker points, clean and adjust. Renew condenser if faulty.
	Ignition failure - In severe rain or after traversing water splash	Dry out ignition leads and distributor cap.
No fuel at jets	No petrol in tank	Refill tank.
	Petrol tank breather choked	Remove petrol cap and clean out breather hole or pipe.
	Sudden obstruction in carburettor(s)	Check jets, filter, and needle valve in float chamber for blockage.
	Water in fuel system	Drain tank and blow out fuel lines.

FAULT DIAGNOSIS - ENGINE

Symptom	Reason/s	Remedy
Intermittent sparking at spark plug	Ignition leads loose	Check and tighten as necessary at spark plug and distributor cap ends.
	Battery leads loose on terminals	Check and tighten terminal leads.
	Battery earth strap loose on body attachment point	Check and tighten earth lead to body attachment point.
	Engine earth lead loose	Tighten lead.
	Low tension leads to SW and CB terminals on coil loose	Check and tighten leads if found loose.
	Low tension lead from CB terminal side to distributor loose	Check and tighten if found loose.
	Dirty, or incorrectly gapped plugs	Remove, clean, and regap.
	Dirty, incorrectly set, or pitted contact breaker points	Clean, file smooth, and adjust.
	Tracking across inside of distributor cover	Remove and fit new cover.
	Ignition too retarded	Check and adjust ignition timing.
	Faulty coil	Remove and fit new coil.
Fuel shortage at engine	Mixture too weak	Check jets, float chamber needle valve, and filters for obstruction. Clean as necessary. Carburettor(s) incorrectly adjusted.
	Air leak in carburettor(s)	Remove and overhaul carburettor.
	Air leak at inlet manifold to cylinder head, or inlet manifold to carburettor	Test by pouring oil along joints. Bubbles indicate leak. Renew manifold gasket as appropriate.
Mechanical wear	Incorrect valve clearances	Adjust rocker arms to take up wear.
	Burnt out exhaust valves	Remove cylinder head and renew defective valves.
	Sticking or leaking valves	Remove cylinder head, clean, check and renew valves as necessary.
	Weak or broken valve springs	Check and renew as necessary.
	Worn valve guides or stems	Renew valve guides and valves.
	Worn pistons and piston rings	Dismantle engine, renew pistons and rings.
Fuel/air mixture leaking from cylinder	Burnt out exhaust valves	Remove cylinder head, renew defective valves.
	Sticking or leaking valves	Remove cylinder head, clean, check, and renew valves as necessary.
	Worn valve guides and stems	Remove cylinder head and renew valves and valve guides.
	Weak or broken valve springs	Remove cylinder head, renew defective springs.
	Blown cylinder head gasket (Accompanied by increase in noise)	Remove cylinder head and fit new gasket.
	Worn pistons and piston rings	Dismantle engine, renew pistons and rings.
	Worn or scored cylinder bores	Dismantle engine, rebore, renew pistons & rings.
Incorrect adjustments	Ignition timing wrongly set. Too advanced or retarded	Check and reset ignition timing.
	Contact breaker points incorrectly gapped	Check and reset contact breaker points.
	Incorrect valve clearances	Check and reset rocker arm to valve stem gap.
	Incorrectly set spark plugs	Remove, clean and regap.
	Carburation too rich or too weak	Tune carburettor(s) for optimum performance.
Carburation and ignition faults	Dirty contact breaker points	Remove, clean, and replace.
	Fuel filters blocked causing top end fuel starvation	Dismantle, inspect, clean, and replace all fuel filters.
	Distributor automatic balance weights or vacuum advance and retard mechanisms not functioning correctly	Overhaul distributor.
	Faulty fuel pump giving top end fuel starvation	Remove, overhaul, or fit exchange reconditioned fuel pump.

FAULT DIAGNOSIS - ENGINE

Symptom	Reason/s	Remedy
Oil being burnt by engine	Badly worn, perished or missing valve stem oil seals	Remove, fit new oil seals to valve stems.
	Excessively worn valve stems and valve guides	Remove cylinder head and fit new valves and valve guides.
	Worn piston rings	Fit oil control rings to existing pistons or purchase new pistons.
	Worn pistons and cylinder bores	Fit new pistons and rings, rebore cylinders.
	Excessive piston ring gap allowing blow-by.	Fit new piston rings and set gap correctly.
	Piston oil return holes choked	Decarbonise engine and pistons.
Oil being lost due to leaks	Leaking oil filter gasket	Inspect and fit new gasket as necessary.
	Leaking rocker cover gasket	" " " " " " "
	Leaking timing case joint	" " " " " " "
	Leaking sump gasket	" " " " " " "
	Loose sump plug	Tighten, fit new gasket if necessary.
Excessive clearances due to mechanical wear	Worn valve gear (Noisy tapping from rocker box)	Inspect and renew rocker shaft, rocker arms, and ball pins as necessary.
	Worn big end bearing (Regular heavy knocking)	Drop sump, if bearings broken up clean out oil pump and oilways, fit new bearings. If bearings not broken but worn fit bearing shells.
	Worn timing chain and gears (Rattling from front of engine)	Remove timing cover, fit new timing wheels and timing chain.
	Worn main bearings (Rumbling and vibration)	Drop sump, remove crankshaft, if bearings worn but not broken up, renew. If broken up strip oil pump and clean out oilways.
	Worn crankshaft (Knocking, rumbling and vibration)	Regrind crankshaft, fit new main and big end bearings.

Chapter 2 Cooling system

Contents

Specifications

Type	Pressurised, forced circular
Coolant capacity (including heater) 1300 cc	10.3 pts (5.8 litres)
1600 cc	11.3 pts (6.3 litres)
Fan type 1300 cc	7 blade) 12 in (304.8 mm)
	10 blade) diameter
1600 cc	7 blade 12.5 in (317.5 mm)
	diameter
Radiator pressure cap rating	13 lb in^2 (0.91 kg cm^2)

Thermostat

Type	Wax
Opening temperature	85 - 89°C (185 - 192°F) ± 3°
Fully opening temperature	99 - 102°C (210 - 216°F)
Fan belt free play	½ in (12.5 mm)

Tightening torque

Fan blades	5 - 7 lb ft (0.69 - 0.97 kg m)
Water pump to block bolts	5 - 7 lb ft (0.69 - 0.97 kg m)
Thermostat housing bolts	12 - 15 lb ft (1.66 - 2.07 kg m)

1 General description

1 The engine cooling system is of thermo-syphon, impeller
assisted type. The system is pressurised by means of the spring
loaded radiator filler cap which prevents loss of coolant down
the overflow pipe and prevents premature boiling by increasing
the boiling point of the coolant.

2 If the water temperature goes above this increased boiling
point the extra pressure in the system forces the internal part of
the cap off its seat, thus exposing the overflow pipe down which
the steam from the boiling water escapes thereby relieving the
pressure. It is therefore important to check that the radiator cap
is in good condition and that the spring behind the sealing washer
has not weakened. Most garages have a special machine in which
radiator caps can be tested. The cooling system comprises the
radiator; top and bottom water hoses; heater hoses; the impeller
water pump (mounted on the front of the engine, it carries the
fan blades, and is driven by the fan belt); the thermostat; and
radiator drain tap.

3 The system functions in the following fashion. Cold water in
the bottom of the radiator circulates up the lower radiator hose
to the water pump where it is pushed round the water passages in
the cylinder block, helping to keep the cylinder bores and pistons
cool.

The water then travels up into the cylinder head and circulates round the combustion spaces and valve seats absorbing more
heat, and then, when the engine is at its proper operating temperature, travels out of the cylinder head, past the open thermostat into the upper radiator hose and so into the radiator header
tank.

The water travels down the radiator where it is rapidly cooled
by the in-rush of cold air through the radiator core, which is
created by both the fan and the motion of the car. The water,
now cold, reaches the bottom of the radiator, when the cycle is
repeated.

When the engine is cold the thermostat (a valve which
opens and closes according to the temperature of the water)
maintains the circulation of the same water in the engine.

Only when the correct minimum operating temperature has
been reached, as shown in the Specifications does the thermostat
begin to open, allowing water to return to the radiator.

2 Cooling system - draining

1 With the car on level ground drain the system as follows:-

2 If the engine is cold remove the filler cap from the radiator by
turning the cap anti-clockwise. If the engine is hot having just
been run, then turn the filler cap very slightly until the pressure

in the system has had time to disperse. Use a rag over the cap to protect your hand from escaping steam. If, with the engine very hot, the cap is released suddenly, the drop in pressure can result in the water boiling. With the pressure released the cap can be removed.

3   If anti-freeze is in the radiator drain it into a clean bucket or bowl for re-use.

4   Place the heater control in the HOT position and unscrew the radiator drain plug (Fig 2 : 1). The plug is the captive type and will cause considerable spray of coolant being drained, so use a sizeable bowl if the coolant is being retained.

5   Screw in the radiator drain plug as soon as draining is complete but do not overtighten.

3   Cooling system - flushing

1   With time the cooling system will gradually lose its efficiency as the radiator becomes choked with rust scales, deposits from the water and other sediment. To clean the system out, remove the radiator cap, unscrew the radiator drain plug and leave a hose running in the radiator cap orifice for ten to fifteen minutes.

2   Then close the drain tap and refill with water and a proprietary cleansing compound. Run the engine for 10 to 15 minutes and then drain it and flush out thoroughly for a further ten minutes. All sediment and sludge should now have been removed.

3   In very bad cases the radiator should be reverse flushed. This can be done with the radiator in position. Place a hose over the open radiator drain plug. Water, under pressure, is then forced up through the radiator and out of the header tank filler orifice.

4   The hose is then removed and placed in the filler orifice and the radiator washed out in the usual fashion.

4   Cooling system - filling

1   Close the radiator drain tap.

2   Fill the system slowly to ensure that no air locks develop. If a heater is fitted, check that the valve to the heater unit is open, otherwise an air lock may form in the heater. The best type of water to use in the cooling system is rain water, so use this whenever possible.

3   Do not fill the system higher than within ½ in of the filler orifice. Overfilling will merely result in wastage, which is especially to be avoided when anti-freeze is in use.

4   Only use anti-freeze mixture with a glycerine or ethylene base.

5   Replace the filler cap and turn it firmly clockwise to lock it in position.

5   Radiator - removal, inspection, cleaning and replacement

1   To remove the radiator first drain the cooling system as described in Section 2.

2   Undo the wire clips which hold the top and bottom radiator hoses on the radiator and then pull off the two hoses (Fig 2 : 2).

3   Undo and remove the two bolts and washers on either side of the radiator which hold it in place. It may be helpful to remove the battery to give better access to the top right hand bolt (Fig 2 : 3).

4   Having removed the bolts lift the radiator out of the engine compartment.

5   With the radiator out of the car any leaks can be soldered up or repaired with a substance such as 'Cataloy'. Clean out the inside of the radiator by flushing as detailed in Section 3. When the radiator is out of the car it is advantageous to turn it upside down for reverse flushing. Clean the exterior of the radiator by hosing down the radiator matrix with a strong jet of water to clear away road dirt, dead flies etc.

6   Inspect the radiator hoses for cracks, internal or external perishing, and damage caused by over-tightening of the hose clips.

7   Note the method of connecting the overflow pipe using a

FIG 2 : 1 LOCATION OF THE RADIATOR DRAIN PLUG

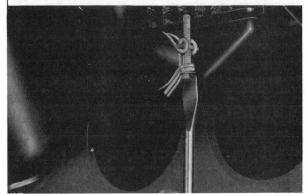
FIG 2 : 2 UNSCREWING THE RADIATOR UPPER AND LOWER HOSE CLIPS

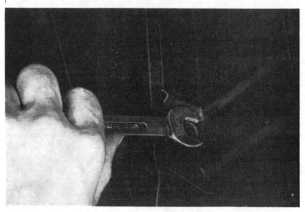
FIG 2 : 3 UNSCREWING A RADIATOR SECURING BOLT

plastic connector from the inside of the filler neck (Fig 2 : 4).

8   Renew hoses, clips and drain tap rubber sealing washer as necessary.

9   Refitting is a reversal of removal.

6   Thermostat - removal, testing and replacement

1   Release the radiator pressure cap and drain sufficient coolant from the system to reduce the level to below that of the thermostat housing (approx. 4 pts.).

2   Unscrew and remove the two bolts which secure the upper thermostat housing and lift the housing off. Do not use a screwdriver in the mating faces but, if it is stuck, tap the elbow gently with a block of wood or soft faced hammer.

3   Peel off the gasket and lift out the thermostat (Fig 2 : 5). If the thermostat is stuck in its seating, carefully cut round the joint between the body and thermostat periphery. Do not try and lever the thermostat out by its bridge piece.

4   If the thermostat is suspect, check it by suspending it in water (away from the sides of the vessel) (Fig 2 : 6) and gradually heating the water. Use an accurate thermometer and check its performance. The unit should start to open at between 85° and 89° C (210° and 216°F). If the thermostat does not operate correctly, renew it with one of similar type.

5   When replacing the thermostat in its housing, first clean the seating recess and use a new gasket with jointing compound such as Hermetite Red. The aluminium components of the housing are liable to show pitting or corrosion and where this is apparent first rub the mating face of the upper housing elbow on a perfectly flat sheet of emery cloth in order to improve the sealing when bolted up.

6   Refit the securing bolts and replace the drained coolant in the system, topping up if necessary.

7   Water pump - removal and replacement

1   Drain the cooling system as described in Section 2, retaining the coolant if required.

2   Disconnect the top and bottom radiator hoses and remove the radiator as described in Section 5.

3   Slacken the dynamo or alternator mounting bolts and the adjustment strap bolt (arrowed for alternator Fig 2 : 7) and pivot the unit towards the engine.

4   Remove the fan belt over the dynamo or alternator pulley, (Fig 2 : 8).

5   Unscrew and remove the four bolts which secure the fan and pulley to the water pump flange and lift the fan and pulley away.

6   Remove the heater hose from the water pump outlet.

7   Unscrew and remove the three water pump securing bolts and withdraw the water pump and gasket from its location on the front face of the cylinder block.

8   Refitting is a reversal of removal but use a new gasket and do not overtighten the fan securing bolts. Adjust the fan belt tension as described in Section 9, and refill the cooling system as described in Section 4.

8   Water pump - dismantling and reassembly

1   It is recommended that when the water pump is in need of repair it should be exchanged for a factory reconditioned unit. However, where the necessary tools and experience are available, carry out the following procedure:

2   Refer to Fig 2 : 9 and remove the bearing retainer clip (3) from the housing.

3   With a suitable extractor or press (Fig 2 : 8) remove the pulley hub (6) from the pump shaft (7).

4   Press the impeller (10) seal assembly (9) slinger (8) and shaft and bearing assembly (7) out of the pump body, making sure

FIG 2 : 4 DISCONNECTING THE RADIATOR OVERFLOW HOSE

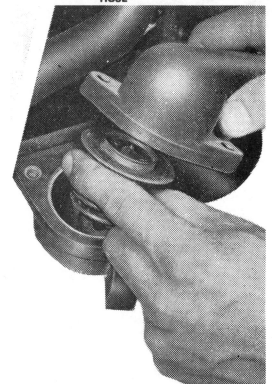

FIG 2 : 5 REMOVING THE THERMOSTAT

FIG 2 : 6 ALTERNATOR MOUNTING AND ADJUSTER STRAP BOLTS

FIG 2 : 7 REMOVING THE FAN BELT

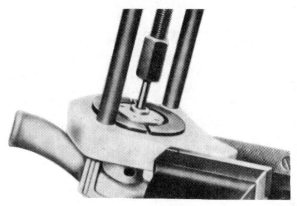

FIG 2 : 8 REMOVING THE PULLEY HUB FROM THE WATER PUMP SHAFT

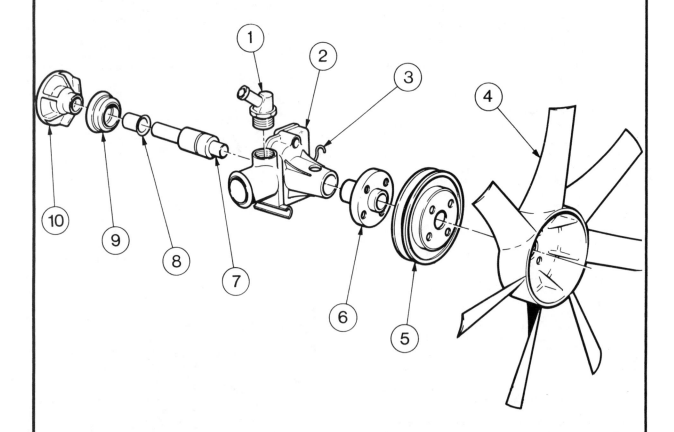

FIG 2 : 9 EXPLODED VIEW OF THE WATER PUMP

1 Heater connection	3 Bearing retainer	5 Fan pulley	8 Slinger
2 Pump body	4 Cooling fan	6 Pulley hub	9 Seal assembly
		7 Shaft and bearing assembly	10 Impeller

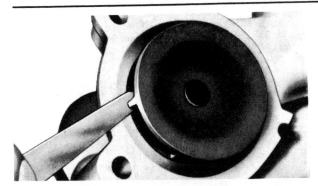

FIG 2 : 10 CHECKING THE IMPELLER BLADE TO BODY CLEARANCE

that the force is exerted only on the outer diameter of the bearing.

5 Press the impeller off the shaft.

6 Remove the seal assembly from the shaft and the slinger which will probably have to be split with a sharp chisel in order to remove it.

7 The shaft and bearing assembly cannot be separated and must be renewed as a combined unit. Press the shaft and bearing assembly into the pump body. Enter the assembly from the rear, short end of the shaft first. When the bearing is flush with the front of the pump, insert the retaining clip.

8 Press the pump pulley hub on to the front end of the shaft until the shaft end and hub faces are flush.

9 Press a new slinger (flanged end first) onto the shaft so that its non flanged end is positioned ½ in (12.5 mm) from the shaft end.

10 Push the new seal over the shaft and into the counterbore in the water pump body.

11 Press the impeller on to the shaft until a clearance of 0.030 in (0.76 mm) can be measured with a feeler gauge (Fig 2 : 10). Note that the clearance is between the impeller blade and housing faces. Do not overpress the impeller onto the shaft as this will compress the slinger and necessitate dismantling again and renewal of the slinger.

12 Check for smooth operation but do not confuse the resistance of the new seal assembly with binding of the pump components.

13 After refitting the water pump as described in Section 7, check for leaks behind the pump pulley flange.

9 Fan belt - adjustment

1 The belt tension is correct when there is ½ in (12.5 mm) of total free movement at the mid way position of the belt between the dynamo or alternator pulley wheel and the water pump pulley wheel (Fig 2 : 11).

2 To adjust the belt, slacken the body and strap mounting bolts, (Fig 2 : 6) and move the charging unit in or out until the correct tension is obtained. The operation will be easier and more precise if the mounting bolts are loosened only just sufficiently to permit the dynamo or alternator to move stiffly.

3 If difficulty is experienced in moving the dynamo or alternator away from the engine, a long spanner or screwdriver placed behind the dynamo and resting against the cylinder block serves as a very good lever and can be held in this position while the dynamo securing bolts are tightened down.

10 Fan belt - removal and replacement

1 If the fan belt is worn or has stretched unduly it should be replaced. The most usual reason for replacement is that the belt has broken in service. It is therefore recommended that a spare belt is always carried.

2 Removal of an old belt is described in Section 7 : 3 and 4 to which reference should be made. If the belt has broken then the dynamo or alternator mounting bolts and adjustment strap must be loosened and the unit pushed in towards the engine

FIG 2 : 11 SECTION OF FAN BELT TO CHECK FOR FREE PLAY

before the new fan belt can be fitted. Do not try to force a new belt over the pulleys with the original adjustment undisturbed.

3 Adjust the belt as described in the preceding section and re-adjust after 500 miles (800 km) running.

11 Temperature gauge - fault finding

1 If the temperature gauge fails to work, either the gauge, the sender unit, the wiring or the connections are at fault.

2 It is not possible to repair the gauge or the sender unit and they must be replaced by new units if at fault.

3 First check the wiring connections and if sound, check the wiring for breaks using an ohmmeter. The sender unit and gauge should be tested by substitution.

12 Temperature gauge and sender unit - removal and replacement

1 For details of how to remove and replace the temperature gauge see Chapter 10.

2 To remove the sender unit, disconnect the wire leading into the unit at its connector and undo the unit with a spanner. The unit is located in the cylinder head just below the water outlet elbow on the left side. Replacement is a reversal of the above procedure but check the condition of the sealing washer and renew if necessary.

13 Anti-freeze mixture

1 In circumstances where it is likely that the temperature will drop to below freezing it is essential that some of the water is drained and an adequate amount of ethylene glycol anti-freeze such as Fords Long Life Anti-Freeze Ford Part No.M97B18-C or Bluecol is added to the cooling system.

2 If either of the above anti-freezes are not available at the time, any anti-freeze which conforms with specification BS3151 or BS3152 can be used. Never use an anti-freeze with an alcohol base as evaporation is too high.

3 Either of the above mentioned anti-freezes can be left in the cooling system for up to two years, but after six months it is advisable to have the specific gravity of the coolant checked at your local garage, and thereafter once every three months.

4 Below are the amounts of anti-freeze by percentage volume which should be added to ensure adequate protection down to the temperature given.

Amount of A.F.	Protection to
50%	-37°C (-34°F)
40%	-25°C (-13°F)
30%	-16°C (+3°F)
25%	-13°C (+9°F)
20%	-9°C (+15°F)
15%	-7°C (+20°F)
10%	-4°C (+25°F)

FAULT DIAGNOSIS - COOLING SYSTEM

Symptom	Reason/s	Remedy
Heat generated in cylinder not being successfully disposed of by radiator	Insufficient water in cooling system	Top up radiator
	Fan belt slipping (accompanied by a shrieking noise on rapid engine acceleration)	Tighten fan belt to recommended tension or replace if worn.
	Radiator core blocked or radiator grill restricted	Reverse flush radiator, remove obstructions.
	Bottom water hose collapsed, impeding flow	Remove and fit new hose.
	Thermostat not opening properly	Remove and fit new thermostat.
	Ignition advance and retard incorrectly set (accompanied by loss of power, and perhaps, misfiring)	Check and reset ignition timing.
	Carburettor(s) incorrectly adjusted (mixture too weak)	Tune carburettor(s).
	Exhaust system partially blocked	Check exhaust pipe for constrictive dents and blockages.
	Oil level in sump too low	Top up sump to full mark on dipstick.
	Blown cylinder head gasket (water/steam being forced down the radiator overflow pipe under pressure)	Remove cylinder head, fit new gasket.
	Engine not yet run-in	Run-in slowly and carefully.
	Brakes binding	Check and adjust brakes if necessary.
Too much heat being dispersed by radiator	Thermostat jammed open	Remove and renew thermostat.
	Incorrect grade of thermostat fitted allowing premature opening of valve	Remove and replace with new thermostat which opens at a higher temperature.
	Thermostat missing	Check and fit correct thermostat.
Leaks in system	Loose clips on water hoses	Check and tighten clips if necessary.
	Top, bottom, or by-pass water hoses perishing and leaking	Check and replace any faulty hoses.
	Radiator core leaking	Remove radiator and repair.
	Thermostat gasket leaking	Inspect and renew gasket.
	Radiator pressure cap spring worn or seal ineffective	Renew radiator pressure cap.
	Blown cylinder head gasket (pressure in system forcing water/steam down overflow pipe	Remove cylinder head and fit new gasket.
	Cylinder wall or head cracked	Dismantle engine, dispatch to engineering works for repair.

Chapter 3 Fuel system and carburation

Contents

Specifications

Fuel pump

Type ... ...   Mechanical, driven by eccentric on camshaft

Delivery pressure ... ...   3.5 to 5.0 lb in^2 (0.25 to 0.35 kg cm^2)

Carburettor

Type ... ...   Autolite, single venturi, downdraught

Model reference (manual choke)

*1   [1300 cc low compression ... ...   71 - 1W - 9510 - JA

    [1300 cc high compression ... ...   71 - 1W - 9510 - KA

*2   [1600 cc low compression ... ...   71 - 1W - 9510 - BJA

    [1600 cc high compression ... ...   71 - 1W - 9510 - VA

(automatic choke)

*3   [1600 cc low compression ... ...   71 - 1W - 9510 - BNA

    [1600 cc high compression ... ...   71 - 1W - 9510 - ZA

*see carburettor data.

Carburettor data

	1	2	3
Throttle barrel diameter	1.34 in (34 mm)	1.42 in (36 mm)	1.42 in (36 mm)
Venturi diameter	0.98 in (25 mm)	1.10 in (28 mm)	1.10 in (28 mm)
Main jet	125	145	145
Idling speed (rev/min)	700	700	700
Fast idle (choke fully open) (rev/min)	1400/1600	1000	2050/2250

Fuel tank capacity ... ...   11.9 gals (54.0 litres)

Minimum octane rating (HC)   98

Torque wrench settings

	lb ft	kg m
Fuel pump to cylinder block	12 to 15	1.7 to 2.1
Carburettor flange nuts	12 to 15	1.7 to 2.1
Manifolds to cylinder head	15 to 18	2.1 to 2.5
Exhaust downpipe to manifold flange coupling nuts	15 to 20	2.0 to 2.7

1 General description

1   The fuel system comprises an 11.9 gal. (54 litres) fuel tank; a mechanically (camshaft) operated pump; and an Autolite single venturi, downdraught type carburettor; together with the necessary fuel lines, line filter and fuel contents gauge and tank transmitter unit.
2   The fuel tank is vented to atmosphere via the filler cap.

2 Air cleaner - removal, element renewal, replacement

1   Raise the bonnet and unscrew and remove the two air cleaner lid securing wing nuts. Lift off the lid.
2   Lift out the paper filtering element (Fig 3 : 1) and if the vehicle has covered 5000 miles (8000 km) since it was originally fitted, or if the vehicle has been operating in exceptionally dusty conditions, renew it. At more frequent intervals, withdraw the element and shake or blow the accumulated dust from it and replace.
3   The air inlet spout on the air cleaner body may be swivelled so that the S (summer) or W (winter) arrows are aligned according to season. It is important to position the air intake appropriately in order to draw in warm air from the exhaust pipe region during winter conditions to prevent the carburettor icing and to minimise condensation in the rocker box.

3 Fuel pump - description

1   The mechanical fuel pump is mounted on the right hand side of the cylinder block (Fig 3 : 2) and is connected to fuel tank and carburettor by braid covered nylon pipes.
2   Additional to the fuel pump integral filter, a line filter is interposed in the pump to carburettor fuel line (Fig 3 : 3).
3   The fuel pump is driven by means of its rocker arm bearing against an eccentric on the camshaft.
4   Although the type of pump fitted is similar, one of two designs may be encountered: Fig 3 : 4 which is of all metal construction and Fig 3 : 5 which incorporates a glass dome. The operating principle of both is similar.
5   As the engine camshaft rotates, the eccentric moves the pump pivoted rocker arm outwards which in turn draws the diaphragm pull rod and diaphragm (9) (Fig 3 : 7) down against the pressure of the diaphragm spring. The vacuum thus created in the pump chamber draws in fuel from the tank through the filter element (4) and non return valve.
6   The actuating (rocker) arm is held in constant contact with the camshaft eccentric by a return spring (14) and as the camshaft continues to rotate, the eccentric profile allows the rocker arm to move inwards. The diaphragm spring is therefore free to push the diaphragm upwards and force the fuel in the pump chamber out of the carburettor through a second non return valve.
7   When the carburettor float chamber is full, the needle valve will close to prevent further fuel from flowing from the pump. The pressure thus created in the pump to carburettor fuel line will hold the diaphragm downwards against the pressure of the diaphragm spring and it will remain in this mode until the needle valve in the carburettor opens to admit more fuel.

4 Fuel pump - sediment removal

1   Every 5000 miles (8000 km) either unscrew the knurled nut on the top of the glass dome (Fig 3 : 6) or remove the centre screw (Fig 3 : 8) according to type of fuel pump fitted.
2   Remove the sediment bowl and filter and wash the filter in clean fuel. Clean the interior of the bowl and check that the sealing rings are in good condition, or renew them.
3   Refit the sediment bowl and filter but do not overtighten either type of securing screw. Check for leaks with the engine

FIG 3 : 1 THE AIR CLEANER WITH LID REMOVED

FIG 3 : 2 FUEL PUMP LOCATION

FIG.3.3. FUEL LINE FILTER

FIG 3 : 4 FUEL PUMP WITH METAL DOME

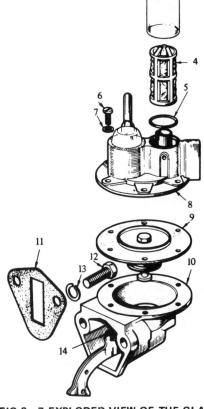

FIG 3 : 7 EXPLODED VIEW OF THE GLASS DOME TYPE
OF FUEL PUMP

1	Dome retaining clamp	8	Upper pump body
2	Finger nut	9	Diaphragm
3	Glass dome	10	Lower pump body
4	Filter element	11	Gasket
5	Dome to body retaining ring	12	Bolt
6	Screw	13	Spring washer
7	Spring washer	14	Actuating arm return spring

FIG 3 : 5 FUEL PUMP WITH GLASS DOME

FIG 3 : 6 KNURLED SECURING NUT FITTED TO GLASS
DOME TYPE FUEL PUMP

FIG 3 : 8 REMOVING THE METAL DOME FROM A FUEL
PUMP

running.

5 Fuel line filter - cleaning

1 Remove the fuel lines from the filter by slackening the securing clips (Fig 3 : 3).
2 Note the direction of fuel flow arrow moulded on the exterior surface of the filter (Fig 3 : 9).
3 Using a tyre pump or air line, blow through the filter in the reverse direction to the fuel flow.
4 Refit the filter noting that it is fitted the correct way round and tighten the securing clips.

6 Fuel pump - testing

Presuming that the fuel lines and unions are in good condition and that there are no leaks anywhere, check the performance of the fuel pump in the following manner: Disconnect the fuel pipe at the carburettor inlet union, and the high tension lead to the coil, and with a suitable container or a large rag in position to catch the ejected fuel, turn the engine over on the starter motor solenoid. A good spurt of petrol should emerge from the end of the pipe every second revolution.

7 Fuel pump - removal and replacement

1 Remove the spring type pipe clip from the pump inlet line and the pinch bolt type clip from the outlet line (Fig 3 : 2).
2 Unscrew and remove the two securing bolts which hold the pump to the crankcase.
3 Lift the pump away with a downward sweeping motion to permit the actuating arm to pass through the crankcase orifice. Retain any packing pieces or gaskets.
4 Replacement is a reversal of removal but ensure that the mating faces are clean and renew suspect thin gaskets and replace the original packing piece.

8 Fuel pump - dismantling, inspection and reassembly

1 Having removed the fuel pump from the cylinder block as described in the preceding Section, consideration should be given to purchasing a new pump if a considerable mileage has been covered. If anything more than the diaphragm, return spring or bowl sealing washer is faulty, it will not be economical to service the individual components.
2 Scratch an alignment mark on the mating edges of the upper and lower bodies and unscrew and remove the upper to lower body securing screws.
3 Separate the bodies and carefully drill out the staking which secures the actuating (rocker) arm retaining pin.
4 Tap out the pin and then withdraw the actuating arm sufficiently far to enable the diaphragm stem to be disengaged from it.
5 Remove the diaphragm and lower seal.
6 Inspect the condition of the diaphragm, seals and springs and renew if they have deteriorated.
7 Reassembly is a reversal of dismantling but remember to stake the actuating arm retaining pin and align the mating marks made on the upper and lower body flange edges.

9 Fuel tank - removal and replacement

1 Remove the filler cap and syphon the contents into a clean container.
2 The fuel tank is located below the luggage boot and held in position by two retaining straps. The tank filler neck protrudes through the right hand corner body panel.
3 Disconnect the electrical connections and fuel feed pipe from

the transmitter unit plate which is located on the front face of the tank and accessible from below the car (Fig 3 : 10).
4 Unscrew the tank strap securing nuts (Fig 3 : 10) and lower the tank to the ground, but this will necessitate releasing the filler neck and manoeuvring it as the tank is withdrawn.
5 Replacement is a reversal of removal.

10 Fuel tank - servicing

1 A drain plug is not fitted to the fuel tank and in the event of an accumulation of water or sediment, the tank should be removed as described in the preceding Section; the tank transmitter unit should be removed as described in the following Section; and the tank shaken vigorously using two or three changes of paraffin until the tank is clean.
2 Should a leak develop in the fuel tank do not be tempted to solder over the hole. Fuel tank repair is a specialist job and unless lengthy safety precautions are observed can be a very dangerous procedure. It is probably as cheap these days to buy a new tank rather than have the faulty one repaired.

11 Fuel gauge sender unit - removal and replacement

1 Disconnect the battery, syphon the fuel into a suitable container, jack up the rear of the car and support on blocks or axle stands in order to provide good working space.
2 Disconnect the electrical lead and fuel line from the tank transmitter unit which is located on the front face of the fuel tank.
3 Unless a special tool is available, use a cold chisel and hammer to rotate the transmitter unit out of engagement with the locking ring and then withdraw the transmitter unit and rubber sealing ring, taking care not to catch or distort the float or arm during the process.
4 Refitting is a reversal of removal.

12 Accelerator linkage - adjustment

1 Unscrew the accelerator outer cable locknuts which are situated on either side of the support bracket (Fig 3 : 12).
2 Detach the throttle return spring.
3 Depress the accelerator pedal as far as it will go.
4 With the carburettor butterfly in this fully open position, adjust the nut which is furthest from the open end of the threaded portion of the outer cable until all slackness is removed from the inner cable and the butterfly is just maintained in the fully open position without any strain. It will be helpful for an assistant to keep the accelerator pedal fully depressed during the adjustment period.
5 Tighten the outer cable locknut, release the accelerator pedal and fit the return spring.

13 Accelerator linkage - removal and replacement

1 Prise the accelerator pedal lobes outwards and disengage it from the shaft spigot. Remove the spring (Fig 3 : 13).
2 Pull off the accelerator cable retaining clip from the shaft extension and disconnect the inner cable (Fig 3 : 14).
3 Pull out the two shaft retaining clips (Fig 3 : 15) rotate one of the square section bushes so that it will pass through the cut-out in the bracket and withdraw the shaft.
4 Slide off the retaining clip from the inner cable socket to throttle shaft lever ball connection (Fig 3 : 16) and disconnect the inner cable.
5 Remove the cable bracket securing screw from the engine rear bulkhead (Fig 3 : 17).
6 Refitting is a reversal of removal but grease the cable to shaft connections and adjust the cable as described in the preceding Section.

FIG 3 : 9 FUEL FLOW DIRECTIONAL ARROW ON FILTER

FIG 3 : 10 LOCATION OF FUEL TANK TRANSMITTER UNIT

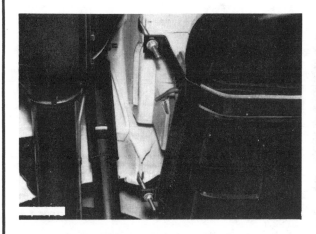

FIG 3 : 11 FUEL TANK SECURING STRAP AND NUTS

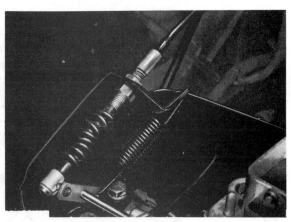

FIG 3 : 12 ACCELERATOR OUTER CABLE ADJUSTER NUT AND LOCKNUT

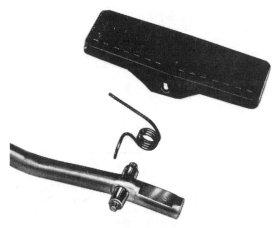

FIG 3 : 13 ACCELERATOR PEDAL AND SPRING

FIG 3 : 14 ACCELERATOR INNER CABLE TO PEDAL SHAFT CONNECTION COMPONENTS

FIG 3 : 15 ACCELERATOR PEDAL SHAFT TO BRACKET ASSEMBLY

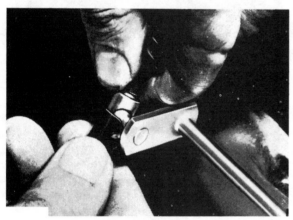

FIG 3 : 16 ACCELERATOR INNER CABLE TO THROTTLE SHAFT LEVER CONNECTION

FIG 3 : 17 ACCELERATOR CABLE BULKHEAD BRACKET LOCATION

14 Manual choke cable - removal, replacement, adjustment

1   Disconnect the inner and outer choke cables at their connections with the carburettor. The inner cable is secured by a pinch screw and the outer cable by a screwed clamp (Fig 3 : 18).
2   Depress the small plunger which retains the choke control knob on its arm and pull off the knob.
3   Remove the retaining screw and withdraw the shrouds from the steering column.
4   Slacken the locking nut and withdraw the choke cable and lever assembly from the steering column bracket (Fig 3 : 19).
5   Refitting is a reversal of removal but adjust the inner and outer cable clamps at the carburettor so that with the choke control knob slightly out, the choke plate at the carburettor is fully released.

15 Carburettors - general description

1   An Autolite single choke downdraught carburettor is fitted to 1300 and 1600 cc models and the differences in jet and choke sizes to cater for the two engine capacities are given in Specifications.
2   When buying a new carburettor, ensure that the part number of the new unit matches the one listed in Specifications for the particular model vehicle.
3   Certain 1600 cc models are fitted with automatic chokes. The incorporation of this device does not alter the internal layout of the carburettor. Both manual and automatic choke types of carburettor are shown in Figs 3 : 20 and 3 : 21.
4   Every 6000 miles (9650 km) check the carburettor slow running as described in Section 21, and clean the sediment from the carburettor bowl.

16 Carburettor - removal and replacement

1   Remove the air cleaner as described in Section 2.
2   Disconnect the vacuum pipe from the carburettor.
3   Disconnect the fuel inlet and vent pipes, (arrowed in Fig 3 : 22).
4   Free the throttle control shaft from the throttle lever by removing the securing clip as shown in Fig 3 : 23.
5   With manual choke carburettors, release the choke inner and outer cables at the carburettor as described in Section 14 : 1.
6   On cars fitted with an automatic choke carburettor, partially drain the cooling system and simply free the two hoses from the automatic choke unit.
7   On all models undo the two nuts and spring washers which hold the carburettor to the inlet manifold and remove the carburettor.
8   Replacement is a straightforward reversal of the removal sequence but note the following points:-
a)   Remove the old inlet manifold to carburettor gasket, clean the mating flanges and fit a new gasket in place.
b)   After reconnecting the manual choke ensure that the choke opens and closes fully with slack in the cable when the choke control is pushed right in.

17 Carburettors - dismantling and reassembly - general

1   With time the component parts of the Autolite carburettor will wear and petrol consumption will increase. The diameter of drillings and jets may alter, and air and fuel leaks may develop round spindles and other moving parts. Because of the high degree of precision involved it is recommended that an exchange rebuilt carburettor is purchased. This is one of the few instances where it is better to buy a new component rather than to rebuild the old one.
2   It may be necessary to partially dismantle the carburettor to clear a blocked jet or to renew the accelerator pump diaphragm.

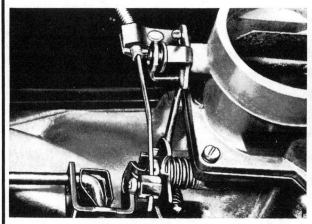

FIG 3 : 18 CHOKE CABLE CONNECTIONS AT CARBUR—
ETTOR

FIG 3 : 19 REMOVING THE CHOKE CONTROL FROM
THE STEERING COLUMN BRACKET

FIG 3 : 20 MANUAL CHOKE TYPE CARBURETTOR

FIG 3 : 21 AUTOMATIC CHOKE TYPE CARBURETTOR

FIG 3 : 22 LOCATION OF THE CARBURETTOR FUEL
INLET AND VENT PIPES

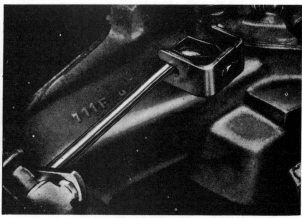

FIG 3 : 23 THROTTLE SHAFT TO CARBURETTOR
THROTTLE LEVER CONNECTION

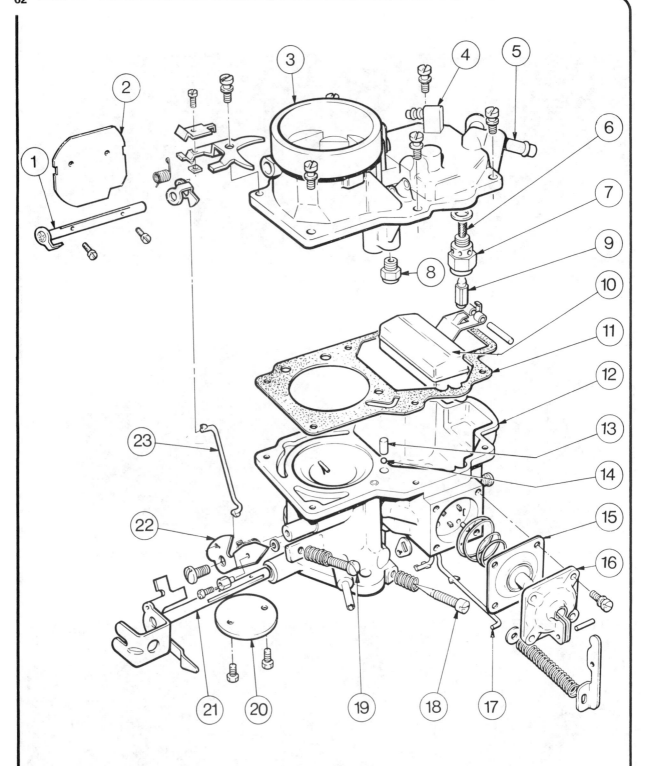

FIG 3 : 24 EXPLODED VIEW OF THE MANUAL CHOKE TYPE CARBURETTOR

1 Choke plate shaft	7 Needle valve housing	13 Weight	18 Volume control screw
2 Choke plate	8 Main jet	14 Ball	19 Throttle stop screw
3 Upper body	9 Needle valve	15 Accelerator pump	20 Throttle plate
4 External vent	10 Float	diaphragm	21 Throttle shaft
5 Fuel inlet	11 Gasket	16 Accelerator pump cover	22 Fast idle cam
6 Filter	12 Lower body	17 Accelerator pump rod	23 Choke operating link

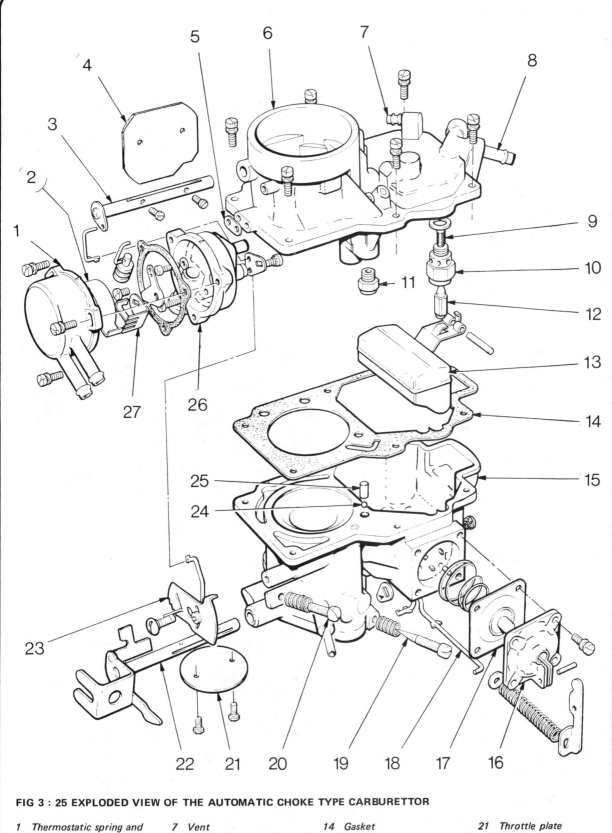

FIG 3 : 25 EXPLODED VIEW OF THE AUTOMATIC CHOKE TYPE CARBURETTOR

1 Thermostatic spring and housing	7 Vent	14 Gasket	21 Throttle plate
2 Thermostatic spring	8 Fuel inlet	15 Lower body	22 Throttle plate shaft
3 Choke plate shaft	9 Filter	16 Accelerator pump cover	23 Fast idle cam
4 Choke plate	10 Needle valve housing	17 Diaphragm	24 Ball
5 Gasket	11 Main jet	18 Pump rod	25 Weight
6 Upper body	12 Needle valve	19 Volume control screw	26 Housing
	13 Float	20 Throttle stop screw	27 Lever

The accelerator pump itself may need attention and gaskets may need renewal. Providing care is taken there is no reason why the carburettor may not be completely reconditioned at home, but ensure a full repair kit can be obtained before you strip the carburettor down. NEVER poke out jets with wire or similar to clean them but blow them out with compressed air or air from a car tyre pump.

---

18 Carburettor - dismantling and reassembly

---

1   The instructions given in this Section are to be read in conjunction with Fig 3 : 24 which shows a manual choke type carburettor in exploded form. Where an automatic choke type carburettor is fitted, these instructions fully apply but should be read in conjunction with Fig 3 : 25 and note taken of the different component key numbers used.

2   Unscrew and remove the six screws and their washers which hold the upper body (3) to the lower body (12).

3   Lift the upper body from the lower body (Fig 3 : 26) and at the same time disengage the choke link (23). This will require the twisting of the upper body to permit the stamped ends of the links to take up the necessary alignment and so enable them to pass through the contoured holes in the fast idle cam. Check that the gasket (11) comes away with the upper body and do not operate the throttle linkage, or the accelerator pump discharge valve components may be ejected and drop past the throttle butterfly into the engine interior and necessitate the removal of the cylinder head. On carburettors fitted with an automatic choke, undo the screw which holds the fast idle cam and rod assembly to the lower body (Fig 3 : 27).

4   Turn the upper body over and withdraw the pivot pin and float (Fig 3 : 28).

5   Unscrew and remove the inlet needle valve (9) housing (7) and retain the seating washer. Separate the filter.

6   With automatic choke carburettors, note the position of the mating marks on the two halves of the thermostatic spring housing, remove the retaining screws and remove the housing (Fig 3 : 29).

7   Unscrew and remove the choke thermostatic lever retaining screw (Fig 3 : 30) and withdraw the piston, link and operating lever.

8   Remove the choke link operating shaft and plate assembly taking care not to damage the plastic bush (Fig 3 : 31).

9   On all models, invert the lower body and shake out the accelerator pump ball valve (14) and weight (13).

10 Unscrew the choke plate (2) retaining screws and withdraw plate and shaft (1). Slip off the control lever and spring.

11 Unscrew and remove the main jet (8) from the upper body, (Fig 3 : 32).

12 Remove the screw from the accelerator pump rod (17) operating link (Fig 3 : 33) and remove the arm, pump rod and spring.

13 Remove the four securing screws from the accelerator pump cover and remove the cover, arm, diaphragm (15) and return spring (Fig 3 : 34).

14 Unscrew and remove the cheese-headed screw which retains the fast idle cam (22) and lift the cam and return spring away.

15 Remove the two screws which retain the throttle plate (20) to the shaft (21) and remove the plate and shaft.

16 Remove the idling mixture (volume control) screw (18) and throttle stop screw (19) and their springs.

17 The carburettor is now completely dismantled and all worn components and gaskets should be renewed. Check the jet sizes with those listed in Sepcifications in case incorrect parts have previously been fitted. Blow all jets and carburettor passages through with compressed air and maintain absolute cleanliness during reassembly.

18 Reassembly is a reversal of the dismantling sequence but the following points must be observed:-

19 Position the accelerator pump rod plate with the '0' mark as shown in Fig 3 : 33.

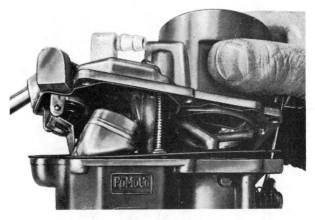

FIG 3 : 26 WITHDRAWING THE UPPER BODY FROM THE CARBURETTOR

FIG 3 : 27 AUTOMATIC CHOKE FAST IDLE CAM ASSEMBLY SECURING SCREW

FIG 3 : 28 REMOVING THE CARBURETTOR FLOAT AND PIVOT PIN

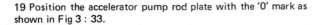

FIG 3 : 29 REMOVING THE CARBURETTOR AUTOMATIC CHOKE OUTER HOUSING

FIG 3 : 30 REMOVING THE CHOKE THERMOSTATIC LEVER RETAINING SCREW

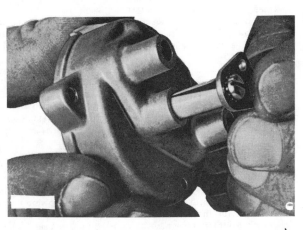

FIG 3 : 31 REMOVING THE CHOKE LINK OPERATING SHAFT/PLATE ASSEMBLY

FIG 3 : 32 LOCATION OF THE CARBURETTOR MAIN JET

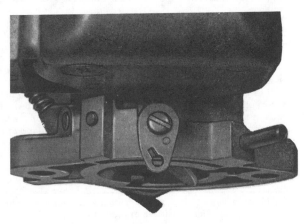

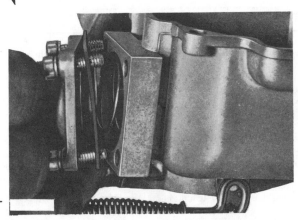

FIG 3 : 33 REMOVING THE ACCELERATOR PUMP ROD OPERATING LINK RETAINING SCREW

FIG 3 : 34 REMOVING THE COVER FROM THE ACCELER-ATOR PUMP

20 Locate the throttle plate in the shaft slot so that the indentations are furthest away from the mixture control screw (Fig 3 : 35).

21 Remember to locate the ball first and then the weight in the lower body accelerator pump orifice.

22 Replace the filter in the needle valve housing and insert the needle valve as shown in Fig 3 : 36. Retain the valve in position with the float and float pivot pin. Check the float level setting as described in Section 19.

23 Check the accelerator pump adjustment as described in Section 20.

24 Check the idling adjustment as described in Section 21.

25 Check the choke and fast idling adjustment as described in Sections 22 or 23 according to type.

26 Where an automatic choke is fitted, check the adjustment as described in Section 23 and remember to top up the cooling system after the hoses are fitted.

19 Float level - adjustment

1 The position of the float is important to the maintenance of the correct fuel level in the float chamber. If the fuel level is too low then fuel starvation will result. If the fuel level is too high, flooding will occur which will be evidenced by leakage at the carburettor body joint.

2 With the upper body held in a vertical position, and the float fully depressing the needle valve, measure the distance between the bottom of the float and the face of the upper body as indicated in Fig 3 : 38. This should be 1.08 in (27.43 mm) for 1300 cc engine carburettors or 1.10 in (27.93 mm) for 1600 cc engine carburettors, and can be reset if necessary by bending the tab resting against the needle valve.

3 Now allow the float to hang down and measure the distance between the bottom of the float and the face of the upper body as indicated in Fig 3 : 37. This should be 0.26 in (6.60 mm) greater than that measured in Paragraph 2, and can be reset if necessary by bending the tab resting against the needle valve.

20 Accelerator pump - adjustment

1 Unscrew the throttle stop screw until the throttle butterfly is fully closed.

2 Depress the diaphragm plunger fully and by using a suitable gauge (twist drill) check that it is a sliding fit between the plunger and operating lever. The correct gap is 1/10 in (2.54 mm) and can only be adjusted by opening or closing the pump rod (17) gooseneck.

21 Slow running - adjustment

1 If available the idling adjustment is best made with the aid of a vacuum gauge. Disconnect the blanking plug on the inlet manifold and connect a suitable adaptor and gauge.

2 Ensure the engine is at its normal operating temperature and then turn in the throttle stop screw (19) to obtain a fast idle.

3 Turn the volume control screw (18) in either direction until a maximum reading is obtained on the gauge.

4 Re-adjust the idling speed as required and continue these adjustments until the maximum vacuum reading is obtained with the engine running smoothly at about 600 rev/min.

5 To adjust the slow running without a vacuum gauge turn the throttle stop screw (19) clockwise so the engine is running at a fast idle, then turn the volume control screw (18) in either direction until the engine just fires evenly. Continue the adjustments until the engine will run as slowly as possible, but smoothly, with regular firing and no hint of stalling.

22 Choke and fast idling - adjustment (manual)

1 With the air cleaner removed, rotate the choke lever until it is hard against its stop.

2 Depress the choke plate and check the gap between the edge of the plate and the inside of the carburettor air intake (Fig 3 : 39). Use a twist drill for this measurement which should be (1300 cc) 0.13 in (3.30 mm); (1600 cc) 0.14 in (3.55 mm).

3 If the gap is incorrect, bend the tab on the choke spindle.

4 The following fast idle check and any necessary adjustment should only be made after the choke has been checked and adjusted:

5 If the engine is cold run it until it reaches its normal operating temperature and then allow it to idle naturally.

6 Hold the choke plate in the fully open vertical position and turn the choke lever until it is stopped by the choke linkage. With the choke lever in this position the engine speed should rise to about 1,000 rev/min as the fast idle cam will have opened the throttle flap very slightly. (Fig 3 : 40).

7 Check how much radial movement is needed on the throttle lever to obtain this result and then stop the engine.

8 With a pair of mole grips clamp the throttle lever fully open on the stop portion of the casting boss and bend down the tab to decrease, or up to increase, the fast idle speed.

9 Remove the grips and check again if necessary repeating the operation until the fast idling is correct. It may also be necessary to adjust the slow idling speed and recheck the choke.

23 Choke and fast idling - adjustment (Automatic)

1 The automatic choke (Fig 3 : 25) fitted to certain 1600 cc models operated by means of a water actuated bi-metallic spring which rotates the choke spindle which in turn opens and closes the choke plate.

2 To adjust the automatic choke, remove the outer choke housing retaining screws and remove the housing (1) (Fig 3 : 25).

3 Depress the vacuum piston until the vacuum bleed port is revealed. Insert a length of wire 0.040 in (1.01 mm) thick suitably bent, (Fig 3 : 41) into the port and then release the piston to trap the wire. With the piston and wire in this position, close the choke plate until its movement is stopped by the linkage. Partially open the throttle to permit the fast idle tab to clear the cam.

4 Use a twist drill to check that the gap between the bottom of the choke plate and the carburettor body is 0.15 in (3.81 mm). If necessary, bend the extension of the choke thermostat lever (the portion which abuts the piston operating lever) to adjust the clearance.

5 Close the choke plate by means of the spring operated lever then open the throttle fully and hold it against the stop. Again using a twist drill, check that the clearance between the bottom of the choke plate and the carburettor body is 0.30 in (7.62 mm) (Fig 3 : 42). Adjust if necessary by bending the projection on the fast idle cam.

6 With the choke plate pull-down correctly adjusted and held in the pull-down position, check that the throttle lever fast idle tab is in the first or high speed step (arrowed on cam) on the fast idle cam (Fig 3 : 43). If necessary, bend the fast idle rod at its existing bend to achieve this result.

24 Fuel system - fault finding

There are three main types of fault the fuel system is prone to, and they may be summarized as follows:-
a) Lack of fuel at engine
b) Weak mixture
c) Rich mixture

25 Lack of fuel at engine

1 If it is not possible to start the engine, first positively check

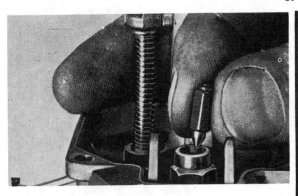

FIG 3 : 35 CORRECT POSITIONING OF THE THROTTLE PLATE IN ITS SHAFT

FIG 3 : 36 METHOD OF INSERTING THE NEEDLE VALVE IN ITS HOUSING

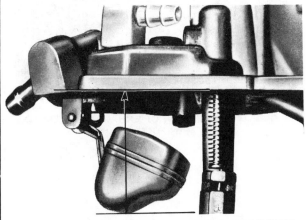

FIG 3 : 37 CHECKING THE FLOAT ADJUSTMENT WITH UPPER BODY HORIZONTAL

FIG 3 : 38 CHECKING THE FLOAT ADJUSTMENT WITH UPPER BODY VERTICAL

FIG 3 : 39 CHECKING CHOKE PLATE ADJUSTMENT ON A MANUAL CHOKE CARBURETTOR

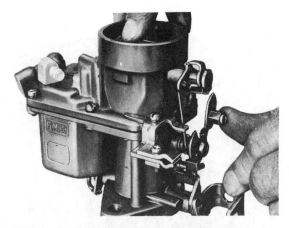

FIG 3 : 40 CHECKING FAST IDLE SETTING ON A MANUAL CHOKE CARBURETTOR

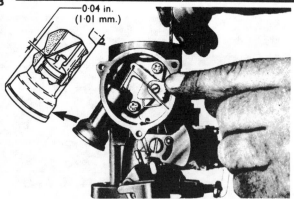

FIG 3 : 41 CHECKING CHOKE PLATE ADJUSTMENT ON AN AUTOMATIC CHOKE CARBURETTOR

FIG 3 : 42 CHECKING FAST IDLE SETTING ON AN AUTOMATIC CHOKE CARBURETTOR

FIG 3 : 43 CHECKING POSITION OF FAST IDLE LEVER TAB ON AUTOMATIC CHOKE CARBURETTOR

FIG 3 : 44 CONNECTION OF EXHAUST SYSTEM TO MANIFOLD

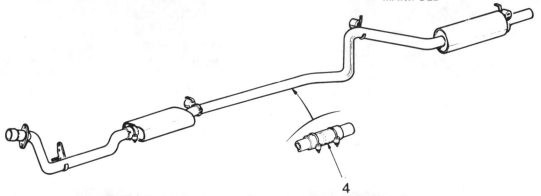

FIG 3 : 45 LAYOUT OF EXHAUST SYSTEM (4 THE SERVICE JOIN)

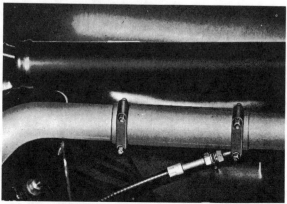

FIG 3 : 46 ADJUSTABLE BRACKET AT EXHAUST DOWN PIPE

FIG 3 : 47 CONNECTING JOINT AND CLAMPS FOR USE WHEN RENEWING SECTIONS OF THE EXHAUST SYSTEM

that there is fuel in the fuel tank, and then check the ignition system as detailed in Chapter 4. If the fault is not in the ignition system then disconnect the fuel inlet pipe from the carburettor and turn the engine over by the starter relay switch.

2   If petrol squirts from the end of the inlet pipe, reconnect the pipe and check that the fuel is getting to the float chamber. This is done by unscrewing the bolts from the top of the float chamber and lifting the cover just enough to see inside.

3   If fuel is there then it is likely that there is a blockage in the starting jet which should be removed and cleaned.

4   No fuel in the float chamber is caused either by a blockage in the pipe between the pump and float chamber or a sticking float chamber valve.

5   If it is decided that it is the float chamber valve that is sticking, remove the fuel inlet pipe, and lift away the cover, complete with valve and floats.

6   Remove the valve spindle and valve and thoroughly wash them in petrol. Petrol gum may be present on the valve or valve spindle and this is usually the cause of a sticking valve. Replace the valve in the needle valve assembly, ensure that it is moving freely, and then reassemble the float chamber. It is important that the same washer be placed under the needle valve assembly, as this determines the height of the floats and therefore the level of petrol in the chamber.

7   Reconnect the fuel pipe and refit the air cleaner.

8   If no petrol squirts from the end of the pipe leading to the carburettor then disconnect the pipe leading to the inlet side of the fuel pump. If fuel runs out of the pipe then there is a fault in the fuel pump, and the pump should be checked as has already been detailed.

9   No fuel flowing from the tank when it is known that there is fuel in the tank indicates a blocked pipe line. The line to the tank should be blown out. It is unlikely that the fuel tank vent would become blocked, but this could be a reason for the reluctance of the fuel to flow. To test for this, blow into the tank down the filler orifice. There should be no build up of pressure in the fuel tank as the excess pressure should be carried away through the filler cap vent hole.

26 Weak mixture

1   If the fuel/air mixture is weak there are six main clues to this condition:-

a)   The engine will be difficult to start and will need much use of the choke, stalling easily if the choke is pushed in.

b)   The engine will overheat easily.

c)   If the spark plugs are examined (as detailed in the Section on engine tuning), they will have a light grey/white deposit on the insulator nose.

d)   The fuel consumption may be light.

e)   There will be a noticeable lack of power

f)   During acceleration and on the overrun there will be a certain amount of spitting back through the carburettor.

2   As the carburettors are of the fixed jet type, these faults are invariably due to circumstances outside the carburettor. The only usual fault likely in the carburettor is that one or more of the jets may be partially blocked. If the car will not start easily but runs well at speed, then it is likely that the starting jet is blocked,

whereas if the engine starts easily but will not rev. then it is likely that the main jets are blocked.

3   If the level of petrol in the float chamber is low this is usually due to a sticking valve or incorrectly set floats.

4   Air leaks either in the fuel lines, or in the induction system, should also be checked for. Also check the distributor vacuum pipe connection as a leak in this is directly felt in the inlet manifold.

5   The fuel pump may be at fault as has already been detailed.

27 Rich mixture

1   If the fuel/air mixture is rich there are also six main clues to this condition:-

a)   If the spark plugs are examined they will be found to have a black sooty deposit on the insulator nose.

b)   The fuel consumption will be heavy.

c)   The exhaust will give off a heavy black smoke, especially when accelerating.

d)   The interior deposits on the exhaust pipe will be dry, black and sooty (if they are wet, black and sooty this indicates worn bores, and much oil being burnt).

e)   There will be a noticeable lack of power.

f)   There will be a certain amount of back-firing through the exhaust system.

2   The faults in this case are usually in the carburettor and most usual is that the level of petrol in the float chamber is too high. This is due either to dirt behind the needle valve, or a leaking float which will not close the valve properly, or a sticking needle.

3   With a very high mileage (or because someone has tried to clean the jets out with wire), it may be that the jets have become enlarged.

4   If the air correction jets are restricted in any way the mixture will tend to become very rich.

5   Occasionally it is found that the choke control is sticking or has been maladjusted.

6   Again, occasionally the fuel pump pressure may be excessive so forcing the needle valve open slightly until a higher level of petrol is reached in the float chamber.

28 Exhaust system

1   The exhaust system fitted to 1300 and 1600 cc models is shown in Fig 3 : 45.

2   The connection of the system to the exhaust manifold is as shown in Fig 3 : 44.

3   The method of support is by a bracket at the front (Fig 3 : 46), and three rubber insulators.

4   The exhaust system fitted as original equipment comprises only two parts, the downpipe and the expansion box and silencer box assemblies and pipe work.

5   For reasons of economy, the system may be cut and separate front or rear sections incorporated to replace rusted or defective sections without the need to purchase a complete system. A connecting joint and clamps (Fig 3 : 47) are available as service parts.

FAULT DIAGNOSIS - FUEL SYSTEM AND CARBURATION

Symptom	Reason/s	Remedy
Carburation and ignition faults	Air cleaner choked and dirty giving rich mixture	Remove, clean and replace air cleaner.
	Fuel leaking from carburettor, fuel pumps, or fuel lines	Check for and eliminate all fuel leaks. Tighten fuel line union nuts.
	Float chamber flooding	Check and adjust float level.
	Generally worn carburettor	Remove, overhaul and replace.
	Distributor condenser faulty	Remove, and fit new unit.
	Balance weights or vacuum advance mechanism in distributor faulty	Remove, and overhaul distributor.
Incorrect adjustment	Carburettor incorrectly adjusted	
	Mixture too rich	Tune and adjust carburettor
	Idling speed too high	Adjust idling speed.
	Contact breaker gap incorrect	Check and reset gap.
	Valve clearances incorrect	Check rocker arm to valve stem clearances and adjust as necessary.
	Incorrectly set spark plugs	Remove, clean, and regap.
	Tyres under-inflated	Check tyre pressures and inflate if necessary.
	Wrong spark plugs fitted	Remove and replace with correct units.
	Brakes dragging	Check and adjust brakes.
Dirt in system	Petrol tank air vent restricted	Remove petrol cap and clean out air vent.
	Partially clogged filters in pump and carburettor	Remove and clean filters.
	Dirt lodged in float chamber needle housing	Remove and clean out float chamber and needle valve assembly.
	Incorrectly seating valves in fuel pump	Remove, dismantle, and clean out fuel pump.
Fuel pump faults	Fuel pump diaphragm leaking or damaged	Remove, and overhaul fuel pump.
	Gasket in fuel pump damaged	Remove, and overhaul fuel pump.
	Fuel pump valves sticking due to petrol gumming	Remove, and thoroughly clean fuel pump.
Air leaks	Too little fuel in fuel tank (prevalent when climbing steep hills)	Refill fuel tank.
	Union joints on pipe connections loose	Tighten joints and check for air leaks.
	Split in fuel pipe on suction side of fuel pump	Examine, locate, and repair.
	Inlet manifold to block or inlet manifold to carburettor - gasket leaking	Test by pouring oil along joints - bubbles indicate leak. Renew gasket as appropriate.

Chapter 4 Ignition system

Contents

Specifications

Distributor

Type and make	Motorcraft, centrifugal/vacuum automatic advance.
Identification:	
1300 and 1600 HC	71 - BB - 12100 - AMA
1300 LC	71 - BB - 12100 - AKA
1600 LC	71 - BB - 12100 - ANA
Drive	Skew gear from camshaft.
Rotation	Anti-clockwise (viewed from top)
Initial static advance	6⁰ BTDC
Breaker points gap	0.025 in (0.64 mm)
Dwell angle	38 to 40⁰
Firing order	1 - 2 - 4 - 3

Distributor advance characteristics

1300/1600 HC ... ...   Identification No 71BB - 12100 - AMA

Mechanical		Vacuum	
Distributor speed revs/min	Degrees advance (distributor)	Vacuum cm of Hg (in of Hg)	Degrees advance (distributor)
550 and below	-0.5 to +0.5	5.1 (2.0) and below	0
620	-0.5 to +1.5	10.2 (4.0)	0 to 1.0·
900	3.5 to 5.5	12.7 (5.0)	0 to 3.0
1,200	6.8 to 8,8	15.2 (6.0)	2.1 to 5.1
1,500	8.0 to 10.0	17.8 (7.0)	3.7 to 6.7
1,800	9.2 to 11.2	20.3 (8.0)	4.8 to 7.8
2,100	10.5 to 12.5	22.9 (9.0)	5.7 to 8.7
2,300 and above	11.3 to 13.3	25.4 (10.0) and above	6.0 to 9.0

1300 LC ... ...   Identification No 71BB - 12100 - AKA

470 and below	-0.5 to 0.5	7.6 (3.0) and below	0
600	1.0 to 3.0	10.2 (4.0)	0 to 0.5
800	5.0 to 7.0	12.7 (5.0)	0 to 1.0
1,000	8.5 to 10.5	15.2 (6.0)	0 to 2.8
1,200	9.5 to 11.5	17.8 (7.0)	1.0 to 4.0
1,600	11.3 to 13.3	20.3 (8.0)	2.1 to 5.1
2,000	13.3 to 15.3	22.9 (9.0)	3.1 to 6.1
2,300 and above	14.8 to 16.8	25.4 (10.0) and above	4.0 to 7.0

1600 LC ... ...   Identification No 71BB - 12100 - ANA

500 and below	-0.5 to 0.5	7.6 (3.0) and below		0
700	0.5 to 2.5	12.7 (5.0)	0	to 1.2
900	2.8 to 4.8	15.2 (6.0)	0	to 3.0
1,100	4.6 to 6.6	17.8 (7.0)	1.7	to 4.7
1,400	6.4 to 8.4	22.9 (9.0)	4.7	to 7.7
1,700	8.2 to 10.2	27.9 (11.0)	7.1	to 10.1
2,000	10.1 to 12.1	33.0 (13.0)	8.7	to 11.7
2,350 and above	12.3 to 14.3	35.6 (14.0) and above	9.0	to 12.0

Condenser

Capacity ... ...   0.21 to 0.25 m fd

Coil

Make ... ...   Autolite

Type ....   Oil filled for use with 1.5 ohm resistor

Resistance at 20°C (68°F)   ... ...   Primary 0.95 to 1.2 ohms

    Secondary 5900 to 6900 ohms

Spark plugs

Make ... ...   Autolite

Type ... ...   14 mm AG 22

Gap ... ...   0.025 in (0.64 mm)

1 General description

In order that the engine can run correctly it is necessary for an electrical spark to ignite the fuel/air mixture in the combustion chamber at exactly the right moment in relation to engine speed and load. The ignition system is based on feeding low tension voltage from the battery to the coil where it is converted to high tension voltage. The high tension voltage is powerful enough to jump the spark plug gap in the cylinders many times a second under high compression pressures, providing that the system is in good condition and that all adjustments are correct.

The ignition system is divided into two circuits. The low tension circuit and the high tension circuit (Fig 4 : 1).

The low tension (sometimes known as the primary) circuit consists of the battery; lead to the control box; lead to the ignition switch; lead from the ignition switch to the low tension or primary coil windings (terminal SW); and the lead from the low tension coil windings (coil terminal CB) to the contact breaker points and condenser in the distributor.

The high tension circuit consists of the high tension or secondary coil windings; the heavy ignition lead from the centre of the coil to the centre of the distributor cap; the rotor arm; and the spark plug leads and spark plugs.

The system functions in the following manner: Low tension voltage is changed in the coil into high tension voltage by the opening and closing of the contact breaker points in the low tension circuit. High tension voltage is then fed via the carbon brush in the centre of the distributor cap to the rotor arm of the distributor cap, and each time it comes in line with one of the four metal segments in the cap, which are connected to the spark plug leads the opening and closing of the contact breaker points causes the high tension voltage to build up, jump the gap from the rotor arm to the appropriate metal segment and so via the spark plug lead to the spark plug, where it finally jumps the spark plug gap before going to earth.

The ignition is advanced and retarded automatically, to ensure the spark occurs at just the right instant for the particular load at the prevailing engine speed.

The ignition advance is controlled both mechanically and by a vacuum operated system. The mechanical governor mechanism comprises two lead weights, which move out from the distributor shaft as the engine speed rises due to centrifugal force. As they move outwards they rotate the cam relative to the distributor shaft, and so advance the spark. The weights are held in position by two light springs and it is the tension of the springs which is largely responsible for correct spark advancement.

The vacuum control consists of a diaphragm, one side of which is connected via a small bore tube to the carburettor, and the other side to the contact breaker plate. Depression in the inlet manifold and carburettor, which varies with engine speed and throttle opening, causes the diaphragm to move, so moving the contact breaker plate, and advancing or retarding the spark. A fine degree of control is achieved by a spring in the vacuum assembly.

The distributor is mounted on the right hand side of the engine and is driven by the camshaft at half engine speed. The distributor shaft carries a cam which opens the contact breaker points, their closure being effected by a return spring. The points and condenser are mounted on the distributor bore plate. Adjustment is provided to compensate for wear of the rocker arm. At the top of the distributor drive shaft is mounted the rotor arm which connects to the H.T. circuit via a spring terminal and cap mounted carbon brush.

The type of distributor fitted is critical to the particular engine model and reference should be made to Specifications before purchasing a new one. The identification number is located as shown in Fig 4 : 2.

2 Contact breaker - adjustment

1 To adjust the contact breaker points to the correct gap, first pull off the two clips securing the distributor cap to the distributor body, and lift away the cap (photo). Clean the cap inside and out with a dry cloth. It is unlikely that the four segments will be badly burned or scored, but if they are the cap will have to be renewed.

2 Inspect the carbon brush contact located in the top of the cap - see that it is unbroken and stands proud of the plastic surface.

3 Check the contact spring on the top of the rotor arm. It must be clean and have adequate tension to ensure good contact.

4 Gently prise the contact breaker points open to examine the condition of their faces. If they are rough, pitted, or dirty, it will be necessary to remove them for resurfacing, or for replacement points to be fitted.

5 Presuming the points are satisfactory, or that they have been cleaned and replaced, measure the gap between the points by turning the engine over until the heel of the breaker arm is on the highest point of the cam.

6 A 0.025 in (0.64 mm) feeler gauge should now just fit between the points. (See Fig 4 : 3).

7 If the gap varies from this amount slacken the contact plate securing screw.

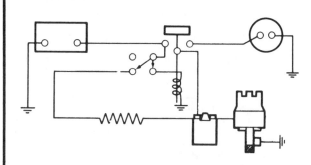

FIG 4 : 1 THE IGNITION CIRCUIT

FIG 4 : 2 POSITION OF DISTRIBUTOR IDENTIFICATION
NUMBER

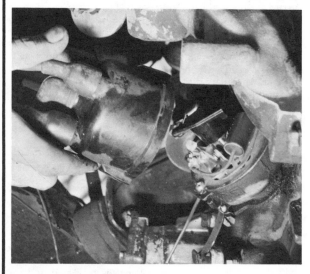

2.1 Lifting away the distributor cap

FIG 4 : 3 TESTING THE CONTACT BREAKER POINTS GAP

FIG 4 : 4 REMOVING THE CONDENSER FROM THE
BASEPLATE

FIG 4 : 5 DISCONNECTING THE DISTRIBUTOR HT LEADS

8   Adjust the contact gap by inserting a screwdriver in the notched hole in the breaker plate. Turn clockwise to increase and anti-clockwise to decrease the gap. When the gap is correct tighten the securing screw and check the gap again.

9   Making sure the rotor is in position replace the distributor cap and clip the spring blade retainers into position.

3   Contact breaker points - removing and replacing

1   If the contact breaker points are burned, pitted or badly worn, they must be removed and either replaced, or their faces must be filed smooth.

2   Lift off the rotor arm by pulling it straight up from the spindle.

3   Slacken the self-tapping screw holding the condenser and low tension leads to the contact breaker and slide out the forked ends of the leads.

4   Remove the points by taking out the two retaining screws and lifting off the points assembly.

5   Replacing the points assembly is a reversal of the removal procedure. Take care not to trap the wires between the points and the breaker plate.

6   When the points are replaced the gap should be set as described in the previous Section.

7   Finally replace the rotor arm and then the distributor cap.

NOTE: Should the contact points be badly worn, a new set should be fitted. As an emergency measure clean the faces with fine emery paper folded over a thin steel ruler. It is necessary to completely remove the built-up deposits, but not necessary to rub the pitted point right down to the stage where all the pitting has disappeared. When the surfaces are flat a feeler gauge can be used and the gap set as described in the preceding Section.

4   Condenser - removal, testing and replacement

1   The purpose of the condenser, (sometimes known as a capacitor) is to ensure that when the contact breaker points open there is no sparking across them which would waste voltage and cause wear.

2   The condenser is fitted in parallel with the contact breaker points. If it develops a short circuit, it will cause ignition failure as the points will be prevented from interrupting the low tension circuit.

3   If the engine becomes very difficult to start or begins to miss after several miles running and the breaker points show signs of excessive burning, then the condition of the condenser must be suspect. A further test can be made by separating the points by hand with the ignition switched on. If this is accompanied by a flash it is indicative that the condenser has failed.

4   Without special test equipment the only sure way to diagnose condenser trouble is to replace a suspected unit with a new one and note if there is any improvement.

5   To remove the condenser from the distributor take off the distributor cap and rotor arm. Slacken the self-tapping screw holding the condenser lead and low tension lead to the points, and slide out the fork on the condenser lead. Undo the condenser retaining screw and remove the condenser from the breaker plate (Fig 4 : 4).

6   To refit the condenser simply reverse the order of removal. Take care that the condenser lead is clear of the moving part of the points assembly.

5   Distributor - lubrication

1   It is important that the distributor cam is lubricated with petroleum jelly at the specified mileages, and that the breaker arm, governor weights, and cam spindle, are lubricated with engine oil once every 6,000 miles (9650 km).

2   Great care should be taken not to use too much lubricant, as any excess that finds its way onto the contact breaker points

could cause burning and misfiring.

3   To gain access to the cam spindle, lift away the rotor arm. Drop no more than two drops of engine oil onto the felt pad. This will run down the spindle when the engine is hot and lubricate the bearings.

4   To lubricate the automatic timing control allow a few drops of oil to pass through the hole in the contact breaker base plate through which the four sided cam emerges. Apply not more than one drop of oil to the pivot post and remove any excess.

6   Distributor - removal

1   To remove the distributor from the engine pull off the four leads from the spark plugs.

2   Disconnect the high tension and low tension leads from the distributor (Fig 4 : 5).

3   Pull off the rubber union holding the vacuum pipe to the distributor vacuum advance housing.

4   Remove the distributor body clamp bolt which holds the distributor clamp plate to the engine and lift out the distributor. BUT SEE NOTE BELOW BEFORE REMOVAL.

NOTE: If it is not wished to disturb the timing, under no circumstances should the body clamp pinch bolt be loosened. For the same reason the precise direction in which the rotor arm points should be noted before it is removed. This enables the drive gear to be settled on the same tooth when the distributor is refitted. While the distributor is removed care must be taken not to turn the engine. If these precautions are observed there will be no need to retime the ignition.

7   Distributor - dismantling

1   With the distributor on the bench - pull off the two spring clips retaining the cover and lift the cover off.

2   Pull the rotor arm off the distributor cam shaft.

3   Remove the points from the breaker plate as detailed in Section 3.

4   Undo the condenser retaining screw and take off the condenser.

5   Next prise off the small circlip from the vacuum unit pivot post.

6   Take out the two screws holding the breaker plate to the distributor body and lift away.

7   Take off the circlip flat washer and wave washer from the pivot post. Separate the two plates by bringing the holding down screw through the key hole slot in the lower plate. Be careful not to lose the spring now left on the pivot post.

8   Pull the low tension wire and grommet from the lower plate.

9   Undo the two screws holding the vacuum unit to the body. Take off the unit (Fig 4 : 7).

10 To dismantle the vacuum unit unscrew the bolt on the end of the unit and withdraw the vacuum spring, stop, and shims.

11 The mechanical advance is next removed but first make a careful note of the assembly, particularly which spring fits which post and the position of the advance springs. Then remove the advance springs.

12 Prise off the circlips from the governor weight pivot pins and take out the weights (Fig 4 : 8).

13 Dismantle the shaft by taking out the felt pad in the top of the spindle. Expand the exposed circlip and take it out (3) (Fig 4 : 6).

14 Now mark which slot in the mechanical advance plate is occupied by the advance stop which stands up from the action plate and lift off the cam spindle.

15 It is only necessary to remove the lower shaft and action plate if it is excessively worn. If this is the case, with a small punch drive out the gear retaining pin and remove the gear with the two washers located above it.

16 Withdraw the shaft from the distributor body and take off the two washers from below the action plate. The distributor is now completely dismantled.

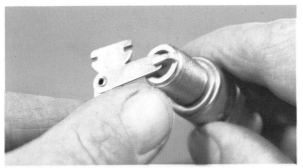

Measuring plug gap. A feeler gauge of the correct size (see ignition system specifications) should have a slight 'drag' when slid between the electrodes. Adjust gap if necessary

Adjusting plug gap. The plug gap is adjusted by bending the earth electrode inwards, or outwards, as necessary until the correct clearance is obtained. Note the use of the correct tool

Normal. Grey-brown deposits lightly coated core nose. Gap increasing by around 0.001 in (0.025 mm) per 1000 miles (1600 km). Plugs ideally suited to engine and engine in good condition

Carbon fouling. Dry, black, sooty deposits. Will cause weak spark and eventually misfire. Fault: over-rich fuel mixture. Check: carburettor mixture settings, float level and jet sizes; choke operation and cleanliness of air filter. Plugs can be re-used after cleaning

Oil fouling. Wet, oily deposits. Will cause weak spark and eventually misfire. Fault: worn bores/piston rings or valve guides; sometimes occurs (temporarily) during running-in period. Plugs can be re-used after thorough cleaning

Overheating. Electrodes have glazed appearance, core nose very white - few deposits. Fault: plug overheating. Check: plug value, ignition timing, fuel octane rating (too low) and fuel mixture (too weak). Discard plugs and cure fault immediately

Electrode damage. Electrodes burned away; core nose has burned, glazed appearance. Fault: initial pre-ignition. Check: as for 'Overheating' but may be more severe. Discard plugs and remedy fault before piston or valve damage occurs

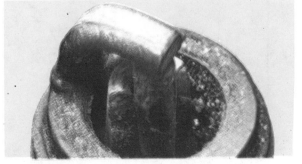

Split core nose (may appear initially as a crack). Damage is self-evident, but cracks will only show after cleaning. Fault: pre-ignition or wrong gap-setting technique. Check: ignition timing, cooling system, fuel octane rating (too low) and fuel mixture (too weak). Discard plugs, rectify fault immediately

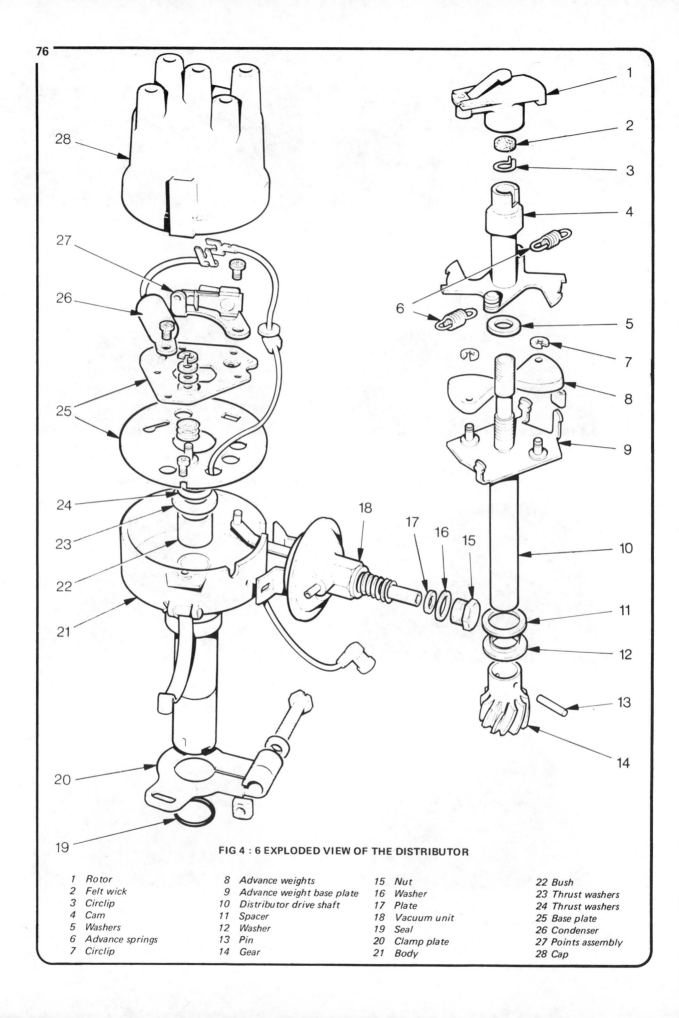

FIG 4 : 6 EXPLODED VIEW OF THE DISTRIBUTOR

1 Rotor	8 Advance weights	15 Nut	22 Bush
2 Felt wick	9 Advance weight base plate	16 Washer	23 Thrust washers
3 Circlip	10 Distributor drive shaft	17 Plate	24 Thrust washers
4 Cam	11 Spacer	18 Vacuum unit	25 Base plate
5 Washers	12 Washer	19 Seal	26 Condenser
6 Advance springs	13 Pin	20 Clamp plate	27 Points assembly
7 Circlip	14 Gear	21 Body	28 Cap

8 Distributor - inspection and repair

1 Check the points as described in Section 3. Check the distributor cap for signs of tracking, indicated by a thin black line between the segments. Replace the cap if any signs of tracking are found.
2 If the metal portion of the rotor arm is badly burned or loose, renew the arm. If only slightly burned clean the end with a fine file. Check that the contact spring has adequate pressure and the bearing surface is clean and in good condition.
3 Check that the carbon brush in the distributor cap is unbroken and stands proud of its holder.
4 Examine the fly weights and pivots for wear and the advance springs for slackness. They can best be checked by comparing with new parts. If they are slack they must be renewed.
5 Check the points assembly for fit on the breaker plate, and the cam follower for wear.
6 Examine the fit of the lower shaft in the distributor body. If this is excessively worn it will be necessary to fit a new assembly.

9 Distributor - reassembly

1 Reassembly is a straightforward reversal of the dismantling process, but there are several points which must be noted:
2 Lubricate with S.A.E.20 engine oil the balance weights and other parts of the mechanical advance mechanism, the distributor shaft, and the portion of the shaft on which the cam bears, during assembly. Do not oil excessively but ensure these parts are adequately lubricated.
3 When fitting the lower shaft, first replace the thrust washers below the action plate before inserting into the distributor body. Next fit the wave washer and thrust washer at the lower end and replace the drive gear. Secure it with a new pin.
4 Assemble the upper and lower shaft with the advance stop in the correct slot (the one which was marked) in the mechanical advance plate.
5 After assembling the advance weights and springs check that they move freely without binding.
6 Before assembling the breaker plates make sure that the three nylon bearing studs are properly located in their holes in the upper breaker plate, and that the small earth spring is fitted on the pivot post.
7 As you refit the upper breaker plate, pass the holding down spindle through the keyhole slot in the lower plate.
8 Hold the upper plate in position by refitting the wave washer, flat washer and large circlip.
9 When all is assembled, remember to set the contact breaker gap to 0.025 in (0.64 mm) as described in Section 2 : 8.
10 If a new gear or shaft is being fitted it is necessary to drill a new pin hole. Proceed as follows:
11 Make a 0.015 in (0.38 mm) forked shim to slide over the drive shaft. (Fig 4 : 9).
12 Assemble the shaft, wave washer, thrust washer, shim and gear wheel in position in the distributor body.
13 Hold the assembly in a large clamp such as a vice or carpenters clamp, using only sufficient pressure to take up all end play.
14 There is a pilot hole in a new gear wheel for drilling the new hole. Set this pilot hole at 90° to the existing hole in an old shaft if the old one is being reused (Fig 4 : 10). Drill a 1/8th in (3.18 mm) hole through both gear and shaft.
15 Fit a new pin in the hole. Release the clamp and remove the shim. The shaft will now have the correct amount of clearance.
16 When fitting an existing gear wheel still in good condition to a new shaft, also drill a new pin hole through the gear wheel at 90° to the existing hole. Secure with a new pin.
17 When replacing the cam spindle (Fig 4 : 11) check that the advance is located in the correct step. Secure with the circlip and replace the lubricating pad.
18 Before reassembly, grease the upper shaft so that the undercut is completely filled, using high melting point type grease.

Distributor - refitting

1 If a new shaft or gear wheel has not been fitted, i.e. the original parts are still being used, it will not be necessary to retime the ignition.
2 Insert the distributor with the vacuum advance assembly to the rear and the mounting plate against the engine block.
3 Notice that the rotor arm rotates as the gears mesh. The rotor arm must settle in exactly the same direction that it was in before the distributor was removed. To do this lift out the assembly far enough to rotate the shaft one tooth at a time, lowering it home to check the direction of the rotor arm. When it points in the desired direction with the assembly fully home, fit the distributor clamp plate bolt.
4 With the distributor assembly fitted reconnect the low tension lead from the side of the distributor to the CB terminal on the coil. Reconnect the H T lead between the centre of the distributor cover and the centre of the coil, and refit the rubber union of the vacuum pipe which runs from the induction manifold to the side of the vacuum advance unit.

11 Spark plugs and leads

1 The correct functioning of the spark plugs is vital for the correct running and efficiency of the engine.
2 At intervals of 6,000 miles (9500 Km) the plugs should be removed, examined, cleaned, and if worn excessively, replaced. The condition of the spark plugs will also tell much about the overall condition of the engine.
3 If the insulator nose of the spark plug is clean and white, with no deposits, this is indicative of a weak mixture, or too hot a plug. (A hot plug transfers heat away from the electrode slowly - a cold plug transfers it away quickly).
4 The plugs fitted as standard are AUTOLITE as listed in Specifications at the beginning of this Chapter. If the tip and insulator nose is covered with hard black looking deposits, then this is indicative that the mixture is too rich. Should the plug be black and oily, then it is likely that the engine is fairly worn, as well as the mixture being too rich.
5 If the insulator nose is covered with light tan to greyish brown deposits, then the mixture is correct and it is likely that the engine is in good condition.
6 If there are any traces of long brown tapering stains on the outside of the white portion of the plug, then the plug will have to be renewed, as this shows that there is a faulty joint between the plug body and the insulator, and compression is being allowed to leak away.
7 Plugs should be cleaned by a sand blasting machine, which will free them from carbon more thoroughly than cleaning by hand. The machine will also test the condition of the plugs under compression. Any plug that fails to spark at the recommended pressure should be renewed.
8 The spark plug gap is of considerable importance, as, if it is too large or too small, the size of the spark and its efficiency will be seriously impaired. The spark plug gap should be set to the figure given in Specifications at the beginning of this Chapter.
9 To set it, measure the gap with a feeler gauge, and then bend open, or close, the outer plug electrode until the correct gap is achieved. The centre electrode should never be bent as this may crack the insulation and cause plug failure if nothing worse.
10 When replacing the plugs, remember to use new plug washers, and replace the leads from the distributor in the correct firing order, which is 1 - 2 - 4 - 3, No 1 cylinder being the one nearest the radiator. No 1 lead from the distributor runs from the 1 o'clock position when looking down on the distributor cap. 2, 3 and 4 are anti-clockwise from No 1 (Fig 4 : 12).
11 The plug leads require no routine attention other than being wiped over regularly and kept clean. At intervals of 6,000 miles (9500 Km) however, pull the leads off the plugs and distributor one at a time and make sure no water has found

78

FIG 4 : 7 REMOVING THE VACUUM UNIT

FIG 4 : 8 REMOVING THE GOVERNOR WEIGHT CIRCLIPS

FIG 4 : 9 TEMPLATE SHIM USED FOR DRILLING NEW SHAFT TENSION PIN HOLE

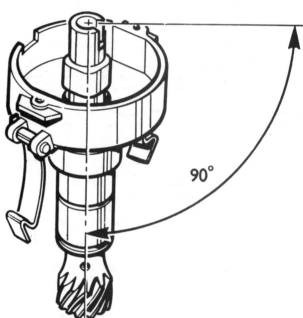

FIG 4 : 10 DISTRIBUTOR SHAFT TENSION PIN HOLE DRILLING DIAGRAM

FIG 4 : 11 FITTING THE DISTRIBUTOR CAM SPINDLE

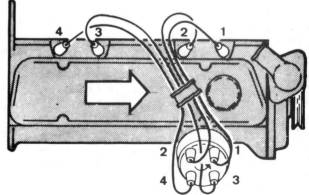

FIG 4 : 12 FITTING SEQUENCE DIAGRAM FOR SPARK PLUG HT LEADS

its way onto the connections. Remove any corrosion from the brass ends, wipe the collars on top of the distributor, and refit the leads.

12 Ignition - timing

1 When a new gear or shaft has been fitted or the engine has been rotated, or if a new assembly is being fitted it will be necessary to retime the ignition. Carry it out as follows:-

2 Set the initial advance to 6° BTDC in the following manner.

3 Turn the engine until No. 1 piston is coming up to TDC on the compression stroke. This can be checked by removing No.1 spark plug and feeling the pressure being developed in the cylinder, or by removing the rocker cover and noting when the valves in No.4 cylinder are rocking, i.e. the inlet valve just opening and exhaust valve just closing. If this check is not made it is all too easy to set the timing 180° out, as both No.1 and 4 cylinders come up to TDC at the same time, but only one is on the firing stroke. The engine can most easily be turned by engaging top gear and edging the car along.

4 Continue turning the engine until the appropriate timing mark on the timing cover is in line with the notch on the crankshaft pulley (Fig 4 : 13). This setting must be correct for the initial advance which is 6° BTDC. (Fig 4 : 14).

5 Now with the vacuum advance unit pointing to the rear of the car, insert the distributor assembly so that the rotor points to No.2 inlet port. The rotor will rotate slightly as the gear drops into mesh.

6 Fit the clamp plate retaining bolt to hold the assembly to the engine block and tighten it.

7 Slacken the distributor clamp pinch bolt (Fig 4 : 15).

8 Gently turn the distributor body until the contact breaker points are just opening when the rotor is pointing at the contact in the distributor cap which is connected to No.1 spark plug. A convenient way is to put a mark on the outside of the distributor body in line with the terminal on cover, so that it shows when the cover is removed.

9 If this position cannot easily be reached check that the drive gear has meshed on the correct tooth by lifting out the distributor once more. If necessary rotate the drive shaft one tooth and try again.

10 Tighten the distributor body clamp enough to hold the distributor, but do not overtighten.

11 Set in this way the timing should be correct, but small adjustments may be made by slackening the distributor clamp bolt once more and rotating the distributor body clockwise to advance and anti-clockwise to retard.

12 The setting of a distributor including the amount of vacuum and mechanical advance can only be accurately carried out on an electronic tester. Alterations to the vacuum advance shims or tension on the mechanical advance unit springs will change the characteristics of the unit.

13 Since the ignition timing setting enables the firing point to be correctly related to the grade of fuel used, the fullest advantage of a change of grade from that recommended for the engine will only be attained by re-adjustment of the ignition setting.

13 Ignition system - fault finding

By far the majority of breakdown and running troubles are caused by faults in the ignition system either in the low tension or high tension circuits.

14 Ignition system - fault symptoms

There are two main symptoms indicating ignition faults, either the engine will not start or fire, or the engine is difficult to start and misfires. If it is a regular misfire, i.e. the engine is only running on two or three cylinders the fault is almost sure to be in the secondary, or high tension circuit. If the misfiring is intermittent, the fault could be in either the high or low tension

FIG 4 : 13 CRANKSHAFT PULLEY AND TIMING CASE TIMING MARKS

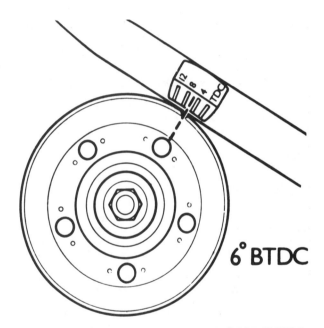

FIG 4 : 14 IGNITION TIMING MARKS SET FOR 6° BTDC

FIG 4 : 15 THE DISTRIBUTOR CLAMP PINCH BOLT

circuits. If the car stops suddenly, or will not start at all, it is likely that the fault is in the low tension circuit. Loss of power and overheating, apart from faulty carburation settings, are normally due to faults in the distributor or incorrect ignition timing.

15 Fault diagnosis - engine fails to start

1 If the engine fails to start and the car was running normally when it was last used, first check there is fuel in the petrol tank. If the engine turns over normally on the starter motor and the battery is evidently well charged, then the fault may be in either the high or low tension circuits. First check the H T circuit. NOTE: If the battery is known to be fully charged; the ignition light comes on, and the starter motor fails to turn the engine CHECK THE TIGHTNESS OF THE LEADS ON THE BATTERY TERMINALS and also the security of the earth lead to its CONNECTION TO THE BODY. It is quite common for the leads to have worked loose, even if they look and feel secure. If one of the battery terminal posts gets very hot when trying to work the starter motor this is a sure indication of a faulty connection to that terminal.

2 One of the commonest reasons for bad starting is wet or damp spark plug leads and distributor. Remove the distributor cap. If condensation is visible internally dry the cap with a rag and also wipe over the leads. Replace the cap.

3 If the engine still fails to start, check that current is reaching the plugs, by disconnecting each plug lead in turn at the spark plug end, and hold the end of the cable about 3/16th in (4.762 mm) away from the cylinder block. Spin the engine on the starter motor.

4 Sparking between the end of the cable and the block should be fairly strong with a regular blue spark. (Hold the lead with rubber to avoid electric shocks). If current is reaching the plugs, then remove them and clean and regap them to 0.025 in (0.64 mm). The engine should now start.

5 If there is no spark at the plug leads take off the H T lead, from the centre of the distributor cap and hold it to the block as before. Spin the engine on the starter once more. A rapid succession of blue sparks between the end of the lead and the block indicate that the coil is in order and that the distributor cap is cracked, the rotor arm faulty or the carbon brush in the top of the distributor cap is not making good contact with the spring on the rotor arm. Possibly the points are in bad condition. Clean and reset them as described in Sections 2 and 3.

6 If there are no sparks from the end of the lead from the coil, check the connections at the coil end of the lead. If they are in order start checking the low tension circuit.

7 Use a 12v voltmeter on a 12v bulb and two lengths of wire. With the ignition switch on and the points open test between the low tension wire to the coil (it is marked S W or +) and earth. No reading indicates a break in the supply from the ignition switch. Check the connections at the switch to see if any are loose. Refit them and the engine should run. A reading shows a faulty coil or condenser or broken lead between the coil and the distributor.

8 Take the condenser wire off the points assembly and with the points open test between the moving point and earth. If there now is a reading then the fault is in the condenser. Fit a new one and the fault is cleared.

9 With no reading from the moving point to earth, take a reading between earth and the CB or - terminal of the coil. A reading here shows a broken wire which will need to be replaced between the coil and distributor. No reading confirms that the coil has failed and must be replaced, after which the engine will run once more. Remember to refit the condenser wire to the points assembly. For these tests it is sufficient to separate the points with a piece of dry paper while testing with the points open.

16 Fault diagnosis - engine misfires

1 If the engine misfires regularly run it at a fast idling speed. Pull off each of the plug caps in turn and listen to the note of the engine. Hold the plug cap in a dry cloth or with a rubber glove as additional protection against a shock from the H T supply.

2 No difference in engine running will be noticed when the lead from the defective circuit is removed. Removing the lead from one of the good cylinders will accentuate the misfire.

3 Remove the plug lead from the end of the defective plug and hold it about 3/16th in (4.762 mm) away from the block. Restart the engine. If the sparking is fairly strong and regular the fault must lie in the spark plug.

4 The plug may be loose, the insulation may be cracked, or the points may have burnt away giving too wide a gap for the spark to jump. Worse still, one of the points may have broken off. Either renew the plug, or clean it, reset the gap, and then test it.

5 If there is no spark at the end of the plug lead, or, if it is weak and intermittent, check the ignition lead from the distributor to the plug. If the insulation is cracked or perished, renew the lead. Check the connections at the distributor cap.

6 If there is still no spark, examine the distributor cap carefully for tracking. This can be recognised by a very thin black line running between two or more electrodes, or between an electrode and some other part of the distributor. These lines are paths which now conduct electricity across the cap thus letting it run to earth. The only answer is a new distributor cap.

7 Apart from the ignition timing being incorrect, other causes of misfiring have already been dealt with under the section dealing with the failure of the engine to start. To recap - these are that:-

a) The coil may be faulty giving an intermittent misfire.

b) There may be a damaged wire or loose connection in the low tension circuit.

c) The condenser may be short circuiting.

d) There may be a mechanical fault in the distributor (broken driving spindle or contact breaker spring).

8 If the ignition timing is too far retarded, it should be noted that the engine will tend to overheat, and there will be a quite noticeable drop in power. If the engine is overheating and the power is down, and the ignition timing is correct then the carburettor should be checked, as it is likely that this is where the fault lies.

Chapter 5 Clutch and actuating mechanism

Contents

Specifications

Type	Single dry plate with diaphragm spring
Diameter	7.5 in (190.5 mm)
Friction lining, outer diameter	7.64 in (194.0 mm)
inner diameter	5.00 in (127.0 mm)
thickness	0.28 in (7.2 mm)
Minimum thickness before renewal	0.08 in (2.0 mm)
Number of driven plate torsion springs	4
Actuation	Cable
Free movement at clutch bellhousing cable abutment	0.12 in (3.5 mm)
Torque wrench settings	
Pressure plate cover to flywheel bolts	15 lb ft (2.07 kg m)

1 General description

1 All models are fitted with a single dry plate diaphragm spring operated clutch. Both 1300 cc and 1600 cc models employ a 7.5 in (190.5 mm) diameter clutch.

2 The unit (Fig 5.1) comprises a pressure plate assembly (1) which contains the pressure plate, diaphragm spring and fulcrum rings. The assembly is bolted and dowelled by means of its cover to the rear face of the flywheel.

3 The driven plate (friction disc) (2) is free to slide along the first motion shaft and is held in position between the flywheel and pressure plate faces by the pressure of the diaphragm spring. The friction lining material is riveted to the driven plate which incorporates a spring cushioned hub to absorb transmission shocks and to assist smooth take offs.

4 The circular diaphragm spring is mounted on shouldered pins and held in place in the cover by two fulcrum rings. The spring itself is held in place by three spring steel clips which are riveted in position.

5 The clutch is actuated by a pendant type foot pedal (8) operated through a cable (7) and release arm (6).

6 Depressing the clutch pedal pushes the release bearing (4) mounted on its retainer (5) forward to bear against the diaphragm spring fingers. This action causes the diaphragm spring outer edge to deflect and move the pressure plate rearwards thus disengaging the pressure plate from the driven plate.

7 When the clutch pedal is released, the diaphragm spring forces the pressure plate into contact with the high friction linings on the clutch disc and at the same time pushes the clutch disc a fraction of an inch forwards on its splines so engaging the clutch disc with the flywheel. The clutch disc is now firmly sandwiched between the pressure plate and the flywheel so the drive is taken up.

8 As the friction linings on the clutch disc wear, the pressure plate automatically moves closer to the disc to compensate. There is therefore no need to periodically adjust the clutch.

2 Clutch cable - removal and replacement

1 Detach the clutch cable support bracket on the clutch bellhousing and swing it aside (Fig 1 : 6).

2 Slacken the clutch cable adjuster nut and locknut.

3 Peel back the rubber gaiter and pull the clutch inner cable from its keyhole type fixing in the clutch release arm (Fig 5 : 2). Do not move the release arm more than ½ in (12.7 mm) during this operation or the arm may become detached from the release bearing retainer and this would necessitate the removal of the gearbox to rectify.

4 Remove the rubber bung from the engine rear bulkhead to provide access to the cable connection on the foot pedal (early models only).

5 Lever the cable eye and pin from the clips on pedal lever, (Fig 5 : 3).

6 Remove the pin from the cable eye and withdraw the clutch cable assembly from the abutment tube in the facia panel.

7 Replacement of the clutch cable is a reversal of removal but adjust the cable after re-fitting as described in Section 4.

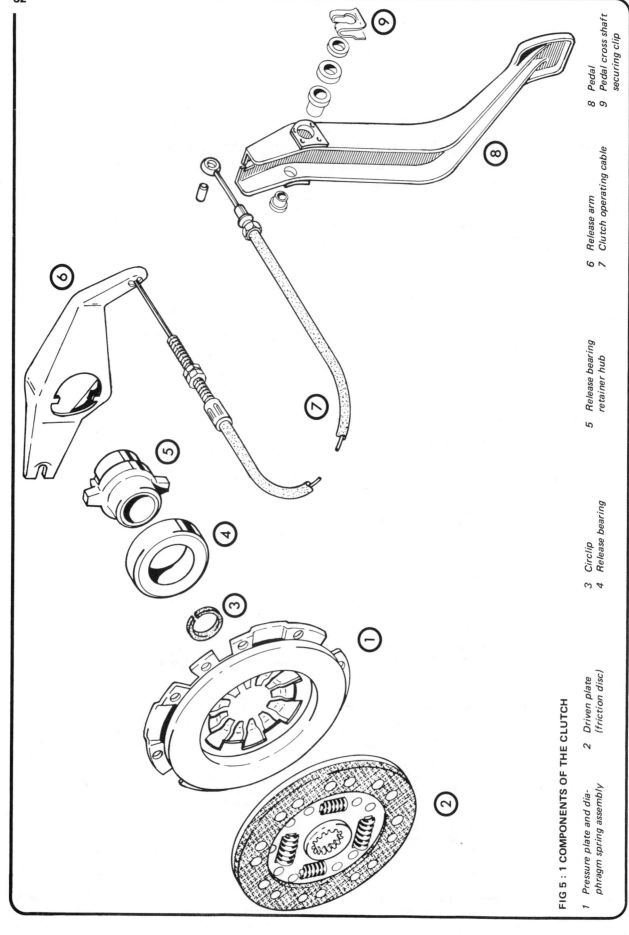

FIG 5 : 1 COMPONENTS OF THE CLUTCH

1	Pressure plate and diaphragm spring assembly	3	Circlip	5	Release bearing retainer hub
2	Driven plate (friction disc)	4	Release bearing	6	Release arm
				7	Clutch operating cable

8 Pedal
9 Pedal cross shaft securing clip

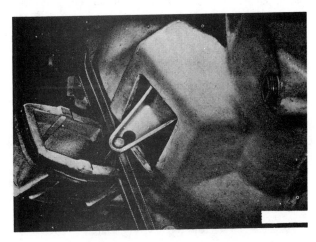

FIG 5 : 2 CLUTCH INNER CABLE TO RELEASE ARM CONNECTION

FIG 5 : 3 REMOVING THE CLUTCH CABLE FROM THE PEDAL LEVER AND THE PEDAL LEVER FROM THE CROSS SHAFT

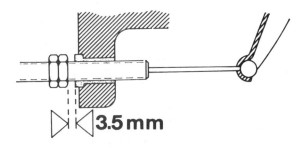

FIG 5 : 4 CLUTCH CABLE NUT TO BELLHOUSING ABUTMENT FREE MOVEMENT DIAGRAM

3 Clutch operating pedal - removal and replacement

1 Disconnect the clutch cable from the clutch pedal as described in the preceding Section.
2 Refer to Ff Fig 5.1 and pull off the retaining clips (9) from the pedal cross shaft.
3 Remove the thrust washer, distance piece and bush, and slide the pedal sideways from the cross shaft.
4 Replacement is a reversal of removal.
5 Adjust the cable as described in Section 4.

4 Clutch operating cable - adjustment

1 Pull the clutch pedal against its return stop.
2 Pull the clutch cable assembly rearwards from its abutment with the clutch bellhousing but without applying any tension to the release arm.
3 Check the clearance between the face of the cable adjuster nut and the face of the abutment. This should measure 0.12 in (3.5 mm) (Fig 5 : 4). The clearance should be checked immediately following two full applications of the clutch pedal.
4 Where the clearance is incorrect, slacken the cable locknut, adjust the cable tension by means of the adjuster nut and finally re-tighten the locknut.

5 Clutch - removal

1 Remove the gearbox as described in Chapter 6.
2 Remove the clutch assembly by unscrewing the six bolts holding the cover to the rear face of the flywheel. Unscrew the bolts diagonally half a turn at a time to prevent distortion to the cover flange.
3 With all the bolts and spring washers removed, lift the clutch assembly off the locating dowels. The driven plate or clutch disc will fall out at this stage as it is not attached to either the clutch cover assembly or the flywheel (Fig 5 : 5).

6 Clutch - replacement

1 It is important that no oil or grease gets on the clutch disc friction linings, or the pressure plate and flywheel faces. It is advisable to replace the clutch with clean hands and to wipe down the pressure plate and flywheel faces with a clean dry rag before assembly begins.
2 Place the clutch disc against the flywheel with the longer end of the hub facing towards the flywheel, (photo). On no account should the clutch disc be replaced with the longer end of the centre hub facing out from the flywheel as, on reassembly, it will be found quite impossible to operate the clutch with the friction disc in this position,
3 Replace the clutch cover assembly loosely on the dowels, (one dowel is arrowed in the photo). Replace the six bolts and spring washers and tighten them finger tight so that the clutch disc is gripped but can still be moved.
4 The clutch disc must now be centralized so that when the engine and gearbox are mated the gearbox input shaft splines will pass through the splines in the centre of the driven plate hub.
5 Centralization can be carried out quite easily by inserting a round bar or long screwdriver through the hole in the centre of the clutch so that the end of the bar rests in the small hole in the end of the crankshaft containing the input shaft bearing bush. Ideally an old Ford input shaft should be used.
6 Using the input shaft bearing bush as a fulcrum, moving the bar sideways or up and down will move the clutch disc in whichever direction is necessary to achieve centralization.
7 Centralization is easily judged by removing the bar and viewing the driven plate hub in relation to the hole in the release bearing. When the hub appears exactly in the centre of the release bearing hole all is correct (photo). Alternatively the input shaft

6.2 Driven plate showing longer hub to flywheel.

6.3 Cover locating dowel.

6.7 Driven plate splined hub centralised with diaphragm spring fingers.

will fit the bush and centre of the clutch hub exactly, obviating the need for visual alignment.

8 Tighten the clutch bolts firmly in a diagonal sequence to ensure that the cover plate is pulled down evenly and without distortion of the flange. Finally tighten the bolts down to a torque of 15 lb ft (2.07 kg m) (Fig 5 : 6).

7 Clutch - dismantling and replacement

1 It is not practical to dismantle the pressure plate assembly and the term 'clutch dismantling and replacement' is the term usually used for simply fitting a new clutch friction plate.

2 If a new clutch disc is being fitted it is false economy not to renew the release bearing at the same time. This will preclude having to replace it at a later date when wear on the clutch linings is still very small.

3 If the pressure plate assembly requires renewal (See Section 8) an exchange unit must be purchased. This will have been accurately set up and balanced to very fine limits.

8 Clutch - inspection

1 Examine the clutch disc friction linings for wear and loose rivets and the disc for rim distortion, cracks, broken hub springs, and worn splines. The surface of the friction linings may be highly glazed, but as long as the clutch material pattern can be clearly seen this is satisfactory (Fig 5 : 7). Compare the amount of lining wear with a new clutch disc at the stores in your local garage, and if the linings are more than three quarters worn replace the disc.

2 It is always best to renew the clutch driven plate as an assembly to preclude further trouble, but, if it is wished to merely re-new the linings, the rivets should be drilled out and not knocked out with a punch. The manufacturers do not advise that only the linings are renewed and personal experience dictates that it is far more satisfactory to renew the driven plate complete than to try and economize by only fitting new friction linings.

3 Check the machined faces of the flywheel and the pressure plate. If either is grooved it should be machined until smooth or renewed.

4 If the pressure plate is cracked or split, or if the pressure of the diaphragm spring is suspect, it is essential that an exchange unit is fitted.

5 Check the release bearing for smoothness of operation. There should be no harshness and no slackness in it. It should spin reasonably freely bearing in mind it has been prepacked with grease.

9 Clutch release bearing - removal and replacement

1 With the gearbox and engine separated to provide access to the clutch, attention can be given to the release bearing located in the bellhousing, over the input shaft.

2 The release bearing is a relatively inexpensive but important component and unless it is nearly new it is a mistake not to re-place it during an overhaul of the clutch.

3 To remove the release bearing, first pull off the release arm rubber gaiter.

4 The release arm and bearing assembly can then be withdrawn from the clutch housing (Fig 5 : 8).

5 To free the bearing from the release arm simply unhook it, and then with the aid of two blocks of wood and a vice press off the release bearing from its hub.

6 Replacement is a straightforward reversal of this procedure.

10 Clutch - faults

There are four main faults to which the clutch and release

FIG 5 : 7 APPEARANCE OF DRIVEN PLATE WITH LININGS
IN GOOD CONDITION

5.8 THE RELEASE ARM AND BEARING ASSEMBLY

FIG 5 : 5 REMOVING THE DRIVEN PLATE AFTER
PRESSURE PLATE ASSEMBLY REMOVAL:
NOTE: THE CORRECT TYPE OF PLATE WILL HAVE ONLY
FOUR TORSION SPRINGS

FIG 5 : 6 TIGHTENING THE PRESSURE PLATE COVER
BOLTS

mechanism are prone. They may occur by themselves or in conjunction with any of the other faults. They are; clutch squeal, slip, spin, and judder.

11 Clutch squeal - diagnosis and cure

1 If on taking up the drive or when changing gear, the clutch squeals, this is a sure indication of a badly worn clutch release bearing.

2 As well as regular wear due to normal use, wear of the clutch release bearing is much accentuated if the clutch is ridden, or held down for long periods in gear, with the engine running. To minimize wear of this component the car should always be taken out of gear at traffic lights and for similar hold-ups.

3 The clutch release bearing is not an expensive item but difficult to get at.

12 Clutch slip - diagnosis and cure

1 Clutch slip is a self-evident condition which occurs when the clutch friction plate is badly worn; the release arm free travel is insufficient; oil or grease have got onto the flywheel or pressure plate faces; or the pressure plate itself is faulty.

2 The reason for clutch slip is that, due to one of the faults listed above, there is either insufficient pressure from the pressure plate, or insufficient friction from the friction plate, to ensure solid drive.

3 If small amounts of oil get onto the clutch, they will be burnt off under the heat of clutch engagement, and in the process, gradually darken the linings. Excessive oil on the clutch will burn off leaving a carbon deposit which can cause quite bad slip, or fierceness, spin and judder.

4 If clutch slip is suspected, and confirmation of this condition is required, there are several tests which can be made:

5 With the engine in second or third gear and pulling lightly up a moderate incline, sudden depression of the accelerator pedal may cause the engine to increase its speed without any increase in road speed. Easing off on the accelerator will then give a definite drop in engine speed without the car slowing.

6 In extreme cases of clutch slip the engine will race under normal acceleration conditions.

7 If slip is due to oil or grease on the linings a temporary cure can sometimes be effected by squirting carbon tetrachloride into the clutch. The permanent cure is, of course, to renew the clutch driven plate and trace and rectify the oil leak.

13 Clutch spin - diagnosis and cure

1 Clutch spin is a condition which occurs when there is a leak in the clutch hydraulic actuating mechanism; the release arm free travel is excessive; there is an obstruction in the clutch either on the primary gear splines, or in the operating lever itself; or the oil may have partially burnt off the clutch linings and have left a resinous deposit which is causing the clutch disc to stick to the pressure plate or flywheel.

2 The reason for clutch spin is that due to any, or a combination of, the faults just listed, the clutch pressure plate is not completely freeing from the centre plate even with the clutch pedal fully depressed.

3 If clutch spin is suspected, the condition can be confirmed by extreme difficulty in changing gear, and very sudden take-up of the clutch drive at the fully depressed end of the clutch pedal travel as the clutch is released.

4 If these points are checked and found to be in order then the fault lies internally in the clutch, and it will be necessary to remove the clutch for examination.

14 Clutch judder - diagnosis and cure

1 Clutch judder is a self-evident condition which occurs when the gearbox or engine mountings are loose or too flexible; when there is oil on the faces of the clutch friction plate; or when the clutch pressure plate has been incorrectly adjusted.

2 The reason for clutch judder is that due to one of the faults just listed, the clutch pressure plate is not freeing smoothly from the friction disc, and is snatching.

3 Clutch judder normally occurs when the clutch pedal is released in first or reverse gears, and the whole car shudders as it moves backwards or forwards.

Chapter 6 Gearbox

Contents

Specifications

Application ... ...   Type 'C' for models with individual front seats
   Type 'D' for models with bench front seats

Type 'C' incorporates remote gear change lever at rear of extension housing.
Type 'D' has gearchange lever mounted on plate just to rear of gearbox rear face

Both models ... ...   Four forward speeds and reverse, synchromesh on all forward gears.

Ratios	Type C	Type D
1st gear	2,97 : 1	3.54 : 1
2nd gear	2.01 : 1	2.40 : 1
3rd gear	1.43 : 1	1.41 : 1
Top gear	1.00 : 1	1.00 : 1
Reverse	3.32 : 1	3.96 : 1

Oil capacity (both models) ... ...   1.58 pints (0.9 litres)
Countershaft gear train end float ... ...   0.008 to 0.020 in (0.205 to 0.505 mm)

Countershaft diameter
   Type C ... ...   0.6818 to 0.6823 in (17.317 to 17.329 mm)
   Type D ... ...   0.6576 to 0.6581 in (16.703 to 16.715 mm)
   Countershaft thrust washers (thickness) ... ...   0.061 to 0.063 in (1.55 to 1.60 mm)

Torque wrench settings (both models)	lb ft	kg m
Gearbox top covers	12 to 15	(1.7 to 2.1)
Gearbox spigot bearing	12 to 15	(1.7 to 2.1)
Extension housing to gearbox	20 to 25	(2.8 to 3.5)

Specifications for Automatic Transmission see page 107

1 General description

1 The gearbox fitted to both the 1300 cc and 1600 cc engined models is a type C (Fig 6 : 1) for cars having individual front seats or a type D (Fig 6 : 2) for cars having a front bench seat.
2 The difference between the two types lies mainly in the gearchange and selector mechanism.
3 The units have four forward speeds, all with synchromesh, and a reverse gear.
4 The gearbox casting is a separate unit from the clutch bellhousing to which it is bolted.

2 Gearbox - removal and replacement

1 The gearbox may be removed as a combined unit with the engine as described in Chapter 1 and then separated. This method should only be employed where major servicing of the engine is also to be undertaken.
2 Where the gearbox only is to be removed, refer to Chapter 1 for a description of operations required to release the gearbox during removal of the combined engine gearbox unit. These operations are summarized in the following paragraphs.
3 Position the vehicle over a pit or raise the rear of the car on

FIG.6.1. TYPE C GEARBOX CASING (REMOTE CONTROL GEAR CHANGE)

FIG.6.2. TYPE D GEARBOX CASING (DIRECT GEAR CHANGE)

FIG 6 : 3 REMOVING THE PLUG WHICH RETAINS THE SELECTOR RAIL SPRING AND DETENT BALL IN POSITION

ramps or axle stands to provide an adequate working clearance which should be slightly greater than the overall depth of the clutch bellhousing.

4 Drain the oil from the gearbox and disconnect the battery negative lead.

5 With type D gearboxes fitted to bench type front seat vehicles, remove the gear lever knob and rubber gaiter. Unscrew the gear-lever turret and withdraw the lever. With type C gearboxes, re-move the centre console, gear lever knob and circlip which retains the lever spring under compression. Bend back the lock tab from the plastic dome nut, unscrew it and withdraw the gear lever (photos).

6 Detach the speedometer cable circlip and withdraw the cable (photo).

7 Mark the edges of the propeller shaft and pinion drive flanges and then detach the rear flange and withdraw the propeller shaft from its connection with the gearbox rear extension housing (photos).

8 Disconnect the exhaust pipe from the manifold (photo).

9 Disconnect the clutch cable from the release arm, peel back the rubber gaiter and remove the outer cable locknut. Unscrew the cable bracket and swing both cable and bracket aside (photo).

10 Disconnect the starter motor lead and remove the starter motor securing bolts (photo).

11 Unscrew and remove the clutch housing to crankcase bolts.

12 Support the engine with a jack and then remove the bolts which secure the gearbox mounting crossmember to the vehicle frame (photo).

13 Lower the jack gently until the gearbox can be withdrawn to the rear from beneath the car (photo). A trolley type jack will facilitate this operation. Do not allow the weight of the gearbox to hang upon the input shaft whilst it is still in engage-ment with the clutch driven plate. Do not release the engine jack more than is absolutely necessary to permit withdrawal of the gearbox, otherwise engine mountings, hoses and controls may be strained.

14 Replacement is a reversal of removal but observe the follow-ing points: Match the propeller shaft/pinion flange marks before mating. Refill the gearbox with the correct grade and quantity of oil after refitting. Adjust the clutch cable as described in Chapter 5.

3 Gearbox - dismantling

1 Remove the clutch release bearing (photo).

2 Detach the clutch release arm (photo).

3 Unscrew and remove the four bolts which secure the clutch bellhousing to the front face of the gearbox (photo).

4 Separate the gearbox and bellhousing units, (photo).

5 Refer to Fig 6 : 4 and remove the four securing bolts from the top cover (1). Lift away the top cover and gasket (2). Carefully retain the two locating pins (6).

6 Using a screwdriver, lever the extension housing rear plug (24) from its seat.

7 Unscrew the blanking plug (7) retaining the spring (8) and ball (9) (Fig 6 : 3).

8 Drive out the spring pin (13) which secures the selector boss (12) to the selector rail (15) as shown in Fig 6 : 5.

9 Withdraw the selector rail through the rear end and at the same time detach the selector boss and lockplate (14).

10 Remove the selector forks (5 and 10) by pushing the synch-ronizer hubs as far to the front of the gearbox as possible. Lift out the forks (Fig 6 : 6) and separate them, if essential, by remov-ing the spring pin.

11 Remove the extension housing oil seal (25) and rear bush (26) if necessary by using a suitable extractor.

12 Unscrew and remove the extension housing securing bolts (Fig 6 : 7).

13 Withdraw the extension housing (22) slightly and rotate it until the cut-a-way is positioned to give access to the counter-shaft (Fig 6 : 8).

2.5A. Removing the gearlever gaiter from a Type 'C' gearbox

2.5B. Bending back a gearlever assembly locking tab, Type 'C'

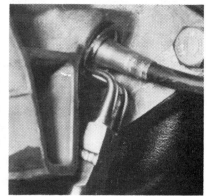

2.6. Withdrawing speedometer cable circlip, Type 'C'

2.7A. Removing propeller shaft flange bolts

2.7B. Removing the propeller shaft sliding sleeve from the gearbox

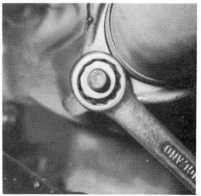

2.8. Removing the exhaust pipe to manifold nuts

2.9. Removing the clutch release arm gaiter and cables

2.10. Removing the starter motor

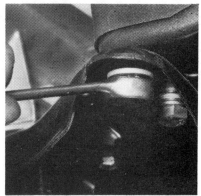

2.12. Unscrewing a gearbox mounting bolt

2.13. Withdrawing the gearbox with the use of a trolley jack

3.1. Detaching the clutch release bearing

3.2. Removing the clutch release arm

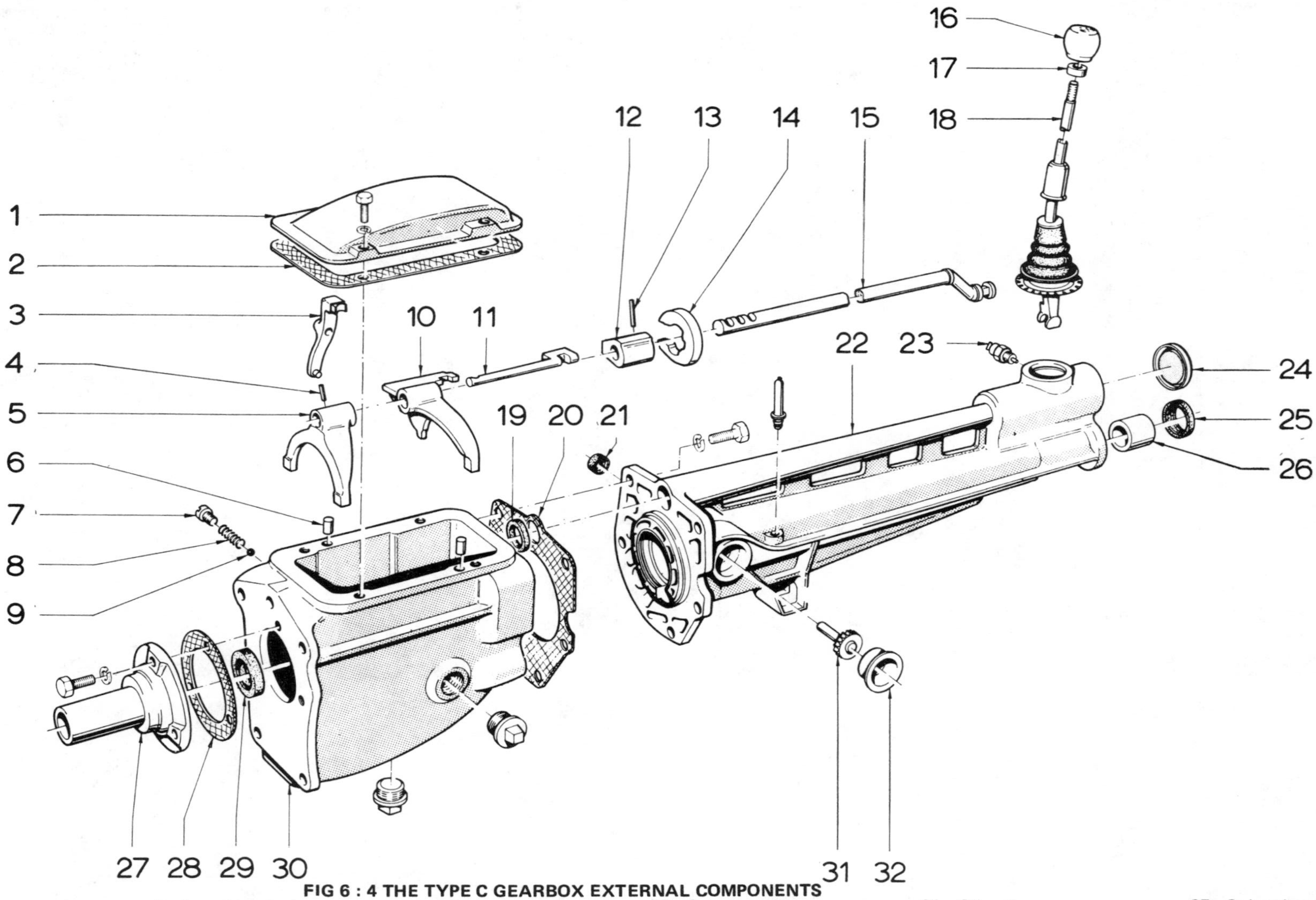

FIG 6 : 4 THE TYPE C GEARBOX EXTERNAL COMPONENTS

1	Top cover	15	Selector rail
2	Gasket	16	Gear lever knob
3	Reverse relay arm	17	Locknut
4	Spring pin	18	Gear lever assembly
5	3rd/top selector	19	Oil seal
	fork	20	Gasket
6	Locating pin	11	Selector fork relay
7	Screwed plug		arm
8	Spring	12	Selector boss
9	Selector rail detent	13	Spring pin
	ball	14	Lock plate
10	1st/2nd selector		

21	Oil seal	27	Spigot bearing
22	Extension housing	28	Gasket
23	Reverse lamp switch	29	Oil seal
24	Extension housing plug	30	Gear case
25	Oil seal	31	Speedometer drive gear
26	Bush	32	Retainer plug

91

3.3 Unscrewing the clutch bellhousing to gearbox bolts

3.4 Separating the gearbox from the clutch bellhousing

FIG 6 : 5 DRIFTING OUT THE SELECTOR BOSS/RAIL SPRING ROLL PIN

FIG 6 : 6 LIFTING OUT THE SELECTOR FORKS

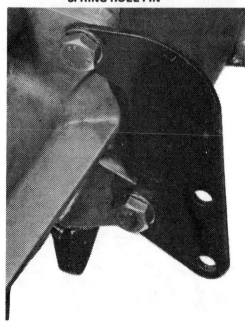

FIG 6 : 7 TWO OF THE FIVE EXTENSION HOUSING TO GEARCASE BOLTS

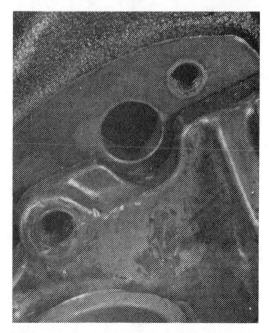

FIG.6.8. ROTATION OF THE EXTENSION HOUSING TO GIVE ACCESS TO THE COUNTERSHAFT

14 Obtain a drift, slightly smaller in diameter than the counter-shaft and drive the countershaft out through the rear of the gearbox. Keep the drift in permanent contact with the end of the countershaft during this operation in order to prevent the countershaft gear train and needle rollers from falling into the gearbox interior (Fig 6 : 9). Carefully lower the countershaft gear train into the bottom of the gearbox (complete with dummy shaft) and then remove the needle rollers.

15 Withdraw the extension housing assembly from the gearbox case (Fig 6 : 10). To accomplish complete withdrawal of the extension housing assembly, it must first be removed only a sufficient distance to enable the needle roller bearings to be removed while the third/top gear synchronizer hub is held forward. Now remove the synchronizer unit.

16 Unscrew and remove the input shaft spigot bearing retaining bolts (Fig 6 : 11).

17 Refer to Fig 6 : 4 and remove the gasket (28) and oil seal (29).

18 Remove the large circlip from the input shaft ball race (photo). (Circlip (6) in Fig 6 : 12).

19 Using a copper drift against the outer bearing rim only (Fig. 6 : 13) drive the input shaft out through the rear end of the gearbox case.

20 Remove circlip (7) (Fig 6 : 12) located in front of the input shaft ball race. Using a press or bearing extractor, remove the bearing from the input shaft, only if essential, due to wear and renewal of the race being required.

21 Lift the countershaft gear train together with thrust washers from the gearbox case. The drift which has acted as a dummy countershaft since the operations described in paragraph 14 may now be withdrawn.

22 From each end of the gear train remove the needle rollers and spacer rings (Fig 6 : 14).

23 Remove the reverse idler shaft (Fig 6 : 15). This is achieved by screwing into the end of the shaft a 5/16 in/24 bolt and by using a nut, washer and distance piece, the shaft may be drawn out (photo). Remove reverse relay arm (3) (Fig 6 : 4) from fulcrum pin.

24 Lever out the speedometer drive retaining plug (Fig 6 : 16) and remove the speedometer drive pinion.

25 Refer to Fig 6 : 12 and remove the mainshaft circlip (3) from the extension housing.

26 Jar the exposed mainshaft at the rear of the extension housing against a wooden block and force the mainshaft assembly from the front end of the extension housing.

27 The gearbox is now dismantled into major components and the gearbox case should be thoroughly cleaned out. Evidence of worn or damaged components will be found in the amount of metal chippings in the base of the casing. Unless the necessary presses and extractors are available, it is unwise to proceed with further dismantling of the shaft assemblies or synchronizer hubs and it is recommended that these parts are taken for reconditioning to a Ford dealer. However, for those who wish to carry out the work, the operations are fully described in the following Sections.

4 Gearbox - examination and renovation

1 Carefully clean and examine all components. Where there are signs of general wear, distortion, chipping, scoring or damage to machined faces then the parts should be renewed.

2 Examine the gear wheels particularly for wear and chipping of teeth. Renew as necessary.

3 Where the countershaft end float is greater than the permitted tolerance of 0.008 to 0.020 in (0.205 to 0.505 mm) renew the thrust washers. It is a feature of the gearbox that circlips 2 and 3 (Fig 6 : 12) are available in various thicknesses to provide an additional means of end float adjustment. All circlips must be renewed if they have been removed during dismantling.

4 Examine the countershaft needle roller bearing surface and if a ridge can be felt then the shaft must be renewed.

5 Refer to Fig 6 : 19 and check the condition of the mainshaft

FIG 6 : 9 THE COUNTERSHAFT EMERGING FROM THE REAR OF THE GEARBOX BEING DRIVEN OUT BY THE DUMMY SHAFT (DRIFT)

FIG 6 : 10 WITHDRAWING THE EXTENSION HOUSING FROM THE GEARCASE

FIG 6 : 11 THE INPUT SHAFT SPIGOT BEARING AND RETAINING BOLTS

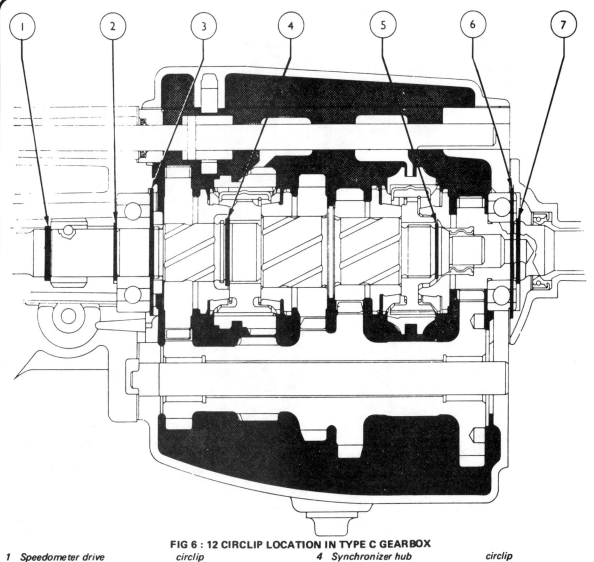

FIG 6 : 12 CIRCLIP LOCATION IN TYPE C GEARBOX

1   Speedometer drive
    gear circlip
2   Mainshaft bearing
    circlip
3   Mainshaft bearing
    circlip
4   Synchronizer hub
    circlip
5   Synchronizer hub
    circlip
6   Input shaft bearing circlip
7   Input shaft bearing circlip

Circlips 2 and 3 are available in a variety of thicknesses to take up mainshaft end-float

3.18. Removing the input shaft bearing
      outer circlip

FIG 6 : 13 DRIFTING OUT THE INPUT SHAFT

94

FIG 6 : 14 THE COUNTERSHAFT, GEARTRAIN, NEEDLE ROLLERS AND SPACERS

FIG 6 : 15 EXTRACTING THE REVERSE IDLER SHAFT

3.23. Removing the reverse idler shaft

FIG 6 : 16 LEVERING OUT THE SPEEDOMETER DRIVE RETAINING PLUG

FIG 6 : 17 SPEEDOMETER DRIVE GEAR AND DETENT BALL

FIG 6 : 18 SYNCHRONIZER UNIT, SHOWING SLEEVE, HUB AND BLOCKER BARS

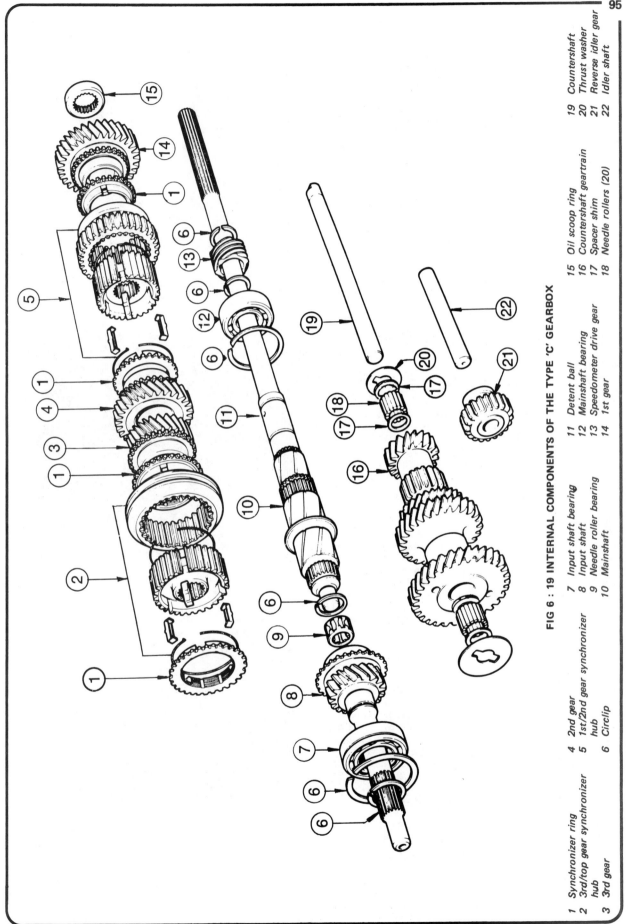

FIG 6 : 19 INTERNAL COMPONENTS OF THE TYPE 'C' GEARBOX

1 Synchronizer ring
2 3rd/top gear synchronizer hub
3 3rd gear
4 2nd gear
5 1st/2nd gear synchronizer hub
6 Circlip
7 Input shaft bearing
8 Input shaft
9 Needle roller bearing
10 Mainshaft
11 Detent ball
12 Mainshaft bearing
13 Speedometer drive gear
14 1st gear
15 Oil scoop ring
16 Countershaft geartrain
17 Spacer shim
18 Needle rollers (20)
19 Countershaft
20 Thrust washer
21 Reverse idler gear
22 Idler shaft

bearing assembly (9) and renew if worn.

6   Examine the synchronizer units (2 and 5). The rings (1) should be renewed to improve the smoothness and speed of gearchanging but wear to other components of the units will necessitate the purchase of the complete remaining assembly.

7   Examine the ends of the selector forks at their points of contact with the channels in the synchronizer unit sleeves. If possible, check for wear by comparing them with new components and renew if necessary.

8   In the rare event of the mainshaft bearing surfaces being scored then renew the shaft.

5   Mainshaft - dismantling and reassembly

1   Refer to Fig 6 : 12 and remove the circlip (5) which is located in front of the 3rd/top gear synchronizer hub.

2   Using a press or extractor engaged behind the rear face of the 3rd gear (3) (Fig 6 : 2) force the mainshaft out of the synchronizer hub.

3   From the splined end of the shaft, remove the speedometer drive locating circlips and withdraw the driven gear (13) retaining the detent ball (Fig 6 : 17).

4   Remove the mainshaft bearing circlip (6) (Fig 6 : 19) and using either a press or an extractor engaging behind the forward face of the 1st gear (14) force the 1st gear, oil scooper ring (15) and bearing (12) from the mainshaft.

5   Remove the circlip from the front of the 1st/2nd gear synchronizer hub (5) and using either a press or an extractor engaged behind the front face of the 2nd gear (4) draw off the gear and synchronizer hub.

6   The synchronizer units may now be dismantled, simply by sliding the sleeve from the hub, detaching the springs and removing the blocker bars (Fig 6 : 18).

7   Reassembly of the synchronizer units is carried out by first fitting the sleeve to the hub so that the mating marks are in alignment. Fit a blocker bar to each of the three hub slots. Fit the two springs one on the front and the other on the rear face of the hub, so that the tagged ends locate in the same blocker bar yet the two springs are staggered to ensure opposite ends of the springs are locating as shown in Fig 6 : 20.

8   Before commencing reassembly of the mainshaft, clean any protective grease from new components (particularly synchronizer units) and lightly lubricate.

9   Slide the second gear onto the mainshaft ensuring that the dog teeth face towards the splined end of the shaft (Fig 6 : 21).

10 Fit the 1st/2nd gear synchronizer ring to the cone of the second gear and then slide the hub assembly on to the mainshaft. Press the hub fully home into its mainshaft location and secure with a new circlip.

11 Fit the synchronizer sleeve, first gear and the oil scoop ring, orientated as shown in Fig 6 : 22.

12 At this stage, particularly where a new extension housing or mainshaft bearing has been purchased, the circlip thickness must be established. Place a spare circlip (2) Fig 6 : 12 (flat side uppermost) in the groove of the ball race seat of the extension housing as shown in Fig 6 : 23. Press the circlip outwards and using a slide gauge, measure accurately the clearance between the ball race shoulder and the circlip upper face. Now measure the width of the ball race which is to be fitted by using a caliper gauge (Fig 6 : 24). By simple subtraction the width of the circlip required to eliminate all end float, after assembly, can be calculated. Circlips are available in a variety of thicknesses.

13 Loosely slide the selected circlip together with the ball race onto the mainshaft and press into position.

14 Fit the speedometer drive gear by first holding the mainshaft so that the detent ball hole is uppermost, insert the ball, locate the drive gear and secure with circlip.

15 Slide third gear (dog teeth forward) onto the mainshaft (Fig 6 : 25).

16 Place the synchronizer ring on the cone.

17 Slide the assembled (see paragraph 7) hub assembly onto the mainshaft so that the wider collar of the hub faces to the rear.

FIG 6 : 20 DIAGRAM SHOWING CORRECT FITTING OF SYNCHRONIZER UNIT SPRING TAGS

FIG 6 : 21 THE CORRECT LOCATION OF 2ND GEAR ON THE MAINSHAFT

FIG 6 : 22 CORRECT SEQUENCE AND ORIENTATION OF SYNCHRONIZER SLEEVE, FIRST GEAR AND OIL SCOOP RING ON MAINSHAFT

FIG 6 : 23 MEASURING MAINSHAFT BEARING RECESS
FOR CIRCLIP THICKNESS CALCULATION

FIG 6 : 24 MEASURING THE WIDTH OF THE MAINSHAFT
BEARING FOR CIRCLIP THICKNESS CALCULATION

FIG 6 : 25 FITTING 3RD GEAR TO THE MAINSHAFT

FIG 6 : 26 LEVERING OUT THE SELECTOR RAIL AND
SPEEDOMETER DRIVE OIL SEALS FROM THE EXTENSION
HOUSING

FIG 6 : 27 FITTING AN EXTENSION HOUSING BUSH

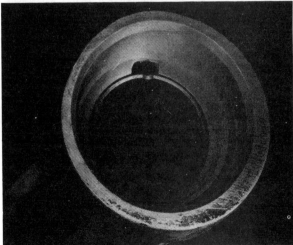

FIG 6 : 28 CORRECT EXTENSION HOUSING AND BUSH
ALIGNMENT

Press the hub on to the shaft until it bears against its shoulder then fit a new circlip.

6 Gearcase - preparation for reassembly

1 Before reassembling the gearbox, the various oil seals must be examined and renewed. It is a wise plan to renew them all at a major overhaul.

2 Lever out the selector rail oil seal from the gearbox case and the speedometer drive oil seal from the extension housing (Fig 6 : 26). Press in new seals.

3 Lever or drift out the extension housing rear oil seal.

4 Should the extension housing bush be scored or worn then it should be extracted or drifted carefully from its location. Drift in a new bush using a tube or mandrel (Fig 6 : 27) so that the cut out of the bush and the oil return groove of the housing are aligned as shown in Fig 6 : 28.

5 Press or drift in a new oil seal (Fig 6 : 29).

7 Gearbox - reassembly

1 Carefully press the mainshaft assembly into the extension housing, ensuring that the splined end of the shaft does not damage the rear oil seal.

2 Engage the circlip previously placed loosely on the shaft (see Section 6 : 13).

3 Fit the speedometer drive pinion and insert a new retainer plug, coated with jointing compound (Fig 6 : 30).

4 Fit the reverse gear relay arm to the fulcrum pin and then the reverse idler gear to the relay arm (groove to the rear). Locate the gear flush with the gear case and using a copper faced hammer, drive the reverse idler shaft into the gearbox case (Fig 6 : 31).

5 Assemble the countershaft gear train by first passing the dummy shaft or drift through the gear bore. Pack the space between the shaft and bore with grease and from each end fit a spacer, needle rollers and second spacer. Coat the countershaft thrust washers with grease and stick them to the internal surfaces of the gearbox case ready for the countershaft to be passed through them. Note the position of the locking tabs when the gear train is correctly positioned (Fig 6 : 32).

6 Carefully cover the countershaft gear train to the bottom of the gearbox case ensuring that the thrust washers are not disturbed (Fig 6 : 33).

7 Where the bearing has been removed from the input shaft, fit a new one by pressing only on the centre track of the bearing. Fit a new circlip.

8 Using a copper drift, drive the input shaft from the inside of the gearbox case until the peripheral circlip recess just appears clear on the outside of the front face of the case. Tap only on the outer bearing track and take care not to damage the gear teeth.

9 Fit the circlip to retain the bearing (Fig 6 : 34).

10 Press a new oil seal into the spigot bearing bush so that the lips of the seal face the gearbox.

11 Lightly grease the running face of the oil seal and fit the spigot bush, using a new gasket, located so that the oil holes are in alignment (Fig 6 : 35). Tighten the bolts which secure the spigot bush to a torque of 12 to 15 lb ft (2.8 to 3.5 kg m). Before fitting the spigot bush it is a wise precaution to tape the input shaft splines so that they do not damage the oil seal as they pass through.

12 Lubricate the needle roller bearing (9) (Fig 6 : 19) and fit it to the input shaft.

13 Slide the top gear synchronizer ring over the cone.

14 Coat the front face of the extension housing with jointing compound and stick a new gasket to it. Now engage the extension housing/mainshaft assembly with the gearbox case. During this operation, push the sleeve of the 3rd/top gear synchronizer hub slightly forward in order to gain sufficient clearance between the hub and the countershaft gear cluster. Check that the top gear synchronizer is returned to its correct position.

FIG 6 : 29 FITTING A NEW EXTENSION HOUSING OIL SEAL

FIG 6 : 30 FITTING A SPEEDOMETER DRIVE PLUG

FIG 6 : 31 FITTING THE REVERSE IDLER SHAFT TO THE GEARBOX

FIG 6 : 32 CORRECT LOCATION OF THE COUNTERSHAFT THRUST WASHERS

FIG 6 : 33 THE COUNTERSHAFT GEARTRAIN RESTING ON THE BOTTOM OF THE GEARCASE PRIOR TO FITTING

FIG 6 : 34 FITTING THE INPUT SHAFT BEARING CIRCLIP

FIG 6 : 35 CORRECT INPUT SHAFT SPIGOT BEARING AND GASKET ALIGNMENT

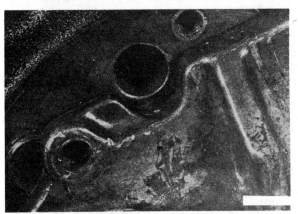

FIG 6 : 36 COUNTERSHAFT HOLE READY TO RECEIVE THE SHAFT

FIG 6 : 37 FITTING THE DUMMY COUNTERSHAFT FROM THE REAR END OF THE GEARCASE

FIG 6 : 38 CORRECT ORIENTATION OF COUNTERSHAFT LUG AFTER INSTALLING

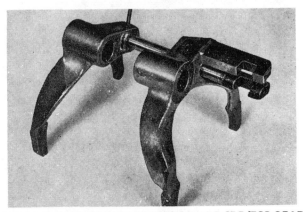

FIG 6 : 39 ASSEMBLING THE 1ST/2ND AND 3RD/TOP GEAR SELECTOR FORKS

FIG 6 : 40 ENGAGING THE SELECTOR FORKS WITH THE SYNCHRONIZER UNIT SLEEVE CHANNELS

15 Rotate the extension housing until the countershaft hole is visible (Fig 6 : 36).

16 Invert the gearbox assembly and engage the countershaft gear train with the mainshaft and input shaft. Check that the countershaft thrust washers are still correctly located and insert the countershaft through the rear end of the box (Fig 6 : 37). Drive it home with a soft faced mallet, keeping it in constant end contact with the dummy shaft, or drift until the latter can be removed. The lug on the rear of the countershaft must take up a horizontal position (Fig 6 : 38) when driven fully home and this must be taken into account during the fitting operation.

17 Rotate the extension housing into its correct position, apply gasket cement to the securing bolts and tighten them to a torque of 20 to 25 lb ft (2.8 to 3.5 kg m).

18 Assemble 1st/2nd and 3rd/top gear selector forks as shown in Fig 6 : 39 using a new spring roll pin.

19 Fit the selector forks to the gearbox by pushing the 1st/2nd and 3rd/top gear synchronizer sleeves to the rear (Fig 6 : 40) and then engaging the forks in the sleeve channels. Arrange the sleeves in the idling position.

20 Grease the selector rail oil seal lips and, keeping the selector relay boss and lock plate in alignment with the rail bore, pass the selector rail through its bore taking care not to damage the oil seal.

21 Secure the selector boss with a new spring roll pin. Fit the detent ball, spring and screw plug (coated with gasket cement) in the sequence shown in Fig 6 : 41.

22 Locate a new gasket and fit the gearbox top cover (Fig 6 : 42) tightening the securing bolts to 12 - 15 lb ft (1.7 to 2.1 kg m).

23 Bolt on the clutch bell housing, insert the clutch release arm and release bearing. The gearbox is now ready for refitting to the car as described in Section 2.

8 Gearbox (Type 'D') - dismantling and reassembly differences

1 This type of gearbox fitted to vehicles having a bench type front seat has certain detail differences (mostly in connection with gearchange selection mechanism) which should be observed. Otherwise all operations as described in the preceding Sections in respect of type C gearboxes will apply.

2 Refer to Figs 6 : 47 and 6 : 48 and remove the gearbox top cover (1) and extension housing top cover (18) (photo).

3 Remove the three coil springs as the top cover is withdrawn (photo).

4 Invert the gearbox and remove the three detent balls into the coil spring orifices.

5 Cut the locking wire from the selector fork using screws and remove the screws (photos).

6 Remove the retainer clip from the 3rd/top gear selector rail.

7 Withdraw the selector rail, retaining the spacer sleeve.

8 Lever out the blanking plug located at the side of the selector rail (Fig 6 : 43) and remove the three detent plungers.

9 Using two screwdrivers as levers, prise out the speedometer drive pinion and extract the 'O' ring seal (Fig 6 : 44).

10 Remove the extension housing fixing bolts and detach the extension housing from the gearbox case.

11 Using a suitable drift, drive the countershaft from the front towards the rear until the countershaft just clears the gearbox case bore. Substitute a dummy shaft for the drift and drive the countershaft from the gearbox (Fig 6 : 45). The dummy shaft must be continuously in contact with the end face of the countershaft during this operation in order to prevent the needle rollers being dislodged. Lower the countershaft gear train complete with dummy shaft to the base of the gearbox case.

12 Drive the mainshaft assembly out through the rear end of the gearbox and dismantle as described for type 'C' gearbox (Section 6).

13 To reassemble, lubricate the input shaft needle roller bearing and fit it to the shaft.

14 Slide the top gear synchronizer ring over the input shaft cone.

15 Slide a new oil seal over the mainshaft and then pass the mainshaft assembly into the gearbox case (Fig 6 : 46) ensuring that the top gear synchronizer sleeve is correctly positioned as shown.

FIG 6 : 41 THE SELECTOR RAIL DETENT BALL, SPRING AND PLUG

FIG 6 : 42 FITTING THE GEARBOX TOP COVER AND GASKET

FIG 6 : 43 LEVERING OUT THE SELECTOR RAIL BLANK-ING PLUG FROM A TYPE 'D' GEARBOX

FIG 6 : 44 REMOVING THE SPEEDOMETER DRIVE PINION FROM A TYPE 'D' GEARBOX

8.2. Unscrewing the extension housing top cover bolts

8.3. Removing the detent coil springs

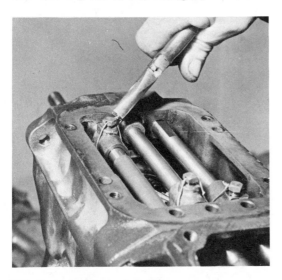

8.5A. Removing selector fork fixing
screw wire.

8.5B. Unscrewing a selector fork fixing
screw

FIG 6 : 45 DRIVING THE COUNTERSHAFT FROM A TYPE 'D' GEARBOX

FIG 6 : 46 FITTING THE MAINSHAFT ASSEMBLY TO A TYPE 'D' GEARBOX

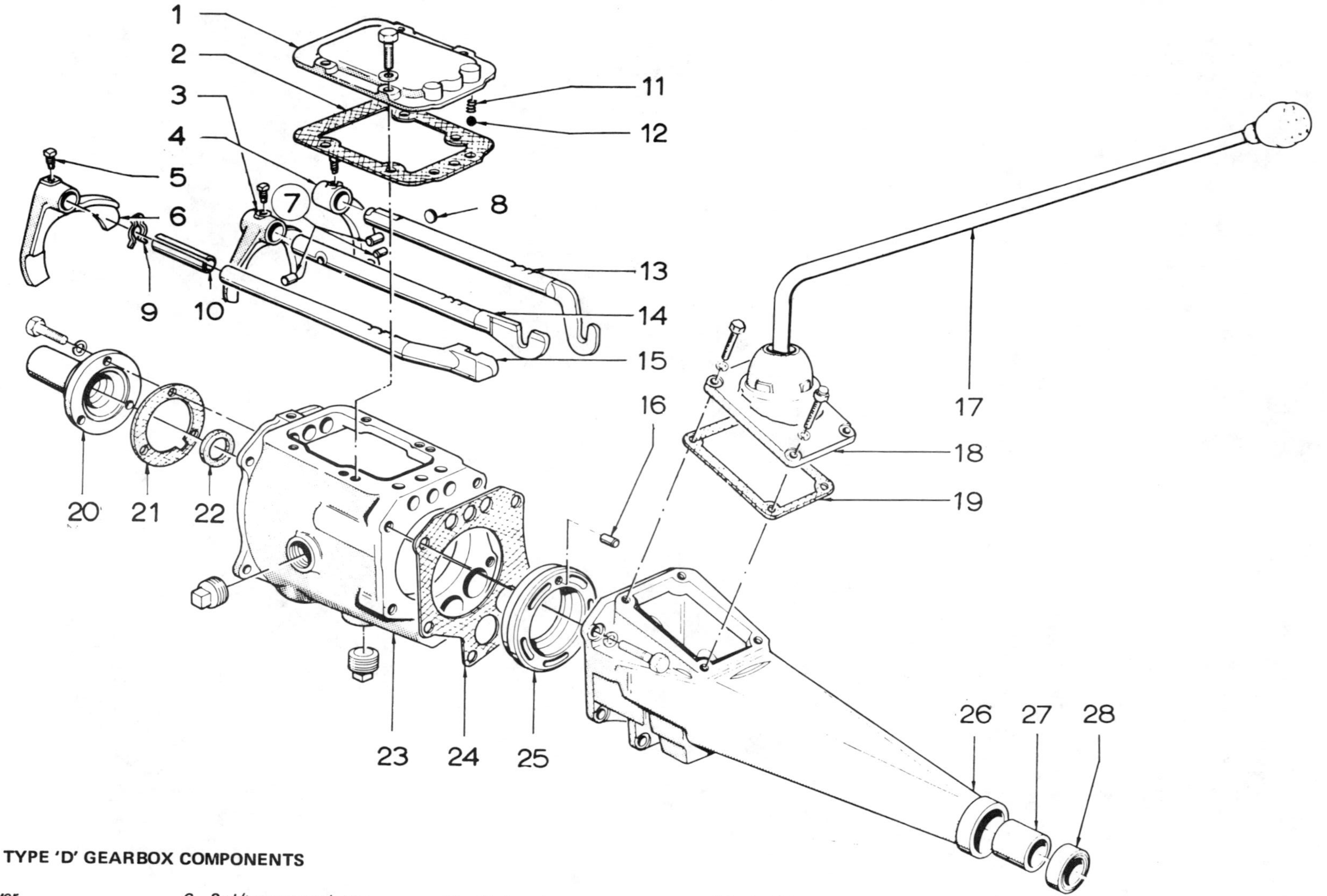

FIG 6 : 47 TYPE 'D' GEARBOX COMPONENTS

1 Top cover
2 Gasket
3 1st/2nd gear selector fork
4 Reverse relay arm
5 Fork securing bolt

6 3rd/top gear selector fork
7 Blocker bars
8 Blanking plug
9 Retainer clip
10 Spacer sleeve

11 Coil spring
12 Detent ball
13 Reverse selector rail
14 1st/2nd gear selector rail

15 3rd/top gear selector rail
16 Locating pin
17 Gear lever
18 Extension housing top cover

19 Gasket
20 Spigot bearing
21 Gasket
22 Oil seal
23 Gearcase
24 Gasket

25 Ball race
26 Extension housing
27 Extension housing rear bush
28 Oil seal

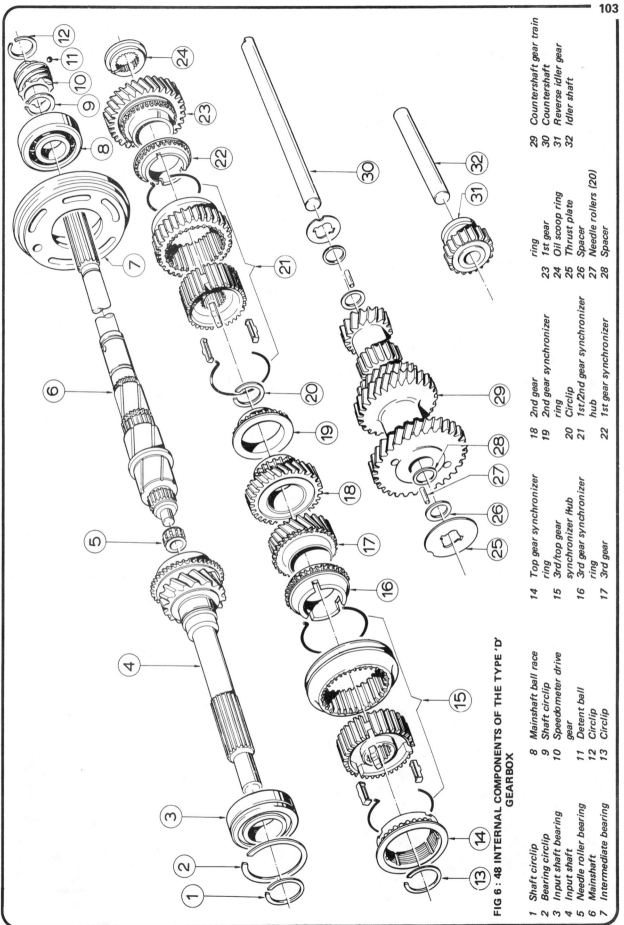

FIG 6 : 48 INTERNAL COMPONENTS OF THE TYPE 'D' GEARBOX

1   Shaft circlip
2   Bearing circlip
3   Input shaft bearing
4   Input shaft
5   Needle roller bearing
6   Mainshaft
7   Intermediate bearing

8   Mainshaft ball race
9   Shaft circlip
10 Speedometer drive gear
11 Detent ball
12 Circlip
13 Circlip

14 Top gear synchronizer ring
15 3rd/top gear synchronizer hub
16 3rd gear synchronizer ring
17 3rd gear

18 2nd gear
19 2nd gear synchronizer ring
20 Circlip
21 1st/2nd gear synchronizer hub
22 1st gear synchronizer ring

23 1st gear
24 Oil scoop ring
25 Thrust plate
26 Spacer
27 Needle rollers (20)
28 Spacer

29 Countershaft gear train
30 Countershaft
31 Reverse idler gear
32 Idler shaft

FIG 6 : 49 CORRECT COUNTERSHAFT LUG ORIENTATION AFTER FITTING THE SHAFT TO A TYPE 'D' GEARBOX

FIG 6 : 50 ALIGNMENT DOWEL ON INTERMEDIATE BEARING RING OF A TYPE 'D' EXTENSION HOUSING

FIG 6 : 51 FITTING THE REVERSE RELAY LEVER TO THE SELECTOR RAIL OF A TYPE 'D' GEARBOX

FIG 6 : 52 ENGAGING THE 1ST/2ND GEAR SELECTOR RAIL WITH THE PRE—ASSEMBLED SELECTOR RODS IN A TYPE 'D' GEARBOX

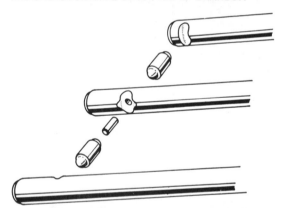

FIG 6 : 53 SELECTOR RAIL DETENT PLUNGERS AND THEIR POSITIONS RELATIVE TO THEIR RESPECTIVE RAILS IN A TYPE 'D' GEARBOX

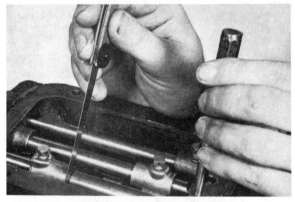

FIG 6 : 54 CHECKING THE END-FLOAT IN A TYPE 'D' GEARBOX

FIG 6 : 55 FITTING A CLIP TO THE SELECTOR RAIL OF A TYPE 'D' GEARBOX

FIG 6 : 56 FITTING THE TOP COVER AND GASKET TO A TYPE 'D' GEARBOX

8.21. 1st/2nd selector rail detent plunger

8.24. Inserting the rear detent balls in their location

8.25. Inserting locking wire in the selector fork fixing screws

FIG 6 : 57 (i) CORRECT ENGAGEMENT OF THE REVERSE RELAY ARM WITH THE REVERSE SELECTOR RAIL OF A TYPE 'D' GEARBOX

FIG 6 : 57 (ii) EXTENSION HOUSING TOP COVER AND VENTILATOR BOLT

16 Invert the gearbox and engage the countershaft gear train with the mainshaft and input shaft. Check that the thrust washers are correctly located.

17 Refer to Section 8 : 16 and fit the countershaft, observing that the final position of the shaft lug is as shown in Fig 6 : 49.

18 Align the locating dowel of the intermediate bearing ring, (Fig 6 : 50) and fit the extension housing, tightening the securing bolts to a torque of 20 to 25 lb ft (2.8 to 3.5 kg m).

19 Fit 1st/2nd gear and 3rd/top gear selector forks to their synchronizer hub channels, then pass the reverse selector rail half way through the right hand gearbox aperture and at this stage fit the reverse relay lever (Fig 6 : 51).

20 Pass the 1st/2nd gear selector rail half way through the centre gearbox aperture engaging as it goes with the pre-assembled selector rods (Fig 6 : 52). Pass the 3rd/top gear selector rod through the spacer sleeve and selector fork whilst they are both held in alignment.

21 Invert the detent plungers into the hole in the side of the gearbox, the two thicker ones located as shown in Fig 6 : 53 and the thinner one positioned in the front end of the 1st/2nd gear selector rail (photo).

22 Push all three selector rails fully home in sequence.

23 Apply gasket cement to the detent plunger hole plug and install it.

24 Insert the rear detent balls in their respective holes and select third gear (photo). Press the appropriate ball downwards with a drift (Fig 6 : 54) and insert a feeler gauge between the spacer sleeve and the selector fork and measure the end float. Select a retainer clip of suitable thickness from the twelve available from Ford dealers which will take up any end float with 3rd gear selected (Fig 6 : 55).

25 Lock the selector fork screws with wire (photo), grease the three detent ball springs and stick them in the cover plate recesses, use a new gasket and fit the top plate all as shown in Fig. 6 : 56. Tighten the bolts to a torque of 12 to 15 lb ft (1.7 to 2.1 kg m).

26 Check that the relay ram engages correctly with the reverse selector rail (visible from within the extension housing top cover), (Fig 6 : 57). (i) Use a new gasket and fit the extension housing top cover, tightening the securing bolts to a torque of 12 to 15 lb ft (1.7 to 2.1 kg m). Note the location of the dual purpose ventilation and securing bolt (Fig 6 : 57) (ii) and check that the hole is kept clear by probing.

27 Fit a new 'O' ring seal and then install the speedometer drive pinion.

FAULT DIAGNOSIS - GEARBOX (MANUAL)

Symptom	Reason	Remedy
General wear	Synchronising cones worn, split or damaged	Dismantle and overhaul gearbox. Fit new gear wheels and synchronising cones.
	Baulk ring synchromesh dogs worn, or damaged	Dismantle and overhaul gearbox. Fit new baulk ring synchromesh.
General wear or damage	Broken selector rod spring	Remove plug and replace spring.
	Gearbox coupling dogs badly worn	Dismantle gearbox. Fit new coupling dogs
	Selector fork rod groove badly worn	Fit new selector fork.
Lack of maintenance	Incorrect grade of oil in gearbox or oil level too low	Drain, refill or top up gearbox with correct grade of oil.
General wear	Bush or needle roller bearings worn or damaged	Dismantle and overhaul gearbox. Renew bearings.
	Gearteeth excessively worn or damaged	Dismantle, overhaul gearbox. Renew gear-wheels.
	Countershaft thrust washers worn allowing excessive end play	Dismantle and overhaul gearbox. Renew thrust washers.
Clutch not fully disengaging	Clutch pedal adjustment incorrect	Adjust clutch pedal correctly.

Automatic transmission

Torque convertor ratio range	Borg Warner type BW 35 Infinitely variable between 1 : 1 and **1.91** : 11 operating in all gears	
Lubricant capacity (dry)	11.25 pints (6.4 litres)	
Gear ratio:		
First	2.395 : 1	
Second	1.450 : 1	
Third	1 : 1	
Reverse	2.094 : 1	
Oil cooler type	Tubes/fins	
Oil cooler hoses:		
Inner diameter	0.272 - 0.300 in (6.91 - 7.62 mm)	
Wall thickness	0.232 - 0.315 in (5.89 - 8.00 mm)	
Torque wrench settings:	lb ft	kg m
Torque convertor to drive plate	25 to 35	(3.5 to 4.1)
Convertor housing to transmission case	8 to 13	(1.1 to 1.8)
Starter inhibitor switch locknut	4 to 6	(0.6 to 0.8)
Centre support to transmission case...	30 to 40	(4.1 to 5.5)
Oil sump to transmission case	8 to 13	(1.1 to 1.8)
Oil drain plug	9 to 12	(1.4 to 1.6)

10 General description

An automatic transmission unit may be fitted as a factory production extra to 1600 over-head valve engined cars.

The system comprises two main components:

1 A three element hydrokinetic torque convertor coupling, capable of torque multiplication at an infinitely variable ratio between 1.91 : 1 and 1 : 1.

2 A torque/speed responsive and hydraulically operated epicyclic gearbox comprising a planetary gearset providing three forward ratios and one reverse ratio.

Due to the complexity of the automatic transmission unit, if performance is not up to standard, or overhaul is necessary, it is imperative that this be left to a main agent who will have the special equipment and knowledge for fault diagnosis and rectification.

The contents of the following Sections are therefore confined to supplying general information and any service information and instruction that can be used by the owner.

11 Fluid level

It is important that transmission fluid manufactured only to the correct specification such as Castrol TQF is used. The capacity of the complete unit is 11.25 pints (6.4 litres). Drain and refill capacity will be less as the torque converter cannot be completely drained, but this operation should not be necessary except for repairs.

12 Maintenance

1 Ensure that the exterior of the converter housing and gearbox is always kept clean of dust or mud, otherwise overheating will occur.

2 Every 6,000 miles (10,000 Km) or more frequently, check the automatic transmission fluid level. With the engine at its normal operating temperature move the selector to the 'P' position and allow the engine to idle for two minutes. With the engine still idling in the 'P' position withdraw the dipstick, wipe it clean and replace it. Quickly withdraw it again and if necessary top up with Castrol TQF automatic transmission fluid. The difference between the 'LOW' and 'FULL' marks on the dipstick is 1 pint (0.50 litre).

3 If the unit has been drained, it is recommended that only new fluid is used. Fill up to the correct 'HIGH' level gradually refilling the unit, the exact amount will depend on how much was left in the converter after draining.

13 Removal and replacement

Any suspected faults must be referred to the main agent before unit removal, as with this type of transmission the fault must be confirmed, using specialist equipment, before it has been removed from the car.

1 Open the engine compartment lid and place old blankets over the wings to prevent accidental scratching of the paintwork.

2 Undo and remove the battery earth connection nut and bolt from the battery terminal.

3 The air cleaner should next be removed. Full information will be found in Chapter 3.

4 Refer to Chapter 10, Sections 23/27 and remove the starter motor.

5 Jack up the front and rear of the car and place on firmly based axle stands. Alternatively place the car on a ramp or over a pit.

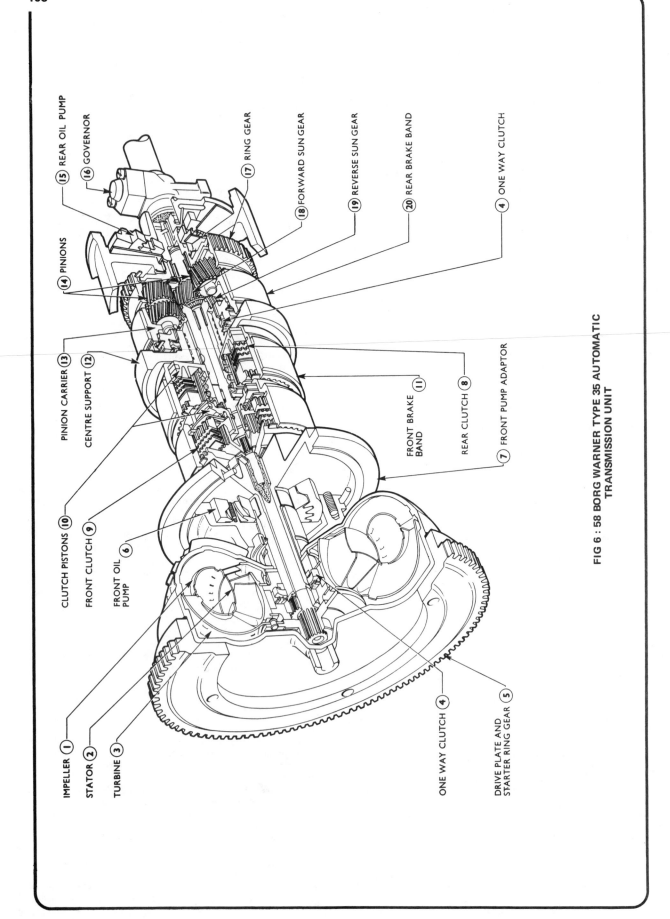

IMPELLER ①
STATOR ②
TURBINE ③

ONE WAY CLUTCH ④

DRIVE PLATE AND
STARTER RING GEAR ⑤

CLUTCH PISTONS ⑩
FRONT CLUTCH ⑨
FRONT OIL
PUMP ⑥

PINION CARRIER ⑬
CENTRE SUPPORT ⑫

PINIONS ⑭

REAR OIL PUMP ⑮
GOVERNOR ⑯

RING GEAR ⑰

FORWARD SUN GEAR ⑱

REVERSE SUN GEAR ⑲

REAR BRAKE BAND ⑳

ONE WAY CLUTCH ④

FRONT BRAKE
BAND ⑪

REAR CLUTCH ⑧

FRONT PUMP ADAPTOR ⑦

FIG 6 : 58 BORG WARNER TYPE 35 AUTOMATIC
TRANSMISSION UNIT

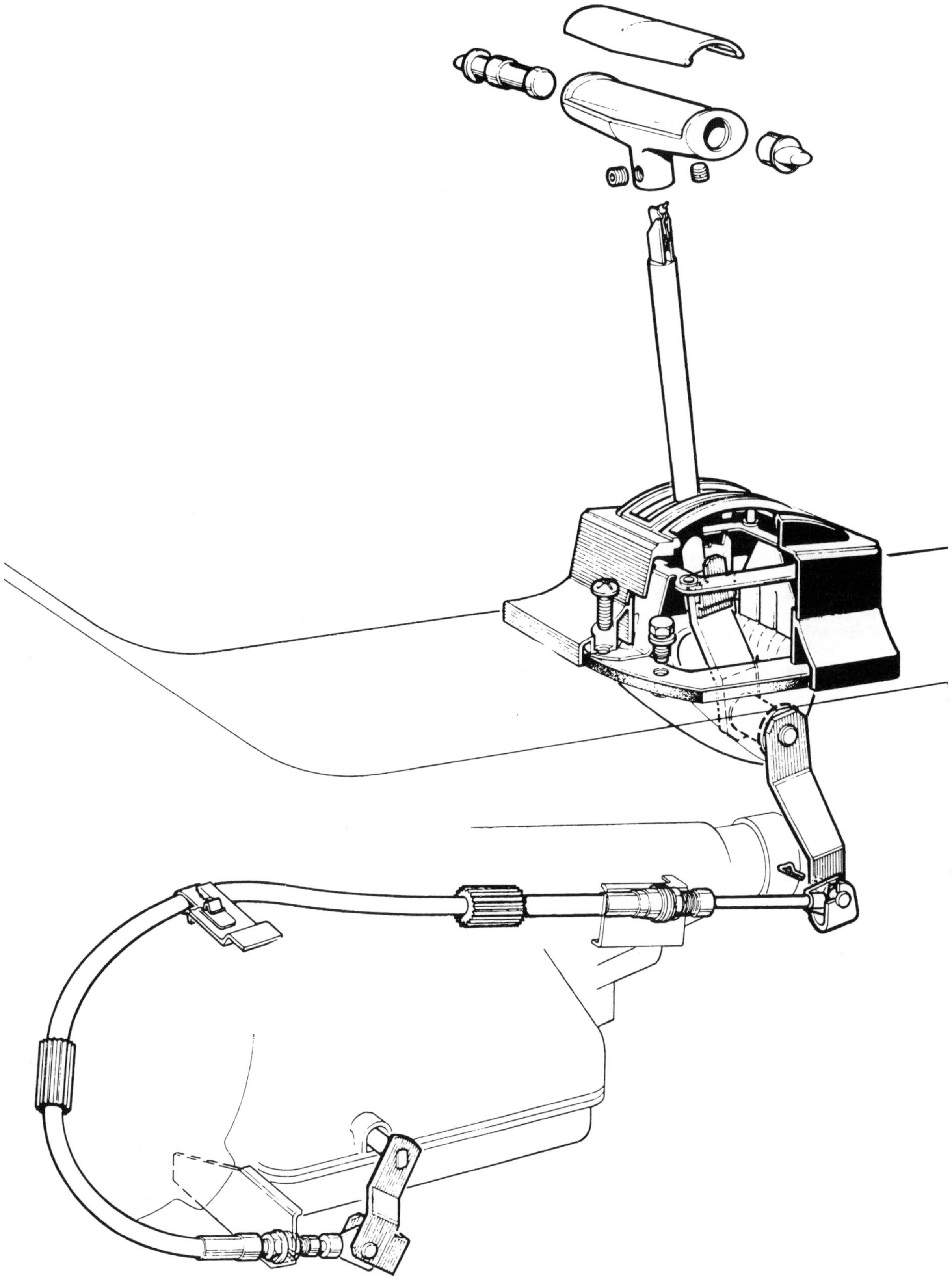

**FIG 6 : 59 SELECTOR LEVER AND CABLE ASSEMBLY —
AUTOMATIC TRANSMISSION**

6 Undo and remove the upper bolts that secure the torque converter housing to the engine. One of these bolts also secures the dipstick tube support bracket.

7 Place a clean container having a capacity of at least 10 pints (5.58 litres) under the automatic transmission unit reservoir. Remove the drain plug and allow the fluid to run out into the container. Refit the drain plug. Take extreme care if the car has just been driven as this oil can be very hot.

8 Unscrew the throttle cable to bracket locknut and slide the nut up the inner cable.

9 Extract the lock pin from the operating arm bolt and remove the bolt and cable from the bracket.

10 Make a note of the electrical cable connections to the reverse inhibitor switch and disconnect the cables from the switch (Fig 6 : 60).

11 Using a pair of circlip pliers contract the speedometer drive cable to transmission casing retaining circlip and withdraw the speedometer inner and outer cable (Fig 6 : 61).

12 Refer to Chapter 7, and remove the propeller shaft. To stop accidental dirt ingress, wrap some polythene around the end of the automatic transmission unit and secure with string or wire.

13 Disconnect the exhaust front stiffener bracket mounting by undoing and removing the two nuts, bolts, spring and plain washers.

14 Undo and remove the two nuts that secure the exhaust down pipe to the manifold studs. Ease the coupling from the studs, lower the downpipe and recover the sealing cone.

15 Extract the spring clip lock pin from the clevis pin connecting the selector cable to the operating arm on the side of the transmission unit. Withdraw the clevis pin (Fig 6 : 62).

16 Unscrew the cable to bracket locknut and slide the nut up the inner cable. Remove the bolt and cable from the bracket.

17 Undo and remove the set bolts and spring washers that secure the torque converter housing cover plate and lift away the cover plate.

18 The torque converter should next be disconnected from the crankshaft driving plate. Rotate the crankshaft until each bolt may be seen through the starter motor aperture. Undo each bolt a turn at a time until all the bolts are free (Fig 6 : 63).

19 Place a piece of soft wood on the saddle of a jack and support the weight across the rear of the engine. Take care to position the jack securely so that it cannot fly out when the automatic transmission unit is being disconnected or reconnected to the rear of the engine.

20 Place an additional jack under the automatic transmission unit and remove the two bolts and spring washers that secure the unit to the crossmember. Also remove the four bolts that locate the crossmember to the underside of the floor panel.

21 Slowly lower the transmission unit and engine jacks until there is sufficient clearance for the dipstick tube to be removed.

22 Withdraw the dipstick and pull the oil filler tube (dipstick tube) sharply from the side of the transmission unit. Recover the 'O' ring (Fig 6 : 64).

23 Undo and remove the remaining bolts and spring washers that secure the converter housing to the engine.

24 Continue to lower the jacks until there is sufficient clearance between the top of the converter housing and underside of the floor for the transmission unit to satisfactorily withdraw.

25 Check that no cables or securing bolts have been left in position and tuck the speedometer cable out of the way.

26 The assistance of at least one person is now required because of the weight of the complete unit.

27 Carefully pull the unit rearwards and, when possible, hold the converter in place in the housing as it will still be full of hydraulic fluid.

28 Finally withdraw the unit from under the car and place on wooden blocks so that the selector lever is not damaged or bent.

29 To separate the converter housing from the transmission case first lift off the converter from the transmission unit, taking suitable precautions to catch the fluid upon separation. Undo and remove the six bolts and spring washers that secure the converter housing to the transmission case. Lift away the converter housing.

30 Refitting the automatic transmission unit is the reverse sequence to removal, but there are several additional points which will assist:

31 If the torque converter has been removed, before refitting the transmission unit it will be necessary to align the front drive tangs with the slots in the inner gear and then carefully replace the torque converter. Take extreme precautions not to damage the oil seal.

32 Adjust the selector cable and inhibitor switch as described later in this Chapter.

33 Refill the transmission unit with Castrol TQF before starting the engine and check the oil level as described in Section 12.

14 Downshift cable - adjustment

Before the cable is adjusted, it is necessary to confirm that it is the cable that needs adjustment and not some other fault. Generally, if difficulty is experienced in obtaining downshift from 2 to 1 in the 'kickdown' position at just below 31 mph it is an indication that the outer cable is too long.

During production of the car, the adjustment is set by a crimped stop on the carburettor end of the inner cable and it is unusual for this setting to change except at high mileages when the inner cable can stretch. To adjust proceed as follows:

1 Apply the handbrake firmly and chock the front wheels for safety reasons.

2 Run the engine until it reaches normal operating temperature, adjust the engine idle speed to approximately 500 rpm with the selector in the 'D' position.

3 Stop the engine and, with an open ended spanner, slacken the locknut and adjust the outer cable control to the stop. Should the stop have been moved, or be loose, it will be necessary to remove the transmission sump pan.

4 Reset the engine idle to normal speed with the selector in the 'N' position. Stop the engine.

5 Wipe the area around the drain plug and sump. Place a clean container of at least 10 pints (5.58 litres) capacity under the pan drain plug. Undo the plug and allow the oil to drain into the container.

6 Undo and remove the fifteen sump pan retaining bolts and spring washers. Take care not to damage the joint between the transmission casing and sump pan.

7 Refer to Fig 6 : 66 and check that the position of the downshift cam is in the idling position as shown in the illustration.

8 Adjust the length of the outer cable so as to remove all the slack from the inner cable.

9 Again refer to Fig 6 : 66 and check the position of the downshift cam with the throttle pedal in the 'kick down' position as shown in the illustration.

10 Refit the sump pan joint, sump pan and retaining bolts with spring washers. Tighten the bolts in a diagonal manner.

11 Refill the transmission with correct hydraulic fluid or use the fluid that was drained originally if it is clean with no streaks showing signs of contamination.

15 Selector linkage - adjustment

1 It is best if this adjustment is carried out with the car placed on ramps. As an alternative the car may be placed on high axle stands.

2 Slacken the locknuts on the outer cable (Fig 6 : 65).

3 Move the selector lever to the 'I' position on the lever quadrant.

4 Position the transmission selector lever in the first location forward from the fully rearward position.

5 Tighten the outer cable locknuts, without moving the selector lever or transmission selector lever.

6 Road test the car and check the six positions of the selector lever.

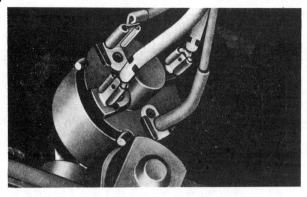

FIG 6 : 60 STARTER INHIBITOR AND REVERSE LIGHT SWITCH

FIG 6 : 61 SPEEDOMETER ATTACHMENT TO TRANSMISS—ION UNIT

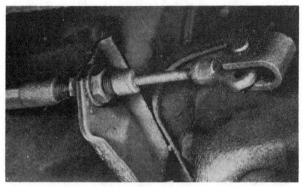

FIG 6 : 62 SELECTOR CABLE ATTACHMENT TO OPERAT—ING ARM

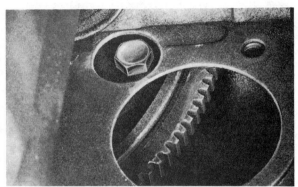

FIG 6 : 63 TORQUE CONVERTER SECURING BOLTS TO CRANKSHAFT DRIVING PLATE

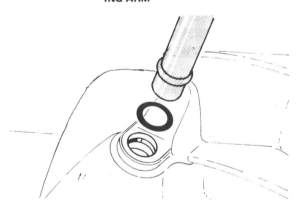

FIG 6 : 64 OIL FILLER AND DIPSTICK TUBE

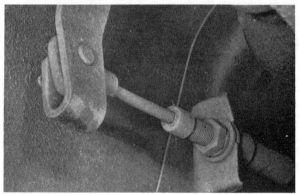

FIG 6 : 65 SELECTOR CABLE ADJUSTMENT POINT

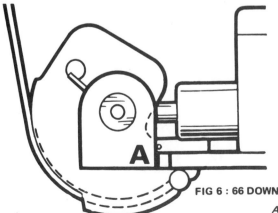

FIG 6 : 66 DOWNSHIFT VALVE CABLE ADJUSTMENT

A Idling position
B Kickdown position

16 Starter inhibitor/reverse light switch - adjustment

1   Select the 'D', 'I' or '2' position. Make a note of the starter inhibitor and reverse light switch cable connections and disconnect the cables from the switch. (See Fig 6 : 60).
2   Connect a test lamp and battery across the two larger reverse light terminals.
3   Undo the locknut and screw out the switch about two turns. Slowly screw in the switch again until the test light connected to the reverse light terminal goes out. Mark the relative position of the switch again.
4   Continue screwing in the switch until the test lamp connected to the starter inhibitor terminal, lights. Mark the relative position of the switch again.
5   Unscrew the switch until it is half way between the two positions and tighten the locknut.
6   Reconnect the cables and check that the starter motor only operates when the selector lever is in the 'P' or 'N' position. Also check that the reverse light only operates with the selector in the 'R' position. If the switch does not operate correctly it should be renewed.

17 Fault diagnosis

Stall test procedure:
The function of a stall test is to determine that the torque converter and gearbox are operating satisfactory.
1   Check the condition of the engine. An engine which is not developing full power will affect the stall test readings.
2   Allow the engine and transmission to reach correct working temperatures.
3   Connect a tachometer to the vehicle.
4   Chock the wheels and apply the handbrake and footbrake.
5   Select 'I' or 'R' and depress the throttle to the 'kick down' position. Note the reading on the tachometer which should be 1,800 rpm. If the reading is below 1,000 rpm suspect the converter for stator slip. If the reading is down to 1,200 rpm the engine is not developing full power. If the reading is in excess of 2,000 rpm suspect the gearbox for brake bind or clutch slip. NOTE: Do not carry out a stall test for a longer period than 10 seconds, otherwise the transmission will become overheated.

Converter - diagnosis
1   Inability to start on steep gradients, combined with poor acceleration from rest and low stall speed (1,000 rpm) indicate that the converter stator uni-directional clutch is slipping. This condition permits the stator to rotate in an opposite direction to the impeller and turbine, and torque multiplication cannot occur.
2   Poor acceleration in third gear above 30 mph (48.3 kpm) and reduced maximum speed indicates that the stator uni-directional clutch has seized. The stator will not rotate with the turbine and impeller and the 'fluid flywheel' phase cannot occur. This condition will also be indicated by excessive overheating of the transmission although the stall speed will be correct.

Road test procedure
1   Check that the engine will only start with the selector lever in the 'P' or 'N' position and that the reverse light operates only in 'R'.
2   Apply the handbrake and with the engine idling select 'N' — 'D', 'N' — 'R' and 'N' — 'I'. Engagement should be positive.
3   With the transmission at normal running temperature select 'D', release the brakes and accelerator with minimum throttle. Check 1 — 2 and 2 — 3 shift speeds and quality of change.
4   At a minimum road speed of 30 mph (48.3 kpm) select 'N' and switch off ignition. Allow the road speed to drop to approximately 28 mph (45.1 kpm) switch on the ignition, select 'D' and the engine should start.
5   Stop the vehicle, select 'D' and re-start, using 'full throttle'. Check 1 — 2 and 2 — 3 shift speeds and quality of change.
6   At 25 mph (40.3 kpm) apply 'full throttle'. The vehicle should accelerate in third gear and should not downshift to second.
7   At a maximum of 45 mph (72.42 kpm) 'kick down' fully, the transmission should downshift to second.
8   At a maximum of 31 mph (49.89 kpm) in third gear 'kick down' fully. The transmission should downshift to first gear.
9   Stop the vehicle, select 'D' and re-starting using 'kick-down' check the 1 — 2 and 2 — 3 shift speeds.
10 At 40 mph (64.4 kpm) in third gear, select 'I' and release the throttle. Check 2 — 3 downshift and engine braking.
11 With 'I' still engaged stop the vehicle and accelerate to over 25 mph (40.3 kpm) using 'kick down'. Check for slip, 'squawk' and absence of upshifts.
12 Stop the vehicle and select 'R'. Reverse using 'full throttle' if possible. Check for slip and clutch 'squawk'.
13 Stop the vehicle on a gradient. Apply the handbrake and select 'P'. Check the parking pawl hold when the handbrake is released. Turn the vehicle around and repeat the procedure. Check that the selector lever is held firmly in the gate in 'P'.

Chapter 7 Propeller shaft

Contents

Specifications

1300 models: Manual gearbox	Single piece
1600 models: Manual gearbox	Single piece
Automatic transmission (and 'export only' manual)	Split type with centre bearing
Single piece type, length	50.75 inch (1289 mm)
Two piece type, length	
Manual gearbox	20.63/29.27 in (524/743.5 mm)
Automatic transmission	22.24/29.27 in (565/743.5 mm)
Single piece type, number of splines	20
Two piece type, number of splines	25
Single piece tube outer diameter	1.18 — 1.19 in (30.127 — 30.163 mm)
Two piece tube outer diameter	
Manual gearbox	1.37 — 1.38 in (34.915 — 34.941 mm)
Automatic transmission	1.19 in (30.163 mm)
Depth of spline: 1300 models	0.046 — 0.053 in (1.17 — 1.35 mm)
1600 models: Manual gearbox	0.046 — 0.053 in (1.17 — 1.35 mm)
Automatic transmission	0.054 — 0.661 in (1.52 — 1.70 mm)
Universal joints	Needle roller bearings

Torque wrench settings:	lb ft	Kg m
Propeller shaft to drive pinion flange	43 — 47	6. — 6.5
Drive shaft centre bearing support bolts	13 — 17	1.8 — 2.3

1 General description

Drive is transmitted from the gearbox to the rear axle by means of a finely balanced tubular propeller shaft. Fitted at each end of the shaft is a universal joint which allows for vertical movement of the rear axle. Each universal joint comprises a four legged centre spider, four needle roller bearings and two yokes.

Fore and aft movement of the rear axle is absorbed by a spline in the front of the propeller shaft which slides over a mating spline on the rear of the gearbox mainshaft.

On some models a split propeller shaft is used whereby a third universal joint is fitted behind the centre bearing. A rubber coupling replaces the conventional universal joint at the front splined end.

All models are fitted with sealed type of universal joints which require no maintenance.

The propeller shaft assembly is a relatively simple component and therefore reliable in service. Unfortunately it is not possible to obtain spare parts for the conventional universal joints; therefore when these are worn a new assembly must be obtained.

2 Propeller shaft - removal and replacement

Single piece propeller shaft:

1 Jack up the rear of the car, or position the rear of the car over a pit.

2 If the rear of the car is jacked up, supplement the jack with support blocks so that danger is minimized should the jack collapse.

3 If the rear wheels are off the ground, place the car in gear and apply the handbrake to ensure that the propeller shaft does not turn when an attempt is made to loosen the four bolts securing the propeller shaft to the rear axle.

4 The propeller shaft is carefully balanced to fine limits and it is important that it is replaced in exactly the same position it was in prior to removal. Scratch marks on the propeller shaft and rear axle flanges to ensure accurate mating when the time comes for reassembly. (See Fig.7 : 2).

5 Unscrew and remove the four bolts and spring washers which hold the flange on the propeller shaft to the flange on the rear axle.

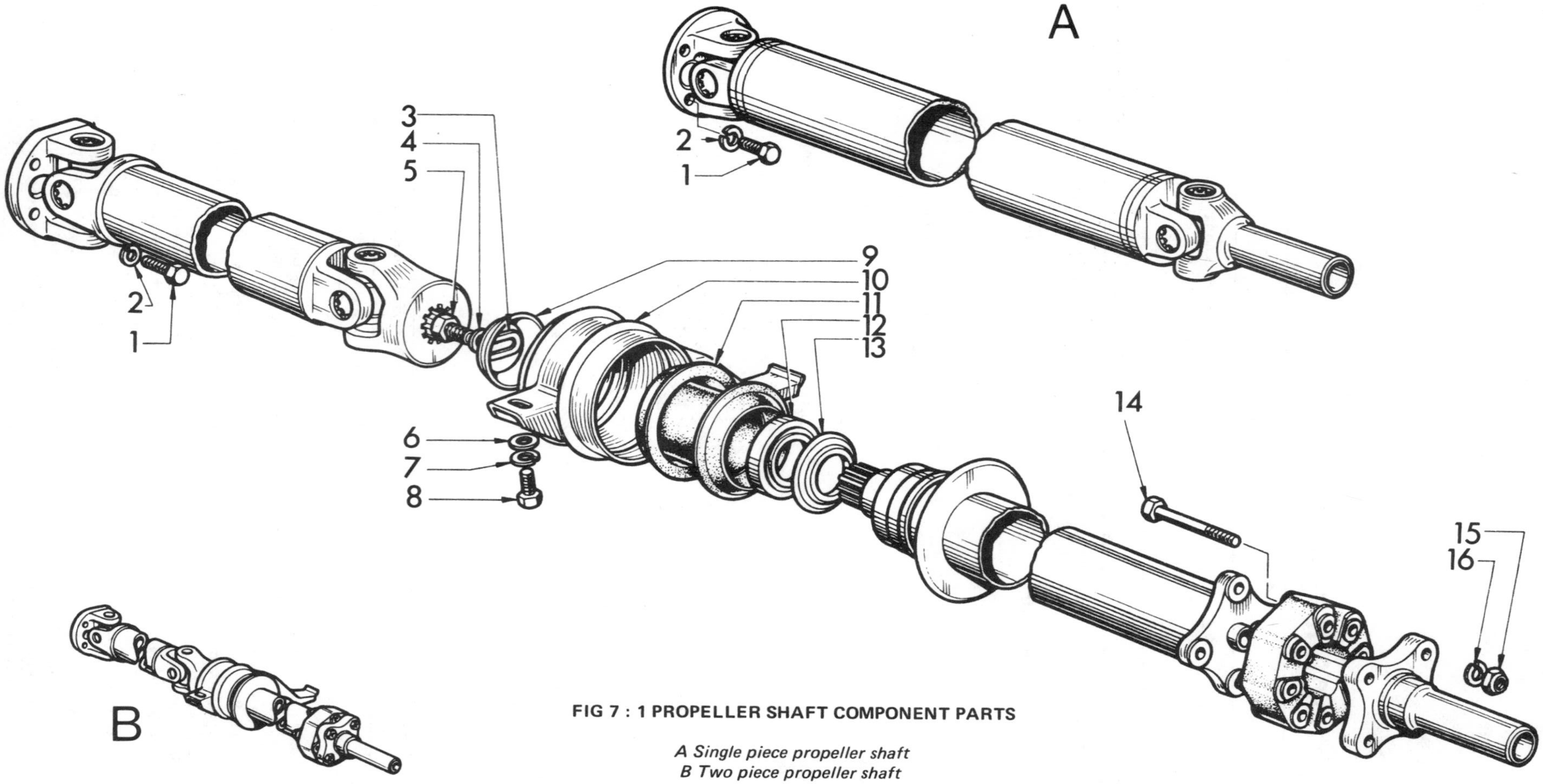

114

A

14

9
10
11
12
13

2
1

3
4
5

6
7
8

15
16

B

FIG 7 : 1 PROPELLER SHAFT COMPONENT PARTS

A Single piece propeller shaft
B Two piece propeller shaft

1 Bolt	10 Bearing housing and re-
2 Spring washer	tainer
3 'U' shaped retainer	11 Rubber bush
4 Bolt	12 Bearing
5 Nut	13 Dust cover
6 Plain washer	14 Bolt
7 Spring washer	15 Nut
8 Bolt	16 Spring washer
9 Dust cover	

6 Slightly push the shaft forward to separate the two flanges, then lower the end of the shaft and pull it rearwards to disengage the gearbox mainshaft splines.

7 Place a large can or a tray under the rear of the gearbox extension to catch any oil which is likely to leak past the oil seal when the propeller shaft is removed.

8 Replacement of the propeller shaft is a reversal of the above procedure. Ensure that the mating marks scratched on the propeller shaft and rear axle flanges line up, and always use new spring washers. Check the oil level in the gearbox and top up if necessary.

Split type propeller shaft:

The removal sequence is basically identical to that for the single piece propeller shaft with the exception that the centre bearing support must be detached from the underside of the body. This should be done before the rear flange securing bolts and spring washers are removed. Support the centre of the propeller shaft during removal.

To detach the centre bearing support, undo and remove the two bolts, spring and plain washers securing it to the underside of the body (Fig.7 : 3).

Replacement is the reverse sequence to removal.

---

3 Propeller shaft centre bearing - removal and replacement

1 Refer to Section 2 and remove the complete propeller shaft assembly.

2 Using a blunt chisel, carefully prise open the centre bearing support retaining bolt locking tab.

3 Slacken the bolt located in the end of the yoke and with a screwdriver ease out the 'U' shaped retainer through the side of the yoke. (These parts are shown in Fig.7 : 4).

4 Mark the propeller shaft and yoke for correct refitting. Disconnect the propeller shaft from the yoke and lift off the insulator rubber together with collar from the ball race.

5 Part the insulator rubber from the collar.

6 Refer to Fig.7 : 5 and using a universal two leg puller draw the bearing together with cup from the end of the propeller shaft.

7 To fit a new bearing and cup onto the end of the propeller shaft use a piece of suitable diameter tube and drive into position.

8 With a pair of pliers bend the six metal tongues of the collar slightly outwards and carefully insert the insulator rubber. It is important that the flange of the insulator rubber when fitted into the support is uppermost. (See 'A' Fig.7 : 4).

9 Using a pair of 'parrot jaw' pliers or a chisel, carefully bend the metal tongues rearwards over the rubber lip as shown in Fig. 7 : 6.

10 Next slide the support with the insulator rubber over the ball race. The semi-circular recess in the support periphery must be positioned towards the front end of the car when fitted. (Fig.7 : 8).

11 Screw the bolt, together with locking tab, into the propeller shaft forward end leaving just sufficient space for the 'U' shaped retainer to be inserted.

12 Assemble the two propeller shaft halves in their original positions as denoted by the two previously made marks, or by the double tooth. (Fig.7 : 7).

13 Refit the 'U' shaped retainer with the tagged end towards the splines (Fig.7 : 9).

14 Finally tighten the retainer securing bolt and bend over the lockwasher.

---

4 Universal joints - tests for wear

1 Wear in the needle roller bearings is characterized by vibration in the transmission, 'clonks' on taking up the drive, and in extreme case of lack of lubrication, metallic squeaking and ultimately grating and shrieking sounds as the bearings break up.

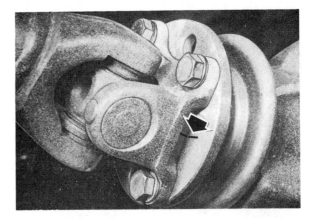

FIG 7 : 2 PROPELLER SHAFT REAR UNIVERSAL JOINT (ARROW SHOWS ALIGNMENT MARKS)

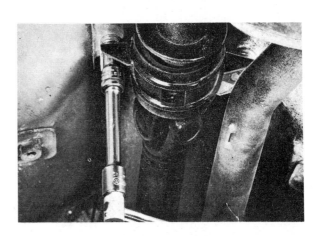

FIG 7 : 3 REMOVAL OF CENTRE BEARING RETAINER SECURING BOLTS

FIG 7 : 4 CENTRE BEARING COMPONENTS

1 Rubber bush
2 Bearing housing and retainer
3 Washer
4 Bolt
5 Dust cover
6 Ball race
7 Dust cover
8 Yoke
9 'U' shaped retainer
('A' shows flange which must be located at top of housing)

FIG 7 : 5 USING UNIVERSAL PULLER TO DRAW OFF
CENTRE BEARING

FIG 7 : 6 USING 'PARROT JAW' PLIERS TO BEND OVER
RUBBER BUSH LOCKING TABS IN HOUSING

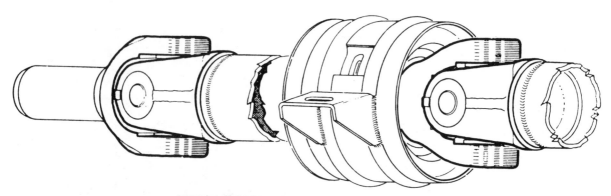

FIG 7 : 7 CORRECT RELATIVE POSITIONS OF THE
PROPELLER SHAFT FORWARD AND CENTRE YOKES

FIG 7 : 8 CENTRE BEARING SUPPORT SEMI-CIRCULAR
RECESS (ARROWED)

FIG 7 : 9 THE CENTRE BEARING AND 'U' SHAPED
RETAINER

2   It is easy to check if the needle roller bearings are worn with
the propeller shaft in position, by trying to turn the shaft with
one hand, the other hand holding the rear axle flange when the
rear universal joint is being checked, and the front half coupling
when the front universal joint is being checked. Any movement
between the propeller shaft and the front half couplings, and
round the rear half couplings, is indicative of considerable wear.
If worn a new assembly will have to be obtained. Check
also by trying to lift the shaft and noticing any movement

of the joints.

3   The centre bearing is a little more difficult to test for wear
when mounted on the car. Undo and remove the two support
securing bolts, spring and plain washers, and allow the propeller
shaft centre to hang down. Test the centre bearing for wear by
grabbing the retainer and rocking it. If movement is evident the
bearing is probably worn and should be renewed as described
in Section 3.

Chapter 8 Rear axle

Contents

Specifications

Type designation	A

Axle ratio: 1300   ... ...   4.11 : 1
1600   ... ...   3.89 : 1
Estate   ... ...   4.11 : 1

Number of gear teeth:
Crownwheel: 1300   37
1600   35
Estate   37
Drive pinion: 1300   9
1600   9
Estate   9

Drive pinion bearing pre-load ... ...   6.8 - 3lb in (8 - 30kgcm)

Crownwheel and pinion backlash   ... ...   0.004 - 0.008 in (0.10 - 0.20 mm)

Number of gears with a differential assembly   2

Thickness of thrust washers - differential:
Pinions   ... ...   0.406 - 0.434 (10.30 - 11.03 mm)
Pinion bearing pre-load   ... ...   0.0012 - 0.004 in (0.03 - 0.10 mm)

Oil capacity ... ...   1.76 pints (1.0 litre)

Torque wrench settings:

	lb ft	kg m
Bearing cap bolts	43 - 49	6. - 6.8
Drive pinion self locking nut	71 - 86	10 - 12
Crownwheel securing bolts	57 - 62	8 - 8.7
Rear axle housing cover	22 - 29	3 - 4
Axle shaft to side flange retainer plate	29 - 36	4 - 5
Propeller shaft to drive pinion flange	43 - 47	6 - 6.5
Propeller shaft centre bearing securing bolts	13 - 17	1.8 - 2.3

1 General description

The rear axle is of the semi-floating type and held in place by two lower swinging arms which are able to pivot on brackets welded to the chassis. Coil springs are located between the under-side of the body and the swinging arms. Longitudinal and diagonal location of the rear axle is also controlled by two upper swing-ing arms which locate between the underside of the body and the outer ends of the final drive housing.

The differential unit is of the two pinion design and driven by a hypoid crownwheel and pinion. It is mounted in a cast iron differential housing into which the halfshaft and hub outer tubes are pressed.

The pinion is mounted on two taper roller bearings which are specially pre-loaded using a spacer and selective shim fitted between the bearings and pinion gear head.

The differential cage is also mounted on two taper roller bearings which are pre-loaded by the differential carrier being spread. The pinion depth of mesh relative to the crownwheel is adjustable by using a selective shim. The drive is taken via two differential side gears to both axle shafts. The axle shafts are splined to the differential side gears and run in ball races at their outer ends. The ball races are fitted with an oil seal which

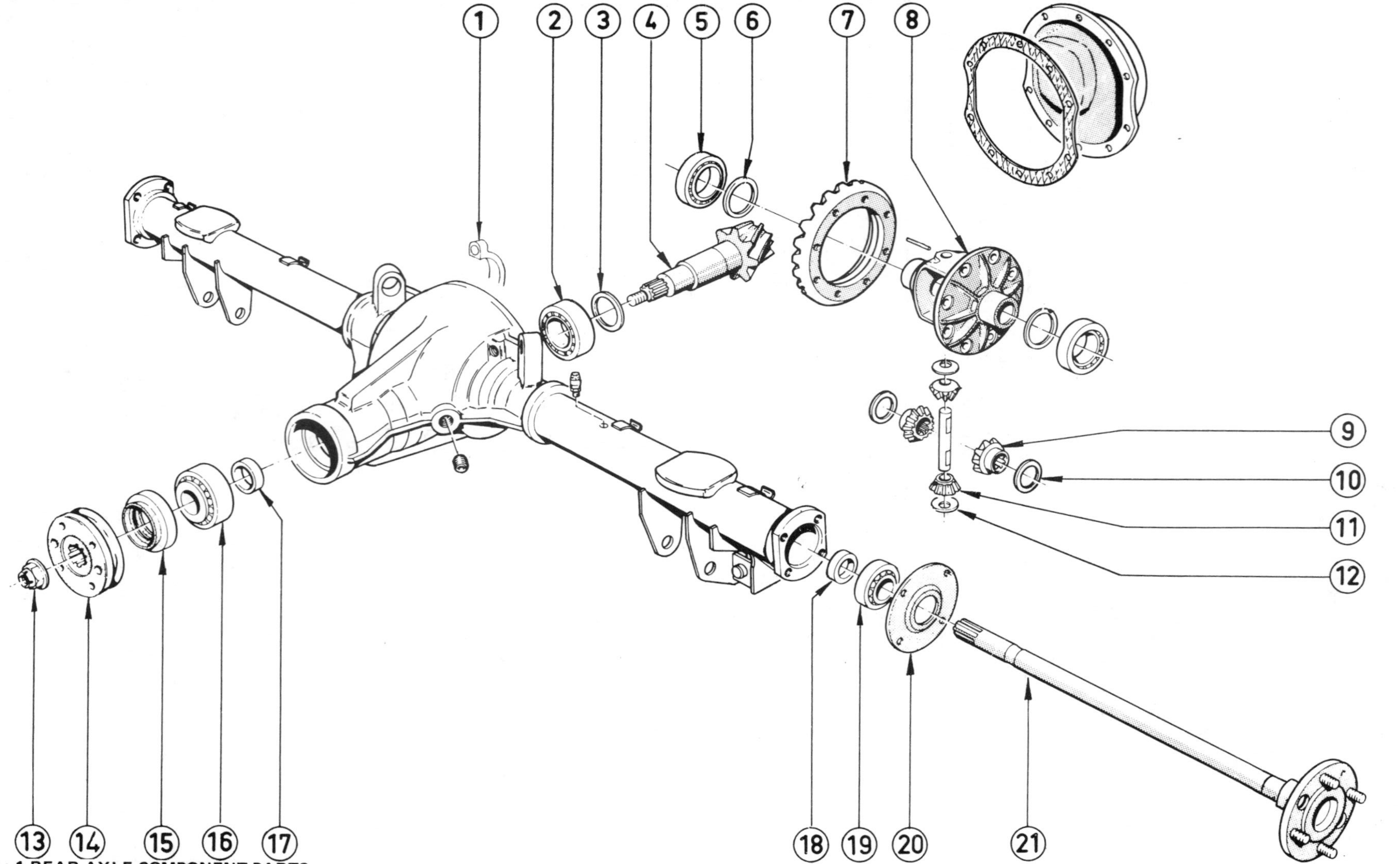

FIG 8 : 1 REAR AXLE COMPONENT PARTS

1 Bearing cap
2 Taper roller bearing
3 Spacer shim, drive pinion

4 Drive pinion gear
5 Taper roller bearing
6 Spacer shim
7 Crown wheel

8 Differential case
9 Side gear
10 Shim
11 Differential pinion

12 Thrust washer, differential pinion
13 Self locking nut
14 Drive pinion flange

15 Oil seal
16 Taper roller bearing, drive pinion
17 Shim, drive pinion

18 Locking sleeve
19 Ball race, axle shaft
20 Retainer plate
21 Axle shaft

seals the axle housing to the outside.

All repairs can be carried out to the component parts by a competent do-it-yourself enthusiast but there are several special tools necessary to enable the differential assembly to be overhauled according to the book'. Further information may be found in Section 8.

It is necessary for the complete rear axle assembly to be removed before the final drive can be dismantled for overhaul.

2 Rear axle - removal and replacement

1 Remove the rear wheel trims and slacken the road wheel nuts. Chock the front wheels, jack up the rear of the car and place on axle stands located beneath the lower radius arms. Remove the two rear wheels.

2 Support the weight of the rear axle by placing the saddle of a jack (preferably trolley type) under the centre of the rear axle.

3 With a scriber or file mark a line across the propeller shaft and pinion driving flanges so that they may be refitted together in their original positions.

4 Undo and remove the four bolts and spring washers securing the propeller shaft and pinion driving flanges and carefully lower the propeller shaft. In the case of models fitted with the split type propeller shaft it is necessary to undo and remove the two bolts with spring and plain washers that secure the centre bearing support to the underside of the body before the propeller shaft can be lowered.

5 Release the handbrake. Undo and remove the two cheese head screws that secure the brake drum to the axle shaft. Using a soft faced hammer carefully tap outwards on the circumference of each brake drum and lift away the brake drums.

6 Using a screwdriver placed between brake shoe and relay lever, lever the handbrake cable relay lever inwards. Grip the handbrake cable and with a pair of pliers release it from the relay lever. Pull the handbrake cable through each brake backplate.

7 Wipe the top of the brake master cylinder reservoir and unscrew the cap. Place a piece of polythene sheeting over the reservoir neck and refit the cap. This is to stop hydraulic fluid syphoning out during subsequent operations.

8 Wipe the area around the brake flexible pipe to metal pipe union just in front of the rear axle and referring to Chapter 9 /3, detach the brake flexible hose from the metal pipe.

9 Undo and remove the bolt, nut and plain washer that secures each upper radius arm to the axle housing.

10 Undo and remove the bolt, nut and plain washer that secures each shock absorber to the rear axle. Contract the shock absorbers.

11 Undo and remove the bolt, nut and plain washer that secures each lower radius arm to the rear axle.

12 The complete rear axle assembly may now be withdrawn from under the rear of the car.

13 To refit the rear axle is the reverse sequence to removal. The two marks previously made on the propeller shaft and pinion flanges should be correctly aligned.

14 The lower radius arm mounting bolts must only be tightened to a torque wrench setting of 42 - 50 lb ft (5.8 - 6.9 kg m) when the road wheels have been refitted and the car is standing on the ground.

15 The centre bearing retaining bolts should be tightened to a torque wrench setting of 13 - 17 lb ft (1.8 - 2.3 kg m).

16 It will be necessary to bleed the brake hydraulic system as described in Chapter 9/2.

17 Check the amount of oil in the rear axle and top up if necessary with Castrol Hypoy.

3 Drive pinion oil seal - removal and replacement

1 This operation may be performed with the rear axle in position or on the bench.

2 With a scriber or file mark a line across the propeller shaft and pinion driving flanges so that they may be refitted together

in their original positions.

3 Undo and remove the four bolts and spring washers securing the propeller shaft and pinion driving flanges and carefully lower the propeller shaft. In the case of models fitted with the split type propeller shaft, it is necessary to undo and remove the two bolts with spring and plain washers that secure the centre bearing support to the underside of the body before the propeller shaft can be lowered.

4 Carefully clean the front of the final drive housing as there will probably be a considerable amount of oil and dirt if the seal has been leaking for a while.

5 Using a mole wrench or large wrench, grip the drive pinion flange and with a socket undo and remove the pinion flange retaining self-locking nut. This nut must be discarded and a new one obtained ready for reassembly.

6 Place a container under the front of the final drive housing to catch any oil that may issue once the oil seal has been removed.

7 Using a universal puller and suitable thrust pad, pull off the drive pinion flange from the drive pinion.

8 Using a screwdriver or small chisel, carefully remove the old oil seal. It will probably be necessary to partially dismantle it. Note which way round it is fitted with the lip facing inwards.

9 Before fitting a new seal, apply some grease to the inner face between the two lips of the seal.

10 Apply a little jointing compound to the outer face of the seal.

11 Using a tubular drift of suitable diameter, carefully drive the oil seal into the final drive housing, Make sure that it is fitted squarely into the housing.

12 Replace the drive pinion flange and once again hold securely with a mole wrench or large wrench. Fit a new self-locking nut and tighten to a torque wrench setting of 71 - 86 lb ft (10 - 12 kg m).

13 Reconnect the propeller shaft, aligning the previously made marks on the flanges, and refit the bolts, with new spring washers. Tighten to a torque wrench setting of 43 - 47 lb ft (6. - 6.5 kg m).

14 With the split type propeller shaft, refit the centre bearing support securing bolts, spring and plain washers and tighten to a torque wrench setting of 13 - 17 lb ft (1.8 - 2.3 kg m).

15 Finally check the oil level in the rear axle and top up if necessary with Castrol Hypoy (photo).

4 Rear cover - removal and replacement

1 Wipe down the rear of the final drive housing to prevent the possibility of dirt entering the rear axle.

2 Using a wide bladed screwdriver carefully prise open the brake pipe securing clip located at the rear of the cover.

3 Place a container of at least 3 pints (1.70 litres) capacity under the rear axle casing to catch the oil as the rear cover is released.

4 Undo and remove the ten bolts and spring washers that secure the rear cover to the final drive housing. Lift away the rear cover and its gaskets. (Fig 8 : 3).

5 Before refitting the rear cover make sure that the mating faces are free from traces of the old gasket or jointing compound.

6 Fit a new gasket and then the rear cover and secure with the ten bolts and spring washers. As the cover bolts protrude into the final drive housing it is important that a suitable oil resistant sealing compound is smeared onto the threads of each bolt before it is fitted.

7 Tighten the cover securing bolts to a torque wrench setting of 22 - 29 lb ft (3 - 4 kg m).

8 Carefully bend up the securing clip so holding the brake pipe firmly against the rear cover.

9 Refill the rear axle with 1.76 pints (1.0 litre) of Castrol Hypoy.

5 Axle shaft - removal and replacement

1 Chock the front wheels, remove the rear wheel trim and

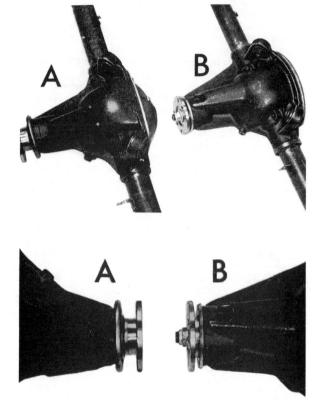

FIG 8 : 2 MAJOR DIFFERENCES BETWEEN TYPE A AND
B − REAR AXLES

3.15 Rear axle combined level and filler plug

slacken the wheel nuts. Jack up the rear of the car and support on firmly based axle stands. Remove the road wheel and release the handbrake.

2 Undo and remove the two cheese head screws that secure the brake drum to the axle shaft. Using a soft faced hammer carefully tap outwards on the circumference of the brake drum and lift away the brake drum.

3 Using a socket wrench placed through the holes in the axle shaft flange, undo and remove the four bolts that secure the bearing retainer plate to the axle casing. (Fig 8 : 4).

4 Place a container under the end of the rear axle to catch any oil that may drain out once the axle shaft has been removed.

5 The axle shaft may now be withdrawn from the rear axle.

6 It is possible for the ball races to bind onto the axle shaft, in which case screw in two long bolts through the rear of the axle tube and so ease the axle shaft assembly out. (Fig 8 : 5).

7 Before refitting the axle shaft assembly, smear a little Castrol LM grease along the length of the axle shaft and also on the ball race to prevent corrosion due to moisture.

8 Insert the axle shaft into the rear axle tube and secure the bearing retainer with the four bolts which should be tightened to a torque wrench setting of 29 - 36 lb ft (4.5 kg m).

9 Refit the brake drum and secure with the two cheese head bolts.

10 Refit the road wheel and lower the car to the ground.

---

6   Axle shaft bearing - removal and replacement

---

1 Refer to Section 5 and remove the axle shaft assembly.

2 Using a 0.315 in (8 mm) diameter drill, bore a hole in the bearing inner ring as shown in Fig 8 : 6. Using a sharp chisel cut the ring across the hole and slide off the ring. A new ring will be required during reassembly.

3 Place the axle shaft upside down in a vice so that the bearing retainer is on the top of the jaws and the axle shaft flange is under them and, using a soft faced hammer, drive the axle shaft through the bearing. This may also be done using a universal puller in reverse, using the feet to push the bearing retainer. It will be necessary to bind the legs together to stop them springing out. Lift away the bearing and retainer noting which way round they are fitted.

4 To fit the new bearing, first slide the bearing retainer along the axle shaft followed by the bearing (the oil seal inside the bearing must be furthermost away from the axle shaft flange).

5 Slide on a new inner ring.

6 Place the axle shaft vertically between the jaws of a bench vice - flange uppermost, so that the inner ring is resting on the top of the vice jaws. Using a soft faced hammer drive the axle shaft through the bearing and inner ring until it is seating fully on the bearing. Alternatively a universal two leg puller can be used, and if it has a hexagonal head on the end of the centre screw it should be tightened to a torque wrench setting of 43 - 58 lb ft (6 - 8 kg m).

7 Refit the axle shaft assembly as described in Section 5.

---

7   Wheel stud - removal and replacement

The usual reasons for renewal of a wheel stud are either the threads have been damaged or the stud has broken, this usually being caused by overtightening of the wheel nuts. To renew a wheel stud, remove the axle shaft assembly as described in Section 5. Using a parallel pin punch of suitable diameter drive the old stud through the flange towards the bearing.

To fit a new stud place it in its hole from the rear of the flange and using a bench vice with a socket placed in front of the stud press it fully home in the flange. This operation is shown in Fig 8 : 7.

FIG 8 : 3 REMOVAL OF REAR COVER AND GASKET

FIG 8 : 4 REMOVAL OF BEARING RETAINER PLATE
SECURING BOLTS

FIG 8 : 5 USING LONG BOLTS TO ASSIST WITHDRAWAL
OF AXLE SHAFT

FIG 8 : 6 DRILLING HOLE IN BEARING INNER RING
PRIOR TO CUTTING WITH CHISEL

FIG 8 : 7 FITTING NEW WHEEL STUD TO AXLE SHAFT
FLANGE

FIG 8 : 8 DIFFERENTIAL CASING AND END CAP IDEN-
TIFICATION MARKS

FIG 8 : 9 USING TWO PIECES OF TAPERED WOOD TO
EASE OUT DIFFERENTIAL HOUSING

FIG 8 : 10 USE OF UNIVERSAL PULLER TO REMOVE
DIFFERENTIAL HOUSING TAPER ROLLER BEARING
CONE

8 Final drive assembly - dismantling, overhaul and reassembly

Most garages will prefer to fit a complete set of gears, bearings, spacers and thrust washers rather than renew parts which may have worn. To do the job properly requires the use of special and expensive tools which the majority of garages do not have.

The primary object of these special tools is to enable the mesh of the crownwheel to the pinion to be very accurately set and thus ensure that noise is kept to a minimum. If any increase in noise cannot be tolerated (providing that the rear axle is not already noisy due to a defective part) then it is best to allow the local Ford garage to carry out the repairs.

Rear axles can be rebuilt without the use of special tools but be prepared for a slight increase in noise.

The rear axle assembly should first be removed from the car as described in Section 2 and then proceed as follows:-

1 Wash down the final drive housing area to remove all traces of dirt. Wipe dry.

2 Support the rear axle on wooden blocks and using a screwdriver prise open the brake pipe securing clip located at the rear of the cover.

3 Place a container of 3 pints (1.70 litres) capacity under the rear axle casing to catch the oil as the rear cover is released.

4 Undo and remove the bolts that secure the rear cover to the final drive housing. Lift away the rear cover and its gasket (Fig 8 : 3). Detach the rear brake pipe from the two rear wheel cylinders.

5 Refer to Section 5 : 2 to 6 inclusive and remove the two axle shaft assemblies.

6 With a scriber mark the relative positions of the two differential casing end caps so that they may be refitted in their original positions (Fig 8 : 8).

7 Undo and remove the bolts that secure each bearing end cap and lift away.

8 Obtain two pieces of 2 inch (50 mm) square wood at least 12 inches long and with a knife taper the ends along a length of 6 inches.

9 Place the tapered ends of the wood levers in the two cut-a-ways of the differential casing and using the rear cover face of the final drive housing as a fulcrum carefully lever the differential assembly from the final drive housing (Fig 8 : 9).

10 If it is necessary to remove the two differential case bearings these may be removed next using a universal two leg puller and suitable thrust pad. Carefully ease each bearing from its location. Recover the shim packs from behind each bearing noting from which side they came. (Fig 8 : 10).

11 Using a scriber mark the relative positions of the crownwheel and differential housing so that the crownwheel may be refitted in its original position.

12 Undo and remove the bolts that secure the crownwheel to the differential housing. Using a soft faced hammer tap the crownwheel from its location on the differential housing (Fig 8 : 12).

13 Using a suitable diameter parallel pin punch tap out the pin that locks the differential pinion gear shaft to the differential housing. NOTE: The hole into which the peg fits is slightly tapered, and the opposite end may be lightly peened over and should be cleaned with a suitable diameter drill.

14 Using a soft metal drift, tap out the differential pinion gear shaft. Lift away the differential pinion gears, side gears and thrust washers taking care to ensure that the thrust washers are kept with their relative gears (Fig 8 : 11).

15 Professional fitters use a special tool for holding the pinion drive flange stationary whilst the nut in the centre of the flange is unscrewed. As it is tightened to a torque wrench setting of 71 - 86 lb ft (10 - 12 kg m), it will require some force to undo it. The average owner will not normally have the use of this special tool so, as an alternative method, clamp the pinion flange in a vice and then undo the nut. Any damage caused to the edge of the flange by the vice should be carefully filed smooth. This nut must not be used again so a new one will be required during reassembly.

16 Using a universal two leg puller and suitable thrust pad draw the pinion drive flange from the end of the pinion shaft.

17 Carefully inspect the large taper roller bearing behind the pinion gear and if it shows signs of wear or pitting or a loose cage, the bearing must be renewed.

18 Using a universal two leg puller and suitable thrust pad draw the bearing from the pinion shaft.

19 The smaller taper roller bearing and oil seal may next be removed from the final drive housing, pinion drive flange end. To do this use a soft metal drift with a tapered end or suitable diameter tube and, working inside the housing, tap the bearing circumference outwards so releasing first the oil seal and then the bearing (Fig 8 : 13).

20 Again using the soft metal drift and working inside the housing, drift out the bearing cups. They must not be used with new bearings.

21 The final drive assembly is now dismantled and should be washed and dried with a clean non-fluffy rag ready for inspection.

22 Carefully inspect all the gear teeth for signs of pitting or wear and, if evident, new parts must be obtained. The crownwheel and pinion are a matched pair so if one of the two requires renewal a new matched pair must be obtained. If wear is evident on one or two of the four differential pinion gears or side gears it is far better to obtain all four gears rather than just replace the worn ones.

23 Inspect the thrust washers for signs of score marks or wear and, if evident, obtain new ones. Before the bearings were removed they should have been inspected for wear and usually if one bearing is worn it is far better to fit a complete new set.

24 With new parts obtained as required, reassembly can begin. First fit the thrust washers to the side gears and place them in position in the differential housing.

25 Place the thrust washer behind the differential pinion gears and mesh these two gears with the side gears through the two apertures in the differential housing. Make sure they are diametrically opposite to each other. Rotate the differential pinion gears through 90° so bringing them into line with the pinion gear shaft bore in the housing.

26 Insert the pinion gear shaft with the locking pin hole in line with the pin hole in the housing. Tap the shaft into position with a soft metal drift.

27 Using feeler gauges as shown in Fig 8 : 14 measure the end float of each side gear. The correct clearance is 0.006 in (0.15 mm) If this figure is exceeded it will be necessary to dismantle the assembly again and fit new thrust washers.

28 Lock the pinion gear shaft using the pin which should be tapped fully home using a suitable diameter parallel pin punch. Peen over the end of the pin hole to stop the pin working its way out.

29 The crownwheel may next be refitted. Wipe the mating faces of the crownwheel and differential housing and if original parts are being used, place the crownwheel into position with the previously made marks aligned. Refit the bolts that secure the crownwheel and tighten these in a progressive and diagonal manner to a final torque wrench setting of 57 - 62 lb ft (8 - 8.7 kg m).

30 Place the shim packs back in their original fitted position on the differential housing bearing location. Using a piece of suitable diameter tube, very carefully fit the differential housing bearings with the smaller diameter of the taper outwards. The bearing cage must not in any way be damaged (Fig 8 : 15).

31 Place the shim behind the head of the pinion gear and using a suitable diameter tube, very carefully fit the larger taper roller bearing onto the pinion shaft. The larger diameter of the bearing must be next to the pinion head (Fig 8 : 16).

32 Using suitable diameter tubes fit the two taper roller bearing cones into the final drive housing making sure that they are fitted the correct way round.

33 Slide the shim and spacer onto the pinion shaft and insert into the final drive housing.

34 Refit the second and smaller diameter taper roller bearing onto the end of the pinion shaft and follow this with a new oil seal. Before the seal is actually fitted apply some grease to the inner face between the two lips of the seal.

FIG 8 : 11 DIFFERENTIAL HOUSING INTERNAL COMPONENTS

FIG 8 : 12 PINION GEAR SHAFT LOCK PIN

FIG 8 : 13 REMOVAL OF DRIVE PINION TAPER ROLLER BEARING AND OIL SEAL

FIG 8 : 14 DETERMINATION OF SIDE GEAR END FLOAT

FIG 8 : 15 USING SUITABLE DIAMETER DRIFT TO FIT NEW TAPER ROLLER BEARING CONE ONTO DIFFERENTIAL HOUSING

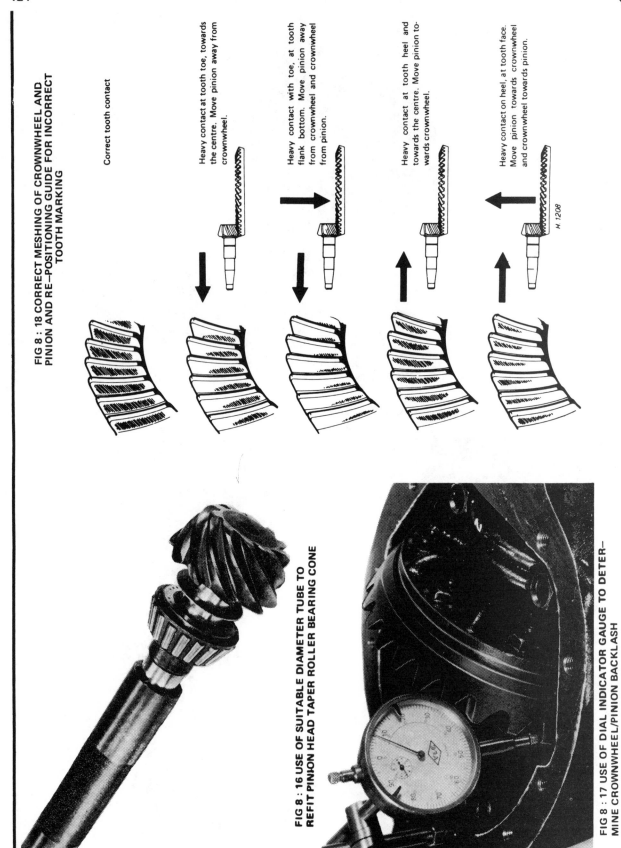

FIG 8 : 18 CORRECT MESHING OF CROWNWHEEL AND PINION AND RE–POSITIONING GUIDE FOR INCORRECT TOOTH MARKING

Correct tooth contact

Heavy contact at tooth toe, towards the centre. Move pinion away from crownwheel.

Heavy contact with toe, at tooth flank bottom. Move pinion away from crownwheel and crownwheel from pinion.

Heavy contact at tooth heel and towards the centre. Move pinion towards crownwheel.

Heavy contact on heel, at tooth face. Move pinion towards crownwheel and crownwheel towards pinion.

H. 1208

FIG 8 : 16 USE OF SUITABLE DIAMETER TUBE TO REFIT PINION HEAD TAPER ROLLER BEARING CONE

FIG 8 : 17 USE OF DIAL INDICATOR GAUGE TO DETER–MINE CROWNWHEEL/PINION BACKLASH

35 Apply a little jointing compound to the outer face of the seal.

36 Using a tubular drift of suitable diameter carefully drive the oil seal into the final drive housing. Make quite sure that it is fitted squarely into the housing.

37 Replace the drive pinion flange and once again hold securely in a bench vice. Fit a new self locking nut and tighten to a torque wrench setting of 71 - 86 lb ft (10 - 12 kg m).

38 Fit the bearing cones to the differential housing bearings and carefully ease the housing into position in the final drive housing.

39 Replace the bearing caps in their original positions. Smear a little jointing compound on the threads of each cap securing bolt and fit into position. When all four bolts have been replaced tighten these up in a diagonal and progressive manner to a final torque wrench setting of 43 - 49 lb ft (6 - 6.8 kg m).

40 If possible mount a dial indicator gauge so that the probe is resting on one of the teeth of the crownwheel and determine the backlash between the crownwheel and pinion (Fig 8 : 17). The backlash may be varied be decreasing the thickness of the shims behind one differential housing bearing and increasing the thickness of shims behind the other, thus moving the crownwheel into or out of mesh as required. The total thickness of the shims must not be changed.

41 The best check the do-it-yourself enthusiast can make to ascertain the correct meshing of the crownwheel and pinion is to smear a little engineer's blue onto the crownwheel and then rotate the pinion. The contact mark should appear right in the middle of the crownwheel teeth. Refer to Fig 8 : 18 where the correct tooth pattern is shown. Also given are incorrect tooth patterns and the method of obtaining the correct pattern. Obviously this will take time and further dismantling, but will be worth it.

42 Before refitting the rear cover make sure that the mating faces are free from traces of the old gasket or jointing compound.

43 Fit a new gasket and then the rear cover and secure with the ten bolts and spring washers. As the cover bolts protrude into the final drive housing it is important that a suitable oil resistant sealing compound is smeared onto the threads of each bolt before it is fitted.

44 Tighten the cover securing bolts to a torque wrench setting of 22 - 29 lb ft (3 - 4 kg m).

45 Carefully bend up the securing clip so holding the brake pipe firmly against the cover.

46 The rear axle may now be refitted to the car as described in Section 2. Refill the rear axle with 1.76 pints (1.0 litre) of Castrol Hypoy.

Chapter 9 Braking system

Contents

Specifications

Type of brakes:	Hydraulic, servo assisted on all four wheels
Front	Dual line disc - self adjusting
Rear	Dual line drum - self adjusting
Handbrake	Mechanical on rear wheels only

Front:

Disc diameter	9.74 in (247.5 mm)
Pad swept area	191.87 in^2 (1254.8 cm^2)
Pad code	2430F.1D330
Max. disc runout	0.002 in (0.05 mm)
Cylinder diameter	2.13 in (54.0 mm)
Minimum pad thickness	0.06 - 0.12 in (1.5 - 3.0 mm)

Rear:

Drum diameter	8.0 in (203.2 mm)
Shoe swept area...	74.39 in^2 (486.5 cm^2)
Wheel cylinder diameter	0.816 in (20.64 mm)
Minimum lining thickness	0.06 in (1.52 mm)

Vacuum servo unit type:	38
Boost ratio	2.2 : 1

Torque wrench settings:	lb ft	kg m
Brake caliper to front suspension	45 - 50	6.22 - 6.91
Brake disc to hub	30 - 34	4.15 - 4.70
Rear brake backplate to axle housing	15 - 18	2.07 - 2.49
Hydraulic pipe unions	5 - 7	0.70 - 1.00
Bleed screw	5 - 7	0.70 - 1.00
Master cylinder - tipping valve securing nut	35 - 45	4.8 - 6.22
Master cylinder to servo	17	2.3

1 General description

Disc brakes are fitted to the front wheels and drum brakes to the rear. Servo assistance from the brake pedal, this being connected to the master cylinder and servo assembly mounted on the bulkhead is available as an option.

The hydraulic system is dual line, the front disc brake calipers have a separate hydraulic system to that of the rear drum brake wheel cylinders so that if failure of the hydraulic pipes to

the front or rear brakes occurs half the braking system is still operative. Servo assistance in this condition is still available.

The front brake disc is secured to the hub flange and the caliper mounted on the steering knuckle and wheel stub so that the disc is able to rotate in between the two halves of the caliper. Inside each half of the caliper is a hydraulic cylinder this being interconnected by a drilling which allows hydraulic fluid pressure to be transmitted to both halves. A piston operates in each cylinder and is in contact with the outer face of the brake pad. By depressing the brake pedal, hydraulic fluid pressure is increased by the servo unit and transmitted to the caliper by a system of metal and flexible hoses whereupon the pistons are moved outwards so pushing the pads onto the face of the disc and slowing down the rotational speed of the disc.

The rear drum brakes have one cylinder operating two shoes. Attached to each of the brake units is an automatic adjuster which operates in conjunction with the handbrake mechanism. The handbrake provides an independent means of rear brake application. When the brake pedal is depressed, hydraulic fluid pressure is increased by the servo unit and is transmitted to the rear brake wheel cylinder by a system of metal and flexible pipes. The pressure moves the pistons outwards so pushing the shoe linings into contact with the inside circumference of the brake drum and slowing down the rotational speed of the drum.

Whenever it is necessary to obtain spare parts for the braking system great care must be taken to ensure that the correct parts are obtained because of the varying types of braking system fitted to the whole of Cortina Mk 111 range.

FIG 9 : 1 BLEED TUBE ON FRONT DISC BRAKE CALIPER BLEED SCREW

2 Bleeding the hydraulic system

1 Removal of all the air from the hydraulic system is essential to the correct working of the braking system. Before undertaking this, examine the fluid reservoir cap to ensure that the vent hole is clear. Check the level of fluid in the reservoir and top up if required.

2 Check all brake line unions and connections for seepage, and at the same time check the condition of the rubber hoses, which may be perished.

3 If the condition of the caliper or wheel cylinders is in doubt, check for possible signs of fluid leakage.

4 If there is any possibility that incorrect fluid has been used in the system, drain all the fluid out and flush through with methylated spirits. Renew all piston seals and cups since these will be affected and could possibly fail under pressure.

5 Gather together a clean jar, a 12 inch length of tubing which fits tightly over the bleed screws, and a tin of the correct brake fluid.

6 To bleed the system, clean the areas around the bleed valves and start on the front right hand bleed screw by first removing the rubber cup over the end of the bleed screw and fitting the bleed tube as shown in Fig 9 : 1.

7 Place the end of the tube in the clean glass jar containing sufficient fluid to keep the end of the tube submerged during the operation.

8 Open the bleed screw a quarter of a turn with a spanner and depress the brake pedal. After slowly releasing the pedal, pause a moment to allow the fluid to recoup in the master cylinder and then depress again. This will force air from the system. Continue until no more air bubbles can be seen coming from the tube. At intervals make certain that the reservoir is kept topped up, otherwise air will enter at this point again (photo).

9 Finally press the pedal down fully and hold it there whilst the bleed screw is tightened. To ensure correct seating it should be tightened to a torque wrench setting of 5 - 7 lb ft (0.70 - 1.00 kg m).

10 Repeat this operation on the second front brake and then the rear brakes starting with the right hand brake unit (photo).

11 When completed check the level of the fluid in the reservoir and then check the feel of the brake pedal, which should be firm and free from any 'spongy' action normally associated with air in the system.

12 It will be noticed that during the bleeding operation the effort required to depress the pedal the full stroke will increase because of the loss of vacuum assistance as it is destroyed by repeated operation of the servo unit. Although the servo unit will be inoperative as far as assistance is concerned it does not affect the brake bleed operation. Never re-use old brake fluid.

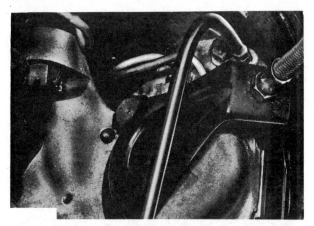

2.8 The master cylinder reservoir must be kept topped up

2.10 Bleed tube on rear drum brake wheel cylinder bleed screw

3   Flexible hose - inspection, removal and replacement

1   Inspect the condition of the flexible hydraulic hoses leading to each of the front disc brake calipers and also the one at the front of the rear axle. If they are swollen, damaged or chafed, they must be renewed.

2   Wipe the top of the brake master cylinder reservoir and unscrew the cap. Place a piece of thin polythene sheet over the top of the reservoir and refit the cap. This is to stop hydraulic fluid syphoning out during subsequent operations.

3   To remove a front flexible hose wipe the union and brackets free of dust and undo the union nuts from the metal pipe ends (Fig 9.2 [i])

4   Undo and remove the locknuts and plain washers securing each flexible hose end to the bracket and lift away the flexible hose from the bracket (Fig 9.2 [ii])

5   To remove the rear flexible hose follow the instructions for the front flexible hose (Fig 9 : 3).

6   Refitting in both cases is the reverse sequence to removal. It will be necessary to bleed the brake hydraulic system as described in Section 2. If one hose has been removed it is only necessary to bleed either the front or rear brake hydraulic system.

4   Front brake pads - inspection, removal and refitting

1   Apply the handbrake, remove the front wheel trim, jack up the front of the car and place on firmly based axle stands. Remove the front wheel (photo).

2   Inspect the amount of friction material left on the pads. The pads must be renewed when the thickness has been reduced to a minimum of 0.12 in (3.0 mm).

3   If the fluid level in the master cylinder reservoir is high, when the pistons are moved into their respective bores to accommodate new pads, the level could rise sufficiently for the fluid to overflow. Place absorbent cloth around the reservoir or syphon a little fluid out so preventing paintwork damage.

4   Using a pair of long nosed pliers extract the two small wire clips that hold the main retaining pins in place (photo).

5   Remove the main retaining pins which run through the caliper, and the metal backing of the pads and the shims (photo).

6   The friction pads can now be removed from the caliper. If they prove difficult to remove by hand a pair of long nosed pliers can be used. Lift away the shims (photo).

7   Carefully clean the recesses in the caliper in which the friction pads and shims lie, and the exposed faces of each piston from all traces of dirt or rust.

8   Using a piece of wood carefully retract the pistons.

9   Fit new friction pads and shims (these can be fitted either way up) and insert the main pad retaining pins. Secure the pins with the small wire clips.

10 Refit the road wheel and lower the car. Tighten the wheel nuts securely.

11 To correctly seat the pistons, pump the brake pedal several times and finally top up the hydraulic fluid in the master cylinder reservoir if necessary.

5   Front brake caliper - removal and refitting

1   Apply the handbrake, jack up the front of the car and place on firmly based axle stands. Remove the front wheel.

2   Wipe the top of the brake master cylinder reservoir and unscrew the cap. Place a piece of thin polythene sheet over the top of the reservoir and refit the cap.

3   Remove the friction pads as described in Section 4.

4   If it is intended to fit new caliper pistons and/or the seals, depress the brake pedal to bring the pistons into contact with the disc and so assist subsequent removal of the pistons.

5   Wipe the area clean around the flexible hose bracket and detach the pipe as described in Section 3. Tape up the end of the pipe to stop the possibility of dirt ingress.

6   Using a screwdriver or chisel bend back the tabs on the locking plate and undo the two caliper body mounting bolts. Lift away the caliper from its mounting flange on the steering knuckle and wheel stub.

7   To refit the caliper, position it over the disc and move it until the mounting bolt holes are in line with the two front holes in the steering knuckle and wheel stub mounting flange.

8   Fit the caliper retaining bolts through the two holes in a new locking plate and insert the bolts through the caliper body. Tighten the bolts to a torque wrench setting of 45 - 50 lb ft (6.22 - 6.91 kg m).

9   Using a screwdriver, pliers or chisel bend up the locking plate tabs so as to lock the bolts.

10 Remove the tape from the end of the flexible hydraulic pipe and reconnect it to the union on the hose bracket. Be careful not to cross thread the union nut during the initial turns. The union nut should be tightened securely, if possible using a torque wrench and special slotted end ring spanner attachment set to 5 - 7 lb ft (0.70 - 1.00 kg m).

11 Push the pistons into their respective bores so to accommodate the pads. Watch the level of hydraulic fluid in the master cylinder reservoir as it can overflow if too high whilst the pistons are being retracted. Place absorbent cloth around the reservoir and syphon out a little fluid.

12 Fit the pads into their respective 'original' positions if being refitted. If new pads are being used it does not matter which side they are fitted. Replace the shims.

13 Insert the two pad and shim retaining pins and secure in position with the spring clips.

14 Bleed the hydraulic system as described in Section 2. Replace the road wheel and lower the car.

6   Front brake caliper - dismantling and reassembly

1   The pistons should be removed first. (See Fig 9 : 4 for the location of the various parts). To do this, half withdraw one piston from its bore in the caliper.

2   Carefully remove the securing circlip and extract the sealing bellows from its location in the lower part of the piston skirt. Completely remove the piston.

3   If difficulty is experienced in withdrawing the pistons, use a jet of compressed air or a foot pump to move it out of its bore.

4   Remove the sealing bellows from its location in the annular ring which is machined in the cylinder bore.

5   Remove the piston sealing ring from the cylinder bore using a small screwdriver but do take care not to scratch the fine finish of the bore.

6   To remove the second piston repeat the procedure described in paragraphs 1 - 5 inclusive.

7   It is important that the two halves of the caliper are not separated under any circumstances. If hydraulic fluid leaks are evident from the joint, the caliper must be renewed.

8   Thoroughly wash all parts in methylated spirits or correct hydraulic fluid. During reassembly new rubber seals must be fitted and these should be well lubricated with clean hydraulic fluid.

9   Inspect the pistons and bores for signs of wear, score marks or damage, and if evident, new parts should be obtained ready for fitting, or a new caliper obtained.

10 To reassemble, fit one of the piston seals into the annular groove in the cylinder bore.

11 Fit the rubber bellows to the cylinder bore groove so that the lip is turned outwards.

12 Lubricate the seal and rubber bellows with correct hydraulic fluid. Push the piston, crown first, through the rubber sealing bellows and then into the cylinder bore. Take care as it is easy for the piston to damage the rubber bellows. This operation is shown in Fig 9 : 6.

13 With the piston half inserted into the cylinder bore, fit the inner edge of the bellows into the annular groove that is in the piston skirt.

14 Push the piston down the bore as far as it will go. Secure the

FIG 9 : 2 FRONT FLEXIBLE HOSE REMOVAL

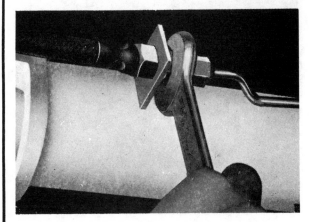

FIG 9 : 3 REMOVAL OF REAR FLEXIBLE HOSE

FIG 9 : 4 FRONT DISC BRAKE CALIPER COMPONENT PARTS

1 Pad shim
2 Brake pad
3 Pad retainer clip
4 Bleed nipple
5 Caliper body
6 Pad retainer
7 Piston bellows retainer
8 Piston bellows
9 Piston
10 Piston seal

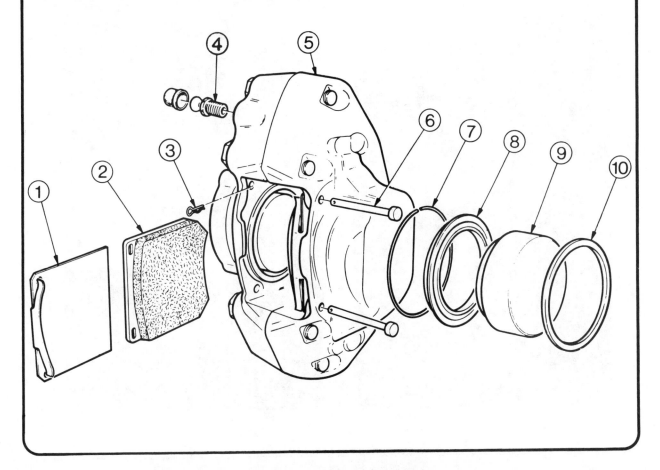

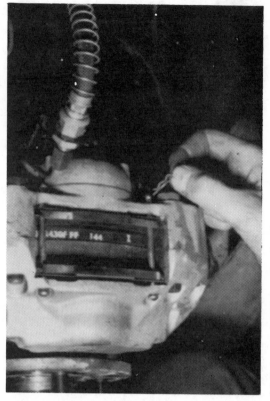

4.4 Removal of retaining pin wire clips

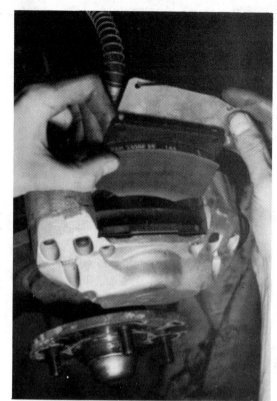

4.6 Pad and shim removal

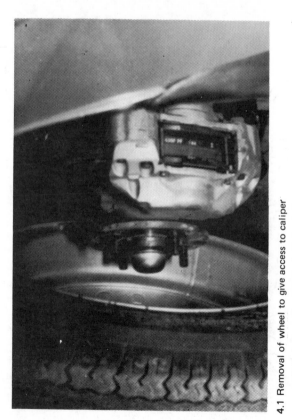

4.1 Removal of wheel to give access to caliper

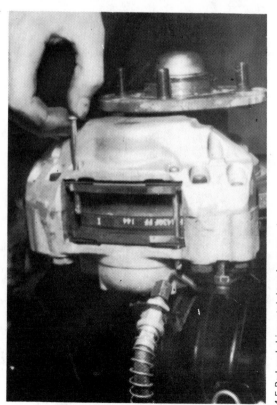

4.5 Pad and shim retaining pin removal

rubber bellows to the caliper with the circlip.

15 Repeat the procedure described in paragraphs 10 to 14 inclusive for the second piston.

16 The caliper is now ready for refitting. It is recommended that the hydraulic pipe end is temporarily plugged to stop any dirt ingress whilst being refitted before the pipe connection is made.

7   Front brake disc and hub - removal and replacement

1 After jacking up the car and removing the front wheel, remove the caliper as described in Section 5.

2 By judicious tapping and levering, remove the dust cap from the centre of the hub.

3 Remove the split pin from the nut retainer and lift away the adjusting nut retainer.

4 Unscrew the adjusting nut and lift away the thrust washer and outer tapered bearing.

5 Pull off the complete hub and disc assembly from the stub axle (Fig 9 : 7).

6 From the back of the hub assembly, carefully prise out the grease seal and lift away the inner tapered bearing.

7 Carefully clean out the hub and wash the bearings with petrol, making sure that no grease or oil is allowed to get onto the brake disc.

8 Should it be necessary to separate the disc from the hub for renewal or regrinding, first bend back the locking tabs and undo and remove the four securing bolts. With a scriber mark the relative positions of the hub and disc to ensure refitting in their original positions and separate the disc from the hub.

9 Thoroughly clean the disc and inspect for signs of deep scoring or excessive corrosion. If these are evident, the disc may be reground but no more than a maximum total of 0.060 .inch (1.524 mm) may be removed. It is, however, desirable to fit a new disc if possible.

10 To reassemble make quite sure that the mating faces of the disc and hub are very clean and place the disc on the hub aligning any previously made marks.

11 Fit the four securing bolts and two new tabwashers (Fig 9 : 8) and tighten the bolts in a progressive and diagonal manner to a final torque wrench setting of 30 - 34 lb ft (4.15 - 4.70 kg m). Bend up the locking tabs.

12 Work some Castrol LM Grease well into the bearings; fully pack the bearing cages and rollers. NOTE: leave the hub and grease seal empty to allow for subsequent expansion of the grease.

13 To reassemble the hub first fit the inner bearing and then gently tap the grease seal back into the hub. A new seal must always be fitted as during removal it was probably damaged. The lip must face inwards to the hub.

14 Replace the hub and disc assembly on the stub axle and slide on the outer bearing and thrust washer (Fig 9 : 9).

15 Refit the adjusting nut and tighten it to a torque wrench setting of 27 lb ft (3.7 kg m) whilst rotating the hub and disc to ensure free movement and centralisation of the bearings. Slacken the nut back by 90° which will give the required end float of 0.001 - 0.005 inch (0.03 - 0.13 mm). Fit the nut retainer and a new split pin but do not lock the split pin yet.

16 At this stage it is advisable, if a dial indicator gauge is available to check the disc for run out. The measurement should be taken as near as possible to the edge of the worn yet smooth part of the disc and must not exceed 0.002 inch (0.05 mm). If the figure obtained is found to be excessive, check the mating surfaces of the disc and hub for dirt or damage, and also check the bearings and cups for excessive wear or damage.

17 If a dial indicator gauge is not available the run out can be checked by means of feeler gauges placed between the casting of the caliper and the disc. Establish a reasonably tight fit with the feeler gauges between the top of the casting and the disc and rotate the disc and hub. Any high or low spot will immediately become obvious by extra tightness or looseness of the fit of the feeler gauges. The amount of run out can be checked by adding

FIG 9 : 6 REFITTING THE PISTON INTO THE CALIPER CYLINDER BORE

FIG 9 : 7 REMOVING THE HUB AND DISC ASSEMBLY FROM THE STUB AXLE

FIG 9 : 8 FITTING DISC SECURING BOLTS AND NEW TAB WASHERS

FIG 9 : 9 REFITTING OUTER BEARING AND THRUST WASHER

or subtracting feeler gauges as necessary. It is only fair to point out that this method is not as accurate as when using a dial gauge owing to the rough nature of the caliper casting (Fig 9 : 10).

18 Once the disc run out has been checked and found to be correct, bend the ends of the split pin back and replace the dust cap.

19 Reconnect the brake hydraulic pipe and bleed the brakes as described in Section 2.

8 Drum brake shoes - inspection, removal and refitting

Refitting new brake linings to shoes is not considered economic, or possible, without the use of special equipment. However, if the services of a local garage or workshop having brake re-lining equipment are available then there is no reason why the original shoes should not be successfully relined. Ensure that the correct specification linings are fitted to the shoes.

1 Chock the frontwheels, jack up the rear of the car and place on firmly based axle stands. Remove the road wheel.

2 Release the handbrake. Undo and remove the drum retaining screws located as shown in Fig 9 : 11 and use a soft faced hammer on the outer circumference of the brake drum to remove the brake drum (photo).

3 Should the situation exist where the shoes foul the drum making removal impossible, the shoes must be collapsed by detaching the handbrake cable from the body mounted brackets and then removing the plunger assembly from the backplate. Whenever the plunger is removed it must be discarded and a new one obtained (see Figs 9 : 12 and 9 : 13).

4 The brake linings should be renewed if they are worn so much that the rivet heads are flush with the surface of the lining. If bonded linings are fitted, they must be renewed when the lining material has worn down to 0.6 inch (1.52 mm) at its thinnest point.

5 Depress each shoe holding down spring and rotate the spring retaining washer through 90° to disengage it from the pin secured to the backplate. Lift away the washer and spring (photo).

6 Ease each shoe from its location slot in the fixed pivot and then detach the other shoe from the wheel cylinder (photo).

7 Note which way round and into which holes in the shoes the two retracting springs fit and detach the retracting springs.

8 Lift away the front shoe followed by the self adjusting pushrod and ratchet assembly.

9 Completely remove the handbrake cable from the body mounted brackets and disconnect the cable from the relay lever (photo).

10 Lift away the rear shoe together with the self adjusting mechanism.

11 If the shoes are to be left off for a while, place a warning on the steering wheel, as accidental depression of the brake pedal will eject the pistons from the wheel cylinder.

12 To remove the relay lever assembly, using a screwdriver prise open the 'U' clip on the rear brake shoe and lift away the relay lever assembly. The 'U' clip must be discarded and a new one obtained ready for reassembly.

13 Thoroughly clean all traces of dust from the shoes, backplates and brake drums using a stiff brush. DO NOT use compressed air. Brake dust can cause judder or squeal and, therefore, it is important to clean out as described.

14 Check that the pistons are free in the cylinder, and the rubber dust covers are undamaged and in position, and that there are no hydraulic brake fluid leaks.

15 Prior to reassembly smear a trace of Castrol PH Brake Grease on the brake shoe support pads, brake shoe pivots and on the ratchet wheel face and threads.

16 To reassemble, first fit the relay lever assembly to the rear brake shoe and retain in position using a new 'U' clip. Using a pair of pliers close up the ends of the clip (Figs 9 : 14 and 9 : 15).

17 Fit the retracting springs to the shoe webs in the same positions as was noted during removal. Replace the adjusting pushrod (photo).

18 Position the rear brake shoe on the fixed pivot and wheel

FIG 9 : 10 DISC RUN OUT CHECK POINTS WHEN USING FEELER GAUGES

FIG 9 : 11 REMOVAL OF BRAKE DRUM RETAINING SCREWS

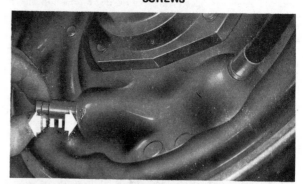

FIG 9 : 12 CHECKING MOVEMENT OF ADJUSTMENT PLUNGERS

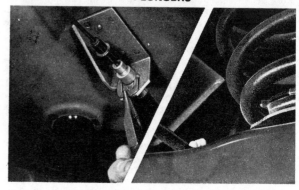

FIG 9 : 13 LH CABLE RETAINING 'U' SHAPED CLIP REMOVAL. RH CABLE RETAINING CLIP ON RADIUS ARM

8.2 Removal of brake drum

8.5 Depressing brake shoe holding spring

8.6 Removal of brake shoes

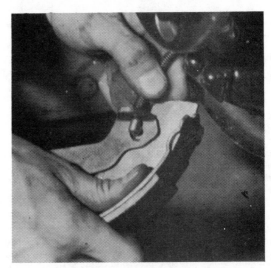

8.9 Disconnection of handbrake cable from relay lever

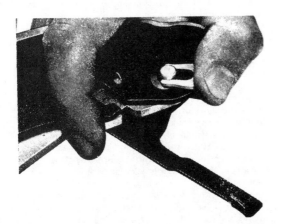

FIG 9 : 14 FITTING NEW 'U' CLIP TO RELAY LEVER PIN

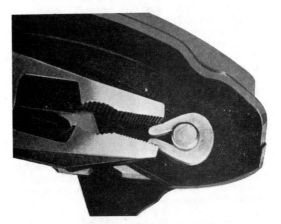

FIG 9 : 15 LOCKING THE ENDS OF THE 'U' CLIP WITH A
PAIR OF PLIERS

cylinder piston extension, and using a screwdriver ease the front shoe into position on the brake backplate and wheel cylinder piston extension.

19 Reconnect the handbrake cable to the relay lever taking care to ensure that it does not foul the adjustment plunger.

20 Refit the handbrake cable to the body mounted brackets.

21 Place each shoe holding down clip on its pin followed by the washer, dished face inwards. Depress and turn the washer through 90º to lock in position. Make sure that each shoe is firmly seated on the backplate.

22 Rotate each adjusting pushrod ratchet until all slack in the pushrod is removed. Check that the adjusting arm positively locates in the ratchet wheel serrations.

23 Refit the brake drum and push it up the studs as far as it will go.

24 The shoes must next be centralised by the brake pedal being depressed firmly several times.

25 Pull on and then release the handbrake lever several times until it is no longer possible to hear the clicking noise of the ratchet being turned by the adjusting arm.

26 Refit the road wheel and lower the car. Road test to ensure correct operation of the rear brakes.

9 Drum brake wheel cylinder - removal, inspection and overhaul

If hydraulic fluid is leaking from the brake wheel cylinder, it will be necessary to dismantle it and replace the seals. Should brake fluid be found running down the side of the wheel or if it is noticed that a pool of liquid forms alongside one wheel and the level in the master cylinder is low, it is indicative of failed seals.

1 Refer to Section 8 and remove the brake drum and shoes. Clean down the rear of the backplate using a stiff brush. Place a quantity of rag under the backplate to catch any hydraulic fluid that may issue from the open pipe or wheel cylinder.

2 Wipe the top of the brake master cylinder reservoir and unscrew the cap. Place a piece of polythene sheet over the top of the reservoir and replace the cap. This is to stop hydraulic fluid syphoning out.

3 Using an open ended spanner, carefully unscrew the hydraulic pipe connection union/s to the rear of the wheel cylinder (Fig 9 : 17). Note that on the left hand wheel cylinder two pipes are attached to it. Note the location of each pipe as these must not be interchanged. To prevent dirt ingress tape over the pipe ends.

4 Undo and remove the two bolts and washers that secure the wheel cylinder to the brake backplate.

5 Withdraw the wheel cylinder from the front of the brake backplate as shown in Fig 9 : 18.

6 To dismantle the wheel cylinder, first ease off each rubber dust cover retaining ring and lift away each rubber dust cover.

7 Carefully lift out each piston together with seal from the wheel cylinder bore. Recover the return spring (Fig 9 : 19).

8 Using the fingers only, remove the piston seal from each piston noting which way round it is fitted (Fig 9 : 20). Do not use a metal screwdriver as this could scratch the piston.

9 Inspect the inside of the cylinder for score marks caused by impurities in the hydraulic fluid. If any are found, the cylinder and pistons will require renewal.

NOTE: If the wheel cylinder requires renewal always ensure that the replacement is exactly similar to the one removed.

10 If the cylinder is sound, thoroughly clean it out with fresh hydraulic fluid.

11 The old rubber seals will probably be swollen and visibly worn. Smear the new rubber seals with hydraulic fluid and refit to the pistons making sure they are the correct way round with the   face of the seal adjacent to the piston rear shoulder (Fig 9 : 20).

12 Wet the cylinder bore and insert the return spring. Carefully insert the pistons, seal end first, into the cylinder making sure that the seals do not roll over as they are initially fitted into the bore.

13 Position the rubber boots on each end of the wheel cylinder and secure in position with the retaining rings.

14 Fit a new ring seal onto the rear of the wheel cylinder and

position this in its slot in the backplate. Secure in position with the two bolts and washers.

15 Reconnect the brake pipe/s to the rear of the wheel cylinder taking care not to cross thread the union nuts. On the left hand wheel cylinder make sure the pipes are connected the correct way round as was noted during removal.

16 Refit the brake shoes and drum as described in Section 8.

17 Refer to Section 2 and bleed the brake hydraulic system.

10 Drum brake backplate - removal and refitting

1 To remove the backplate refer to Chapter 8/5 and remove the axle shaft.

2 Detach the handbrake cable from the handbrake relay lever.

3 Wipe the top of the brake master cylinder reservoir and unscrew the cap. Place a piece of polythene sheet over the top of the reservoir and replace the cap.

4 Using an open ended spanner, carefully unscrew the hydraulic pipe connection union/s to the rear of the wheel cylinder. (Fig. 9 : 17). Note that on the left hand wheel cylinder two pipes are attached to the wheel cylinder. Note the location of each pipe as these must not be interchanged. To prevent dirt ingress tape over the pipe ends.

5 The brake backplate may now be lifted away.

6 Refitting is the reverse sequence to removal. It will be necessary to bleed the brake hydraulic system as described in Section 2.

11 Handbrake - adjustment

1 It is important to check that lack of adjustment is not caused by the cable becoming detached from the body mounted clips; inadequate lubrication of the equaliser bracket and pivot points, or excessive wear of the rear shoe linings.

2 Chock the front wheels. Jack up the rear of the car and support on firmly based axle stands located under the rear axle. Release the handbrake.

3 Check the adjustment of the handbrake by measuring the amount of movement of the adjustment plungers located in the brake backplate. This should be 0.20 - 0.39 inch (5.0 - 10.0 mm) (Fig 9 : 12). If the results obtained differ on one side compared with the other it may be equalised by gripping the handbrake cable at the equaliser bracket and adjusting the position of the cable.

4 If the movement of the adjustment plungers is correct pull on and then release the handbrake lever several times until it is no longer possible to hear the clicking noise of the ratchet being turned by the adjusting arm.

5 If the movement of the adjustment plungers is incorrect the cable may then be adjusted as described in the following paragraphs.

6 Make sure that the handbrake is in the full-off position.

7 Remove all free movement of the adjustment plungers by slackening off the cable as necessary at the right hand cable to body abutment bracket. The relay levers in the rear brake units will automatically return to the fully 'off' position.

8 Now adjust the cable at the right hand cable to body abutment bracket so as to give a plunger free movement of 0.20 - 0.39 inch (5.0 - 10.0 mm) on each brake backplate (Fig 9:21).

9 Equalise the movement of the plungers by gripping the handbrake cable at the equaliser bracket and adjusting the position of the cable.

10 Should adjustment of the cable not alter the plunger free movement it is an indication that the cable is binding or the automatic brake adjuster is not operating correctly - usually due to siezure of the moving parts within the brake unit. It could also be that the adjustment plungers have seized in their locations in the backplates. Further investigation will therefore be necessary.

11 When adjustment is correct tighten the adjuster locknuts.

12 Pull on and then release the handbrake lever several times until it is no longer possible to hear the clicking noise of the

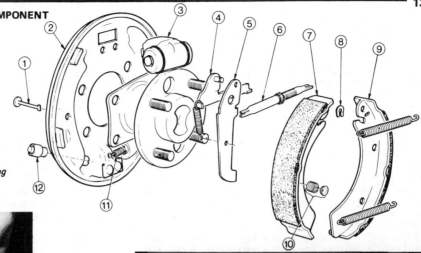

FIG 9 : 16 REAR DRUM BRAKE COMPONENT PARTS

1 Shoe hold down pin
2 Backplate
3 Wheel cylinder
4 Self-adjusting lever
5 Handbrake relay lever
6 Pushrod and ratchet
7 Leading shoe
8 'U' clip
9 Trailing shoe
10 Hold down spring and washer
11 Handbrake cable retracting spring
12 Handbrake adjustment plunger

8.17 Refitting adjusting pushrod and retracting springs

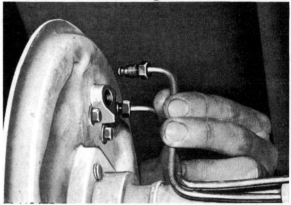

FIG 9 : 17 HYDRAULIC PIPE CONNECTIONS TO LEFT HAND WHEEL CYLINDER

FIG 9 : 18 REMOVAL OF WHEEL CYLINDER FROM BRAKE BACKPLATE

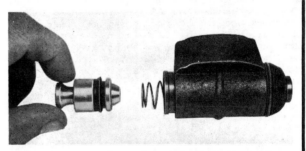

FIG 9 : 19 DISMANTLING WHEEL CYLINDER

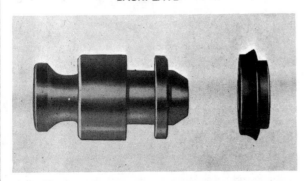

FIG 9 : 20 WHEEL CYLINDER PISTON AND SEAL SHOW—ING WHICH WAY ROUND THE SEAL MUST BE FITTED

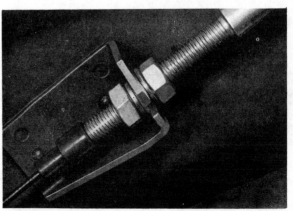

FIG 9 : 21 HANDBRAKE CABLE ADJUSTMENT LOCATION ON BODY MOUNTED BRACKET

ratchet being turned by the adjuster arm.

13 Remove the axle stands and lower the car to the ground.

12 Handbrake cable - removal and replacement

1 Chock the front wheels. Jack up the rear of the car and support on firmly based axle stands located under the rear axle. Release the handbrake. Remove the two rear wheels.

2 Using a pair of pliers, remove the spring clip and withdraw the clevis pin and wave washer that secures the handbrake cable to the handbrake lever. Detach the cable from the handbrake lever (Fig 9 : 22).

3 Undo the cable adjuster nuts and then detach the cable from the clips located under the body and on the radius arm. Using a pair of pliers withdraw the retaining 'U' shaped clip at the adjuster bracket (Fig 9 : 13).

4 Remove the brake drums. If they are tight they may be removed using a soft faced hammer on the outer drum circumference and tapping outwards.

5 Detach the brake cable from each brake unit relay lever and pull the cable rearwards through the rear of the backplate.

6 To refit the cable, first feed the cable ends through the rear of the backplate and reconnect to the relay levers. Replace the brake drums.

7 Attach the cable to the underbody brackets and clips on the radius arms. Take care to make sure that the adjuster is correctly located in its bracket.

8 Position the handbrake cable onto the handbrake lever and retain with the clevis pin, wave washer and spring clip.

9 Refit the rear wheels and referring to Section 11 adjust the handbrake cable.

10 Remove the axle stands and lower the car to the ground.

13 Brake master cylinder - removal and replacement

1 Apply the handbrake and chock the front wheels. Drain the fluid from the master cylinder reservoir and master cylinder by attaching a plastic bleed tube to one of the front brake caliper bleed screws. Undo the screw one turn and then pump the fluid out into a container by means of the brake pedal. Hold the brake pedal against the floor at the end of each stroke and tighten the bleed screw. When the pedal has returned to its normal position, loosen the bleed screw and repeat the process until the reservoir is empty.

2 Wipe the area around the two union nuts on the side of the master cylinder body and using an open ended spanner undo the two union nuts. Take over the ends of the pipes to stop dirt ingress (Fig 9 : 23).

3 Undo and remove the two nuts and spring washers that secure the master cylinder to the rear of the servo unit. Lift away the master cylinder taking care that no hydraulic fluid is allowed to drip onto the paintwork (Fig 9 : 25).

4 Refitting is the reverse sequence to removal. Always start the union nuts before finally tightening the master cylinder nuts. It will be necessary to bleed the hydraulic system and full details will be found in Section 2.

14 Brake master cylinder - dismantling, examination and reassembly

If a replacement cylinder is to be fitted, it will be necessary to lubricate the seals before fitting to the car as they have a protective coating when originally assembled. Remove the blanking plugs from the hydraulic pipe union seating. Inject clean hydraulic fluid into the master cylinder and operate the primary piston several times so the fluid will spread over all the internal working surfaces.

If the master cylinder is to be dismantled after removal proceed as follows:-

1 Undo and remove the two screws and spring washers holding

the reservoir to the master cylinder body (Fig 9 : 24). Lift away the reservoir. Using a suitable sized Allen key or wrench, unscrew the tipping valve nut and lift away the seal. Using a suitable diameter rod, push the primary plunger down the bore, so enabling the tipping valve to be withdrawn.

2 Shake out the parts. Take care that adequate precautions are taken to ensure all parts are caught as they emerge. You can use compressed air.

3 Separate the primary and secondary plungers from the intermediate spring. Use the fingers to remove the gland seal from the primary plunger.

4 The secondary plunger assembly should be separated by lifting the thimble leaf over the shouldered end of the plunger. Using the finger, remove the seal from the secondary plunger.

5 Depress the secondary spring, allowing the valve stem to slide through the keyhole in the thimble, thus releasing the tension on the spring.

6 Detach the valve spacer, taking care of the spring washer which will be found located under the valve head.

7 Examine the bore of the cylinder carefully for any signs of scores or ridges. If this is found to be smooth all over, new seals can be fitted. If, however, there is any doubt of the condition of the bore, then a new cylinder must be fitted.

8 If examination of the seals shows them to be apparently oversize, or swollen, or very loose on the plungers, suspect oil contamination in the system. Oil will swell these rubber seals, and if one is found to be swollen, it is reasonable to assume that all seals in the braking system will need attention.

9 Thoroughly clean all parts in clean hydraulic fluid or methylated spirits. Ensure that the by-pass ports are clear.

10 All components should be assembled wet, by dipping in clean brake fluid. Using fingers only, fit new seals to the primary and secondary plungers ensuring that they are the correct way round. Place the dished washer with the dome against the underside of the valve seat. Hold it in position with the valve spacer, ensuring that the legs face towards the valve seal.

11 Replace the plunger return spring centrally on the spacer, insert the thimble into the spring and depress until the valve stem engages in the keyhole of the thimble.

12 Insert the reduced end of the plunger into the thimble, until the thimble engages under the shoulder of the plunger, and press home the thimble leaf. Replace the intermediate spring between the primary and secondary plungers.

13 Check that the master cylinder bore is clean and smear with clean brake fluid. With the complete assembly suitably wetted with brake fluid, carefully insert the assembly into the bore. Ease the lips of the piston seals into the bore taking care that they do not roll over. Push the assembly fully home.

14 Refit the tipping valve assembly and seal, to the cylinder bore and tighten the securing nut to a torque wrench setting of 35 - 45 lb ft (4.8 - 6.11 kg m).

15 Using a clean screwdriver push the primary piston in and out checking that the recuperating valve opens when the screwdriver is withdrawn and closes again when it is pushed in.

16 Check the condition of the front and rear reservoir gaskets and if there is any doubt as to their condition they must be replaced.

17 Replace the hydraulic fluid reservoir and tighten the two retaining screws.

18 The master cylinder is now ready for refitting to the servo unit. Bleed the complete hydraulic system and road test the car.

15 Brake pedal - removal and replacement

1 Open the bonnet and disconnect the battery.

2 If a manual choke is fitted, remove the choke control knob.

3 Undo and remove the screw and annulus that hold the two halves of the steering column shroud together. Using a knife split the two halves of the column shroud and lift away.

4 Undo and remove the crosshead screws that secure the facia panel to the instrument panel. Lift away the facia panel (Fig 9 : 26).

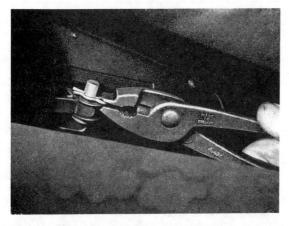

FIG 9 : 22 HANDBRAKE CABLE RETAINING CLEVIS PIN CLIP REMOVAL

FIG 9 : 23 BRAKE MASTER CYLINDER HYDRAULIC PIPE CONNECTIONS

FIG 9 : 24 EXPLODED VIEW OF BRAKE MASTER CYLINDER

1   Reservoir cap
2   Cap seal
3   Seal retainer
4   Reservoir
5   Sealing ring
6   Tipping valve retainer
7   Tipping valve
8   Circlip
9   Gasket
10 Master cylinder body
11 Washer
12 Screw
13 Seal
14 Primary piston
15 Spring
16 Secondary piston
17 Seal
18 Spring retainer thimble
19 Spring
20 Spring retainer
21 Valve
22 Washer
23 Seal

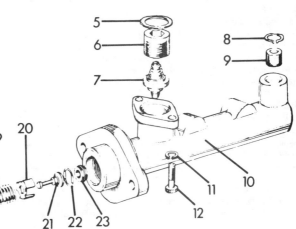

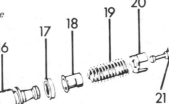

FIG 9 : 25 REMOVAL OF BRAKE MASTER CYLINDER (RESERVOIR REMOVED FOR CLARITY)

FIG 9 : 26 FACIA PANEL RETAINING SCREW REMOVAL

5 Undo and remove the screws that secure the instrument cluster to the instrument panel. Draw the cluster away from the instrument panel by a sufficient amount to give access to the rear. Detach the wiring loom multi-pin connector and the speedometer drive cable (Fig 9 : 27). Lift away the instrument cluster.

6 Detach and lift away the demister duct.

7 Withdraw the spring clip from the brake servo pushrod to brake pedal clevis pin. Lift away the clevis pin and the bushes (Fig 9 : 28).

8 Detach the brake pedal return spring from the brake pedal bracket (Fig 9 : 29).

9 Remove the circlips that secure the pedal shaft to the pedal shaft bracket and carefully push the shaft through the bracket and pedal (Fig 9 : 30).

10 Lift away the brake pedal and split bushes. Remove the half bushes from each side of the brake pedal (Fig 9 : 31).

11 Inspect the bushes for signs of wear and, if evident, they must be renewed.

12 Refitting the brake pedal is the reverse sequence to removal. Lubricate all moving parts with Castrol GTX.

16 Handbrake lever - removal and replacement

1 If a centre console is fitted it must first be removed. It is attached to the transmission cover panels by self tapping screws.

2 Undo and remove the self tapping screws that secure the handbrake lever rubber gaiter to the floor. Slide the gaiter up the handbrake lever.

3 Lift away the carpeting from around the handbrake area.

4 Chock the front wheels and working inside the car remove the spring clip from the primary cable to handbrake lever clevis pin. Withdraw the clevis pin and wave washer (Fig 9 : 32).

5 Undo and remove the two bolts and spring washers that secure the handbrake lever to the floor. The handbrake lever assembly may be lifted away from its location on the floor.

6 Refitting is the reverse sequence to removal. Smear the clevis pin with a little Castrol LM Grease.

17 Vacuum servo unit - description

A vacuum servo unit is fitted into the brake hydraulic circuit in series with the master cylinder, to provide assistance to the driver when the brake pedal is depressed. This reduces the effort required by the driver to operate the brakes under all braking conditions.

The unit operates by vacuum obtained from the induction manifold and comprises basically a booster diaphragm and check valve. The servo unit and hydraulic master cylinder are connected together so that the servo unit piston rod acts as the master cylinder pushrod. The drivers braking effort is transmitted through another pushrod to the servo unit piston and its built in control system. The servo unit piston does not fit tightly into the cylinder, but has a strong diaphragm to keep its edges in constant contact with the cylinder wall, so assuring an air tight seal between the two parts. The forward chamber is held under vacuum conditions created in the inlet manifold of the engine and, during periods when the brake pedal is not in use, the controls open a passage to the rear chamber so placing it under vacuum conditions as well. When the brake pedal is depressed, the vacuum passage to the rear chamber is cut off and the chamber opened to atmospheric pressure. The consequent rush of air pushes the servo piston forward in the vacuum chamber and operates the main pushrod to the master cylinder.

The controls are designed so that assistance is given under all conditions, and, when the brakes are not required, vacuum in the rear chamber is established when the brake pedal is released. All air from the atmosphere entering the rear chamber is passed through a small air filter.

Under normal operating conditions the vacuum servo unit is very reliable and does not require overhaul, except at very high mileages. In this case, it is far better to obtain a service exchange unit, rather than repair the original unit.

18 Vacuum servo unit - removal and replacement

1 Slacken the clip securing the vacuum hose to the servo unit and carefully draw the hose from its union.

2 Refer to Section 13 and remove the master cylinder.

3 Using a pair of pliers remove the spring clip in the end of the brake pedal to pushrod clevis pin. Lift away the clevis pin and the bushes (Fig 9 : 28).

4 Undo and remove the nuts and spring washers that secure the servo unit mounting bracket to the bulkhead. Lift away the servo unit and bracket (Fig 9 : 33).

5 Undo and remove the four nuts and spring washers that secure the bracket to the servo unit.

6 Refitting the servo unit is the reverse sequence to removal. It will be necessary to bleed the brake hydraulic system as described in Section 2.

19 Vacuum servo unit - dismantling, inspection and reassembly

Thoroughly clean the outside of the unit using a stiff brush and wipe with a non-fluffy rag. It cannot be too strongly emphasised that cleanliness is important when working on the servo. Before any attempt is made to dismantle, refer to Fig 9 : 34 where it will be seen that two items of equipment are required: Firstly, a base plate must be made to enable the unit to be safely held in a vice, secondly, a lever must be made similar to the form shown. Without these items it is impossible to dismantle satisfactorily.

To dismantle the unit proceed as follows:

1 Refer to Fig 9 : 35 and using a file or scriber, mark a line across the two halves of the unit to act as a datum for alignment.

2 Fit the previously made base plate into a firm vice and attach the unit to the plate using the master cylinder studs.

3 Fit the lever to the four studs on the rear shell as shown in Fig 9 : 34.

4 Use a piece of long rubber hose and connect one end to the adaptor on the engine inlet manifold and the other end to the non-return valve. Start the engine and this will create a vacuum in the unit so drawing the two halves together.

5 Rotate the lever in an anticlockwise direction until the front shell indentations are in line with the recesses in the rim of the rear shell. Then press the lever assembly down firmly whilst an assistant stops the engine and quickly removes the vacuum pipe from the inlet manifold connector. Depress the operating rod so to release the vacuum, whereupon the front and rear halves should part. If necessary, use a soft faced hammer and lightly tap the front half to break the bond.

6 Lift away the rear shell followed by the diaphragm return spring, the dust cover, end cap and the filter. Also withdraw the diaphragm. Press down the valve rod and shake out the valve retaining plate. Then separate the valve rod assembly from the diaphragm plate.

7 Gently ease the spring washer from the diaphragm plate and withdraw the pushrod and reaction disc.

8 The seal and plate assembly in the end of the front shell are a press fit. It is recommended that, unless the seal is to be renewed, they be left in situ.

9 Thoroughly clean all parts and then inspect for signs of damage, stripped threads etc., and obtain new parts as necessary. All seals should be renewed and for this a 'Major Repair Kit' should be purchased. This kit will also contain two separate greases which must be used as directed, and not interchanged.

10 To reassemble first smear the seal and bearing with grease, Ford number 64949008 EM-IC-14 and refit the rear shell positioning it such that the flat face of the seal is towards the bearing. Press into position and refit the retainer.

11 Lightly smear the disc and hydraulic pushrod with grease Ford number 64949008 EM-IC-14. Refit the reaction disc and pushrod

FIG 9 : 27 INSTRUMENT CLUSTER DRAWN FORWARDS
GIVING SPEEDOMETER CABLE AND WIRING LOOM
MULTIPIN CONNECTOR ACCESS

FIG 9 : 29 BRAKE PEDAL RETURN SPRING LOCATION

FIG 9 : 31 BRAKE PEDAL SPLIT BUSHES

FIG 9 : 33 REMOVAL OF SERVO UNIT MOUNTING
BRACKET SECURING NUTS

FIG 9 : 28 CLEVIS PIN SECURING BRAKE SERVO PUSH
ROD TO BRAKE PEDAL

FIG 9 : 30 PEDAL SHAFT AND PEDAL RETAINING CLIPS

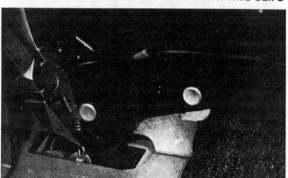

FIG 9 : 32 REMOVAL OF CLEVIS PIN SPRING CLIP

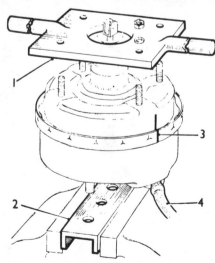

FIG 9 : 34 SPECIAL TOOLS REQUIRED TO
DISMANTLE SERVO UNIT

| 1 | Lever | 3 | Scribe line |
| 2 | Base plate | 4 | Vacuum applied |

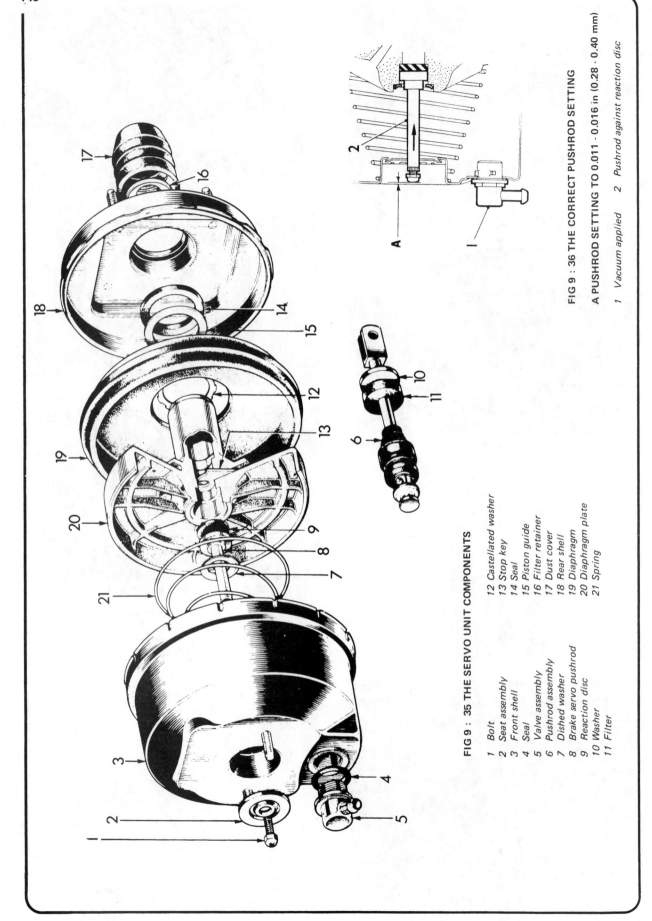

FIG 9 : 35 THE SERVO UNIT COMPONENTS

1 Bolt
2 Seat assembly
3 Front shell
4 Seal
5 Valve assembly
6 Pushrod assembly
7 Dished washer
8 Brake servo pushrod
9 Reaction disc
10 Washer
11 Filter
12 Castellated washer
13 Stop key
14 Seal
15 Piston guide
16 Filter retainer
17 Dust cover
18 Rear shell
19 Diaphragm
20 Diaphragm plate
21 Spring

FIG 9 : 36 THE CORRECT PUSHROD SETTING

A PUSHROD SETTING TO 0.011 - 0.016 in (0.28 - 0.40 mm)

1 Vacuum applied   2 Pushrod against reaction disc

141

to the diaphragm plate and press in the large spring washer. The small spring washer supplied in the 'Major Repair Kit' is not required. It is important that the length of the pushrod is not altered in any way and any attempt to move the adjustment bolt will strip the threads. If a new hydraulic pushrod has been required, the length will have to be reset. Details of this operation are given at the end of this Section.

12 Lightly smear the outer diameter of the diaphragm plate neck and the bearing surfaces of the valve plunger with grease, Ford number 64949008 EM-IC-15. Carefully fit the valve rod assembly into the neck of the diaphragm and fix with the retaining plate.

13 Fit the diaphragm into position and also the non return valve to the front shell. Next smear the seal and plate assembly with grease, Ford number 64949008 EM-IC-15 and press into the front shell with the plate facing inwards.

14 Fit the front shell to the base plate and the lever to the rear shell. Reconnect the vacuum hose to the non return valve and the adaptor on the engine inlet manifold. Position the diaphragm return spring in the front shell. Lightly smear the outer head of the diaphragm with grease, Ford number 64949008 EM-IC-15 and locate the diaphragm assembly in the rear shell. Position the rear shell assembly on the return spring and line up the previously made scribe marks.

15 The assistant should start the engine. Watching one's fingers very carefully, press the two halves of the unit together and using the lever tool, turn clockwise to lock the two halves together. Stop the engine and disconnect the hose.

16 Press a new filter into the neck of the diaphragm plate, refit the end cap and position the dust cover onto the special lugs of the rear shell.

17 Hydraulic pushrod adjustment only applies if a new pushrod has been fitted.. It will be seen from Fig 9 : 36 that there is a bolt screwed into the end of the pushrod. The amount of protrusion has to be adjusted in the following manner: remove the bolt and coat the threaded portion with Loctite Grade B. Reconnect the vacuum hose to the adaptor on the inlet valve and non return valve. Start the engine and screw the prepared bolt into the end of the pushrod. Adjust the position of the bolt head so that it is 0.11 to 0.061 in (0.28 - 0.40 mm) below the face of the front shell as shown by dimension 'A' in Fig 9 : 36. Leave the unit for a minimum of 24 hours to allow the Loctite to set hard.

18 Refit the servo unit to the car as described in the previous Section. To test the servo unit for correct operation after overhaul, first start the engine and run for a minimum period of two minutes and then switch off. Wait for ten minutes and apply the footbrake very carefully, listening to hear the rush of air into the servo unit. This will indicate that vacuum was retained and, therefore that the servo unit is operating correctly.

---

20 Stop light switch - removal and replacement

---

1 Open the bonnet and disconnect the battery.

2 If a manual choke control is fitted remove the choke control knob.

3 Undo and remove the screw and annulus that holds the two halves of the steering column shroud together. Using a knife split the two halves of the column shroud and lift away.

4 Undo and remove the crosshead screws that secure the facia panel to the instrument panel. Lift away the facia panel.

5 Undo and remove the screws that secure the instrument cluster to the instrument panel. Draw the cluster away from the instrument panel by a sufficient amount to give access to the rear. Detach the wiring loom multi pin connector and the speedometer drive cable. Lift away the instrument cluster.

6 Detach the electric cables from the switch. Undo and remove the switch locknut and remove the switch.

7 Refitting the switch is the reverse sequence to removal.

FAULT DIAGNOSIS - BRAKING SYSTEM

Symptom	Reason/s	Remedy
Leaks and air bubbles in hydraulic system	Brake fluid level too low	Top up master cylinder reservoir. Check for leaks.
	Caliper leaking	Dismantle caliper, clean, fit new rubbers and bleed brakes.
	Master cylinder leaking (bubbles in master cylinder fluid)	Dismantle master cylinder, clean and fit new rubbers. Bleed brakes.
	Brake flexible hose leaking	Examine and fit new hose if old hose leaking. Bleed brakes.
	Brake line fractured	Replace with new brake pipe. Bleed brakes
	Brake system unions loose	Check all unions in brake system and tighten as necessary. Bleed brakes.
Normal wear	Pad linings over 75% worn	Fit replacement pads.
Incorrect adjustment	Brakes badly out of adjustment	Jack up car and adjust brakes.
Brake pad renewal	New linings not yet bedded-in	Use brakes gently until springy pedal feeling leaves.
Excessive wear or damage	Brake discs badly worn or cracked	Fit new brake discs.
Lack of maintenance	Master cylinder securing nuts loose	Tighten master cylinder securing nuts. Ensure spring washers are fitted.
Leaks or bubbles in hydraulic system	Caliper leaking	Dismantle caliper, clean, fit new rubbers and bleed brakes.
	Master cylinder leaking (bubbles in master cylinder reservoir)	Dismantle master cylinder, clean and fit new rubbers and bleed brakes. Replace cylinder if internal walls scored.
	Brake pipe line or flexible hose leaking	Fit new pipeline or hose.
	Unions in brake system loose	Examine for leaks, tighten as necessary.
Lining type or condition	Pad shoe linings badly worn	Fit replacement brake shoes and linings.
	New pads recently fitted - not yet bedded-in	Use brakes gently until braking effort normal.
	Harder linings fitted than standard causing increase in pedal pressure	Remove pads and replace with normal units.
Oil or grease leaks	Linings and brake drums contaminated with oil, grease or hydraulic fluid	Rectify source of leak, clean brake drums, fit new linings.
Oil or grease leaks	Linings and discs contaminated with oil, grease or hydraulic fluid	Ascertain and rectify source of leak, clean discs, fit new pads
Lack of maintenance	Tyre pressures unequal	Check and inflate as necessary
	Radial ply tyres fitted at one end of car only	Fit radial ply tyres of the same make to all four wheels
	Brake caliper loose	Tighten backplate securing nuts and bolts
	Brake pads fitted incorrectly	Remove and fit correct way round.
	Different type of linings fitted at each wheel	Fit the pads specified by the manufacturers all round.
	Anchorage for front suspension or rear suspension loose	Tighten front and rear suspension pick-up points including spring anchorage.
	Brake discs badly worn, cracked or distorted	Fit new brake discs.
Incorrect adjustment	Brake shoes adjusted too tightly	Slacken off brake pad adjusters

Chapter 10 Electrical system

Contents

Specifications

Battery...	Lead acid 12 volt	
Earthed terminal...	Negative (−)	
Capacity at 20 hr rate		
Standard (a)...	38 amp/hr	Plates per cell 9
Optional (b)...	44 amp/hr	Plates per cell 9
Optional (c)...	55 amp/hr	Plates per cell 11
Optional (d)...	66 amp/hr	Plates per cell 13
Specific gravity charged	1.270 to 1.290 at a temperature of 25°C (77°F)	

Starter motor

System...	Inertia or pre-engaged
Type	Make:
A	Lucas M35G Inertia
B	Lucas M35GPE pre-engaged
C	Lucas M35JPE pre-engaged

	M35G (Inertia) or M35 GPE (Solenoid)	M35JPE (Solenoid)
Number of brushes	4	4
Brush material	Carbon	Carbon
Min. brush length..	0.35 in (9.0 mm)	0.38 in (9.5 mm)
Brush spring pressure	14.9 oz (420 gm)	17 oz (480 gms;)
Commutator min. diameter..	1.338 in (34 mm)	—
Armature endfloat	0.005–0.150 in	0.005–0.150 in
	(0.1–0.3 mm)	(0.1–0.3 mm)
Number of pinion gear teeth	10	10
Number of flywheel ring teeth..	110	135
Direction of rotation..	clockwise	clockwise
Max. output	620 watts	700 watts
Voltage	12	12

Dynamo   ... ...   Lucas C–40
Speed (ratio to engine) ... ...   1.5 : 1
Brush length ... ...   0.718 in (18.23 mm)
Maximum charge... ... ...   22 amps
Maximum output.. ... ...   264 watts
Fan belt tension ... ...   0.5 in (13 mm) total free movement

Control unit ... ...   Lucas RB340
Setting at 20°C (68°F) 3000 rpm Dynamo:
Setting... ... ...   14.7 – 15.3 volts
Checking ... ...   14.4 – 15.6 volts
Cut in voltage .. ..   12.6 – 13.4 volts
Drop off voltage ... ...   9.25 – 11.25 volts
Air gap settings:
Voltage and current regulator ... ...   0.045 – 0.049 in (1.14 – 1.24 mm)
Cut out relay ... ...   0.035 – 0.045 in (0.9 – 1.1 mm)

Alternator
Application ... ...   Type
1600 ... ...   15 ACR Possible alternative fitment 28 GI
1600 with heated backlight.. ... ...   17 ACR Possible alternative fitment 35 A–KI

Lucas specifications
System voltage..   12
Earth polarity... ... ...   Negative (–)
Rotation (drive end)... ... ...   Clockwise
Nominal rated output at 14.0 volts and 6,000 rpm ... ...   34 amps (15 ACR) or 36 amps (17 ACR)
Number of poles   12
Stator phases   3
Stator windings ... ...   Star
Max. continuous speed (rpm)   12,500
Stator winding resistance (ohms per phase)... ... ...   0.133
Rotor winding resistance (ohms at 20°C) ... ...   4.33 ± 5% (15 ACR) or 4.165 ± 5% (17 ACR)
Slip ring end brush length (new) ... ...   0.5 in (13 mm)
Brush spring tension... ... ...   7–10 oz (198–283 gms)
Regulating voltage (11 TR) volts 14.0–14.4

Bosch specifications
System voltage   12
Earth polarity .. ..   Negative (–)
Rotation (drive end)... ... ...   Clockwise
Max. run out of slip rings ... ...   0.001 in (0.3 mm)
Carbon brush min. length ... ...   0.563 in (14 mm)
Min. diameter of slip rings ... ...   1.25 in (31.5 mm)
Max. current ... ...   28 amps (28 GI) or 35 amps (35A–KI)
Speed ratio to engine ... ...   1 : 1.9

Fuse unit
Number of fuses   7
Additional fuses - head relay   2
Fuse rating   ... ...   8 amps

Windscreen wiper... ... ...   2 speed self parking
Horn.. ... ...   Single tone horn, 4.5 in (114.3 mm)

Bulbs

	Quantity	Description	Fitting
Headlight	2	Sealed or semi-sealed	Bayonet
Front direction indicator	2	32 CP	Bayonet
Rear direction indicator..	2	32 CP	Bayonet
Rear stop/tail	2	4/32 CP	Bayonet
Number plate - saloon	1	4 CP	Bayonet
- estate	2	4 CP	Bayonet
Reverse	2	32 CP	Bayonet
Interior - saloon	1	6 watt	Festoon
- estate	2	6 watt	Festoon
Instrument panel warning light..	4	1 CP	Wedge base
Instrument panel illumination...	8	1 CP	Bayonet

Torque wrench settings

	lb ft	kg m
Starter motor retaining bolts	20—25	2.76—3.46
Alternator fan pulley nut	25—29	3.5 —4.0
Alternator mounting bolts	15—18	2.07—2.49
Alternator mounting brackets...	20—25	2.76—3.46

1 General description

The electrical system is of the 12 volt negative earth type and the major components comprise a 12 volt battery of which the negative terminal is earthed; an alternator or dynamo which is driven from the crankshaft pulley; and a starter motor.

The battery supplies a steady amount of current for the ignition, lighting, and other electrical circuits and provides a reserve of electricity when the current consumed by the electrical equipment exceeds that being produced by the alternator or dynamo. The alternator has its own integral regulator which ensures a high output if the battery is in a low state of charge or the demand from the electrical equipment is high, and a low output if the battery is fully charged and there is little demand from the electrical equipment.

The dynamo is of the two brush type and works in conjunction with the voltage regulator and cut out. The dynamo is cooled by a multi-bladed fan mounted behind the dynamo pulley which blows air through cooling holes in the dynamo end brackets. The output from the dynamo is controlled by the regulator which ensures a high output if the battery is in a low state of charge or the demand from the electrical equipment high, and a low output if the battery is fully charged and there is little demand from the electrical equipment.

When fitting electrical accessories to cars with a negative earth system it is important, if they contain Silicone Diode or Transistors, that they are connected correctly, otherwise serious damage may result to the components concerned. Items such as radios, tape recorders, electronic ignition systems, electronic tachometer, automatic dipping etc., should all be checked for correct polarity.

It is important that the battery positive lead is always disconnected if the battery is to be boost charged when an alternator is fitted. Also if body repairs are to be carried out using electronic arc welding equipment the alternator must be disconnected otherwise serious damage can be caused to the more delicate instruments. When the battery has to be disconnected it must always be reconnected with the negative terminal earthed.

2 Battery - removal and replacement

1   The battery is on a carrier fitted to the left hand wing valance of the engine compartment. It should be removed once every three months for cleaning and testing. Disconnect the positive and then the negative leads from the battery terminals by undoing and removing the plated nuts and bolts. Note that two cables are attached to the positive terminal.

2   Unscrew and remove the bolt, and plain washer that secures the battery clamp plate to the carrier. Lift away the clamp plate. Carefully lift the battery from its carrier and hold it vertically to

ensure that none of the electrolyte is spilled.

3   Replacement is a direct reversal of this procedure. NOTE - Replace the negative lead before the positive lead and smear the terminals with vaseline to prevent corrosion; NEVER use an ordinary grease.

3 Battery - maintenance and inspection

1   Normal weekly battery maintenance consists of checking the electrolyte level of each cell to ensure that the separators are covered by ¼ inch (6.35 mm) of electrolyte. If the level has fallen, top up the battery using distilled water only. Do not overfill. If a battery is overfilled or any electrolyte spilled, immediately wipe away the excess as electrolyte attacks and corrodes any metal it comes into contact with very rapidly.

2   If the battery has the Auto-fil device as fitted on original production of the car, a special topping up sequence is required. The white balls in the Auto-fil battery are part of the automatic topping up device which ensures correct electrolyte level. The vent chamber should remain in position at all times except when topping up or taking specific gravity readings. If the electrolyte level in any of the cells is below the bottom of the filling tube top up as follows:

a)   Lift off the vent chamber cover.

b)   With the battery level, pour distilled water into the trough until all the filling tubes and trough are full.

c)   Immediately replace the cover to allow the water in the trough and tubes to flow into the cells. Each cell will automatically receive the correct amount of water.

3   As well as keeping the terminals clean and covered with petroleum jelly, the top of the battery, and especially the top of the cells, should be kept clean and dry. This helps prevent corrosion and ensures that the battery does not become partially discharged by leakage through dampness and dirt.

4   Once every three months remove the battery and inspect the battery securing bolts, the battery clamp plate, tray and battery leads for corrosion (white fluffy deposits on the metal) which are brittle to touch. If any corrosion is found clean off the deposit with ammonia and paint over the clean metal with an anti-rust/anti-acid paint.

5   At the same time inspect the battery case for cracks. If a crack is found, clean and plug it with one of the proprietary compounds marketed by such firms as Holts for this purpose. If leakage through the crack has been excessive then it will be necessary to refill the appropriate cell with fresh electrolyte as detailed later. Cracks are frequently caused to the top of the battery cases by pouring in distilled water in the middle of winter AFTER instead of BEFORE a run. This gives the water no chance to mix with the electrolyte and so the former freezes and splits the battery case.

6   If topping up the battery becomes excessive and the case has

been inspected for cracks that could cause leakage, but none are found, the battery is being overcharged and the voltage regulator will have to be checked and reset.

7   With the battery on the bench at the three monthly interval check, measure the specific gravity with a hydrometer to determine the state of charge and condition of the electrolyte. There should be very little variation between the different cells and, if a variation in excess of 0.025 is present it will be due to either:

a) Loss of electrolyte from the battery at sometime caused by spillage or a leak, resulting in a drop in the specific gravity of the electrolyte when the deficiency was replaced with distilled water instead of fresh electrolyte.

b) An internal short circuit caused by buckling of the plates or similar malady pointing to the likelihood of total battery failure in the near future.

8   The specific gravity of the electrolyte for fully charged conditions at the electrolyte temperature indicated, is listed in Table A. The specific gravity of a fully discharged battery at different temperatures of the electrolyte is given in Table B.

TABLE A

Specific gravity - battery fully charged
1.268 at 100°F or 38°C electrolyte temperature
1.272 at 90°F or 32°C   "   "
1.276 at 80°F or 27°C   "   "
1.280 at 70°F or 21°C   "   "
1.284 at 60°F or 16°C   "   "
1.288 at 50°F or 10°C   "   "
1.292 at 40°F or 4°C   "   "
1.296 at 30°F or 1.5°C   "   "

TABLE B

Specific gravity - battery fully discharged
1.098 at 100°F or 38°C electrolyte temperature
1.102 at 90°F or 32°C   "   "
1.106 at 80°F or 27°C   "   "
1.110 at 70°F or 21°C   "   "
1.114 at 60°F or 16°C   "   "
1.118 at 50°F or 10°C   "   "
1.122 at 40°F or 4°C   "   "
1.126 at 30°F or 1.5°C   "   "

4   Battery - electrolyte replenishment

1   If the battery is in a fully charged state and one of the cells maintains a specific gravity reading which is 0.025 or more lower than the others and a check of each cell has been made with a voltmeter to check for short circuits (a four to seven second test should give a steady reading of between 1.2 and 1.8 volts) then it is likely that electrolyte has been lost from the cell with the low reading at some time.

2   Top up the cell with a solution of 1 part sulphuric acid to 2.5 parts of water. If the cell is already fully topped up draw some electrolyte out of it with a pipette. The total capacity of each cell is 0.75 pint (0.426 litre).

3   When mixing the sulphuric acid and water NEVER ADD WATER TO SULPHURIC ACID - always pour the acid slowly onto the water in a glass container. IF WATER IS ADDED TO SULPHURIC ACID IT WILL EXPLODE.

4   Continue to top up the cell with the freshly made electrolyte and then recharge the battery and check the hydrometer readings.

5 Battery - charging

1   In winter time when heavy   demand is placed upon the battery such as when starting from cold, and when much electrical equipment is continually used, it is a good idea to occasionally have

the battery fully charged from an external source at the rate of 3.5 to 4 amps.

2   Continue to charge the battery at this rate until no further rise in specific gravity is noted over a four hour period.

3   Alternatively, a trickle charger, charging at the rate of 1.5 amps can be safety used overnight.

4   Specially rapid 'boost' charges which are claimed to restore the power of the battery in 1 to 2 hours are most dangerous as they can cause serious damage to the battery plates through over-heating.

5   While charging the battery note that the temperature of the electrolyte should never exceed 100°F.

6   Dynamo - routine maintenance

1   Routine maintenance consists of checking the tension of the fan belt, and lubricating the dynamo rear bearing once every 6,000 miles (10,000 Km) or 6 months.

2   The fan belt should be tight enough to ensure no slip between the belt and the dynamo pulley. If a shrieking noise comes from the engine when the unit is accelerated rapidly, it is likely that it is the fan belt slipping. On the other hand, the belt must not be too taut or the bearings will wear rapidly and cause dynamo failure or bearing seizure. Ideally 0.5 inch (12.7 mm) of total free movement should be available at the fan belt midway between the fan and the dynamo pulley.

3   To adjust the fan belt tension, slightly slacken the three dynamo retaining bolts, and swing the dynamo on the upper two bolts outwards to increase the tension, and inwards to lower it.

4   It is best to leave the bolts fairly tight so that considerable effort has to be used to move the dynamo, otherwise it is difficult to get the correct setting. If the dynamo is being moved outwards to increase the tension and the bolts have only been slackened a little, a long spanner acting as a lever placed behind the dynamo with the lower end resting against the block works very well in moving the dynamo outwards. Retighten the dynamo bolts and check that the dynamo pulley is correctly aligned with the fan belt.

5   Lubrication of the dynamo consists of inserting three drops of engine oil in the small oil hole in the centre of the commutator end bracket. This lubricates the rear bearing. The front bearing is pre-packed with grease and requires no attention.

7   Dynamo - testing in position

1   If, with the engine running, no charge comes from the dynamo, or the charge is very low, first check that the fan belt is in place and is not slipping. Then check that the leads from the control box to the dynamo are firmly attached and that one has not come loose from its terminal.

2   The lead from the larger 'D' terminal on the dynamo should be connected to the 'D' terminal on the control box, and similarly the 'F' terminals on the dynamo and control box should also be connected together. Check that this is so and that the leads have not been incorrectly fitted. Ensure that a good connection exists to control box terminal 'E'.

3   Make sure none of the electrical equipment (such as the lights or radio) is on and then pull the leads off the dynamo terminals marked 'D' and 'F'. Join the terminals together with a short length of wire.

4   Attach to the centre of this length of wire the negative clip of a 0 - 30 volts voltmeter and run the other clip to earth on the dynamo yoke. (Fig.10.2). Start the engine and allow it to idle at approximately 750 rpm. At this speed the dynamo should give a reading of about 15 volts on the voltmeter. There is no point in raising the engine speed above a fast idle as the reading will then be inaccurate.

5   If a reading of between 4 to 6 volts is recorded it is likely that the armature winding is at fault.

6   If no reading is recorded then check the brushes and brush connections. If a very low reading of approximately 1 volt is

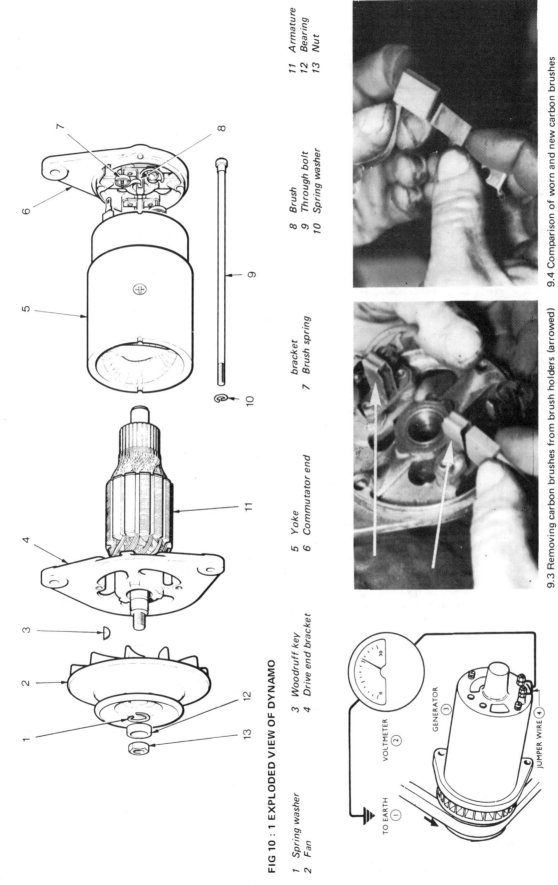

FIG 10 : 1 EXPLODED VIEW OF DYNAMO

1	Spring washer	3	Woodruff key	5	Yoke	7	Brush spring	8	Brush	11	Armature
2	Fan	4	Drive end bracket	6	Commutator end bracket			9	Through bolt	12	Bearing
								10	Spring washer	13	Nut

9.3 Removing carbon brushes from brush holders (arrowed)

9.4 Comparison of worn and new carbon brushes

FIG 10 : 2 DYNAMO OUTPUT TEST

observed then the field winding may be suspect.

7   If the voltmeter shows a good reading then with the temporary
link still in position connect both leads from the control box to
'D' and 'F' on the dynamo ('D' to 'D' and 'F' to 'F'). Release the
lead from the 'D' terminal at the control box end and clip one
lead from the voltmeter to the end of the cable, and the other
lead to a good earth. With the engine running at the same speed
as previously an identical voltage to that recorded at the dynamo
should be noted on the voltmeter. If the voltage is the same as
recorded at the dynamo then check the 'F' lead in similar fashion.
If both readings are the same as the dynamo then it will be necessary to test the control box.

8   Dynamo - removal and replacement

1   Slacken the two dynamo retaining bolts, and the nut on the
sliding link, and move the dynamo in towards the engine so that
the fan belt can be removed.
2   Disconnect the two leads from the dynamo terminals.
3   Remove the nut from the sliding link bolt, and remove the
two upper bolts. The dynamo is then free to be lifted away from
the engine.
4   Replacement is a reversal of the above procedure. Do not
finally tighten the retaining bolt and the nut on the sliding link
until the fan belt has been tensioned correctly (see Section 6 for
details).

9   Dynamo - dismantling and inspection

Before attempting to strip the dynamo fully, which is really
quite difficult to do well, make sure the individual parts are
available. Apart from changing the brushes it is probably cheaper
in the end to have an auto-electrician look at the dynamo or to
exchange it.
1   Mount the dynamo in a vice and unscrew and remove the two
through bolts from the commutator end bracket.
2   Mark the commutator end bracket and the dynamo casing so
that the end bracket can be replaced in its original position. Pull
the end bracket off the armature shaft. NOTE - Some versions of
the dynamo may have a raised pip on the edge of the casing. If
so, marking the end bracket and casing is unnecessary. A pip may
also be found on the drive end bracket at the opposite end of the
casing.
3   Lift the two brush springs and draw the brushes out of the
brush holders (photo).
4   Measure the brushes and if worn down to 0.281 inch (7.144
mm) or less unscrew the screws holding the brush leads to the
end bracket. Take off the brushes complete with leads. Old and
new brushes are compared in the photograph.
5   If no locating pip can be found, mark the drive end bracket
and the dynamo casing so that the drive end bracket can be replaced in its original position. Then pull the drive end bracket
complete with armature out of the casing.
6   Check the condition of the ball bearing in the drive end plate
by firmly holding the plate and noting if there is visible side
movement of the armature shaft in relation to the end plate. If
play is present the armature assembly must be separated from
the end plate. If the bearing is sound there is no need to carry
out the work described in the following two paragraphs.
7   Hold the armature in one hand (mount it carefully in a vice if
preferred), and undo the nut holding the pulley wheel and fan in
place. Pull off the pulley wheel and fan.
8   Next move the woodruff key from its slot in the armature
shaft and also the bearing locating ring.
9   Place the drive end bracket across the open jaws of a vice
with the armature downwards and gently tap the armature shaft
from the bearing in the end plate with the aid of a suitable drift.
10 Carefully inspect the armature and check it for open or short
circuited windings. It is a good indication of an open circuited
armature when the commutator segments are burnt. If the armature has short circuited the commutator segments will be very

badly burnt, and the overheated armature windings badly dis-
coloured. If open or short circuits are suspected then test by
substituting the suspect armature for a new one.
11 Check the resistance of the field coils. To do this, connect an
ohmmeter between the field terminals and the yoke and note the
reading on the ohmmeter which should be about 6 ohms. If the
ohmmeter reading is infinity this indicates an open circuit in the
field winding. If the ohmmeter reading is below 5 ohms this
indicates that one of the field coils is faulty and must be replaced.
12 Field coil replacement involves the use of a wheel operated
screwdriver, a soldering iron, caulking and riveting. This operation
is considered to be beyond the scope of most owners. Therefore,
if the field coils are at fault either purchase a rebuilt dynamo, or
take the casing to a Ford garage or electrical engineering works
for new field coils to be fitted.
13 Next check the condition of the commutator. If it is dirty and
blackened clean it with a petrol dampened rag. If the commutator
is in good condition the surface will be smooth and quite free
from pits or burnt areas, and the insulated segments clearly
defined.
14 If, after the commutator has been cleaned pits and burnt spots
are still present, wrap a strip of glass paper round the commutator
taking great care to move the commutator ¼ of a turn every ten
rubs till it is thoroughly clean.
15 Check the bush bearing in the commutator end bracket for
wear by noting if the armature spindle rocks when placed in it.
If worn it must be renewed.
16 The bush bearing can be removed by a suitable extractor or
by screwing an inch tap four or five times into the bush. The tap
complete with bush is then pulled out of the end bracket.
17 NOTE - The new bush bearing is of the porous bronze type
and it is essential that it is allowed to stand in SAE 30 engine oil
for 24 hours before fitment. In an emergency the bush can be
immersed in hot oil (100°C) for 2 hours.
18 Carefully fit the new bush into the end plate, pressing it in
until the end of the bearing is flush with the inner side of the end
plate. If available press the bush in with a smooth shouldered
mandrel the same diameter as the armature shaft.

10 Dynamo - repair and reassembly

1   To renew the ball bearing fitted to the drive end bracket,
using a pair of circlip pliers or screwdriver remove the circlip that
retains the bearing. Carefully press or drift out the old bearing.
2   Thoroughly clean the bearing housing and the new bearing and
pack with a high melting point grease.
3   Place the bearing on the end bracket and gently tap into place
with the aid of a suitable diameter drift.
4   Refit the drive end bracket to the armature shaft. Do not try
and force the bracket on but, with the aid of a suitable socket
abutting the bearing, tap the bearing in gently, so pulling the end
bracket down with it.
5   Slide the spacer up the shaft and refit the woodruff key.
6   Replace the fan and pulley wheel and then fit the spring
washer and nut and tighten the latter. The drive bracket end of
the dynamo is now fully assembled.
7   If the brushes are little worn and are to be used again, ensure
that they are placed in the same holders from which they were
removed. When refitting brushes, either new or old, check that
they move freely in their holders. If either brush sticks, clean with
a petrol moistened rag and if still stiff, lightly polish the sides of
the brush with a very fine file until the brush moves quite freely
in its holder.
8   Tighten the two retaining screws and washers which hold the
wire leads to the brushes in place.
9   It is far easier to slip the end piece with brushes over the commutator, if the brushes are raised in their holders and held
in this position by the pressure of the springs resting against
their flanks.
10 Refit the armature to the casing and then the commutator
end plate and screw up the two through bolts.

11 Control box - general description

The control box comprises the voltage regulator and the cut-out. The voltage regulator controls the output from the dynamo depending on the state of the battery and the demands of the electrical equipment and ensures that the battery is not overcharged. The cut-out is really an automatic switch and connects the dynamo to the battery when the dynamo is turning fast enough to produce a charge. Similarly it disconnects the battery from the dynamo when the engine is idling or stationary so that the battery does not discharge through the dynamo.

12 Cut-out and regulator contacts - maintenance

1   Every 12,000 miles (20,000 Km) check the cut-out and regulator contacts. If they are dirty or rough or burnt, place a piece of fine glass paper (DO NOT USE EMERY PAPER OR CARBORUNDUM PAPER) between the cut-out contacts, close them manually and drive the glass paper through several times.
2   Clean the regulator contacts in exactly the same way, but use emery or carborundum paper and not glass paper. Carefully clean sets of contacts from all traces of dust with a rag moistened in methylated spirits.

13 Regulator - adjustment

1   If the battery is being undercharged check that the fan belt is not slipping and the dynamo is producing its correct output. Check the battery lead terminals for secureness on their posts. If the battery is being overcharged this points fairly definitely to an incorrectly set regulator.
2   Checking the action of the regulator and cut-out is not difficult but must be completed as quickly as possible (NOT more than 30 seconds for each test), to avoid errors caused by heat of the coils. Essential test equipment comprises a 0-25 volt voltmeter and a moving coil −40 to +40 ammeter and an air temperature gauge. Also required is a special adjusting tool illustrated in Fig 10:5.
3   The regulator portion of the three bobbin type control box comprises the voltage regulator and the current regulator. The third bobbin at the 'B' terminal end is the cut-out.
4   To test the regulator take off the control box cover and slip a piece of thin card between the cut-out points. Connect the voltmeter between the control box terminal 'D' and a good earth. Start and run the engine at about 3,000 rpm when a steady reading on the voltmeter should be given as shown in Table A.

TABLE A
Air temperature	Type RB 340 Open circuit voltage
10°C or 50°F	14.9 to 15.5
20°C or 68°F	14.7 to 15.3
30°C or 86°F	14.5 to 15.1
40°C or 104°F	14.3 to 14.9

5   If the reading fluctuates by more than 0.3 volts then it is likely that the contact points are dirty. If the reading is steady but incorrect turn the voltage adjustment cam clockwise with the special Lucas tool to increase the setting, and anticlockwise to lower it.
6   Stop the engine and then restart it, gradually increasing the speed. If the voltage continues to rise with a rise in engine speed this indicates short circuited or fused points or a faulty magnet coil. If this is the case the only remedy is to fit an exchange control box.
7   The dynamo should be able to provide 22 amps at 3,000 rpm irrespective of the state of the battery.
8   To test the dynamo output take off the control box cover, and short out the voltage regulator contacts by holding them together with a bulldog clip.
9   Pull off the Lucas connectors from the control box terminals 'B' and connect an ammeter reading to 40 amps to the two cables

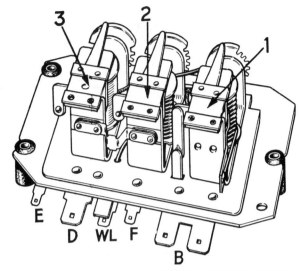

FIG 10 : 3 LUCAS RB340 CONTROL BOX WITH COVER REMOVED

1   Cut out   3   Voltage regulator
2   Current regulator

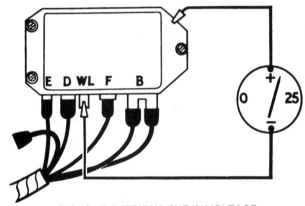

FIG 10 : 4 CHECKING CUT-IN VOLTAGE

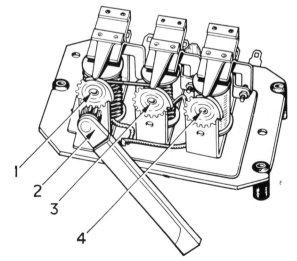

FIG 10 : 5 ADJUSTING THE CUT-OUT WITH SPECIAL LUCAS TOOL

1   Cut-out   3   Current regulator
2   Special tool   4   Voltage regulator

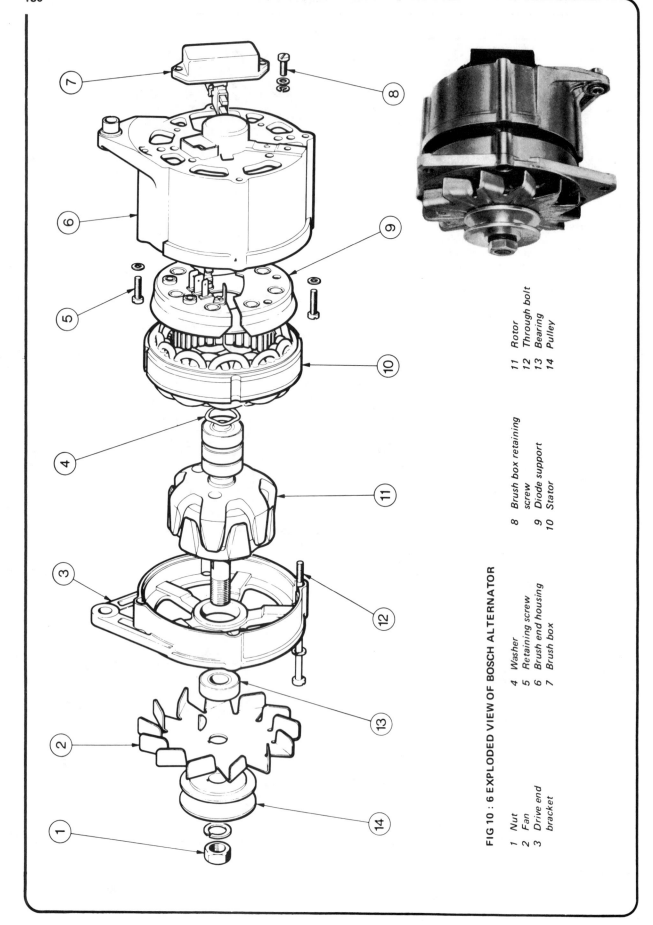

FIG 10 : 6 EXPLODED VIEW OF BOSCH ALTERNATOR

1 Nut
2 Fan
3 Drive end
    bracket

4 Washer
5 Retaining screw
6 Brush end housing
7 Brush box

8 Brush box retaining
    screw
9 Diode support
10 Stator

11 Rotor
12 Through bolt
13 Bearing
14 Pulley

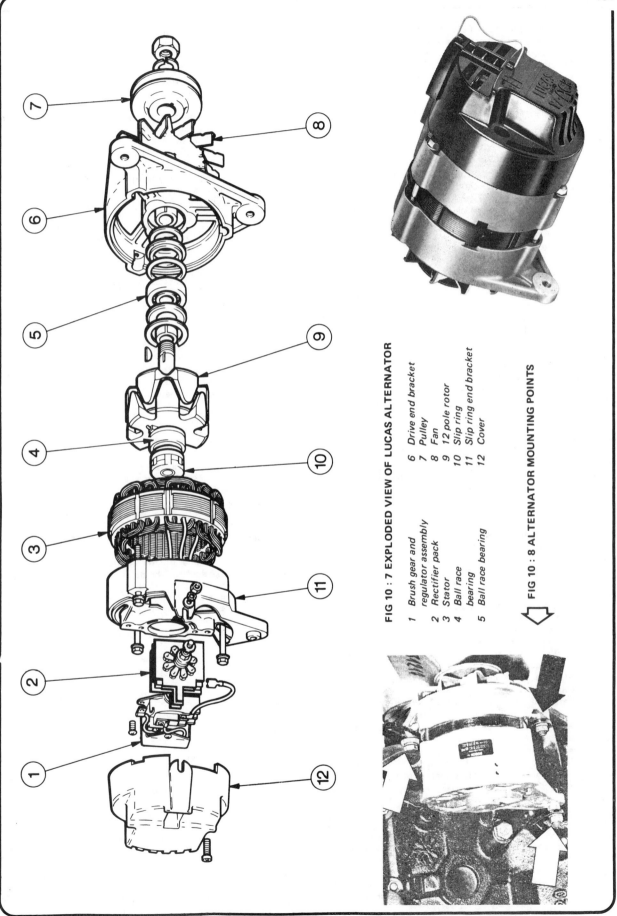

FIG 10 : 7 EXPLODED VIEW OF LUCAS ALTERNATOR

1 Brush gear and
  regulator assembly
2 Rectifier pack
3 Stator
4 Ball race
  bearing
5 Ball race bearing

6 Drive end bracket
7 Pulley
8 Fan
9 12 pole rotor
10 Slip ring
11 Slip ring end bracket
12 Cover

FIG 10 : 8 ALTERNATOR MOUNTING POINTS

just disconnected and to ONE of the 'B' Lucar connectors.

10 Turn on all the lights and other electrical equipment and start the engine. At about 3,000 rpm the dynamo should be giving between 21 and 23 amps as recorded on the ammeter. If the ammeter needle flickers it is likely that the contact points are dirty.

11 To increase the current turn the cap on top of the current regulator clockwise, and to lower it, anticlockwise.

14 Cut-out - adjustment

1   Check the voltage required to operate the cut-out by connecting a voltmeter between the control box terminal 'WL' and a good earth as shown in Fig.10:4. Remove the control box cover, start the engine and gradually increase its speed until the cut-outs close. This should occur when the reading is between 12.7 and 13.3 volts.

2   If the reading is outside these limits turn the adjusting cam on the cut-out relay a fraction at a time clockwise to raise the voltage cut-in point and anticlockwise to lower it.

3   To adjust the drop off voltage bend the fixed contact blade carefully. The adjustment to the cut-out should be completed within 20 seconds of starting the engine as otherwise heat build up from the shunt coil will affect the readings.

4   If the cut-out fails to work, clean the contacts, and, if there is still no response, renew the cut-out and regulator unit.

15 Alternator - general description

The main advantage of an alternator lies in its ability to provide a high charge at low revolutions.

An important feature of the alternator is a built in output control regulator, based on 'thick film' hybrid integrated micro-circuit technique, which results in the alternator being a self contained generating and control unit.

The system provides for direct connection of a charge indicator light, and eliminates the need for a field switching relay or warning light control unit, necessary with former systems.

The alternator is of rotating field, ventilated design. It comprises principally, a laminated stator on which is wound a star connected 3-phase output winding; a twelve pole rotor carrying the field windings - each end of the rotor shaft runs in ball race bearings which are lubricated for life; natural finish aluminium die cast end brackets, incorporated the mounting lugs; a rectifier pack for converting the AC out-put of the machine to DC for battery charging; and an output control regulator.

The rotor is belt driven from the engine through a pulley keyed to the rotor shaft. A pressed steel fan adjacent to the pulley draws cooling air through the machine. This fan forms an integral part of the alternator specifications. It has been designed to provide adequate air flow with a minimum of noise, and to withstand the high stresses associated with maximum speed. Rotation is clockwise viewed on the drive end. Maximum continuous rotor speed is 12,500 rpm.

Rectification of alternator output is achieved by six silicone diodes housed in a rectifier pack and connected as a 3-phase full-wave bridge. The rectifier pack is attached to the outer face of the slip ring end bracket and contains also three 'field' diodes; at normal operating speeds, rectified current from the stator output windings flows through these diodes to provide self-excitations of the rotor fields, via brushes bearing on face-type slip rings.

The slip rings are carried on a small diameter moulded drum attached to the rotor shaft outboard of the slip ring end bearing. The inner ring is centred on the rotor shaft axle, while the outer ring has a mean diameter of ¾ inch approximately. By keeping the mean diameter of the slip rings to a minimum, relative speeds between brushes and rings, and hence wear, are also minimal. The slip rings are connected to the rotor field winding by wires carried in grooves in the rotor shaft.

The brush gear is housed in a moulding screwed to the outside of the slip ring end bracket. This moulding thus encloses the slip

ring and brush gear assembly, and, together with the shielded bearing, protects the assembly against the entry of dust and moisture.

The regulator is set during manufacture and requires no further attention. Briefly, the 'thick' film regulator comprises resistors and conductors screen printed onto a 1 inch square alumina substrate. Mounted on the substrate are Lucas semi-conductor dice consisting of three transistors, a voltage reference diode and a field recirculation diode, and also two capacitors. The internal connections between these components and the substrate are made by special connectors. The whole assembly is 0.0625 in (1.588 mm) thick, and is housed in a recess in an aluminium heat sink, which is attached to the slip ring end bracket. Complete hermetic sealing is achieved by a silicone rubber encapsulant to provide environmental proctection.

Electrical connections to external circuits are brought out to Lucar connector blades, these being grouped to accept a moulded connector socket which ensures correct connections.

16 Alternator - routine maintenance

1   The equipment has been designed for the minimum amount of maintenance in service. The only items subject to wear being the brushes and bearings.

2   Brushes should be examined after about 75,000 miles (120,000 km) and renewed if necessary. The bearings are pre-packed with grease for life, and should not require further attention.

3   Check the fan belt every 3,000 miles (5,000 km) for correct adjustment which should be 0.5 in (12.70 mm) total movement at the centre of the run between the alternator and water pump pulleys.

17 Alternator - special procedures

Whenever the electrical system of the car is being attended to, or external means of starting the engine are used, there are certain precautions that must be taken otherwise serious and expensive damage can result.

1   Always make sure that the negative terminal of the battery is earthed. If the terminal connections are accidentally reversed or if the battery has been reverse charged the alternator diodes will burn out.

2   The output terminal on the alternator marked 'BAT' or B+ must never be earthed but should always be connected directly to the positive terminal of the battery.

3   Whenever the alternator is to be removed or when disconnecting the terminals of the alternator circuit always disconnect the battery earth terminal first.

4   The alternator must never be operated without the battery to alternator cable connected.

5   If the battery is to be charged by external means always disconnect both battery cables before the external charge is connected.

6   Should it be necessary to use a booster charger or booster battery to start the engine always double check that the negative cable is connected to negative terminal and the positive cable to positive terminal.

18 Alternator - removal and refitting

1   Disconnect the battery leads.

2   Note the terminal connections at the rear of the alternator and disconnect the plug or multi pin connector.

3   Undo and remove the alternator adjustment arm bolt, slacken the alternator mounting bolts and push the alternator inwards towards the engine. Lift away the fan belt from the pulley. (Fig. 10:8).

4   Remove the remaining two mounting bolts and carefully lift the alternator away from the car.

5   Take care not to knock or drop the alternator otherwise this

can cause irreparable damage.

6 Refitting the alternator is the reverse sequence to removal. Adjust the fan belt so that it has 0.5 in (12.70 mm) total movement at the centre of the run between the alternator and water pump pulleys.

19 Alternator - fault finding and repair

Due to the specialist knowledge and equipment required to test or service an alternator it is recommended that if the performance is suspect, the car be taken to an auto electrician who will have the facilities for such work. Because of this recommendation information is limited to the inspection and renewal of the brushes. Should the alternator not charge or the system be suspect the following points may be checked before seeking further assistance.

1 Check the fan belt tension as described in Section 16.
2 Check the battery as described in Section 3.
3 Check all electrical cable connections for cleanliness and security.

20 Alternator brushes (Lucas) - inspection, removal and refitting

1 Refer to Fig.10:7 and undo and remove the two screws that hold on the end cover. Lift away the end cover.
2 The brush holder moulding should be removed by undoing the two securing bolts and disconnecting the 'Lucar' connection to the diode plate.
3 With the brush holder moulding removed and the brush assemblies still in position, check that they protrude from the face of the moulding by at least 0.2 in (5 mm). Also check that when depressed, the spring pressure is 7 - 10 oz (198 - 283 gms) when the end of the brush is flush with the face of the brush moulding. To be done with any accuracy this requires a push type spring scale.
4 Should either of the foregoing requirements not be fulfilled the spring assemblies must be renewed. This can be done by simply removing the holding screws of each assembly and replacing them.
5 With the brush holder moulding removed the slip rings on the face end of the rotor are exposed. These can be cleaned with a petrol soaked cloth and any signs of burning may be removed very carefully with fine glass paper. On no account should any other abrasive be used or any attempt at machining be made.
6 When the brushes are refitted they should slide smoothly in their holders. Any sticking tendency may first be rectified by wiping with a petrol soaked cloth, or if this fails, by carefully polishing with a very fine file where any binding marks may appear.
7 Reassemble in the reverse order of dismantling. Make sure that leads which may have been connected to any of the screws are reconnected correctly.

21 Alternator brushes (Bosch) - inspection, removal and refitting

1 Undo and remove the two screws, spring and plain washers that secure the brush box to the rear of the brush end housing (see Fig.10:6). Lift away the brush box.
2 Check that the carbon brushes are able to slide smoothly in their guides without any sign of binding.
3 Measure the length of the brushes and if they have worn down to 0.35 in (9 mm) or less they must be renewed.
4 Hold the brush wire with a pair of engineer's pliers and unsolder it from the brush box. Lift away the two brushes.
5 Insert the new brushes and check to make sure that they are free to move in their guides. If they bind lightly polish with a very fine file.
6 Solder the brush wire ends to the brush box taking care that no solder is allowed to pass to the stranded wire.
7 Whenever new brushes are fitted new springs should be fitted.
8 Refitting the brush box is the reverse sequence to removal.

22 Starter motor - general description

The starter motor fitted to engines covered by this manual may be either of the inertia or pre-engaged type of Lucas manufacture.

The principle of operation of the inertia type starter motor is as follows: When the ignition is switched on and the switch operated, current flows from the battery to the starter motor solenoid switch which causes it to become energised. Its internal plunger moves inwards and closes an internal switch so allowing full starting current to flow from the battery to the starter motor. This causes a powerful magnetic field to be induced into the field coils which causes the armature to rotate.

Mounted on helical splines is the drive pinion which, because of the sudden rotation of the armature, is thrown forwards along the armature shaft and so into engagement with the flywheel ring gear. The engine crankshaft will then be rotated until the engine starts to operate on its own, and at this point, the drive pinion is thrown out of mesh with the flywheel ring gear.

The pre-engaged starter motor operates by a slightly different method using end face commutator brushes instead of brushes located on the side of the commutator.

The method of engagement on the pre-engaged starter differs considerably in that the drive pinion is brought into mesh with the starter ring gear before the main starter current is applied.

When the ignition is switched on, current flows from the battery to the solenoid which is mounted on the top of the starter motor. The plunger in the solenoid moves inwards so causing a centrally pivoted engagement lever to move in such a manner that the forked end pushes the drive pinion into mesh with the starter ring gear. When the solenoid plunger reaches the end of its travel, it closes an internal contact and fully starting current flows to the starter field coils. The armature is then able to rotate the crankshaft so starting the engine.

A special one way clutch is fitted to the starter drive pinion so that when the engine just fires and starts to operate on its own, it does not drive the starter motor.

23 Starter motor (inertia) - testing on engine

1 If the starter motor fails to operate, then check the condition of the battery by turning on the headlamps. If they glow brightly for several seconds and then gradually dim, the battery is in an uncharged condition.
2 If the headlamps continue to glow brightly and it is obvious that the battery is in good condition then check the tightness of the battery terminal to its connection on the body frame. Check the tightness of the connections at the relay switch and at the starter motor. Check the wiring with a voltmeter for breaks or shorts.
3 If the wiring is in order then check that the starter motor switch is operating. To do this, press the rubber covered button in the centre of the relay switch under the bonnet. If it is working, the starter motor will be heard to 'click', as it tries to rotate. Alternatively check it with a voltmeter.
4 If the battery is fully charged, the wiring in order, and the switch working but the starter motor fails to operate then it will have to be removed from the car for examination. Before this is done, however, ensure that the starter pinion has not jammed in mesh with the flywheel. Check by turning the square end of the armature shaft with a spanner. This will free the pinion if it is stuck in engagement with the flywheel teeth.

24 Starter motor (inertia) - removal and replacement

1 Disconnect the positive and then the negative terminals from the battery. Also disconnect the starter motor cable from the terminal on the starter motor end cover.
2 Undo and remove the nuts, bolts and spring washers which secure the starter motor to the clutch and flywheel housing. Lift

the starter motor away by manipulating the drive gear out from the ring gear area and then from the engine compartment.

3   Refitting is the reverse procedure to removal. Make sure that the starter motor cable, when secured in position by its terminal, does not touch any part of the body or power unit which could damage the insulation.

25 Starter motor (inertia) - dismantling and reassembly

1   With the starter motor on the bench, loosen the screw on the cover band and slip the cover band off. With a piece of wire bent into the shape of a hook, lift back each of the brush springs in turn and check the movement of the brushes in their holders by pulling on the flexible connectors. If the brushes are so worn that their faces do not rest against the commutator, or if the ends of the brush leads are exposed on their working face, they must be renewed.

2   If any of the brushes tend to stick in their holders then wash them with a petrol moistened cloth and, if necessary, lightly polish the sides of the brush with a very fine file until it moves quite freely in its holder.

3   If the surface of the commutator is dirty or blackened, clean it with a petrol dampened rag. Secure the starter motor in a vice and check it by connecting a heavy gauge cable between the starter motor terminal and a 12 volt battery.

4   Connect the cable from the other battery terminal to earth in the starter motor body. If the motor turns at high speed it is in good order.

5   If the starter motor still fails to function or if it is wished to renew the brushes then it is necessary to further dismantle the motor.

6   Lift the brush springs with the wire hook, and lift all four brushes out of their holders one at a time.

7   Remove the terminal nuts and washers from the terminal post on the commutator end bracket.

8   Unscrew the two through bolts which hold the end plates together and pull off the commutator end bracket. Also remove the driving end bracket which will come away complete with the armature.

9   At this stage, if the brushes are to be renewed, their flexible connectors must be unsoldered and the connectors of new brushes soldered in their place. Check that the new brushes move freely in their holders as detailed above. If cleaning the commutator with petrol fails to remove all the burnt areas and spots, then wrap a piece of glass paper round the commutator and rotate the armature.

10   If the commutator is very badly worn, remove the drive gear as detailed below. Then mount the armature in a lathe and with the lathe turning at high speed, take a very fine cut out of the commutator and finish the surface by polishing with glass paper. DO NOT UNDERCUT THE MICA INSULATORS BETWEEN THE COMMUTATOR SEGMENTS.

11   With the starter motor dismantled, test the four field coils for an open circuit. Connect a 12 volt battery with a 12 volt bulb in one of the leads between the field terminal post and the tapping point of the field coils to which the brushes are connected. An open circuit is proved by the bulb not lighting.

12   If the bulb lights, it does not necessarily mean that the field coils are in order, as there is a possibility that one of the coils will be earthed to the starter yoke or pole shoes. To check this, remove the lead from the brush connector and place it against a clean portion of the starter yoke. If the bulb lights, the field coils are earthing. Replacement of the field coils calls for the use of a wheel operated screwdriver, a soldering iron, caulking and riveting operations and is beyond the scope of the majority of owners. The starter yoke should be taken to a reputable electrical engineering works for new field coils to be fitted. Alternatively, purchase an exchange Lucas starter motor.

13   If the armature is damaged, this will be evident after visual inspection. Look for signs of burning, discolouration, and for conductors that have lifted away from the commutator.

14   With the starter motor stripped down, check the condition of

the bushes. They should be renewed when they are sufficiently worn to allow visible side movement of the armature shaft.

15   The old bushes are simply driven out with a suitable drift and the new bushes inserted by the same method. As the bushes are of the phosphor bronze type it is essential that they are allowed to stand in engine oil for at least 24 hours before fitment. Alternatively soak in oil at 100°C for 2 hours.

16   To dismantle the starter motor drive, first use a press to push the retainer clear of the circlip which can then be removed. Lift away the retainer and main spring.

17   Slide the remaining parts with a rotary action of the armature shaft.

18   It is most important that the drive gear is completely free from oil, grease and dirt. With the drive gear removed, clean all parts thoroughly in paraffin. UNDER NO CIRCUMSTANCES OIL the drive components. Lubrication of the drive components could easily cause the pinion to stick.

19   Reassembly of the starter motor drive is the reverse sequence to dismantling. Use a press to compress the spring and retainer sufficiently to allow a new circlip to be fitted to its groove on the shaft. Remove the drive from the press.

20   Reassembly of the starter motor is the reverse sequence to dismantling.

26 Starter motor (pre-engaged) - testing on engine

1   If the starter motor fails to operate then check the condition of the battery by turning on the headlamps. If they glow brightly for several seconds and then gradually dim the battery is in an uncharged condition.

2   If the headlights continue to glow brightly and it is obvious that the battery is in good condition, then check the tightness of the battery wiring connections (and in particular the earth lead from the battery terminal to its connection on the body frame). If the positive terminal on the battery becomes hot when an attempt is made to work the starter this is a sure sign of a poor connection on the battery terminal. To rectify remove the terminal, clean the mating faces thoroughly and reconnect. Check the connections on the rear of the starter solenoid. Check the wiring with a voltmeter or test lamp for breaks or shorts.

3   Test the continuity of the solenoid windings by connecting a test lamp circuit comprising a 12 volt battery and low wattage bulb between the 'STA' terminal and the solenoid body. If the two windings are in order the lamp will light. Next connect the test lamp (fitted with a high wattage bulb) between the solenoid main terminals. Energise the solenoid by applying a 12 volt supply between the unmarked Lucar terminal and the solenoid body. The solenoid should be heard to operate and the test bulb light. This indicates full closure of the solenoid contacts.

4   If the battery is fully charged, the wiring in order, the starter/ignition switch working and the starter motor still fails to operate then it will have to be removed from the car for examination. Before this is done ensure that the starter motor pinion has not jammed in mesh with the flywheel by engaging a gear (not automatic) and rocking the car to and fro. This should free the pinion if it is stuck in mesh with the flywheel teeth.

27 Starter motor (pre-engaged) - removal and replacement

Removal is basically identical to that for the inertia type starter motor with the exception of the cables at the rear of the solenoid. Note these connections and then detach the cable terminal from the solenoid.

28 Starter motor (pre-engaged type B) - dismantling and reassembly

1   Having removed the starter motor from the car the solenoid unit may be removed after disconnecting the link cable to the motor from the main terminal.

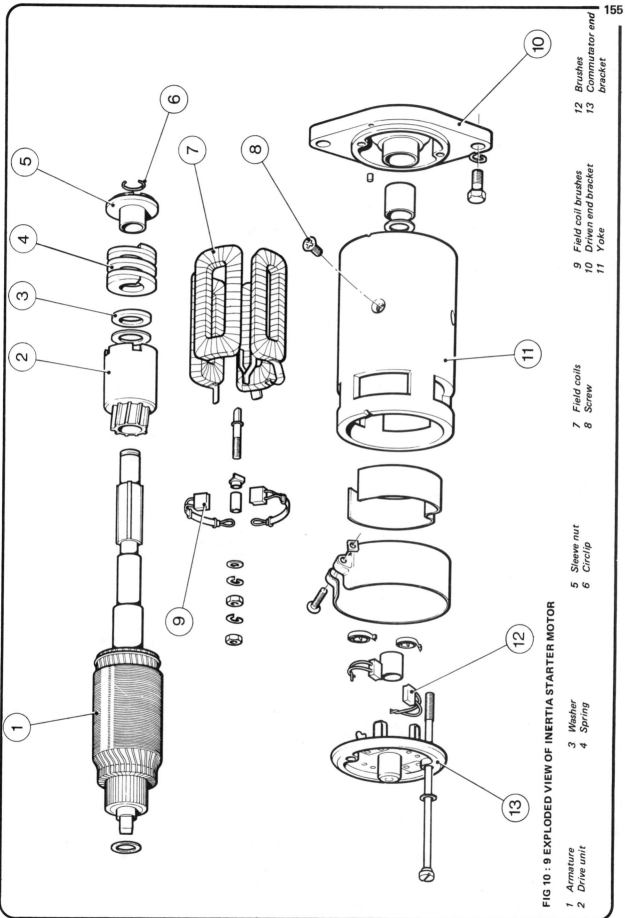

FIG 10 : 9 EXPLODED VIEW OF INERTIA STARTER MOTOR

1	Armature	3	Washer	5	Sleeve nut
2	Drive unit	4	Spring	6	Circlip

7	Field coils	9	Field coil brushes	12	Brushes
8	Screw	10	Driven end bracket	13	Commutator end bracket
		11	Yoke		

2 The solenoid plunger can be then disengaged from the lever in the drive end bracket.

3 Take off the brush gear band cover and lift out the two insulated brushes from their holders. Then remove the two through bolts which hold both end covers to the yoke.

4 Take the end bracket off the commutator and then slacken the locknut on the eccentric pivot bolt and unscrew the pivot bolt from the drive end bracket.

5 The armature can now be removed from the drive end bracket and the engaging lever after that. Note which way round the lever goes.

6 If the thrust collar on the armature shaft is depressed a small jump ring is revealed. Remove this and the collar and the drive unit can be drawn off. The driving pinion and clutch are a single assembly but can be separated from the grooved operating bush by pushing back the bush to reveal another jump ring. This can be removed, thus releasing the bush from the spindle.

7 Checking of the armature field coils and subsequently bearing bushes and brush gear should be carried out as described in Section 25.

8 Reassembly is a reversal of the removal procedure. All the components of the drive pin and bearings should be liberally greased on assembly. Adjustment of the eccentric pin may be necessary. The best way is to connect a 6 volt supply between the small terminal of the solenoid and the solenoid casing (Fig. 10:12). This will draw in the plunger as far as the springs, which the lower power will not permit it to overcome. If the pinion is held back lightly (towards the armature) to take up any lost motion, the gap between the end of the pinion and the thrust collar should be 0.010 inch (0.28 mm). The eccentric pin should be moved to achieve this. The arrow head on the pivot bolt should point only towards the arrowed arc marked in the bracket, as the adjustment range is through 180° only.

29 Starter motor bushes (pre-engaged Type B) - inspection, removal and replacement

1 With the starter motor stripped down check the condition of the bushes. They should be renewed when they are sufficiently worn to allow visible side movement of the armature shaft.

2 The old bushes are simply driven out with a suitable drift and the new bushes inserted by the same method. As the bushes are of the phosphor bronze type, it is essential that they are allowed to stand in Castrol GTX for at least 24 hours before fitment. If time does not allow this, place the bushes in oil at 100°C (212°F) for 2 hours.

30 Starter motor (pre-engaged Type C) - dismantling and reassembly

1 With the starter motor on the bench, loosen the screw on the cover band and slip the cover band off. With a piece of bent wire in the shape of a hook lift back each of the brush springs in turn and check the movement of the brushes in their holders by pulling on the flexible connectors. If the brushes are so worn that their faces do not rest against the commutator or if the ends of the brush leads are exposed on their working faces they must be renewed.

2 If any of the brushes tend to stick in their holders then wipe them with a petrol moistened cloth and if necessary, lightly polish the sides of the brushes with a very fine file, until the brushes move quite freely in their holders.

3 Undo the large nut holding the heavy duty cable to the lower solenoid terminal (marked STA). Remove the nut, spring washer and cable connector.

4 Undo and remove the nuts and spring washers that secure the solenoid to the drive end bracket. Carefully withdraw the solenoid from its mounting. It will be observed that the plunger will be left attached to the engagement lever.

5 Lift the plunger return spring from the plunger and put in a safe place. Disengage the end of the plunger from the top of the engagement lever.

6 Undo the locknut securing the eccentric pivot pin to the starter motor body. This will be found towards the top of the drive end bracket. Unscrew the eccentric pivot pin.

7 Unscrew and remove the two through bolts and spring washers from the rear of the commutator end bracket which will release the yoke from the end bracket. With a scriber mark the relative position of the drive end bracket and yoke. To separate the two parts, using a soft faced hammer tap on the end bracket whilst holding the yoke.

8 Pull the commutator end bracket off the rear of the yoke. Lift off the steel thrust washer and fibre thrust washer from the spigot on the end of the commutator (if these washers are fitted). Also lift away the rubber grommet located at the top of the yoke and commutator end bracket.

9 Carefully withdraw the armature with the drive pinion assembly and engagement lever from the fixing bracket.

10 If it is necessary to dismantle the starter pinion drive, place the armature between soft jaws in a bench vice and using a universal puller draw the jump ring from the armature.

11 Tap down the circlip retaining cover and remove the washer, circlip and cover. The pinion assembly may now be removed.

12 Draw the actuating bush towards the pinion so as to expose the circlip, and remove the circlip, bush, spring and large washer. It is very important that the one way clutch is not gripped in the vice at the point adjacent to the pinion whilst this is being carried out otherwise the clutch will be damaged.

13 The drive pinion and one way clutch are serviced as a complete assembly so if one part is worn or damaged a new assembly must be obtained.

14 At this stage if the brushes are to be renewed, their flexible connectors must be cut leaving 0.25 in (7 mm) attached to the field coils. Discard the old brushes. Solder new brushes to the flexible connector stubs. Check that the new brushes move freely in their holders as described in paragraph 2.

15 If cleaning the commutator with petrol fails to remove all the burnt areas and spots, then wrap a piece of glass paper round the commutator and rotate the armature.

16 If the commutator is very badly worn remove the drive gear, if still in place on the armature, and mount the armature in a lathe. With the lathe turning at high speed take a very fine cut out of the commutator and finish the surface by polishing with glass paper. DO NOT UNDERCUT THE MICA INSULATORS BETWEEN THE COMMUTATOR SEGMENTS.

17 With the starter motor dismantled test the four field coils for an open circuit. Connect a 12 volt battery with a 12 volt bulb in one of the leads between the field terminal post and the tapping point of the field coils to which the brushes are connected. An open circuit is proved by the bulb not lighting.

18 If the bulb lights, it does not necessarily mean that the field coils are in order as there is a possibility that one of the coils will be earthed to the starter yoke or pole shoes. To check this, remove the lead from the brush connector and place it against a clean portion of the starter yoke. If the bulb lights the field coils are earthing. Replacement of the field coils calls for the use of a wheel operated screwdriver, a soldering iron, caulking and riveting operations and is beyond the scope of the majority of owners. The starter yoke should be taken to a reputable electrical engineering works for new field coils to be fitted. Alternatively, purchase an exchange Lucas starter motor.

19 If the armature is damaged this will be evident after visual inspection. Look for signs of burning, discolouration, and for conductors that have lifted away from the commutator.

20 Reassembly is the reverse sequence to dismantling but it will be necessary to adjust the pinion movement.

21 Once the starter motor has been completely reassembled, test for correct operation by securing it in a vice and connecting a heavy gauge cable between the starter motor solenoid lower terminal and a 12 volt battery. Connect the cable from the other battery terminal to earth on the starter motor body. If the motor turns at high speed it is in good order.

22 Disconnect the heavy duty cable from the lower terminal marked 'STA' and by referring to Fig.10:12 connect a 6 volt

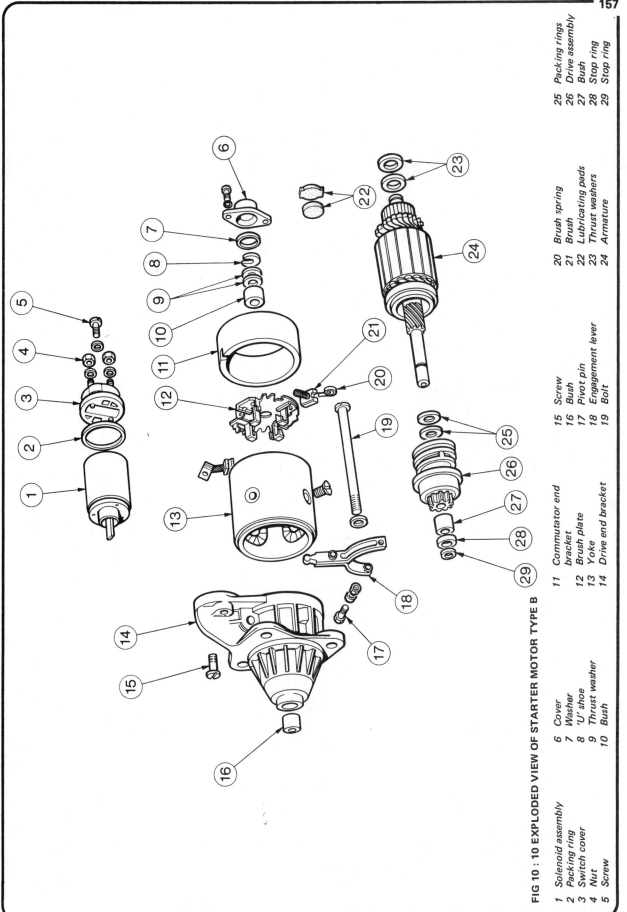

FIG 10 : 10 EXPLODED VIEW OF STARTER MOTOR TYPE B

1 Solenoid assembly
2 Packing ring
3 Switch cover
4 Nut
5 Screw

6 Cover
7 Washer
8 'U' shoe
9 Thrust washer
10 Bush

11 Commutator end bracket
12 Brush plate
13 Yoke
14 Drive end bracket

15 Screw
16 Bush
17 Pivot pin
18 Engagement lever
19 Bolt

20 Brush spring
21 Brush
22 Lubricating pads
23 Thrust washers
24 Armature

25 Packing rings
26 Drive assembly
27 Bush
28 Stop ring
29 Stop ring

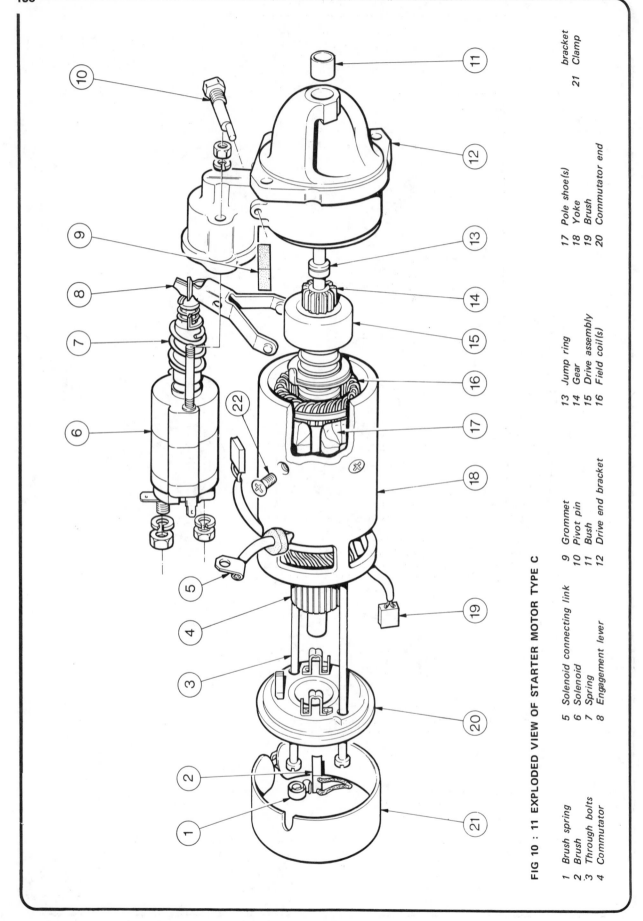

FIG 10 : 11 EXPLODED VIEW OF STARTER MOTOR TYPE C

1 Brush spring	5 Solenoid connecting link	9 Grommet	13 Jump ring	17 Pole shoe(s)
2 Brush	6 Solenoid	10 Pivot pin	14 Gear	18 Yoke
3 Through bolts	7 Spring	11 Bush	15 Drive assembly	19 Brush
4 Commutator	8 Engagement lever	12 Drive end bracket	16 Field coil(s)	20 Commutator end bracket
				21 Clamp

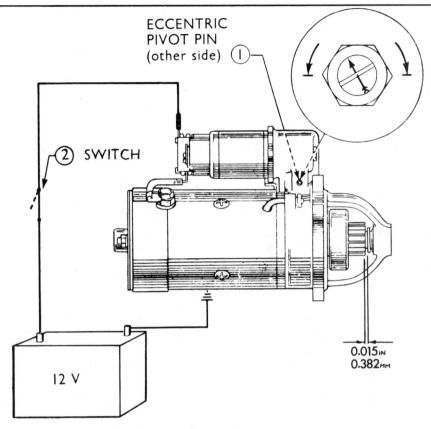

FIG 10 : 12 SETTING ECCENTRIC PIN

battery to the starter motor as shown. Do not make the final battery connection yet.

23 Undo but do not remove the eccentric pin locknut on the side of the fixing bracket. Then screw the eccentric pin in fully.

24 Now make the final battery connection so energising the solenoid full in winding and hold in winding which will, via the engaging lever move the pinion to its engagement position.

25 Refer to Fig 10.12 and locate a feeler gauge between the pinion and thrust washer. With the fingers gently press the pinion towards the motor, so that any lost motion in the linkage may be taken up.

26 With a screwdriver rotate the eccentric pin until the gap is between 0.005–.015 in (0.127–0.382 mm). Finally tighten the eccentric pin locknut.

31 Flasher circuit - fault tracing and rectification

1 The actual flasher unit consists of a small alloy container positioned at the rear of the instrument panel.

2 If the flasher unit works twice as fast as usual when indicating either right or left turns, this is an indication that there is a broken filament in the front or rear indicator bulb on the side operating quickly.

3 If the external flashers are working but the internal flasher warning light has ceased to function, check the filament of the warning bulb and replace as necessary.

4 With the aid of the wiring diagram check all the flasher circuit connections if a flasher bulb is sound but does not work.

5 With the ignition switched on check that the current is reaching the flasher unit by connecting a voltmeter between the 'plus' terminal and earth. If it is found that current is reaching the unit, connect the two flasher unit terminals together and operate the direction indicator switch. If one of the flasher warning lights comes on this proves that the flasher unit itself is at fault and must be replaced as it is not possible to dismantle and repair it.

32 Windscreen wiper mechanism - maintenance

1 Renew the windscreen wiper blades at intervals of 12,000 miles (20,000 km) or 12 months, or more frequently if found necessary.

2 The washer round the wheelbox spindle can be lubricated with several drops of glycerine every 6,000 miles (10,000 km). The windscreen wiper linkage pivots may be lubricated with a little Castrol GTX.

33 Windscreen wiper blades - removal and replacement

1 Lift the wiper arm away from the windscreen and remove the old blade by turning it in towards the arm and then disengage the arm from the slot in the blade.

2 To fit a new blade, slide the end of the wiper arm into the slotted spring fastening in the centre of the blade. Push the blade firmly onto the arm until the raised portion of the arm is fully home in the hole in the blade.

34 Windscreen wiper arms - removal and replacement

1 Before removing a wiper arm, turn the windscreen wiper switch on and off to ensure the arms are in their normal parked position parallel with the bottom of the windscreen.

2 To remove the arm, pivot the arm back and pull the wiper arm head off the splined drive. If the arm proves difficult to remove a screwdriver with a long blade can be used to lever the wiper arm head off the spline. Care must be taken not to damage the splines.

3 When replacing an arm position it so it is in the correct relative parked position and then press the arm head onto the

splined drive until it is fully home on the splines.

35 Windscreen wiper mechanism - fault diagnosis and rectification

1   Should the windscreen wipers fail, or work very slowly, then check the terminals on the motor for loose connections and make sure the insulation of all wiring has not been damaged thus causing a short circuit. If this is in order then check the current the motor is taking by connecting an ammeter in the circuit and turning on the wiper switch. Consumption should be between 2.3 and 3.1 amps.
2   If no current is passing through the motor, check that the switch is operating correctly.
3   If the wiper motor takes a very high current check the wiper blades for freedom of movement. If this is satisfactory check the gearbox cover and gear assembly for damage.
4   If the motor takes a very low current ensure that the battery is fully charged. Check the brush gear and ensure the brushes are bearing on the commutator. If not, check the brushes for freedom of movement and, if necessary, renew the tension springs. If the brushes are very worn they should be replaced with new ones. Check the armature by substitution if this part is suspect.

36 Windscreen wiper linkage - removal and replacement

1   For safety reasons disconnect the battery. Undo and remove the fixing screw and unclip the plastic wiper motor cover. Lift away the cover.
2   Undo and remove the bolts that secure the wiper assembly mounting bracket to the scuttle panel. Note that one of the bolts retains the earth wire terminal. Detach the multi pin plug from the motor.
3   Carefully lever off the wiper system linkage from the windscreen wiper motor. Undo and remove the three bolts and spring washers that secure the motor to the bracket assembly.
4   Undo and remove the bolts that secure the heater unit and draw the heater unit box to one side just sufficiently for the wiper motor and bracket assembly to be withdrawn.
5   Refer to Section 34 and remove the wiper arms and blades.
6   Carefully unscrew the spindle nuts and washers and, working within the engine compartment, lift away the wiper linkage.
7   Refitting is the reverse sequence to removal. Lubricate all moving parts with the exception of the wiper spindles with Castrol GTX. Lubricate the wiper spindles with three drops of glycerine.

37 Windscreen wiper motor - removal and replacement

1   Refer to Section 36 and follow the sequence described in paragraphs 1 to 3 inclusive.
2   Undo and remove the bolts that secure the heater hose and pull the heater box to one side. Lift away the windscreen wiper motor from the mounting bracket and the operating arm from the motor.
3   Refitting the windscreen wiper motor is the reverse sequence to removal.

38 Windscreen wiper motor - dismantling, inspection and reassembly

1   Refer to Fig.10:14 and undo and remove the two crosshead screws that secure the gearbox cover plate to the gearbox.
2   Undo and remove the nut that secures the operating arm to the gear shaft. Lift away the operating arm, wave and plain washer.
3   Release the spring clips that secure the case and armature to the gearbox. Lift away the case and armature.
4   Wipe away all the grease from inside the gearbox and using a pair of circlip pliers remove the circlip that secures the gear to

the shaft. Separate the gear from the shaft.
5   Undo and remove the screw that secures the brush mounting plate, detach the wiring loom plug and remove the brushes.
6   Clean all parts and then inspect the gears and brushes for wear and damage. Refit the spindle and check for wear in its bush in the gearbox body. Obtain new parts as necessary.
7   Reassembly is the reverse sequence to dismantling. Pack the gearbox with Castrol LM Grease.

39 Horn - fault tracing and rectification

1   If the horn works badly or fails completely, first check the wiring leading to the horn for short circuits and loose connections. Also check that the horn is firmly secured and that there is nothing lying on the horn body.
2   Using a test lamp check the wiring to the number 5 fuse on the fusebox located in the engine compartment. Check that the fuse has not blown.
3   If the fault is an internal one it will be necessary to obtain a replacement horn.
4   To remove the horn disconnect the battery and remove the radiator grille as described in Chapter 12/32.
5   Detach the lead at the rear of the horn and then undo and remove the retaining bolt, spring, horn bracket and star washer.
6   Refitting the horn is the reverse sequence to removal.

40 Headlight assembly - removal and replacement

1   Open the bonnet and for safety reasons disconnect the battery.
2   Undo and remove the nine crosshead screws that secure the radiator grille to the front body panels. Lift away the radiator grille.
3   **Sealed beam unit.** Undo and remove the three inner bezel retaining screws that secure the sealed beam unit to the backplate, (photo).
4   Carefully lift away the bezel and sealed beam unit (photo). Detach the plug from the rear of the sealed beam unit (photo). Note: On some models the side light bulb holder is attached to the plug.
5   Fit the plug to the new sealed beam unit and refit the unit and radiator grille, this being the reverse sequence to removal.
6   **Semi-sealed beam unit.** Detach the bulb holder from the lens by rotating in an anti-clockwise direction and pulling away the bulb holder. Lift away the bulb as shown in Fig.10:15.
7   Refitting the new bulb and the radiator grille is the reverse sequence to removal.

41 Headlight - alignment

1   It is always advisable to have the headlights aligned using special optical beam setting equipment but if this is not available the following procedure may be used for single headlight units:
2   Position the car on level ground 1 ft (3 m) in front of a dark wall or board. The wall or board must be at right angles to the centre line of the car.
3   Draw a vertical line on the board in line with the centre line of the car (Fig.10:15)
4   Bounce the car on its suspension to ensure correct settlement and then measure the height between the ground and the centre of the headlights.
5   Draw a horizontal line across the board at this measured height. On this horizontal line mark a cross either side of the vertical line equal to half the distance between the centres of the two headlights. Switch the headlights on to main beam.
6   By careful adjustment of the two plastic adjusters at the rear of the headlight assembly (accessible from within the engine compartment) set the centres of each beam onto the crosses which have been previously marked on the board or wall.
7   Bounce the car once more and recheck the setting. Now lower the beams by about 1.5 in (38.1 mm) so as not to dazzle other

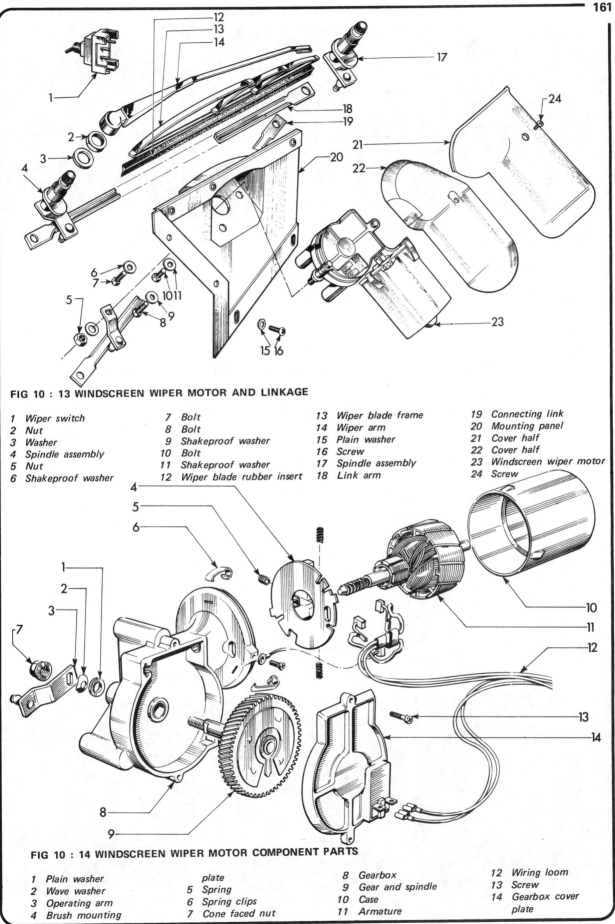

FIG 10 : 13 WINDSCREEN WIPER MOTOR AND LINKAGE

1 Wiper switch	7 Bolt	13 Wiper blade frame	19 Connecting link
2 Nut	8 Bolt	14 Wiper arm	20 Mounting panel
3 Washer	9 Shakeproof washer	15 Plain washer	21 Cover half
4 Spindle assembly	10 Bolt	16 Screw	22 Cover half
5 Nut	11 Shakeproof washer	17 Spindle assembly	23 Windscreen wiper motor
6 Shakeproof washer	12 Wiper blade rubber insert	18 Link arm	24 Screw

FIG 10 : 14 WINDSCREEN WIPER MOTOR COMPONENT PARTS

1 Plain washer	plate	8 Gearbox	12 Wiring loom
2 Wave washer	5 Spring	9 Gear and spindle	13 Screw
3 Operating arm	6 Spring clips	10 Case	14 Gearbox cover
4 Brush mounting	7 Cone faced nut	11 Armature	plate

162

40.3. Three inner bezel retaining screws removal

40.4A. Lifting away inner bezel

40.4B. Removal of plug from rear of sealed beam unit

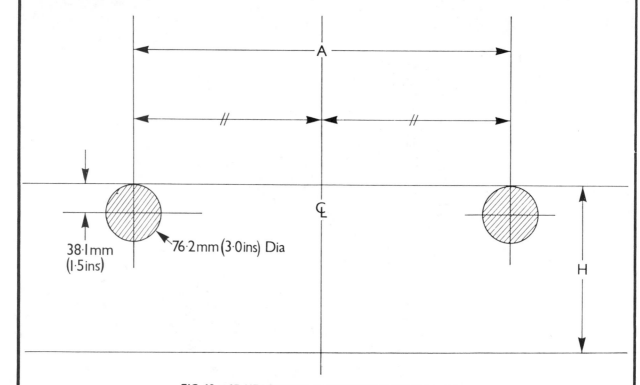

38·1mm (1·5ins)

76·2mm (3·0ins) Dia

A

C$_L$

H

FIG 10 : 15 HEADLIGHT ALIGNMENT SETTING MARK POSITIONS
NOTE: CENTRE OF MAIN BEAM BRIGHT SPOT TO BE WITHIN THE 3 IN. (76.2 MM) DIAMETER SHADED AREA

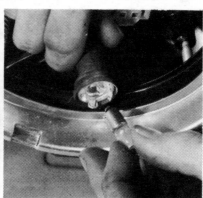

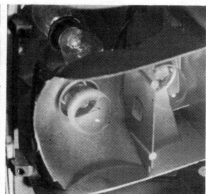

42.2A. Side light bulb holder removal

42.2B. Side light bulb removal

44.5. Three bulbs are used in the light cluster

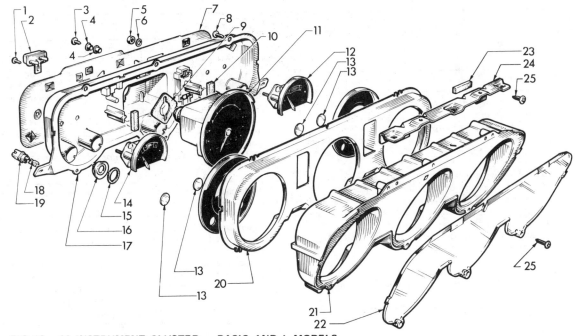

FIG 10 : 16 INSTRUMENT CLUSTER – BASIC AND L MODELS

1 Screw	7 Printed circuit	13 Lens	19 Bulb holder
2 Voltage regulator	8 Screw	14 Fuel gauge	20 Cluster front cover
3 Screw	9 Gasket	15 Washer	21 Cluster frontice
4 Shaped bush	10 Foam pad	16 Light holder	22 Cluster glass
5 Nut	11 Speedometer	17 Cluster body	23 Packing
6 Spring washer	12 Temperature gauge	18 Bulb capless type	24 Cluster top rail
			25 Screw

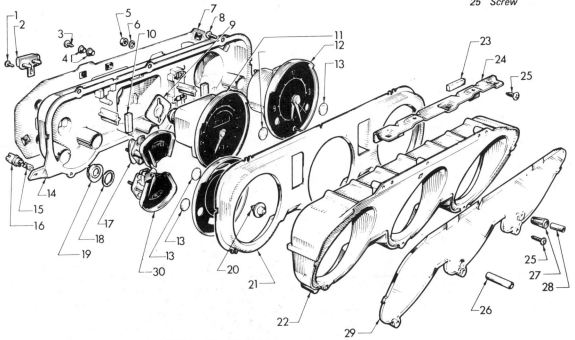

FIG 10 : 17 INSTRUMENT CLUSTER - XL MODELS

1 Screw	9 Gasket	17 Fuel gauge	25 Screw
2 Voltage regulator	10 Foam pad	18 Washer	26 Trip reset knob
3 Screw	11 Speedometer	19 Light holder	27 Tapered insert
4 Shaped bush	12 Clock	20 Shaped clip	28 Clock winder knob
5 Nut	13 Lens	21 Cluster front cover	29 Cluster glass
6 Spring washer	14 Cluster body	22 Cluster frontice	30 Temperature gauge
7 Printed circuit	15 Bulb - capless type	23 Packing	
8 Screw	16 Bulb holder	24 Cluster top rail	

road users and to compensate for those occasions when there is weight in the back of the car.

42 Side light bulb - removal and refitting

1 Models fitted with 'sealed beam' type headlights have the sidelight bulb mounted on the connecting plug at the rear of the sealed beam unit. To remove the bulb is a simple matter of pulling away from the connecting plug once the headlight unit has been removed as described in Section 40. Refitting is a reversal of removal.

2 Models fitted with 'semi-sealed' type headlights have the sidelight bulb inserted in the rear of the outer reflector and lens assembly. To remove the bulb refer to Section 40 and remove the headlight unit and then detach the bulb holder from the reflector. Press in and turn the bulb in an anti-clockwise direction to release the bayonet fixing and lift away the bulb. Refitting is a reversal of the removal procedure (photos).

43 Front direction indicator light assembly and bulb - removal and replacement

1 Working under the wheel arch disconnect the electric cable to the light assembly.

2 Undo and remove the retaining nut and push the light assembly forwards away from its location in the front wing.

3 Refitting is the reverse sequence to removal.

4 If it is necessary to only remove the bulb, undo and remove the two crosshead screws that secure the lens to the light body. Lift away the lens.

5 To detach the bulb, press in and turn in an anticlockwise direction to release the bayonet fixing and lift away the bulb. Refitting the bulb and lens is the reverse sequence to removal. Make sure that the lens gasket is correctly fitted to prevent dirt and water ingress.

44 Rear direction indicator, stop and tail light assembly and bulb - removal and replacement

1 Open the luggage compartment and detach the cables from the rear of the unit noting the location of the cable.

2 Undo and remove the nuts that secure the rear light assembly to the rear wing. Lift away the rear light assembly.

3 Refitting is the reverse sequence to removal.

4 Should it be necessary to fit a new bulb, undo and remove the four crosshead screws that secure the lens to the light body. Lift away the lens and its sealing washer.

5 Remove the applicable bulb by pressing and turning it in an anti-clockwise direction (photo).

6 Refitting the bulb and lens is the reverse sequence to removal. Take care to ensure that the lens sealing washer is correctly fitted to prevent dirt and water ingress.

45 Rear number plate light assembly and bulb - removal and replacement

1 Undo and remove the two crosshead screws that secure the light assembly to the bumper, or if screws are not used, simply unclip the complete light assembly. Detach the electric cable and lift away the lamp.

2 Undo and remove the two crosshead screws that secure the lens to the assembly. Lift away the lens and sealing washer (early type only).

3 To remove the bulb, press and turn in an anti-clockwise direction or unclip the bulb retainer, invert the light assembly and recover the bulb.

4 Refitting the bulb, lens and assembly is the reverse sequence to removal. Take care to ensure that the lens sealing washer is correctly fitted to prevent dirt and water ingress.

46 Interior light - removal and replacement

1 Very carefully pull the interior light assembly from its location in the roof panel.

2 Disconnect the wires from the terminal connectors and lift away the light unit.

3 If the bulb requires renewal either lift the bulb from its clips (festoon type) or press and turn in an anti-clockwise direction (bayonet cap type).

4 Refitting the interior light is the reverse sequence to removal.

47 Instrument cluster and printed circuit - removal and replacement

1 Open the bonnet and for safety reasons disconnect the battery.

2 If a manual choke control is fitted pull off the choke control knob.

3 Undo and remove the screw and annulus that holds the two halves of the steering column shroud together. Using a knife split the two halves of the column shroud and lift away.

4 Undo and remove the crosshead screws that secure the facia panel to the instrument panel. Lift away the facia panel.

5 Undo and remove the screws that secure the instrument cluster to the instrument panel. Draw the cluster away from the instrument panel by a sufficient amount to give access to the car. Detach the wiring loom multi pin connector and also the speedometer drive cable by depressing the knurled pad on the speedometer cable ferrule and pull the cable from the speedometer head. Lift away the instrument cluster.

6 Remove the eight illuminating bulbs and voltage regulator unit (retained by one crosshead screw) from the rear of the instrument cluster.

7 Undo and remove the instrument securing nuts and very carefully detach the printed circuit.

8 Refitting the printed circuit, instrument cluster and facia is the reverse sequence to removal.

48 Instrument cluster glass or bulb - removal and replacement

Glass:

Refer to Section 47 and remove the instrument cluster as described in paragraphs 1 to 5 inclusive. The glass may be removed once the screws have been removed. If a clock is fitted the control knob must be removed. Refitting the glass is the reverse sequence to removal.

Bulb:

Refer to Section 47 and remove the instrument cluster and relevant bulb as described in paragraphs 1 to 6 inclusive. Refitting is the reverse sequence to removal.

49 Voltage regulator - removal and replacement

1 Refer to Section 47 and remove the instrument cluster as described in paragraphs 1 to 5 inclusive. Undo and remove the crosshead screw that secures the voltage regulator to the cluster and lift away the regulator.

2 Refitting the voltage regulator is the reverse sequence to removal.

50 Speedometer head - removal and replacement

1 Refer to Section 47 and remove the instrument cluster as described in paragraphs 1 to 6.

2 Undo and remove the crosshead screws that secure the speedometer head to the instrument cluster. Lift away the speedometer head.

3 Refitting the speedometer head is the reverse sequence to removal.

51 Speedometer inner and outer cable - removal and replacement

1 Working under the car using a pair of circlip pliers remove the circlip that secures the speedometer cable to the gearbox extension housing. If a circlip is not used on the speedometer cable, undo and remove the bolt, and spring washer that secures the forked plate to the extension housing. Lift away the forked plate and withdraw the speedometer cable.

2 Remove the clip that secures the speedometer outer cable to the bulkhead.

3 Working under the facia depress the knurled pad on the speedometer cable ferrule and pull the cable from the speedometer head.

4 Remove the grommet that seals the cable at the bulkhead. Withdraw the speedometer cable.

5 Refitting the speedometer cable is the reverse sequence to removal.

6 It is possible to remove the inner cable from the outer cable whilst still attached to the car. Follow the instructions in paragraphs 1 and 3 and pull the inner cable from the outer cable.

52 Fuel tank indicator unit - removal and replacement

1 With the level of petrol in the tank lower than the bottom of the indicator unit wipe the area around the unit free of dirt.

2 Detach the fuel tank indicator unit cable from its terminal connector.

3 Using two crossed screwdrivers in the slots of the indicator unit body or a soft metal drift carefully unlock the indicator unit. Lift away the indicator unit and sealing ring.

4 Refitting the indicator unit is the reverse sequence to removal. Always fit a new seal in the recess in the tank to ensure no leaks develop.

53 Light switch - removal and replacement

1 Disconnect the battery. Pull the knob from the switch stalk and using a pair of pliers unscrew the bezel.

2 Working under the dash panel pull the wiring loom from its retaining clips.

3 Pull the light switch rearwards from its location and detach the wiring loom plug from the back of the switch.

4 Refitting the light switch is the reverse sequence to removal.

54 Direction indicator switch - removal and replacement

1 Open the bonnet and for safety reasons disconnect the battery.

2 If a manual choke control is fitted, pull off the choke control knob.

3 Undo and remove the screw and annulus that holds the two halves of the steering column shroud together. Using a knife split the two halves of the column shroud and lift away.

4 Detach the multi pin plug from the underside of the switch.

5 Undo and remove the two screws and shake-proof washer located on the lever side of the switch and detach the switch assembly from the steering column (Fig.10:19).

6 Refitting the direction indicator switch is the reverse sequence to removal. Before the shroud is refitted check that the switch and self cancelling system operates correctly, for this the battery will have to be reconnected.

55 Ignition switch and lock - removal and replacement

1 Open the bonnet and for safety reasons disconnect the battery.

2 Make a careful note of the cable connections to the ignition

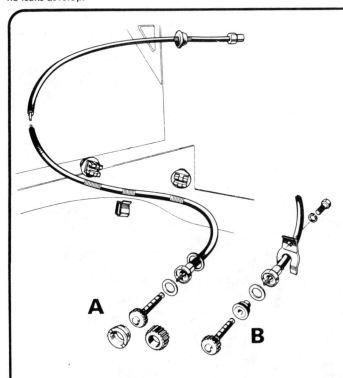

FIG 10   18 SPEEDOMETER CABLE AND DRIVEN
GEAR

A Manual and automatic transmission
B Alternative automatic transmission

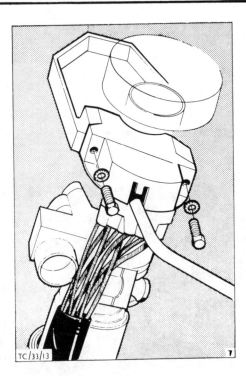

FIG 10 : 19 DIRECTION INDICATOR SWITCH

switch and lock body. Detach these cables.

3 Carefully unscrew the chrome bezel that secures the lock to the switch panel.

4 Using a suitable diameter drill remove the headless bolts that clamp the lock to the steering column. An alternative method is to use a centre punch and unscrew the bolts. Lift away the complete assembly. NOTE - New shear bolts will be required during reassembly.

5 To refit, place the lock assembly with the key in the lock onto the steering column. Withdraw the lock so as to allow the pawl to enter the steering shaft.

6 Position the loose half of the clamp on the lock and engage new shear bolts in their tapped holes. Tighten the bolts a turn at a time until the heads shear off. Whilst the bolts are being tightened continually check that operation of the pawl is smooth and free.

7 Refitting is now the reverse sequence to removal.

56 Windscreen wiper switch - removal and replacement

1 Pull the heater control knobs from their respective operating levers. It will be necessary to tap out the dowel pin of the lower knob. Take care not to bend the operating lever.

2 Working under the dashboard carefully press out the operating lever bezel.

3 Remove the radio switch bezel (if fitted).

4 Pull the windscreen wiper switch knob from the switch stalk and unscrew the bezel. Detach the plug from the rear of the switch and finally remove the switch.

5 Refitting the switch is the reverse sequence to removal.

57 Fuses

The fuses are located on a block which is mounted on the engine compartment inner wing panel and upon inspection it will be seen that there are seven fuses. Their function is shown on the plastic cover (photo).

There are three unused connections, these being 1, 2 and 7 and these may be used for the fitment of accessories. Fuses numbered 2 and 7 are connected via the ignition switch whilst fuse 1 is connected to a direct current supply and is live all the time.

There are two additional fuses mounted on the inner wing panel these being integral with the headlamp relay. All fuses have an 8 amp rating.

Fuse	Function
1	Interior lights, warning indicator system, clock, cigar lighter, glove box lamp.
2	Rear number plate light, instrument panel lights, switching stage indicator lights.
3	Tail light RH, side light RH.
4	Tail light, LH, side light LH.
5	Horn, heater blower motor, current control heated rear window.
6	Windscreen wiper motor, foot operated windscreen wiper motor, reverse light.
7	Flasher system, stop light, voltage divider.
8	Main beam RH and LH.
9	Dipped beam RH and LH.

Before any fuse that has blown is renewed, it is important to find the cause of the trouble and for it to be rectified, as a fuse acts as a safety device and protects the electrical system against expensive damage should a fault occur.

58 Additional fitments - hazard warning and heated rear window

1 Most Cortinas are fitted with a hazard warning flasher system. This operates all flashers at once and is activated by a switch on the fascia. A warning light operates near the switch too. It should be dealt with in the same way as the indicator flashing system.

2 Heated rear windows are also becoming a standard fitment. Again a fascia mounted switch activates them and a fascia warning light is fitted. The heating element is very delicate and great care should be taken, even when cleaning the window on the inside. If failure is indicated check the switching/circuitry/fuse first in the normal manner. If the element is suspect have a glass specialist look at it. They are costly!

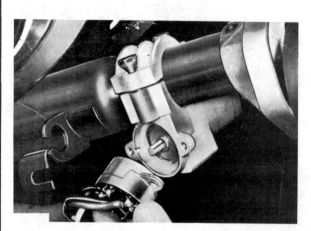

FIG 10 : 20 IGNITION SWITCH AND LOCK REMOVAL

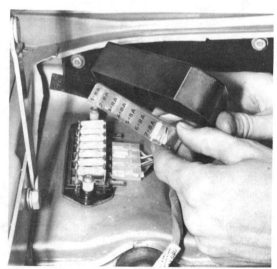

57. Fuse block with outer and inner covers removed

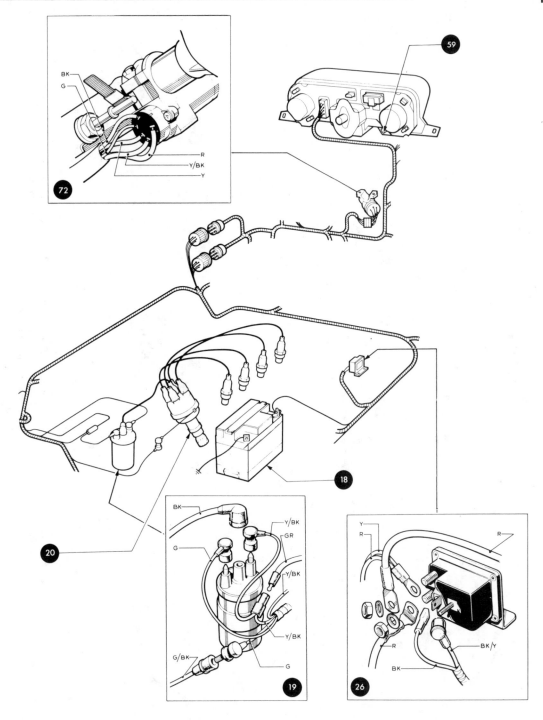

IGNITION SYSTEM - LOOM DIAGRAM AND LAYOUT

18 Battery (RHD)	20 Distributor	(manual transmission)	72 Ignition switch
19 Ignition coil	26 Starter solenoid	59 Generator warning lamp	

COLOUR CODE

R	Red	Y	Yellow	BK	Black	LG	Light Green
BL	Blue	P	Purple	W	White	O	Orange
BR	Brown	PK	Pink	G	Green	GR	Grey

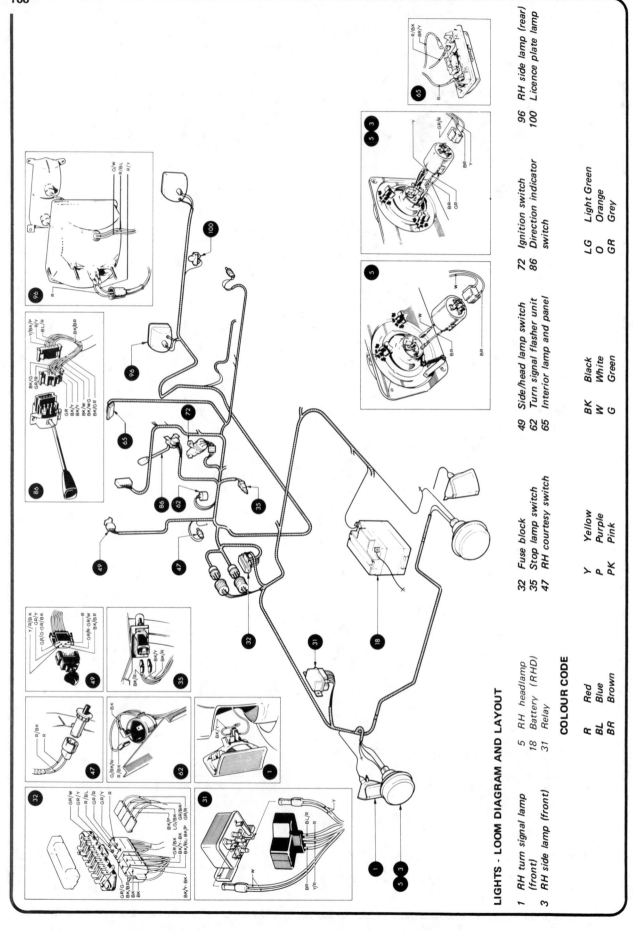

LIGHTS - LOOM DIAGRAM AND LAYOUT

1	RH turn signal lamp (front)	5	RH headlamp	49	Side/head lamp switch	96	RH side lamp (rear)
3	RH side lamp (front)	18	Battery (RHD)	62	Turn signal flasher unit	100	Licence plate lamp
		31	Relay	65	Interior lamp and panel		
		32	Fuse block	72	Ignition switch		
		35	Stop lamp switch	86	Direction indicator switch		
		47	RH courtesy switch				

COLOUR CODE

R	Red	Y	Yellow	BK	Black	LG	Light Green
BL	Blue	P	Purple	W	White	O	Orange
BR	Brown	PK	Pink	G	Green	GR	Grey

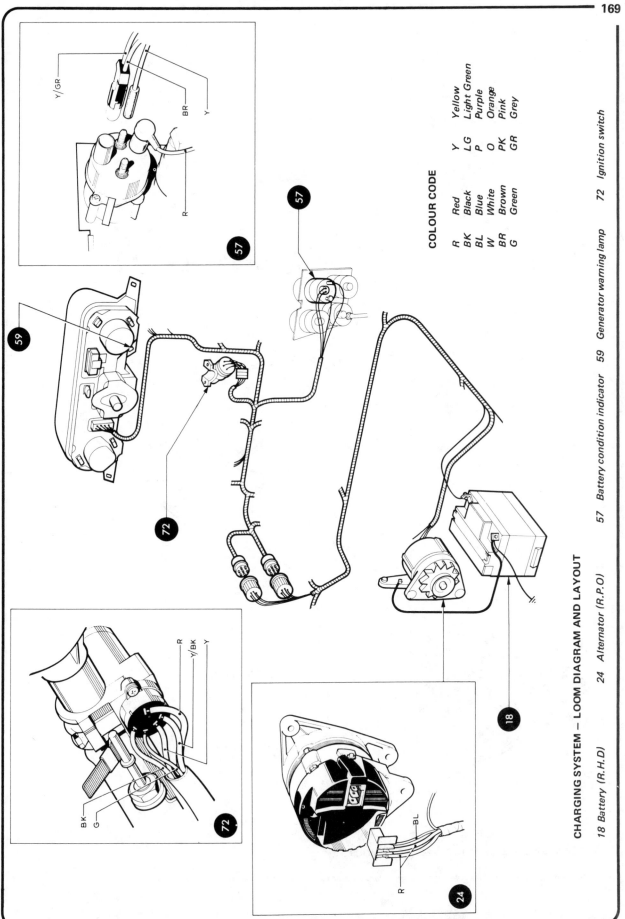

COLOUR CODE

R	Red	Y	Yellow
BK	Black	LG	Light Green
BL	Blue	P	Purple
W	White	O	Orange
BR	Brown	PK	Pink
G	Green	GR	Grey

CHARGING SYSTEM – LOOM DIAGRAM AND LAYOUT

18 Battery (R.H.D)   24 Alternator (R.P.O)   57 Battery condition indicator   59 Generator warning lamp   72 Ignition switch

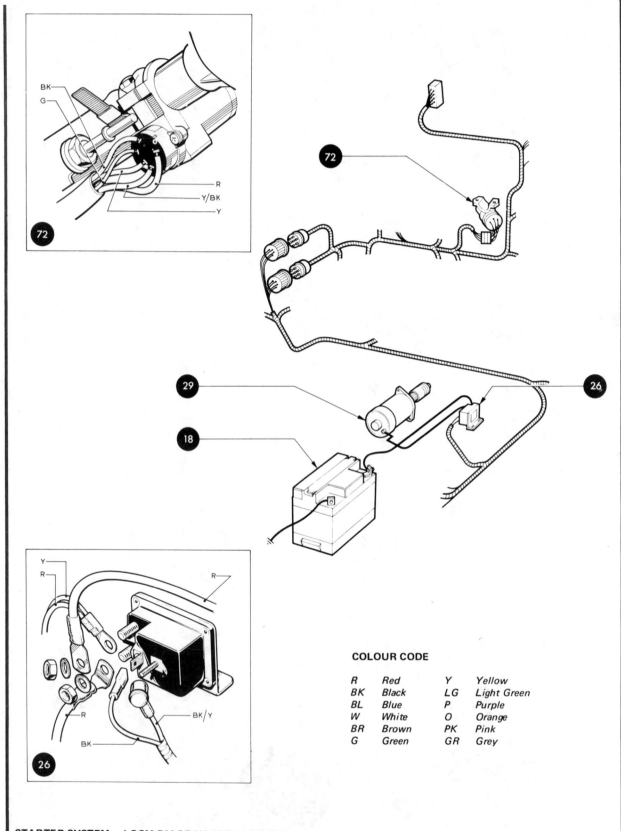

COLOUR CODE

R	Red	Y	Yellow
BK	Black	LG	Light Green
BL	Blue	P	Purple
W	White	O	Orange
BR	Brown	PK	Pink
G	Green	GR	Grey

STARTER SYSTEM – LOOM DIAGRAM AND LAYOUT

18 Battery (R.H.D.) 26 Starter solenoid (manual transmission) 29 Inertia starter motor (manual transmission) 72 Ignition switch

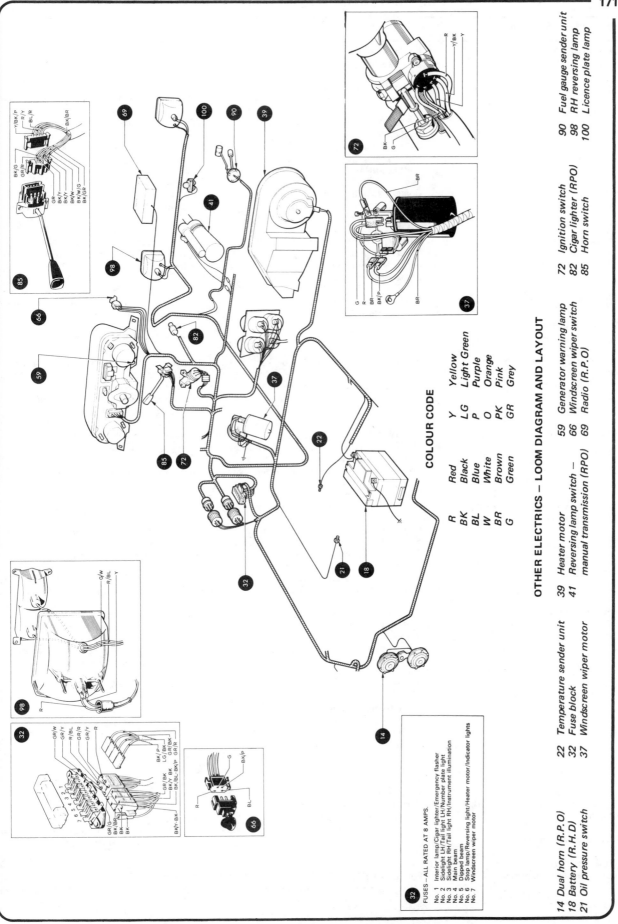

COLOUR CODE

R	Red	Y	Yellow
BK	Black	LG	Light Green
BL	Blue	P	Purple
W	White	O	Orange
BR	Brown	PK	Pink
G	Green	GR	Grey

OTHER ELECTRICS – LOOM DIAGRAM AND LAYOUT

FUSES – ALL RATED AT 8 AMPS.

No. 1 Interior lamp/Cigar lighter/Emergency flasher
No. 2 Sidelight LH/Tail light LH/Number plate light
No. 3 Sidelight RH/Tail light RH/Instrument illumination
No. 4 Main beam
No. 5 Dipped beam
No. 6 Stop lamp/Reversing light/Heater motor/Indicator lights
No. 7 Windscreen wiper motor

14 Dual horn (R.P.O)	22 Temperature sender unit	39 Heater motor	59 Generator warning lamp	90 Fuel gauge sender unit
18 Battery (R.H.D)	32 Fuse block	41 Reversing lamp switch –	66 Windscreen wiper switch	98 RH reversing lamp
21 Oil pressure switch	37 Windscreen wiper motor	manual transmission (RPO)	69 Radio (R.P.O)	100 Licence plate lamp
			72 Ignition switch	
			82 Cigar lighter (RPO)	
			85 Horn switch	

FAULT DIAGNOSIS - ELECTRICAL SYSTEM

Symptom	Reason/s	Remedy
No electricity at starter motor	Battery discharged	Charge battery.
	Battery defective internally	Fit new battery.
	Battery terminal leads loose or earth lead not securely attached to body	Check and tighten leads.
	Loose or broken connections in starter motor circuit	Check all connections and tighten any that are loose.
	Starter motor switch or solenoid faulty	Test and replace faulty components with new.
Electricity at starter motor : faulty motor	Starter motor pinion jammed in mesh with flywheel gear ring	Disengage pinion by turning squared end of armature shaft.
	Starter brushes badly worn, sticking, or brush wires loose	Examine brushes, replace as necessary, tighten down brush wires.
	Commutator dirty, worn or burnt	Clean commutator, recut if badly burnt.
	Starter motor armature faulty	Overhaul starter motor, fit new armature.
	Field coils earthed	Overhaul starter motor.
Electrical defects	Battery in discharged condition	Charge battery.
	Starter brushes badly worn, sticking, or brush wires loose	Examine brushes, replace as necessary, tighten down brush wires.
	Loose wires in starter motor circuit	Check wiring and tighten as necessary.
Dirt or oil on drive gear	Starter motor pinion sticking on the screwed sleeve	Remove starter motor, clean starter motor drive.
Mechanical damage	Pinion or flywheel gear teeth broken or worn	Fit new gear ring to flywheel, and new pinion to starter motor drive.
Lack of attention or mechanical damage	Pinion or flywheel gear teeth broken or worn	Fit new gear teeth to flywheel, or new pinion to starter motor drive.
	Starter drive main spring broken	Dismantle and fit new main spring.
	Starter motor retaining bolts loose	Tighten starter motor securing bolts. Fit new spring washer if necessary.
Wear or damage	Battery defective internally	Remove and fit new battery.
	Electrolyte level too low or electrolyte too weak due to leakage	Top up electrolyte level to just above plates.
	Plate separators no longer fully effective	Remove and fit new battery.
	Battery plates severely sulphated	Remove and fit new battery.
Insufficient current flow to keep battery charged	Fan/dynamo belt slipping	Check belt for wear, replace if necessary, and tighten.
	Battery terminal connections loose or corroded	Check terminals for tightness, and remove all corrosion.
	Dynamo not charging properly	Remove and overhaul dynamo.
	Short in lighting circuit causing continual battery drain	Trace and rectify.
	Regulator unit not working correctly	Check setting, clean and replace if defective.
Dynamo not charging	Fan belt loose and slipping, or broken	Check, replace and tighten as necessary.
	Brushes worn, sticking, broken or dirty	Examine, clean or replace brushes as necessary.
	Brush springs weak or broken	Examine and test. Replace as necessary.
	Commutator dirty, greasy, worn, or burnt	Clean commutator and undercut segment separators.
	Armature badly worn or armature shaft bent	Fit new or reconditioned armature.
	Commutator bars shorting	Undercut segment separations.
	Dynamo bearings badly worn	Overhaul dynamo, fit new bearings.
	Dynamo field coils burnt, open, or shorted	Remove and fit rebuilt dynamo.
	Commutator no longer circular	Recut commutator and undercut segment separators.
	Pole pieces very loose	Strip and overhaul dynamo. Tighten pole pieces.
Regulator or cut-out fails to work correctly	Regulator incorrectly set	Adjust regulator correctly.
	Cut-out incorrectly set	Adjust cut-out correctly.
	Open circuit in wiring of cut-out and regulator unit	Remove, examine and renew as necessary.
Alternator not charging		Take car to specialist Auto-Electrician.

FUEL GAUGE

Fuel gauge gives no reading	Fuel tank empty!	Fill fuel tank.
	Electric cable between tank sender	Check cable for earthing and joints for

Symptom	Reason/s	Remedy
	unit and gauge earthed or loose	tightness.
	Fuel gauge case not earthed	Ensure case is well earthed.
	Fuel gauge supply cable interrupted	Check and replace cable if necessary.
	Fuel gauge unit broken	Replace fuel gauge.
Fuel gauge registers full all the time	Electric cable between tank unit and gauge broken or disconnected	Check over cable and repair as necessary.
HORN		
Horn operates all the time	Horn push either earthed or stuck down	Disconnect battery earth. Check and rectify source of trouble.
	Horn cable to horn push earthed	Disconnect battery earth. Check and rectify source of trouble.
Horn fails to operate	Blown fuse	Check and renew if broken. Ascertain cause
	Cable or cable connection loose, broken or disconnected	Check all connections for tightness and cables for breaks.
	Horn has an internal fault	Remove and overhaul horn.
Horn emits intermittent or unsatisfactory noise	Cable connections loose	Check and tighten all connections.
	Horn incorrectly adjusted	Adjust horn until best note obtained.
LIGHTS		
Lights do not come on	If engine not running, battery discharged	Push-start car, charge battery.
	Light bulb filament burnt out or bulbs broken	Test bulbs in live bulb holder.
	Wire connections loose, disconnected or broken	Check all connections for tightness and wire cable for breaks.
	Light switch shorting or otherwise faulty	By-pass light switch to ascertain if fault is in switch and fit new switch as appropriate.
Lights come on but fade out	If engine not running battery discharged	Push-start car, and charge battery.
Lights give very poor illumination	Lamp glasses dirty	Clean glasses.
	Reflector tarnished or dirty	Fit new reflectors.
	Lamps badly out of adjustment	Adjust lamps correctly.
	Incorrect bulb with too low wattage fitted	Remove bulb and replace with correct grade.
	Existing bulbs old and badly discoloured	Renew bulb units.
	Electrical wiring too thin not allowing full current to pass	Re-wire lighting system.
Lights work erratically - flashing on and off, especially over bumps	Battery terminals or earth connection loose	Tighten battery terminals and earth connection.
	Lights not earthing properly	Examine and rectify.

Chapter 11 Suspension and steering

Contents

Specifications

Front suspension	Independent, coil spring, long and short swinging arms. Double acting, hydraulic, telescopic shock absorbers.
Number of turns per spring	7.2 or 7.5
Identification...	Coded with different paint colours. For replacement using spring of same colour coding
Toe in	0.16 in (3.9 mm)
*Castor	$3^o 9' \pm 0^o 30'$
*Camber	$0^o 37' \pm 0^o 30'$
*KPI	$3^o 35' \pm 0^o 30'$
Toe out on turns	20° back lock, front lock 19° 35° back lock, front lock $32^o 18'$

*Vehicle to be fitted with kerb height gauges - see text.

Rear suspension type	Radius arms, coil springs Double acting, hydraulic, telescopic shock absorbers
1300 cc and 1600 cc standard engine	
Spring wire diameter	
Standard	0.516 in (13.1 mm)
Heavy duty	0.563 in (14.3 mm)
Coil inside diameter	
Standard	4.05 in (102.8 mm)
Heavy duty	3.95 in (100.4 mm)
Number of turns	
Standard	6.3
Heavy duty	6.8
Free spring length	11.4 in (290 mm)
Fitted height:	
Standard	8.488 in (215.6 mm)
Heavy duty	9.192 in (233.5 mm)
Spring rate:	
Standard	26.6 mm/100 Kg
Heavy duty	19.95 mm/100 Kg
Steering type	Rack and pinion
Steering wheel diameter	15.51 x 14.53 in (394 x 369 mm)
Turns - lock to lock...	3.7

Steering ratio	18.7 : 1	
Steering gear adjustment	Shims	
Minimum turning circle diameter	31ft 10 in (9.7 m)	
Maximum turning angle:		
Outer wheel	38º 48'	
Inner wheel	35º 36'	
Lubricant capacity	0.25 pint (0.14 litre)	
Lubricant type	Castrol Hypoy 90	

Wheels and tyres:

Wheel size	4½J x 13 (standard) 5½J x 13 (optional)
Tyres	The size and tyre pressure depend on the vehicle specification and optional equipment fitted. See manufacturer's recommendations.

Torque wrench settings:

Front suspension:	lb ft	kg m
¼ in - 20 UNC	5 - 7	0.69 - 0.97
5/16 in - 18 UNC	12 - 15	1.66 - 2.07
5/16 in - 24 UNF	12 - 15	1.66 - 2.07
3/8 in - 16 UNC	17 - 22	2.35 - 3.04
3/8 in - 24 UNF	22 - 27	3.04 - 3.73
7/16 in - 14 UNC	30 - 35	4.15 - 4.84
7/16 in - 20 UNF	40 - 45	5.53 - 6.22
½ in - 13 UNC	45 - 50	6.22 - 6.91
½ in - 20 UNF	50 - 60	6.91 - 8.29
9/16 in - 12 UNC	60 - 70	8.29 - 9.67
9/16 in - 18 UNF	65 - 75	8.98 - 10.37
5/8 in - 11 UNC	75 - 85	10.37 - 11.75
5/8 in - 18 UNF	100 - 110	13.82 - 15.20

Rear suspension:		
*Upper radius arm to body	42 - 50	5.8 - 6.9
*Upper radius arm to axle	42 - 50	5.8 - 6.9
*Lower radius arm to body	42 - 50	5.8 - 6.9
*Lower radius arm to axle	42 - 50	5.8 - 6.9
Coil spring to bottom plate	28 - 34	3.9 - 4.8

*These bolts must be tightened after the vehicle has been lowered to the ground.

Steering:		
Steering gear to crossmember	15 - 18	2.1 - 2.4
Track rod end to steering arm	18 - 22	2.5 - 3.0
Coupling to pinion spline	12 - 15	1.7 - 2.1
Universal joint to steering shaft spline	12 - 15	1.7 - 2.1
Steering wheel to steering shaft	20 - 25	2.8 - 3.4
Track rod end locknut	40 - 45	5.5 - 6.3
Track rod end ball housing	33 - 37	4.6 - 5.2
Pinion pre-load cover	6 - 8	0.9 - 1.1
Rack slipper cover	6 - 8	0.9 - 1.1
Pinion turning torque	5 - 15 lb in	6 - 17 kg cm
Wheel nuts	50 - 55	7.0 - 7.7

1 General description

The independent front suspension comprises short and long swinging arms with coil springs and hydraulic double acting shock absorbers which operate on the lower swinging arms. The main suspension framework is located on the underbody side member and acts as a mounting point for the wishbone type upper and single lower swinging arms. Attached to the upper frame are rubber bump stops to absorb excessive swinging arm movement. The suspension arms are mounted on rubber bushes and carry the stub axle ball joints at their outer ends.

Located on each axle stub are two taper roller bearings and these run in cups which are pressed into the wheel hubs. To keep the grease in the hub is a spring loaded neosprene seal located in the inner end of the hub. The wheel studs are splined and pressed into the hub flange.

Bolted to the lower arm are rubber mounted tie bars which control the suspension castor angle. The tie bars are connected to a stabilizer bar via a bolt and spacer and bushed at its connection points. It is mounted in split bushes which are clipped to brackets which are bolted to the body side members.

The rear suspension comprises lower and upper radius arms and coil spring. The two lower radius arms are in position in the axial direction of the vehicle and the two upper radius arms are in a diagonal position so as to absorb any forces created during cornering. All four radius arms are mounted in insulated rubber blocks. Fitted between the rear axle casing and underside of the body are rubber mounted double acting hydraulic telescopic shock absorbers.

The coil springs are mounted on the lower radius arms and locate on a rubber ring between the spring and underside of the body.

The steering gear is of the rack and pinion type and is located on the front crossmember by two 'U' shaped clamps. The pinion is connected to the steering column by a flexible coupling. Above the flexible coupling the steering column is split by a universal joint that is designed to collapse on impact thus minimizing injury to the driver in the event of an accident.

Turning the steering wheel causes the rack to move in a lateral direction and the track rods attached to either end of the rack pass this movement to the steering arms on the stub axle assemblies thereby moving the road wheels.

Two adjustments are possible on the steering gear, namely rack slipper bearing adjustment and pinion bearing pre-load adjustment, but the steering gear must be removed from the car to carry out these adjustments. Both adjustments are made by varying the thickness of shim packs.

The two track rods are adjustable in length to allow adjustment of the toe in setting, and make sure the wheel lock angles are correct. Lock stops are built in to the steering gear and are not adjustable.

2 Front hub bearings - removal and replacement

1 Refer to Chapter 9/5: 1, 2, 3, 5 and 6 and remove the disc brake caliper.
2 By judicious tapping and levering remove the dust cap from the centre of the hub.
3 Remove the split pin from the nut retainer and lift away the adjusting nut retainer (Fig 11 : 1).
4 Unscrew the adjusting nut and lift away the thrust washer and outer tapered bearing.
5 Pull off the complete hub and disc assembly from the stub axle.
6 From the back of the hub assembly carefully prise out the grease seal noting which way round it is fitted as shown in Fig 11 : 2. Lift away the inner tapered bearing.
7 Carefully clean out the hub and wash the bearings with petrol making sure that no grease or oil is allowed to get onto the brake disc.
8 Using a soft metal drift carefully remove the inner and outer bearing cups.
9 To fit new cups make sure they are the right way round and using metal tubes of suitable size carefully drift them into position.
10 Pack the cone and roller assembly with Castrol LM grease working the grease well into the cage and rollers. NOTE: leave the hub and grease seal empty to allow for subsequent expansion of the grease.
11 To reassemble the hub, first fit the inner bearing and then gently tap the grease seal back into the hub. A new seal must always be fitted as during removal it was probably damaged. The lip must face inwards to the hub.
12 Replace the hub and disc assembly on the stub axle and slide on the outer bearing and thrust washer.
13 Refit the adjusting nut and tighten it to a torque wrench setting of 27 lb ft (3.7 kg m) whilst rotating the hub and disc to ensure free movement and centralisation of the bearing. (Fig 11 : 3). Slacken the nut back by 90° which will give the required end float of 0.001 - 0.005 inch (0.03 - 0.13 mm). Fit the nut retainer and new split pin. Bend over the ears of the split pin.
14 Refit the dust cap to the centre of the hub.
15 Refit the caliper as described in Chapter 9/5.

3 Front hub bearings - adjustment

1 To check the condition of the hub bearings, jack up the front of the car and support on firmly based stands. Grasp the road wheel at two opposite points to check for any rocking movement in the wheel hub. Watch carefully for any movement in the steering gear which can easily be mistaken for hub movement.
2 If a front wheel hub has excessive movement, this is adjusted by removing the hub cap and then tapping and levering the dust cap from the centre of the hub.
3 Remove the split pin from the nut retainer and lift away the adjusting nut retainer.
4 If a torque wrench is available tighten the centre adjusting nut to a torque wrench setting of 27 lb ft (3.73 kg m) as shown

in Fig 11 : 3 and then slacken the nut back until an end float of 0.001 - 0.005 inch (0.03 - 0.13 mm) is obtained. Replace the nut retainer, and lock with a new split pin.
5 Assuming a torque wrench is not available however, tighten the centre adjusting nut until a slight drag is felt on rotating the wheel. Then loosen the nut very slowly until the wheel turns freely again and there is just a perceptible end float. Refit the nut retainer and lock with a new split pin.
6 Refit the dust cap to the centre of the hub.

4 Front hub - removal and replacement

1 Follow the instructions given in Section 2 up to and including paragraph 5.
2 Bend back the locking tab and undo the four bolts holding the hub to the brake disc.
3 If a new hub assembly is being fitted it is supplied complete with new cups and bearings. The bearing cups will already be fitted in the hub. It is essential to check that the cups and bearings are of the same manufacture, this can be done by reading the name on the bearings and by looking at the initial letter stamped on the hub, 'T' stands for Timken and 'S' for Skefco.
4 Clean with scrupulous care the mating surfaces of the hub and check for blemishes or damage. Any dirt or blemishes will almost certainly give rise to disc run-out. Using new locking tabs bolt the disc and hub together and tighten the bolts to a torque wrench setting of 30 - 34 lb ft (4.15 - 4.70 kg m).
5 To grease and reassemble the hub assembly follow the instructions given in Section 2 paragraph 10 onwards.

5 Front axle assembly - removal and replacement

1 Chock the rear wheels, jack up the vehicle and support the body on firmly based axle stands. Remove the front wheels.
2 Using a garage crane or overhead hoist support the weight of the engine.
3 Wipe the top of the brake master cylinder reservoir and unscrew the cap. Place a piece of polythene sheet over the top of the reservoir and refit the cap. This is to stop hydraulic fluid syphoning out during subsequent operations.
4 Wipe the area around the three way union on the axle frame and detach the main feed pipe to the union. Place some tape over the end of the pipe and open union to stop dirt ingress.
5 Slacken the steering column clamp plate and carefully withdraw the column.
6 Undo and remove the engine mounting securing nuts at the underside of the mounting. There is one nut to each mounting, as shown in Fig 11 : 4.
7 Using a garage hydraulic jack or blocks support the weight of the front axle assembly.
8 Undo and remove the bolts which secure the front axle assembly to the body side members (Fig 11 : 5). Carefully lower the complete assembly and draw forwards from under the front of the vehicle.
9 Refitting the front axle assembly is the reverse sequence to removal. It will be necessary to bleed the brake hydraulic system as described in Chapter 9/2.

6 Front axle assembly - overhaul

After high mileage it may be considered necessary to overhaul the complete front axle assembly. It is far better to remove the complete unit as described in Section 5 and dismantle it rather than to work on it still mounted on the car. Then proceed as follows:
1 Refer to Chapter 9/5 and remove the caliper.
2 Prise off the hub dust cap and withdraw the split pin and nut retainer. Undo and remove the nut (Fig 11 : 1).
3 Carefully pull the hub and disc assembly from the axle stub.
4 Undo and remove the ball stud securing nuts and then using a

FIG 11 : 1 FRONT HUB AND BEARINGS

FIG 11 : 2 FRONT HUB OIL SEAL REMOVAL

FIG 11 : 3 TIGHTENING THE FRONT HUB ADJUSTMENT NUT

FIG 11 : 4 ENGINE MOUNTING SECURING NUT

FIG 11 : 5 FRONT AXLE SECURING BOLTS TO BODY SIDE MEMBER

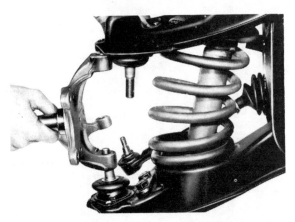

FIG 11 : 6 REMOVAL OF STUB AXLE ASSEMBLY

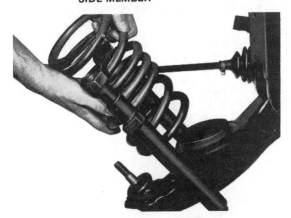

FIG 11 : 7 FRONT COIL SPRING WITH COMPRESSOR FITTED

universal balljoint separator, release the balljoint taper pins from their stub axle locations.

5 Next remove the track rod ends from their locations on the stub axles and remove the stub axle assembly as shown in Fig 11 : 6.

6 Withdraw the long bolt that secures the upper arm to the axle frame and lift away the upper arm.

7 It is necessary to compress the spring. For this either make up a spring compressor tool comprising two parts as shown in Fig 11 : 7 or borrow this from the local Ford garage quoting tool number P 4045. Do not attempt to use any makeshift tools as this can be very dangerous.

8 Using the spring compressors, contract the spring by at least 2 inches (50.8 mm).

9 Undo and remove the upper and lower shock absorber retaining nuts (lower fixing) and bolt (upper fixing). The shock absorber may now be lifted away through the coil spring and lower arm aperture.

10 Undo and remove the bolts that secure the tie bar to the lower arm. The lower arm should now be pulled down until there is sufficient clearance for the coil spring to be lifted away.

11 Bend back the lock tabs and unscrew and remove the four bolts that secure the steering 'U' shaped rack brackets to the front axle frame. Lift away the steering rack assembly.

12 Undo and remove the nut and bolt that secures the lower arm to the front axle frame. Lift away the lower arm.

13 Using a suitable diameter drift or long bolt, piece of metal tube, packing washers and nut, remove the lower arm bush.

14 The operations described in paragraphs 1 - 13 should now be repeated for the second front suspension assembly. It will be necessary to release the coil spring compressor.

15 Undo and remove the nuts that secure the tie bars to the axle frame. Lift away the connecting link, tie bar and stabilizer bar assembly (if fitted).

16 Undo and remove the nuts and washers from each of the connecting links and part the stabilizer bar from the tie bars.

17 It is now beneficial to cut away the bushes in the tie bar and stabilizer which will make removal far easier.

18 Pull out the two bump stop rubbers from the axle frame.

19 Undo and remove the three way union retaining nut, release the brake pipe from its mounting clips and lift away the complete brake pipe assembly.

20 Dismantling is now complete. Wash all parts and wipe dry ready for inspection. Inspect all bushes for signs of wear and all parts for damage or excessive corrosion and, if evident, new parts must be obtained. If one coil spring requires renewal the second one must also be renewed as it will have settled over a period of time. If the brake pipe has corroded now is the time to obtain a new one.

21 During reassembly it is important that none of the rubber mounted bolts are fully tightened until the weight of the vehicle is taken on the front wheels.

22 Position the three way union and brake pipe on the front axle frame and secure in position with the nut and clips.

23 Replace the rubber bump stops. If they are difficult to insert in their locations smear with a little washing up liquid.

24 Fit new end bushes to the stabilizer and tie bar and then locate the connecting links in the stabilizer.

25 Next locate the connecting links in the tie bar and stabilizer bar bushes. Secure with their nut and washers.

26 Screw the nuts on the tie bar ends and follow with the washer together with the bush. Locate the tie bars in their respective positions on the frame and loosely refit the spacer, bush, nut and washer.

27 Using a bench vice and suitable diameter tube fit a new bush to the lower arm.

28 Locate the lower arm in the frame and line up the holes with a screwdriver. Refit the pivot bolt and washers making sure the bolt head is towards the front of the axle frame.

29 Refit the tie bar to the lower suspension arm and retain with the two nuts and bolts.

30 Place the coil spring between the frame and lower arm. Insert the shock absorber through the lower arm and spring and secure

the shock absorber in position with the bolt (upper fixing) and nuts (lower fixing).

31 Unscrew the spring compressor and repeat the operations in paragraphs 24 to 30 for the second front suspension assembly.

32 Check the condition of the steering rack mounting rubbers and obtain new if necessary. Position the steering rack on the axle frame and secure to the mounting brackets with the 'U' clamps. Always use a new locking plate under the bolt heads. Tighten the bolts to a torque wrench setting of 15 - 18 lb ft (2.1 - 2.4 kg m), and bend up the locking plate.

33 Place the upper suspension arm on the axle frame, insert the pivot bolt through the arm and frame holes so that the head is towards the front of the axle frame. Secure with the washer and nut. Repeat this operation for the second upper suspension arm.

34 Connect the stub axle assembly to the suspension arm balljoints, locate the track rod ends in the stub axle and tighten all the nuts. The track rod end to steering arm nuts should be tightened to a torque wrench setting of 18 - 22 lb ft (2.5 - 3 kg m).

35 Refer to Section 4 and refit the hub and disc assemblies.

36 Refer to Chapter 9/5 and refit the caliper.

37 The complete front axle assembly may now be refitted to the car as described in Section 5.

7 Front axle mounting bushes - removal and replacement

1 Refer to Section 5, and remove the front axle assembly.

2 Using a piece of tube about 4 inches (101.6 mm) long and suitable diameter, a long bolt and nut and packing washers, draw the bushes from the side member.

3 New bushes may now be fitted using the reverse procedure as was used for removal.

4 Refit the front assembly as described in Section 5.

8 Stub axle - removal and replacement

1 Refer to Section 2 and remove the front hub and disc assembly.

2 Undo and remove the three bolts and spring washers that secure the brake disc splash shield to the stub axle.

3 Extract the split pins and then undo and remove the castellated nuts that secure the three balljoint pins to the stub axle.

4 Using a universal balljoint separator, separate the balljoint pins from the stub axle. Lift away the stub axle.

5 Refitting the stub axle is the reverse sequence to removal. The track rod end to steering arm retaining nut must be tightened to a torque wrench setting of 18 - 22 lb ft (2.5 - 3.0 kg m).

6 If a new stub axle has been fitted it is recommended that the steering geometry and front wheel toe in be checked. Further information may be found in Section 21.

9 Lower suspension arm - removal and replacement

1 Chock the rear wheels, jack up the front of the car and place on firmly based axle stands. Remove the road wheel.

2 Undo and remove the bolt that secures the brake pipe bracket and carefully push the pipes to one side.

3 It is now necessary to compress the spring. For this either make up a spring compressor tool comprising two parts as shown in Fig 11 : 7 or borrow this from the local Ford garage quoting tool number P 4045. Do not attempt to use any makeshift tools as this can be very dangerous.

4 Using the spring compressor, contract the spring by at least 2 inches (50.8 mm).

5 Undo and remove the upper and lower shock absorber retaining nuts (lower fixing) and bolt (upper fixing). The shock absorber may now be lifted away through the coil spring and lower arm aperture.

6 Withdraw the split pin, undo and remove the castellated nut that secures the lower wishbone balljoint pin to the stub axle. Using a universal balljoint separator, separate the balljoint pin

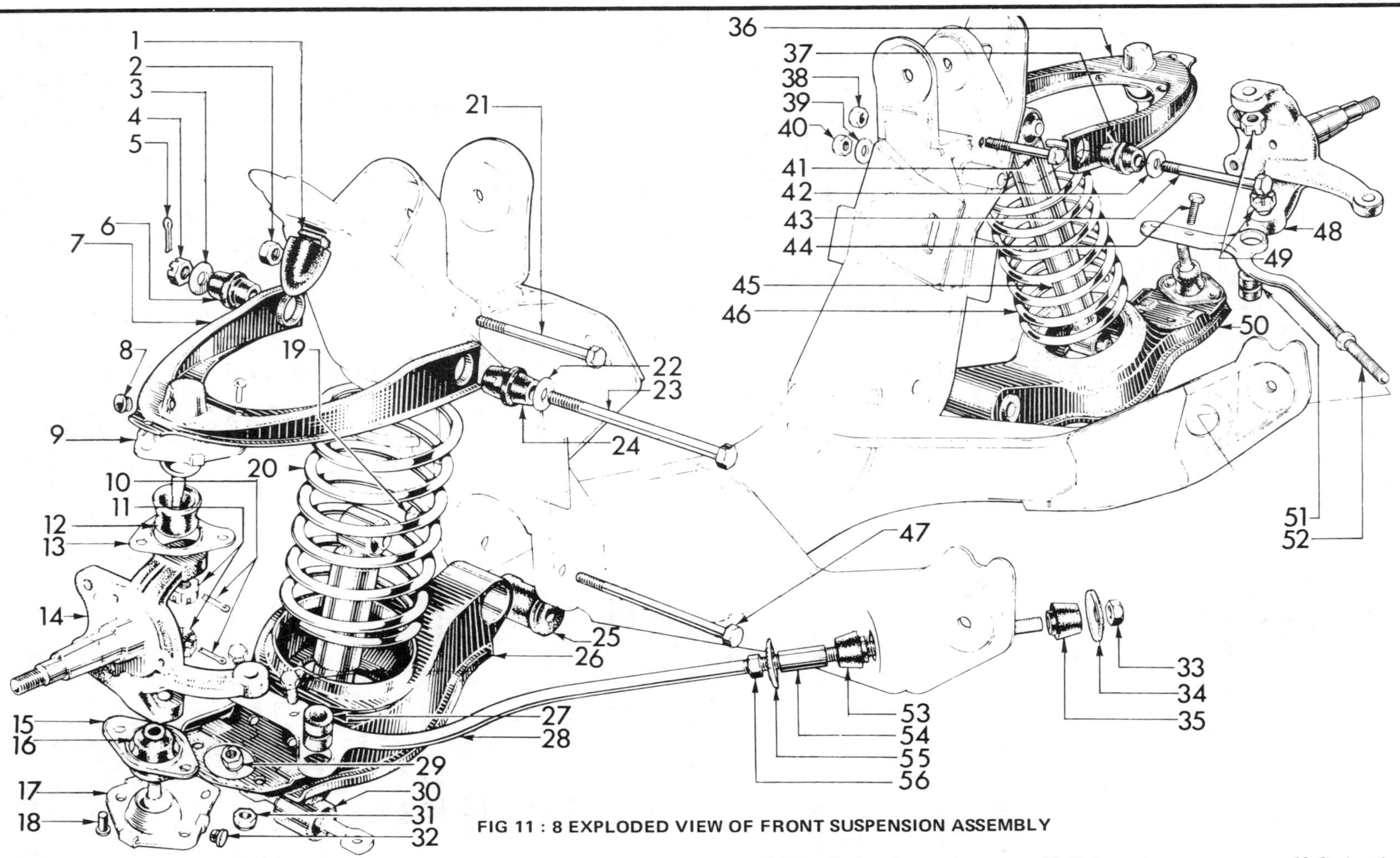

FIG 11 : 8 EXPLODED VIEW OF FRONT SUSPENSION ASSEMBLY

1 Bump rubber	21 Bolt	39 Plain washer
2 Nut	22 Plain washer	40 Nut
3 Plain washer	23 Bolt	41 Bolt
4 Castellated nut	24 Bush	42 Plain washer
5 Split pin	25 Bush	43 Bolt
6 Bush	26 Lower suspension arm	44 Bolt
7 Upper arm	27 Bush	45 Shock absorber
8 Rubber plug	28 Tie bar	46 Coil spring
9 Ball joint	29 Nut	47 Bolt
10 Split pin	30 Shock absorber	48 Stub axle
11 Castellated nut	31 Nut	49 Castellated nut
12 Rubber boot	32 Rubber plug	50 Lower suspension arm
13 Retaining plate	33 Nut	51 Bush
14 Stub axle	34 Dished washer	52 Tie bar
15 Retaining plate	35 Bush	53 Bush
16 Rubber boot	36 Upper arm	54 Spacer
17 Balljoint	37 Bush	55 Dished washer
18 Rivet	38 Nut	56 Nut
19 Nut		
20 Coil spring		

from the stub axle.

7   The lower suspension arm may now be parted and the coil spring removed.

8   Undo the tie bar locknut and remove the two bolts and nuts that secure the tie bar to the lower arm.

9   Undo and remove the bolt that secures the lower arm to the front axle frame. The lower suspension arm can now be lifted rearwards and downwards away from the front axle frame.

10 To fit a new bush first remove the old bush by using a piece of tube about 4 inches (101.6 mm) long and suitable diameter, a long bolt and nut and packing washer, draw the bush from the lower suspension arm. Fitting a new bush is the reverse sequence to removal.

11 Refitting the lower suspension arm is the reverse sequence to removal. The lower arm retaining bolts must be tightened once the car has been lowered to the ground.

12 If a new lower steering arm has been fitted it is recommended that the steering geometry and front wheel toe in be checked. Further information may be found in Section 21.

10 Stabilizer bar - removal and replacement

1   Undo and remove the bolt that secures each stabilizer bar mounting bush clip to the stabilizer bar mounting bracket.

2   Release the clips and then undo and remove the three bolts and spring washers that secure each mounting bracket to the body side member.

3   Undo and remove the two nuts, dished washer and upper bushes and detach the connecting links from their locations in the stabilizer bar. The stabilizer bar may now be lifted away from the underside of the car.

4   Refitting the stabilizer bar is the reverse sequence to removal.

11 Stabilizer bar mounting bushes - removal and replacement

1   Undo and remove the bolt that secures each stabilizer bar mounting bush clip to the stabilizer bar mounting brackets.

2   Using a metal bar such as a tyre lever, carefully ease the stabilizer bar downwards and push the split mounting bushes and washers clear of their locations.

3   Push the new bushes and washers onto the bar in their approximate positions and then align the bushes with the stabilizer bar mounting brackets and refit the retaining clips and bolts.

12 Stabilizer bar connecting link bush - removal and replacement

1   Refer to Section 10 and remove the stabilizer bar.

2   Using a sharp knife or hacksaw blade, cut the cone ends off the connecting link bushes and discard the bushes.

3   Using a bench vice, a piece of tube of suitable diameter and a socket, fit the connecting link bushes.

4   Refit the stabilizer bar as described in Section 10.

13 Front shock absorber - removal and replacement

1   Chock the rear wheels, jack up the front of the car and place on firmly based stands. Remove the road wheel.

2   Locate a small jack under the lower suspension arm and partially compress the coil spring.

3   Undo and remove the shock absorber top mounting bolt.

4   Undo and remove the two nuts that secure the shock absorber lower mounting. The shock absorber may now be lifted away through the coil spring and lower arm aperture.

5   Examine the shock absorber for signs of damage to the body, distorted piston rod, loose mounting or hydraulic fluid leakage. If evident, a new unit should be fitted.

6   To test for shock absorber efficiency hold the unit in the vertical position and gradually extend and contract it between its maximum and minimum limits ten times. It should be

apparent that there is equal resistance on both directions of movement. If this is not apparent a new unit should be fitted - always renew shock absorbers in pairs.

8   Refitting the shock absorbers is the reverse sequence to removal.

14 Tie bar - removal and replacement

1   Chock the rear wheels, jack up the front of the car and place on firmly based axle stands. Remove the road wheel.

2   Undo and remove the bolts that secure the tie bar to the lower suspension arm.

3   Extract the split pin from the end of the bar. Undo and remove the forward of the two nuts that secure the tie bar to the chassis frame member.

4   Where fitted, disconnect the stabilizer bar connecting link.

5   Remove the bush and spacer assembly from the threaded end of the tie bar. Lift away the tie bar.

6   If it is necessary to fit new bushes, use a sharp knife or hacksaw blade and cut the cone ends from the tie bar bush. Discard the old bush.

7   Using a tube of suitable diameter, a socket and bench vice, fit a new tie bar end bush.

8   Refitting the tie bar is the reverse sequence to removal. It is recommended that the steering geometry and front wheel toe in be checked. Further information will be found in Section 21.

15 Rear suspension and rear axle - removal and replacement

1   Chock the front wheels, jack up the rear of the car and support the body on firmly based stands. Remove the rear wheels.

2   Unscrew the two cheese head screws that secure the brake drum to the hub.

3   Release the handbrake and using a soft faced hammer on the outer circumference of a brake drum remove the brake drum.

4   Should the situation exist whereby the shoes foul the drum making removal impossible, the shoes must be collapsed by detaching the handbrake cable from the body mounted brackets, and then the plunger assembly removed from the backplate. Whenever the plunger is removed it must be discarded and a new one obtained.

5   Completely remove the handbrake cable from the body mounted brackets and disconnect the cable from the relay lever, inwards. Grip the handbrake cable end with a pair of pliers and release it from the end of the relay lever. Pull the handbrake cable through each brake backplate.

6   With a scriber or file, mark a line across the propeller shaft and pinion driving flanges so that they may be refitted together in their original positions.

7   Undo and remove the four bolts and spring washers securing the propeller shaft driving flanges and carefully lower the propeller shaft. For models fitted with the split type propeller shaft, it is necessary to undo and remove the two bolts with spring and plain washers that secure the centre bearing support to the underside of the body before the propeller shaft can be removed.

8   Wipe the top of the brake master cylinder reservoir and unscrew the cap. Place a piece of polythene sheeting over the reservoir neck and refit the cap. This is to stop hydraulic fluid syphoning out during subsequent operations.

9   Wipe the area around the brake flexible pipe to metal pipe, union just in front of the rear axle and referring to Chapter 9/3, detach the flexible hose from the metal pipe.

10 Slacken the nut which secures the lower radius arms to the rear axle casing. Carefully position a jack under one radius arm and very slightly compress the spring. Remove the nut and bolt from the front mounting. Now lower the jack so allowing the spring to extend. When the spring is fully extended lift it away and recover the rubber ring from the upper spring mounting.

11 Support the weight of the rear axle by placing the saddle of a jack (preferably trolley type) under the centre of the rear axle.

12 Undo and remove the nut and bolt securing the top of the

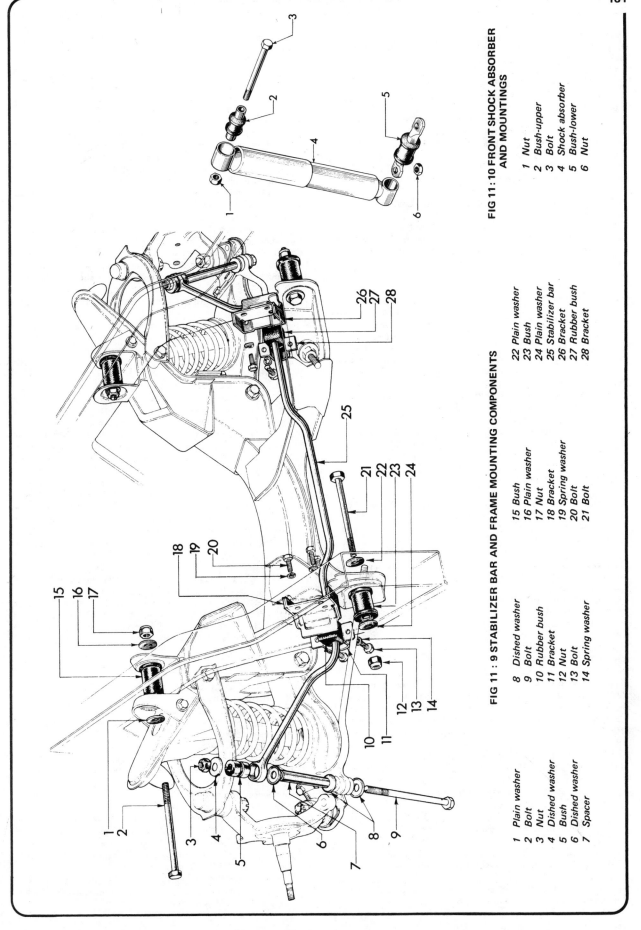

FIG 11 : 10 FRONT SHOCK ABSORBER AND MOUNTINGS

1 Nut
2 Bush-upper
3 Bolt
4 Shock absorber
5 Bush-lower
6 Nut

FIG 11 : 9 STABILIZER BAR AND FRAME MOUNTING COMPONENTS

1 Plain washer
2 Bolt
3 Nut
4 Dished washer
5 Bush
6 Dished washer
7 Spacer

8 Dished washer
9 Bolt
10 Rubber bush
11 Bracket
12 Nut
13 Bolt
14 Spring washer

15 Bush
16 Plain washer
17 Nut
18 Bracket
19 Spring washer
20 Bolt
21 Bolt

22 Plain washer
23 Bush
24 Plain washer
25 Stabilizer bar
26 Bracket
27 Rubber bush
28 Bracket

shock absorber to the body mounted bracket.

13 Undo and remove the nut and bolt that secures the radius arm to the underside of the body.

14 Repeat the operations in paragraphs 10, 12, and 13 for the second side of the rear suspension assembly.

15 The rear suspension and axle assembly may now be withdrawn from under the rear of the car.

16 Refitting the rear suspension and axle assembly is the reverse sequence to removal. The two marks previously made on the propeller shaft and pinion flanges should be correctly aligned.

17 The lower radius arm mounting bolts must only be tightened to a torque wrench setting of 42 - 50 lb ft (5.8 - 6.9 kg m), when the road wheels have been refitted and the car is standing on the ground.

18 It will be necessary to bleed the brake hydraulic system as described in Chapter 9/2.

19 The brake shoes must be centralised by the brake pedal being depressed firmly several times. Pull on and then release the handbrake lever until it is no longer possible to hear the clicking noise of the ratchet being turned by the adjusting arms.

16 Rear suspension upper radius arm - removal and replacement

1 Chock the front wheels, jack up the rear of the car and support the body on firmly based stands. Remove the rear wheels.

2 Support the weight of the rear axle then undo and remove the nut and bolt securing the radius arm. Should it be found that the bolt is trapped by a spring coil undo and remove the shock absorber lower mounting nut and bolt. This will enable the rear axle to drop slightly, thereby extending the spring enough for the through bolt to be removed through the spring coils.

3 Lift away the upper radius arm.

4 Should it be necessary to fit new mounting insulator bushes, the bushes may be removed using a piece of tube about 4 inches (101.6 mm) long and of suitable diameter, a long bolt and nut and packing washers, and drawing out the old bushes.

5 Fitting new bushes is the reverse procedure as was used for removal.

6 Refitting is the reverse sequence to removal. The upper radius arm attachments to the body and axle must be tightened to a torque wrench setting of 42 - 50 lb ft (5.8 - 6.9 kg m), when the car has been lowered to the ground.

17 Rear suspension lower radius arm - removal and replacement

1 Chock the front wheels, jack up the rear of the car and support the body on firmly based axle stands. Remove the rear wheels.

2 Support the weight of the rear axle and then undo and remove the two radius arm mounting through bolt nuts. Remove the front mounting through bolts and carefully lower the jack. This will remove the load from the rear coil spring.

3 Remove the second radius arm mounting through bolt and lift away the radius arm and coil spring. Recover the upper spring rubber bush. Finally detach the spring from the radius arm.

4 Should it be necessary to fit new mounting insulator bushes, the bushes may be removed using a piece of tube about 4 inches (101.6 mm) long and of suitable diameter, a long bolt and nut and packing washers, and drawing out the old bushes.

5 Fitting new bushes is the reverse procedure as was used for removal. NOTE that the two bushes are of different diameters.

6 Refitting the lower radius arm is the reverse sequence to removal. The upper spring rubber bush must be refitted correctly. The attachments to the body and axle must be tightened to a torque wrench setting of 42 - 50 lb ft (5.8 - 6.9 kg m), when the car has been lowered to the ground.

18 Rear suspension bump rubber - removal and replacement

Removal of a bump rubber is simply a matter of pulling it downwards from its mushroom shaped mounting stud. Refitting

is a reversal of the removal procedure.

19 Rear shock absorber - removal and replacement

1 Chock the front wheels, jack up the rear of the car and support the axle on firmly based stands. Remove the rear wheel.

2 Undo and remove the shock absorber upper and lower mounting nuts and bolts. Lift away the shock absorbers.

3 Should it be necessary to fit new rubber bushes, use a suitable diameter drift and drive out the spacer sleeve and then the rubber bushes. Refitting new bushes is the reversal of the removal sequence.

4 Examine the shock absorber for signs of damage to the body, distorted piston rod or hydraulic leakage. If evident, a new unit should be fitted.

5 To test for damper efficiency, hold the unit in the vertical position and gradually extend and contract the unit between its maximum and minimum limits ten times. It should be apparent that there is equal resistance in both directions of movement. If this is not apparent a new unit should be fitted. Always renew shock absorbers in pairs.

6 Refitting the shock absorber is the reverse sequence to removal.

20 Steering - lubrication

Lubrication of the rack and pinion during normal service operation is not necessary as the lubricant is contained on the assembly by rubber gaiters. However should a loss occur due to a leak from the rack housing or rubber gaiters then the correct amount of oil should be inserted using an oil can. Obviously before replenishment is carried out the source of leak must be found and rectified.

To top up the oil in the rack and pinion assembly, remove the clip from the rubber gaiter on the right hand end of the steering rack housing and rotate the steering wheel until the rack is in the normal straight ahead position. Allow any remaining oil to seep out so that it is not overfilled. Using an oil can filled with Castrol Hypoy 90 insert the nozzle into the end of the rack housing and refill with not more than 0.25 pint (0.14 litre) of oil.

Reposition the gaiter and tighten the clip quickly to ensure minimum loss of oil and then move the steering wheel from lock to lock very slowly to distribute the oil in the housing.

IMPORTANT: If any time the car is raised from the ground and the front wheels are clear and suspended, do not use any excessive force or rapid movement when moving the wheels, especially from one lock to the other, otherwise damage could occur to the steering mechanism.

21 Front wheel - alignment

The front wheels are correctly aligned when they are turning in at the front 0.000 - 0.16 in (0.000 - 3.9 mm). It is important that this measurement is taken on a centre line drawn horizontally and parallel with the ground through the centre line of the hub. The exact point should be in the centre of the side wall of the tyre and not on the wheel rim which could be distorted and so give inaccurate readings.

The adjustment is effected by loosening the lock nut on each tie rod balljoint and also slackening the rubber gaiter clip holding it to the tie rod, both tie rods are then turned equally until the adjustment is correct.

Measurement of the steering angles as well as the toe in requires the use of special equipment and the job is best left to the local Ford garage. If the wheels are not in alignment or the steering angles incorrect, tyre wear will be heavy and uneven, and the steering will be stiff and unresponsive.

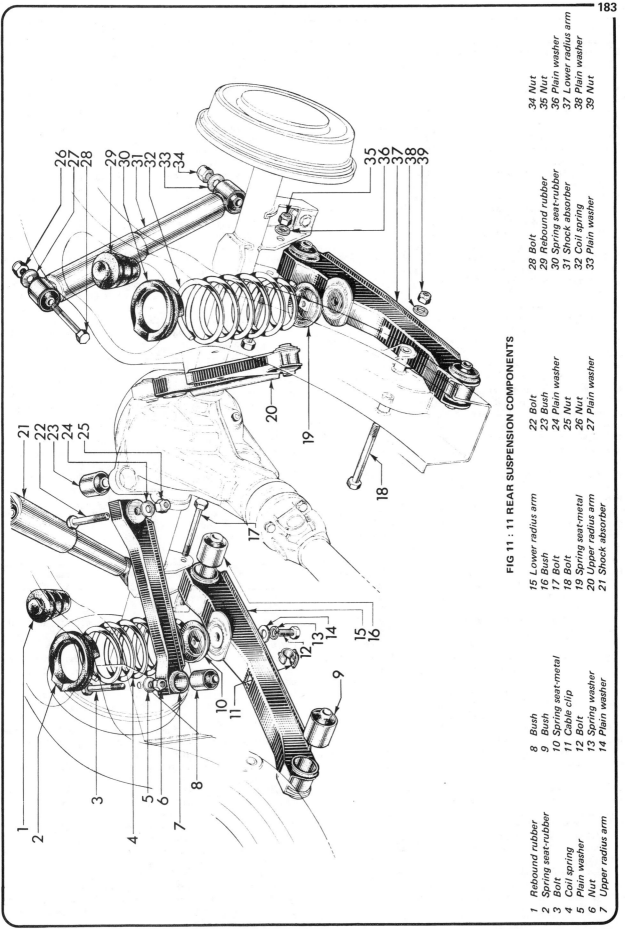

FIG 11 : 11 REAR SUSPENSION COMPONENTS

1 Rebound rubber	15 Lower radius arm	28 Bolt
2 Spring seat-rubber	16 Bush	29 Rebound rubber
3 Bolt	17 Bolt	30 Spring seat-rubber
4 Coil spring	18 Bolt	31 Shock absorber
5 Plain washer	19 Spring seat-metal	32 Coil spring
6 Nut	20 Upper radius arm	33 Plain washer
7 Upper radius arm	21 Shock absorber	34 Nut
8 Bush	22 Bolt	35 Nut
9 Bush	23 Bush	36 Plain washer
10 Spring seat-metal	24 Plain washer	37 Lower radius arm
11 Cable clip	25 Nut	38 Plain washer
12 Bolt	26 Nut	39 Nut
13 Spring washer	27 Plain washer	
14 Plain washer		

22 Steering wheel - removal and replacement

1 If a steering wheel embellishment is fitted, undo and remove the two crosshead screws that secure it to the spokes. The screw heads will be found on the underside of the spokes. Lift away the embellishment.

2 With the front wheels in the straight ahead position note the position of the spokes of the steering wheel and mark the hub of the steering wheel and inner shaft to ensure correct positioning upon refitting.

3 Using a socket or box spanner of correct size slacken and remove the steering wheel nut. Remove the wheel by thumping the rear of the rim adjacent to the spokes with the palms of the hands which should loosen the hub splines from the steering shaft splines. Lift away the steering wheel.

4 Replacement is the reverse procedure to removal. Correctly align the two marks previously made to ensure correct positioning of the spokes. Do not thump the steering wheel as it could cause the inner shaft to collapse. Refit the nut and tighten to a torque wrench setting of 20 - 25 lb ft (2.8 - 3.4 kg m).

23 Steering column assembly - removal and replacement

1 Bend back the lock washer tabs and undo and remove the two bolts that secure the clamp bar to the upper universal joint assembly. Lift away the lockwasher and clamp bar.

2 Undo and remove the nut, spring washer and long bolt that holds the two halves of the column shroud. Lift away the annulus from the top of the shroud. Pull off the choke control knob (if a manual choke is fitted). Using a knife, separate the two halves of the shroud and lift away.

3 Slacken the choke control locknut on the bracket positioned at the side of the steering column. Release the choke outer cable from the bracket by sliding it through the slot in the bracket.

4 Locate the ignition switch wiring loom multi pin connector located half way down the column and detach the connector and two singer connectors.

5 Undo and remove the two bolts and shakeproof washers that secure the direction indicator switch. Lift away the switch.

6 Remove the steering wheel as described in Section 22.

7 Lift away the direction indicator self cancel cam and spring from the inner shaft.

8 Detach the brake pedal return spring from the pedal assembly.

9 Undo and remove the bolts and spring washers that secure the steering column mounting bolts to the underside of the dash panel.

10 Pull the column assembly into the car and lift away. Take care not to touch the headlining or trim, with the column.

11 To refit the steering column locate it in its approximate position making sure that the grommets located at the bottom of the assembly locates in the dash panel. The triangular shaft locates in the universal joint clamp.

12 Refitting is now the reverse sequence to removal. Make sure that the ear on the self cancel cam is adjacent to the cancelling lever of the indicator switch when the front wheels are in the straight ahead position. When refitting the steering wheel do not thump it as the inner shaft could collapse. Finally before the steering wheel nut is replaced, check that the direction indicator's self cancel operates correctly.

24 Steering column shaft - removal and replacement

1 Refer to Section 23 and remove the steering column assembly.

2 Lift away the lower bearing cover. Using a pointed chisel carefully prise open the staking and ease out the lower bearing. (Fig 11 : 13).

3 With a pair of circlip pliers contract and withdraw the circlip and plain washer from the top end of the shaft.

4 Again with the circlip pliers, remove the upper bearing top retaining circlip.

5 Using a soft faced hammer carefully tap the shaft down through the outer tube and then remove the top bearing together with its cover.

6 The shaft may now be completely removed from the outer tube. Finally remove the upper bearing lower retaining circlip.

7 Inspect the shaft for signs of collapse. The total length of the shaft must be 31.12 $\pm$ 0.02 in (790.5 $\pm$ 0.5 mm) and if it is shorter it may be carefully pulled back to the optimum length. Grasp both ends and try twisting. If backlash is evident a new shaft must be obtained. Check that the steering wheel location splines are in good order and not worn.

8 To reassemble, first fit a new upper bearing lower retainer circlip. Insert the shaft into the outer tube and slide the upper bearing onto the shaft until it locates on its splines in front of the circlip.

9 Fit the upper bearing cover and push the shaft into its final fitted position in the outer tube. Locate and fit a new upper bearing top retaining circlip.

10 Next fit the plain washer and secure the assembly with a new shaft retaining circlip.

11 Fit a new lower bearing and secure it in position by staking it in the place provided. Refit the lower bearing cover.

25 Steering column flexible coupling and universal joint assembly - removal and replacement

1 Undo and remove the nut, clamp bolt and spring washer that secures the flexible coupling bottom half to the pinion shaft.

2 Bend back the lock tabs and undo and remove the two bolts securing the universal joint lock bar to the lower steering shaft. Lift away the tab washer and lock bar.

3 The lower steering shaft may now be lifted away.

4 To refit place the lower steering shaft in its approximate fitted position and align the master splines on the shaft and pinion. Connect the shaft to the pinion.

5 Position the triangular clamp on the bottom of the steering column and secure with the clamp bar bolts and tab washer. Tighten the bolts fully and lock by bending up the tabs.

6 Refit the flexible coupling bottom half clamp bolt spring washer and nut. Tighten to a torque wrench setting of 12 - 15 lb ft (1.7 - 2.1 kg m).

26 Rack and pinion steering gear - removal and replacement

1 Before starting this operation set the steering wheel to the straight ahead position.

2 Jack up the front of the car and place blocks under the wheels. Lower the car slightly so that the track rods are in a near horizontal position.

3 Undo and remove the nut, bolt and spring washer that secures the flexible coupling bottom half clamp to the pinion shaft.

4 Bend back the lock tabs and then undo and remove the bolts that secure the steering gear assembly to the mountings on the front axle frame. Lift away the bolts, lock washers and 'U' shaped clamps.

5 Withdraw the split pins and undo and remove the castellated nuts from the ends of each track rod where they join the steering arms. Using a universal balljoint separator, separate the track rod ball pins from the steering arms and lower the steering gear assembly downwards out of the car.

6 Before replacing the steering gear assembly make sure the wheels have remained in the straight ahead position. Also check the condition of the mounting rubbers round the housing and if they appear worn or damaged they must be renewed.

7 Check that the steering rack is also in the straight ahead position. This can be done by ensuring that the distances between the ends of both track rods and the rack housing on both sides are the same.

8 Place the steering gear assembly in its location on the front axle frame and at the same time mate up the splines on the pinion shaft with the splines in the clamp on the steering column

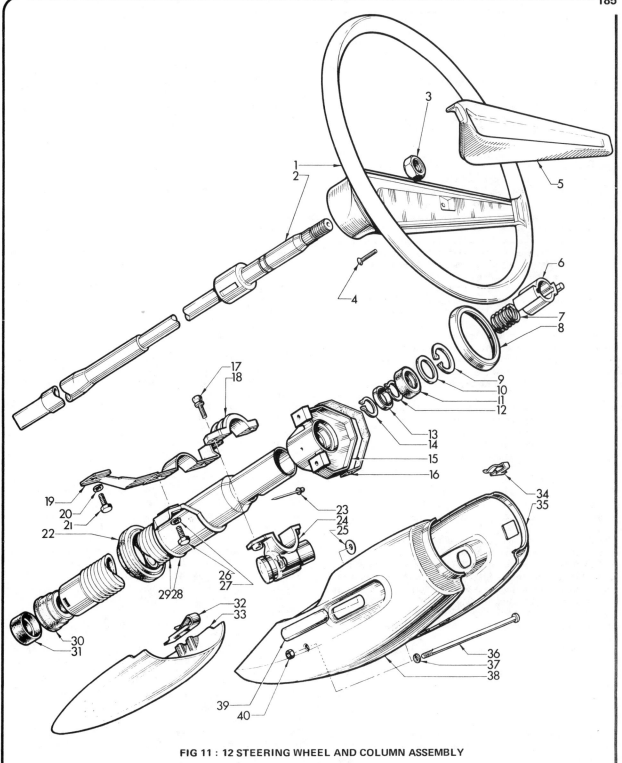

FIG 11 : 12 STEERING WHEEL AND COLUMN ASSEMBLY

1 Steering wheel	12 Circlip	23 Rivet	33 Column shroud half
2 Steering shaft	13 Upper bearing	24 Bracket	(alternative)
3 Nut	14 Circlip	25 Clip	34 Clip
4 Screw	15 Bracket - upper	26 Bolt	35 Column shroud half
5 Embellisher	16 Bracket surround	27 Spring washer	36 Bolt
6 Self cancel cam	17 Bolt	28 Outer tube	37 Spring washer
7 Spring	18 Bracket end cap	29 Collapsible outer tube	38 Column shroud half
8 Annulus	19 Bracket - lower	30 Lower bearing	39 Chrome finisher (auto-
9 Circlip	20 Spring washer	31 Bearing cover	matic choke only)
10 Plain washer	21 Bolt	32 Spire nut	40 Nut
11 Bearing cover	22 Rubber grommet		

flexible column. There is a master spline so make sure these are in line.

9 Replace the two 'U' shaped clamps using new locking tabs under the bolts, tighten the bolts to a torque wrench setting of 12 - 15 lb ft (1.7 - 2.1 kg m). Bend up the locking tabs.

10 Refit the track rod ends into the steering arms, replace the castellated nuts and tighten them to a torque wrench setting of 18 - 22 lb ft (2.5 - 3.0 kg m). Use new split pins to lock the nuts.

11 Tighten the clamp bolt on the steering column flexible coupling to a torque wrench setting of 12 - 15 lb ft (1.7 - 2.1 kg m), having first double checked that the pinion is correctly located on the splines.

12 Jack up the car, remove the blocks from under the wheels and lower the car to the ground. The toe in must now be checked and further information will be found in Section 21.

---

27 Rack and pinion steering gear - adjustments

1 For the steering gear to function correctly, two adjustments are necessary. These are pinion bearing pre-load and rack damper adjustment. Care must be taken not to overtighten otherwise seizure may take place. Double check all readings.

2 To carry out these adjustments, remove the steering gear from the car as described in Section 26, then mount the steering gear assembly in a soft jawed vice so that the pinion is in a horizontal position, and the rack damper cover plate to the top.

3 Remove the rack damper cover plate by undoing and removing the two retaining bolts and spring washers. Lift away the cover plate, gasket and shims. Also remove the small spring and the recessed yoke, which bears onto the rack. These parts are shown in Fig 11 : 14.

4 Now remove the pinion bearing pre-load cover plate from the base of the pinion, by undoing and removing the two bolts and spring washers. Lift away the cover-plate, gasket and shims.

5 To set the pinion bearing pre-load replace the cover plate with the shim pack (0.093 in shim uppermost). Tighten the bolts down evenly, and firmly until the cover plate makes contact. Leave out the gasket at this stage.

6 Measure the gap between the cover plate and pinion housing. This gap should be 0.011—0.013 in. (0.28—0.33 mm). Take several readings near each bolts to ensure the inner plate is parallel. Note the final reading.

7 Building up a shim pack to the required thickness and use at least two shims in addition to the 0.093 in. shim which must always be fitted next to the cover BUT subtract 0.001 inch from your final reading before doing so. Select your shims from those given in a shim pack and make it within 0 to plus 0.025 of this figure. For example if the final reading was 0.028 in. the shim pile selected should be within 0.027 to 0.0295 when measured with a micrometer. Shim thicknesses available are given below.

Part No.	Material	Thickness
71 BB - 3K544 - AA	Steel	0.005 in (0.13 mm)
71 BB - 3K544 - BA	Steel	0.007 in (0.19 mm)
71 BB - 3K544 - CA	Steel	0.010 in (0.25 mm)
71 BB - 3K544 - DA	Steel	0.092 in (2.35 mm)
71 BB - 3K544 - LA	Steel	0.002 in (0.05 mm)
71 BB - 3581 - AA	Buna coated flexoid	0.01 in (0.254 mm)

8 With the cover plate removed, make sure that the pinion grease seal is packed with Castrol LM grease. Smear some jointing compound onto the cover plate mating face and refit the cover plate.

9 Smear a little Loctite or similar sealer on the threads of the bolts and tighten them down to a torque wrench setting of 6 - 8 lb ft (0.9 - 1.1 kg m).

10 To reset the rack damper adjustment, replace the yoke in its location on the rack and make sure it is fully home. Using a straight edge and feeler gauges, measure the distance between the top of the slipper and the surface of the pinion housing. Make a note of this dimension.

11 Assemble a shim pack including the gasket whose thickness is greater than the measurement obtained in paragraph 10, by between 0.006 - 0.0005 in (0.152 - 0.013 mm). Shim thicknesses

available are listed below:

Part No.	Material	Thickness
71 BB - 3N597 - AA	Steel	0.005 in (0.127 mm)
71 BB - 3N597 - BA	Steel	0.007 in (0.19 mm)
71 BB - 3N597 - CA	Steel	0.010 in (0.25 mm)
71 BB - 3N597 - DA	Steel	0.015 in (0.38 mm)
71 BB - 3N597 - EA	Steel	0.020 in (0.50 mm)
71 BB - 3N597 - FA	Steel	0.060 in (1.5 mm)
71 BB - 3N598 - AA	Buna coated flexoid	0.010 in (0.25 mm)

12 Fit the spring into the recess in the yoke. Place the shim pack so that the gasket will be next to the cover plate and refit the cover plate. Apply a little Loctite or similar sealing compound to the bolt threads. Tighten down the bolts to a torque wrench setting of 6 - 8 lb ft (0.9 - 1.1 kg m).

---

28 Rack and pinion steering gear - dismantling and reassembly

1 Remove the steering gear assembly from the car as described in Section 26.

2 Undo the track rod balljoint locknuts and unscrew the balljoints. Lift away the plain washer and remove the locknut. To assist in obtaining an approximate correct setting for track rod adjustment mark the threads or count the number of turns required to undo the balljoint.

3 Slacken off the clips securing the rubber gaiter to each track rod and rack housing end. Carefully pull off the gaiters. Have a quantity of rag handy to catch the oil which will escape when the gaiters are removed. Note - On some steering gear assemblies soft iron wire is used instead of clips. Always secure the gaiter with clips.

4 To dismantle the steering gear assembly it is only necessary to remove the tract rod which is furthest away from the pinion.

5 To remove the track rod, place the steering gear assembly in a soft jawed vice. Working on the track rod balljoint, carefully drill out the pin that locks the ball housing to the locknut. Great care must be taken not to drill too deeply or the rack will be irreparably damaged. The hole should be about 0.375 in (9.525 mm) deep.

6 Hold the locknut with a spanner, then grip the ball housing with a mole wrench and undo it from the treads on the rack.

7 Take out the spring and ball seat from the recess in the end of the rack and then unscrew the locknut from the threads on the rack. The spring and ball seal must be renewed during re-assembly.

8 Carefully prise out the pinion dust seal and then withdraw the pinion together with the bearing assembly nearest the flexible coupling. As the bearings utilise bearing tracks and loose balls (fourteen in each bearing) care must be taken not to lose any of the balls or drop them into the steering gear on reassembly.

9 Undo and remove the two bolts and spring washers that secure the rack damper cover. Lift away the cover, gasket, shims, springs and yoke.

10 With the pinion removed, withdraw the complete rack assembly with one track rod still attached from the pinion end of the casing.

11 The remaining pinion bearing assembly may now be removed from the rack housing.

12 It is always advisable to withdraw the rack from the pinion end of the rack housing. This avoids passing the rack teeth through the bush at the other end of the casing and causing possible damage.

13 Carefully examine all parts for signs of wear or damage. Check the condition of the rack support bush at the opposite end of the casing from the pinion. If this is worn renew it. If the rack or pinion teeth are in any way damaged a new rack and pinion will have to be obtained.

14 Take the pinion seal off the top of the casing and replace it

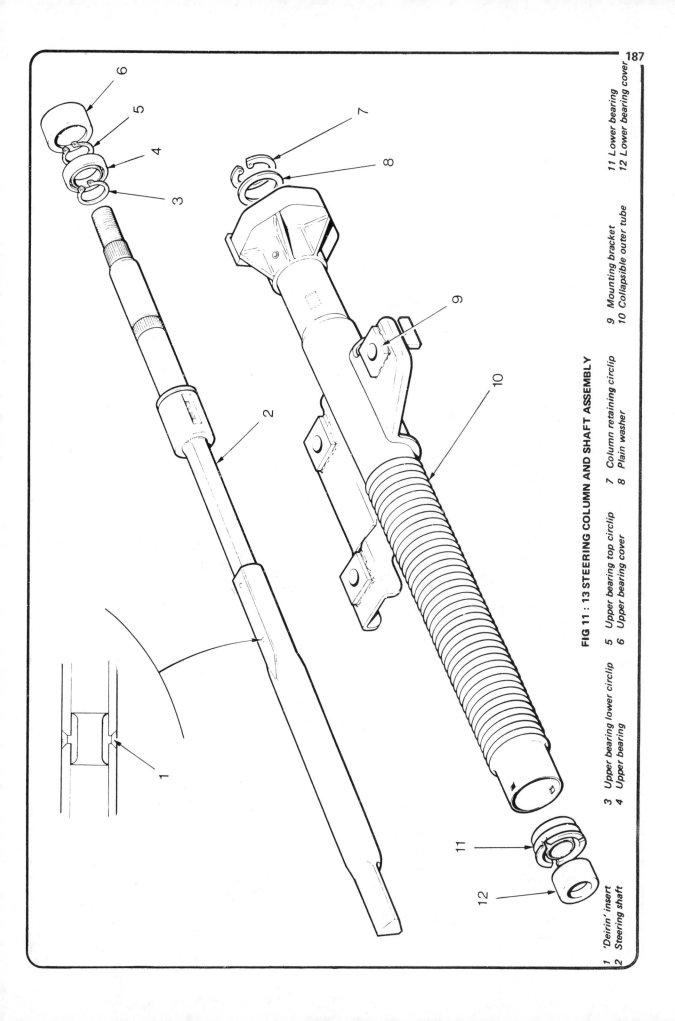

FIG 11 : 13 STEERING COLUMN AND SHAFT ASSEMBLY

1 'Deirin' insert	3 Upper bearing lower circlip	5 Upper bearing top circlip	7 Column retaining circlip	9 Mounting bracket	11 Lower bearing
2 Steering shaft	4 Upper bearing	6 Upper bearing cover	8 Plain washer	10 Collapsible outer tube	12 Lower bearing cover

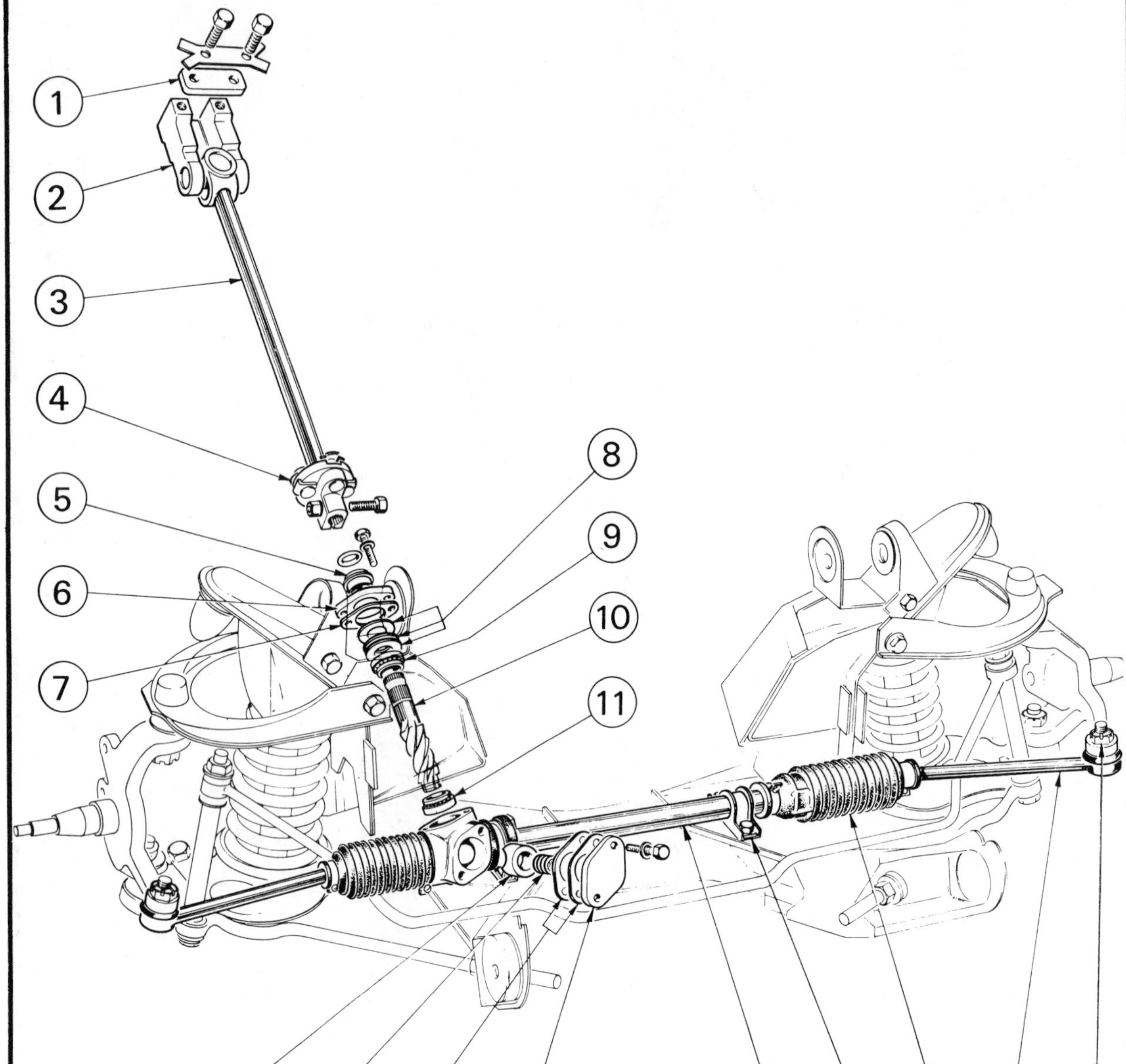

188

FIG.11.14. EXPLODED VIEW OF RACK AND PINION AND LOWER COLUMN ASSEMBLY

1 Clamp bar	6 Pinion cover	11 Lower pinion bearing	16 Rack housing
2 Universal joint assembly	7 Pinion cover jointing gasket	12 Track rod outer ball joint	17 Slipper bearing cover
3 Lower steering shaft	8 Pinion pre-load shims	13 Track rod	18 Slipper pre-load spring
4 Flexible coupling	9 Upper pinion bearing	14 Rack bellows	20 Slipper
5 Pinion cover grease seal	10 Pinion	15 Rack mounting bracket	

with a new seal.

15 To commence reassembly, fit the lower pinion bearing and thrust washer into their recess in the casing. The loose balls can be held in place by a small amount of grease.

16 Replace the rack in the housing from the pinion end and position it in the straight ahead position by equalising the amount it protrudes at either end of the casing.

17 Replace the remaining pinion bearing and thrust washer onto the pinion and fit the pinion into its housing so that the larger master spline on the pinion shaft is parallel to the rack and on the right hand side of the pinion.

18 Replace the rack damper yoke, springs, shims, gasket and cover plate.

19 To replace the track rod that has been removed, start by fitting a new spring and ball seat to the recess in the end of the rack shaft and replace the locknut onto the threads of the rack.

20 Lubricate the ball, ball seat and ballhousing with a small amount of Castrol Hypoy 90. Then slide the ball housing over the track rod and screw the housing onto the rack threads keeping the track rod in the horizontal position until the track rod starts to become stiff to move.

21 Using a normal spring balance, hook it round the track rod 0.5 in (12.70 mm) from the end and check the effort required to move it from the horizontal position.

22 By adjusting the tightness of the ball housing on the rack threads the effort required to move the track rod must be set at 5 lbs (2.8 kg).

23 Tighten the locknut up to the housing and then recheck that the effort required to move the track rod is still correct at 5 lbs (2.8 kg).

24 On the line where the locknut and ball housing meet, drill a 0.125 in (3.175 mm) diameter hole which must be 0.375 in (0.525 mm) deep. Even if the two halves of the old hole previously drilled out align, a new hole must be drilled.

25 Tap a new retaining pin into the hole and peen the end over to secure it.

26 Refit the rubber gaiters and track rod ends ensuring that they are replaced in exactly the same position from which they were removed.

27 Remove the rack damper cover plate and pour in 0.25 pint (0.15 litre) of Castrol Hypoy 90. Then carry out both steering gear adjustments as described in Section 27.

28 After the steering gear has been refitted to the car the toe in must be checked. Further information will be found in Section 21.

---

29 Steering rack rubber gaiter - removal and replacement

1 Jack up the front of the car and place blocks under the wheels. Lower the car slightly so that the track rods are in a near horizontal position.

2 Withdraw the split pin and undo the castellated nut holding the balljoint taper pin to the steering arm. Using a universal balljoint separator part the taper pin from the steering arm.

3 Undo the track rod balljoint locknut and unscrew the balljoint. To assist in obtaining an approximate correct setting for track rod adjustment, mark the threads or count the number of turns required to undo the balljoint.

4 Slacken off the clips securing the rubber gaiter to the track rod and rack housing end. Carefully pull off the gaiter. Have a quantity of rag handy to catch the oil which will escape when the gaiters are removed. Note: On some steering gear assemblies soft iron wire is used instead of clips. Always secure the gaiter with clips.

5 Fitting a new rubber gaiter is now the reverse sequence to removal. It will be necessary to refill the steering gear assembly with Castrol Hypoy 90. Full information will be found in Section 21.

---

30 Track rod end - removal and replacement

Full information will be found in Section 29, omitting paragraphs **4** and **5**.

FAULT DIAGNOSIS - SUSPENSION, DAMPERS AND STEERING

Symptom	Reason/s	Remedy
General wear or damage	Tyre pressures uneven	Check pressures and adjust as necessary.
	Shock absorbers worn	Test, and replace if worn.
	Spring broken	Renew springs.
	Steering gear ball joints badly worn	Fit new ball joints.
	Suspension geometry incorrect	Check and rectify.
	Steering mechanism free play excessive	Adjust or overhaul steering mechanism.
Lack of maintenance or accident damage	Tyre pressure too low	Check pressures and inflate tyres.
	No grease in steering swivels	Re-grease thoroughly.
	No oil in steering gear	Top up steering gear.
	No grease in steering and suspension ball joints	Re-grease thoroughly.
	Front wheel toe-in incorrect	Check and reset toe-in.
	Suspension geometry incorrect	Check and rectify.
	Steering gear incorrectly adjusted too tightly	Check and re-adjust steering gear.
	Steering column badly misaligned	Determine cause and rectify.
General wear or damage	Wheel nuts loose	Check and tighten as necessary.
	Front wheels and tyres out of balance	Balance wheels and tyres.
	Steering ball joints badly worn	Replace steering gear ball joints.
	Hub bearings badly worn	Remove and fit new hub bearings.
	Steering gear free play excessive	Adjust and overhaul steering gear.
	Front springs weak or broken	Inspect and overhaul as necessary.

Chapter 12 Bodywork and underframe

Contents

1 General description

The combined body and underframe is of an all steel welded construction. This makes a very strong and torsionally rigid shell.

The Cortina models are available in either saloon or estate - car versions. There are four forward hinged doors for either version (two door as an option on GT models). The windscreen is slightly curved and is zone toughened. In the event of windscreen shattering this 'zone' breaks into much larger pieces than the rest of the screen thus giving the driver much better vision than would otherwise be possible.

The Aeroflow type of ventilation system is fitted. Air being drawn in through a grille on the scuttle can either be heated or pass straight into the car. Used air passes out through a grille below the rear window.

The estate cars have the same engine and general specifications as the saloon except that the air extraction vents are on the rear quarter panels and the counterbalanced tailgate is fitted with a lock. The loading capacity as a five seater is 33.2 cu ft (0.94 cu m) or as a two seater 63.8 cu ft (1.81 cu m).

Although the wheelbase for the saloon and estate car versions is the same, the overall length of the estate car is 9.3 in (236.22 mm) longer.

For additional occupant safety the instruments and controls are deeply recessed in the facia and thick padding is used to surround the top of the dash panel.

2 Maintenance - bodywork and underframe

1 The condition of your car's bodywork is of considerable importance as it is on this that the second hand value of the car will mainly depend. It is much more difficult to repair neglected bodywork than to renew mechanical assemblies. The hidden portions of the body, such as the wheel arches, the underframe and the engine compartment are equally important, although obviously not requiring such frequent attention as the immediately visible paintwork.

2 Once a year or every 12,000 miles (20,000 km) it is sound to visit your local main agent and have the underside of the body steam cleaned. This will take about 1½ hours. All traces of dirt and oil will be removed and the underside can then be inspected carefully for rust, damaged hydraulic pipes, frayed electrical wiring and similar maladies. The car should be greased on completion of this job.

3 At the same time the engine compartment should be cleaned in a similar manner. If steam cleaning facilities are not available then brush 'Gunk' or a similar cleanser over the whole engine compartment with a stiff paint brush, working it well in where there is an accumulation of oil and dirt. Do not paint the ignition system, and protect it with oily rags when the 'Gunk' is washed off. As the Gunk is washed away it will take with it all traces of oil and dirt, leaving the engine looking clean and bright.

4 The wheel arches should be given particular attention as under sealing can easily come away here and stones and dirt thrown up from the road wheels can soon cause the paint to chip and flake, and so allow rust to set in. If rust is found, clean down the bare metal with wet and dry paper, paint on an anti-corrosive coating such as Kurust, or if preferred, red lead, and renew the paintwork and undercoating.

5 The bodywork should be washed once a week or when dirty. Thoroughly wet the car to soften the dirt and then wash the car down with a soft sponge and plenty of clean water. If the surplus dirt is not washed off very gently, in time it will wear the paint down as surely as wet and dry paper. It is best to use a hose if this is available. Give the car a final wash down and then dry with a soft chamois leather to prevent the formation of spots.

6 Spots of tar and grease thrown up from the road can be removed by a rag dampened with petrol.

7 Once every six months, or every three months if wished, give

the bodywork and chromium trim a thoroughly good wax polish. If a chromium cleaner is used to remove rust on any of the car's plated parts remember that the cleaner also removes part of the chromium, so use sparingly.

3 Maintenance - upholstery and carpets

1 Remove the carpets or mats and thoroughly vacuum clean the interior of the car every three months or more frequently if necessary.
2 Beat out the carpets and vacuum clean them if they are very dirty. If the upholstery is soiled apply an upholstery cleaner with a damp sponge and wipe off with a clean dry cloth.

4 Maintenance - PVC external roof covering

Under no circumstances try to clean any external PVC roof covering with detergents, caustic soaps or spirit cleaners. Plain soap and water is all that is required with a soft brush to clean dirt that may be ingrained. Wash the covering as frequently as the rest of the car.

5 Minor body repairs

1 At some time during the ownership of your car it is likely that it will be bumped or scraped in a mild way, causing some slight damage to the body.
2 Major damage must be repaired by your local Ford agent, but there is no reason why you cannot successfully beat out, repair and re-spray minor damage yourself. The essential items which the owner should gather together to ensure a really professional job are:
a) a plastic filler such as Holts 'Cataloy'.
b) paint whose colour matches exactly that of the bodywork, either in a can for application by a spray gun, or in an aerosol can
c) fine cutting paste
d) medium and fine grade wet and dry paper.
3 Never use a metal hammer to knock out small dents as the blows tend to scratch and distort the metal. Knock out the dent with a mallet or rawhide hammer and press on the underside of the dented surface a metal dolly or smooth wooden block roughly contoured to the normal shape of the damaged area.
4 After the worst of the damaged area has been knocked out, rub down the dent and surrounding area with medium wet and dry paper and thoroughly clean away all traces of dirt.
5 The plastic filler comprises a paste and hardener which must be thoroughly mixed together. Mix only a small quantity at a time as the paste sets hard within five to fifteen minutes depending on the amount of hardener used.
6 Smooth on the filler with a knife or stiff plastic to the shape of the damaged portion and allow to thoroughly dry, a process which takes about six hours. After the filler has dried it is likely that it will have contracted slightly, so spread on a second layer of filler if necessary.
7 Smooth down the filler with fine wet and dry paper wrapped round a small flat block of wood and continue until the whole area is perfectly smooth and it is impossible to feel where the filler joins the rest of the paintwork.
8 Spray on from an aerosol can, or with a spray gun, an anti-rust undercoat, smooth down with wet and dry paper, and then spray on two coats of the final finish using a circular motion.
8 When thoroughly dry, polish the whole area with a fine cutting paste to smooth the re-sprayed area into the remainder of the wing or panel and to remove the small particles of spray paint which will have settled round the area.
10 This will leave the area looking perfect with not a trace of the previous unsightly dent.

6 Major body repairs

1 Because the body is built on the monocoque principle and is integral with the underframe, major damage must be repaired by competent mechanics with the necessary welding and hydraulic straightening equipment.
2 If the damage has been serious it is vital that the body is checked for correct alignment, as otherwise the handling of the car will suffer and many other faults such as excessive tyre wear and wear in the transmission and steering may occur.
3 There is a special body jig which most large body repair shops have and to ensure that all is correct it is important that this jig be used for all major repair work.

7 Maintenance - hinges and locks

Once every 3,000 miles (5,000 km) or 4 months the door, bonnet and boot or tailgate hinges and locks should be oiled with a few drops of oil from an oil can. The door striker plates can be given a thin smear of grease to reduce wear and ensure free movement.

8 Front bumper - removal and replacement

1 Open the bonnet and remove the radiator grille as described in Section 32.
2 Undo and remove the nuts, washer and spacer assemblies that secure the wrap round ends of the bumper bar. Then unscrew the crosshead screws that secure the under riders to the body. (Fig. 12:1).
3 The front bumper assembly may now be lifted away taking care not to scratch the paintwork on the front wings.
4 If it is necessary to detach the under riders from the bumper bar, undo and remove the nut and washer that secure the bracket and under rider to the bumper bar.
5 Refitting the bumper bar and under riders is the reverse sequence to removal. Do not fully tighten the fixings until the bumper bar is perfectly straight and correctly located.

9 Rear bumper - removal and replacement

1 Undo and remove the crosshead screws that secure the number plate light and place to one side.
2 Undo and remove the crosshead screws that secure the under-riders to the body.
3 Open the luggage compartment lid and roll back the matting. Undo and remove the bolts and washers that secure the bumper bar brackets to the body (Fig.12:2).
4 The rear bumper may now be lifted away taking care not to scratch the paintwork on the rear wings.
5 If it is necessary to detach the under riders and brackets undo and remove the bolts, spring and plain washers.
6 Refitting the bumper bar and under riders is the reverse sequence to removal. Do not fully tighten the fixings until the bumper bar is perfectly straight and correctly located.

10 Windscreen glass - removal and replacement

1 If you are unfortunate enough to have a windscreen shatter, or should you wish to renew your present windscreen, fitting a replacement is one of the few jobs which the average owner is advised to leave to a professional. For the owner who wishes to attempt the job himself the following instructions are given:
2 Cover the bonnet with a blanket or cloth to prevent accidental damage and remove the windscreen wiper blades and arms as detailed in Chapter 10/23.
3 Put on a pair of lightweight shoes and get onto one of the front seats. An assistant should be ready to catch the glass as it

is released from the body aperture.

4   Place a piece of soft cloth between the soles of your shoes and the windscreen glass and with both feet on one top corner of the windscreen, push firmly.

5   When the weatherstrip has freed itself from the body aperture flange in that area repeat the process at frequent intervals along the top edge of the windscreen until, from outside the car the glass and weatherstrip can be removed together.

6   If you are having to replace your windscreen due to a shattered screen, remove all traces of sealing compound and broken glass from the weatherstrip and body flange.

7   Now is the time to remove all pieces of glass if the screen has shattered. Use a vacuum cleaner to extract as much as possible. Switch on the heater boost motor and adjust the screen controls to 'screen defrost' but watch out for flying pieces of glass which might have blown out of the ducting.

8   Carefully inspect the rubber moulding for signs of splitting or deterioration.

9   To refit the glass, first fit the weatherstrip onto the glass with the joint at the lower edge.

10 Insert a piece of thick cord into the channel of the weatherstrip with the two ends protruding by at least 12 in (304.8 mm) at the top centre of the weatherstrip.

11 Mix a concentrated soap and water solution and apply to the flange of the windscreen aperture.

12 Offer the screen up to the aperture and with an assistant to press the rubber surround hard against one end of the cord, move round the windscreen, so drawing the lip over the windscreen flange of the body. Keep the draw cord parallel to the windscreen as shown in Fig.12:3. Using the palms of the hands, thump on the glass from the outside to assist the lip in passing over the flange and to seat the screen correctly onto the aperture.

13 To ensure a good watertight joint apply some Seelastik SR51 between the weatherstrip and the body and press the weatherstrip against the body to give a good seal.

14 Any excess Seelastik may be removed with a petrol moistened cloth.

15 A special shaped tool is now required to insert the finisher and full details of this are given in Fig.12:5. A handyman should be able to make up an equivalent tool using netting wire and a wooden file handle.

16 Fit the eye of the tool into the groove and feed in the finisher strip.

17 Push the tool around the complete length of the moulding, feeding the finisher into the channel as the eyelet opens it.

18 Refit the wiper arms and blades and do not forget the Road Fund Tax disc.

11 Door rattles - tracing and rectification

1   The most common cause of door rattle is a misaligned, loose or worn striker plate. However other causes may be:
a) loose door or window winder handles
b) loose or misaligned door lock components
c) loose or worn remote control mechanism

2   It is quite possible for door rattles to be the result of a combination of the above faults so a careful examination should be made to determine the exact cause of the rattles.

3   If striker plate wear or misalignment is the cause of the rattle the plate should be renewed or adjusted as necessary. The procedure for these tasks is detailed in Section 13.

4   Should the window winder handle rattle, this can be rectified easily by inserting a rubber washer between the escutcheon and door trim panel.

5   If the rattle is found to be emanating from the door lock it will in all probability mean that the lock is worn and therefore should be replaced with a new lock unit as described in Section 15.

6   Lastly if it is worn hinge pins causing rattles they should be renewed.

12 Front and rear door - removal and replacement

1   Using a pencil, accurately mark the outline of the hinge relative to the door pillar to assist refitting. It is desirable to have an assistant to take the weight of the door once the hinges have been released. Remove the two bolts that secure each hinge to the pillar and lift away the complete door.

2   For storage it is best to stand the door on an old blanket and allow it to lean against a wall also suitably padded at the top to stop scratching.

3   Refitting the door is the reverse sequence to removal. If after refitting, adjustment is necessary, it should be done at the hinges to give correct alignment, or the striker reset if the door either moves up or down on final closing.

13 Door striker plate - removal, replacement and adjustment

1   If it is wished to renew a worn striker plate, mark its position on the door pillar so a new plate can be fitted in the same position.

2   To remove the plate simply undo and remove the four crosshead screws which hold the plate in position. Lift away the plate (Fig.12:4).

3   Replacement of the door striker plate is the reverse sequence to removal.

4   To adjust the door striker plate, slacken the four crosshead screws and move the striker plate in or out as necessary. Make sure that the lock engages fully when the door is flush with the body exterior line. It is very important that the door is not adjusted to be flush with the body in the safety catch position. When the correct position has been found, tighten the four crosshead screws firmly.

14 Door trim - removal and replacement

1   Using a knife or thin wide bladed screwdriver carefully prise the plastic trim from its recess in the window winder handle. This will expose the handle retaining screw (Fig.12:7).

2   Wind up the window and note the position of the handle. Undo and remove the crosshead retaining screw and lift away the handle.

3   Undo and remove the two crosshead screws that secure the door pull. Lift away the door pull. Unscrew the interior lock knob.

4   Using a screwdriver carefully remove the door lock remote control housing bezel by sliding the bezel towards the hinge end of the door. Lift away the bezel.

5   Insert a thin strip of metal with all the sharp edges removed, or a thick knife blade, between the door and the trim panel. This will release one or two of the trim panel retaining clips without damaging the trim. The panel can now be gently eased off by hand.

6   Carefully remove the plastic weatherproof sheeting. Removal is now complete.

7   Replacement is generally a reversal of the removal procedure. NOTE - When replacing the panel ensure that each of the trim panels retaining clips is firmly located in its hole by sharply striking the panel in the approximate area of each clip with the palm of the hand. This will make sure the trim is seated fully.

15 Door lock assembly - removal and replacement

1   Refer to Section 14 and remove the door interior trim.

2   Carefully ease out the door lock remote control housing assembly clear of its location in the door inner panel. Unhook the remote control rod and remove the remote control unit.

3   Working inside the door shell, carefully prise the two control rods clear of their locations in the lock assembly.

4   Undo and remove the two bolts that secure the door exterior

12.1 FRONT BUMPER BRACKET RETAINING BOLTS

12.2 REMOVAL OF REAR BUMPER BRACKET SECURING BOLTS

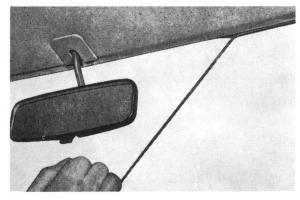

12.3 PULLING DRAW CORD TO LOCATE WEATHERSTRIP IN WINDOW APERTURE

12.4 DOOR STRIKER PLATE

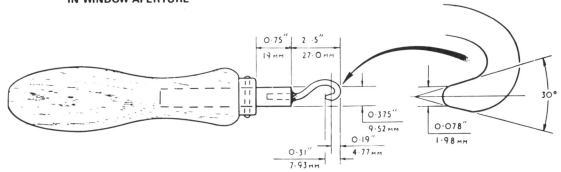

12.5 SPECIAL TOOL FOR INSERTING CHROME MOULDING

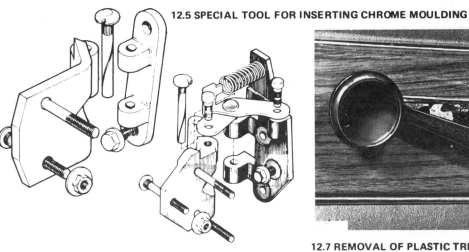

12.6 FRONT AND REAR DOOR HINGES

12.7 REMOVAL OF PLASTIC TRIM FROM WINDOW WINDER HANDLE

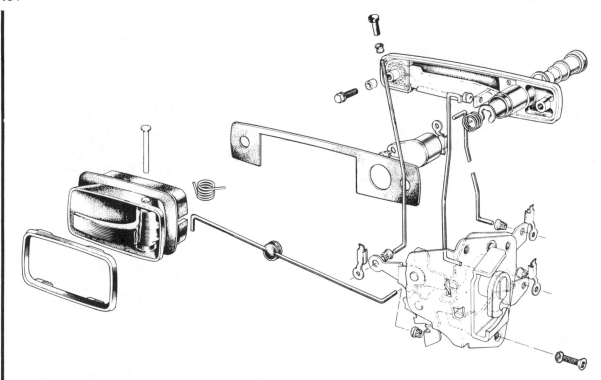

12.8 FRONT DOOR LOCK ASSEMBLY

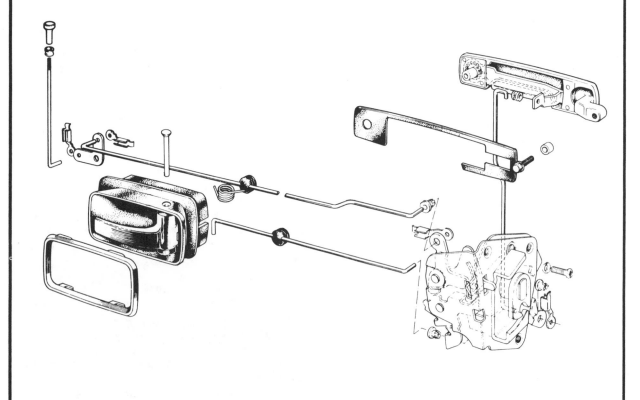

12.9 REAR DOOR LOCK ASSEMBLY

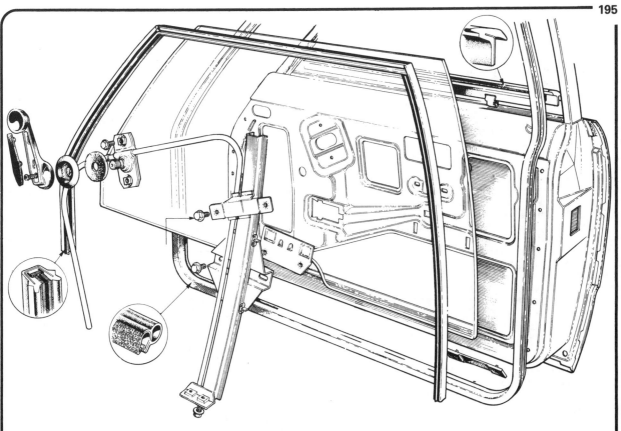

12.10 FRONT DOOR WINDOW REGULATOR AND SEALS

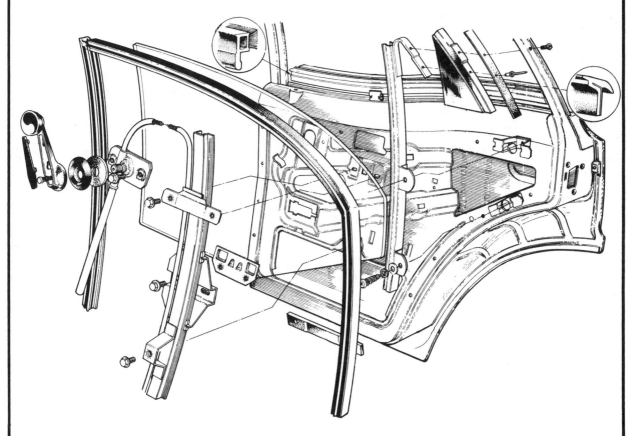

12.11 REAR DOOR WINDOW REGULATOR AND SEALS

handle to the door outer panel. The exterior handle assembly complete with control rods can now be removed.

5   Undo and remove the three crosshead screws and cup shaped shakeproof washers that secure the lock assembly to the door shell. The lock assembly may now be lifted away from inside the door.

6   Refitting the door lock assembly is the reverse sequence to removal. Lubricate all moving parts with a little Castrol LM Grease.

16 Door glass and regulator - removal and replacement

1   Using a screwdriver carefully ease out the door inner and outer weatherstrips from their retaining clips on the door panel.

2   Undo and remove the two bolts that secure the door glass to the window regulator. Tilt the glass as shown in Fig.12:13 and carefully remove the glass upwards.

3   Undo and remove the bolts that secure the window regulator to the door inner panel and lift away the regulator mechanism through the large aperture in the bottom inner panel.

4   Should it be necessary to remove the glass run channel, start at the front lower frame end and carefully ease the glass run channel from its location in the door frame.

5   Refitting the door glass and regulator is the reverse sequence to removal. Lubricate all moving parts with a little Castrol LM grease. Before refitting the trim panel check the operation and alignment of the glass and regulator and adjust if necessary. When all is correct fully tighten all securing bolts.

17 Door outer belt weatherstrip - removal and replacement

1   Wind the window down to its fullest extent. Carefully prise its weatherstrip out of the groove in the door outer bright metal finish moulding.

2   To refit, correctly position the weatherstrip over its groove and using the thumbs carefully press the strip fully into the groove.

3   Wind the window up and check that the weatherstrip is correctly fitted.

18 Bonnet - removal and replacement

1   Open the bonnet and support it open using the bonnet stay. To act as a datum for refitting, mark the position of the hinges relative to the bonnet inner panel.

2   With an assistant hold the bonnet in the open position and release the stay.

3   Undo and remove the two bolts, spring and plain washers that secure each hinge to the bonnet, and lift away the bonnet taking care not to scratch the top of the wings (photos).

4   Lean the bonnet up against a wall, suitably padded to stop scratching the paint.

5   Refitting the bonnet is the reverse sequence to removal. Any adjustment necessary can be made either at the hinges or the bonnet catch.

19 Bonnet lock - adjustment

1   Should it be necessary to adjust the bonnet catch, first slacken the locknut securing the shaft in position.

2   Using a wide bladed screwdriver, screw the shaft in or out as necessary until the correct bonnet front height is obtained. Tighten the locknut.

20 Bonnet release cable - removal, replacement and adjustment

1   Detach the operating cable from the bonnet lock spring and then undo and remove the bolt and clamp that secures the outer

cable to the front panel (Fig.12:14).

2   Working under the dashboard remove the spring clip securing the inner cable clevis pin. Withdraw the clevis pin. It may be found easier if the two bonnet release bracket retaining screws are removed before the clevis pin is withdrawn to give better access. (See Figs.12:15 and 12:16).

3   Release the outer cable from its spring clips and withdraw it from the grommet in the bulkhead.

4   Well lubricate the inner and outer cable and then refit in the reverse sequence to removal.

5   To adjust the cable, slacken the bolt that secures the cable clip nearest to the lock assembly. Push or pull the outer cable as necessary to adjust the inner cable tension and secure in its new position by tightening the clamp bolt.

21 Boot lid - removal and replacement

1   Open the boot lid to its fullest extent. To act as a datum for refitting, mark the position of the hinge relative to the lid inner panel.

2   With an assistant hold the bonnet in the open position and then undo and remove the two bolts, spring and plain washers that secure each hinge to the boot lid. Lift away the boot lid taking care not to scratch the top of the rear wings.

3   Lean the boot lid up against a wall, suitably padded to stop scratching the paint.

4   Refitting the boot lid is the reverse sequence to removal. Any adjustment necessary can be made at the hinge.

22 Boot lid lock - removal and replacement

1   Open the boot lid and carefully withdraw the spring clip located at the end of the lock spindle.

2   Undo and remove the three bolts and spring washers that secure the lock to the bonnet lid (Fig.12:17). Lift away the lock assembly.

3   Refitting the lock assembly is the reverse sequence to removal.

23 Boot lid lock striker plate - removal and replacement

1   Open the boot lid and with a pencil mark the outline of the striker plate relative to the inner rear panel to act as a datum for refitting.

2   Undo and remove the two bolts with spring and plain washers that secure the striker plate. Lift away the striker plate.

3   Refitting the striker plate is the reverse sequence to removal. Line up the striker plate with the previously made marks and tighten the securing bolts.

24 Tailgate assembly - removal and replacement

1   Open the tailgate and with a pencil mark the outline of the hinges relative to the inner panel.

2   With an assistant hold the tailgate in the open position and then undo and remove the bolts, spring and plain washers that secure each hinge to the tailgate. Lift away the tailgate taking care not to scratch the side panels.

3   Refitting the tailgate is the reverse sequence to removal. Any adjustment may be made at the hinges.

25 Tailgate lock - removal and replacement

1   Using a wide bladed screwdriver or a thick knife blade between the tailgate and the trim panel, release one or two of the trim panel retaining clips without damaging the trim. The panel can now be gently eased by hand.

2   Undo and remove the large hexagonal nut that retains the

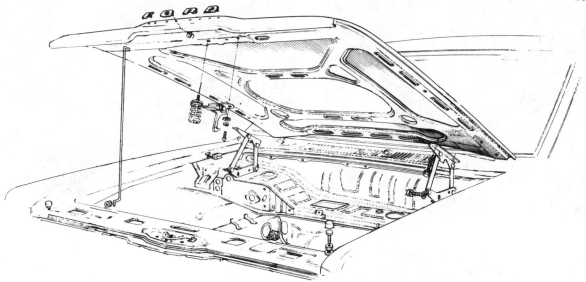

12.12 BONNET AND HINGE ASSEMBLY

12.13 DOOR GLASS REMOVAL

18.3A Slackening the bonnet hinge securing bolts

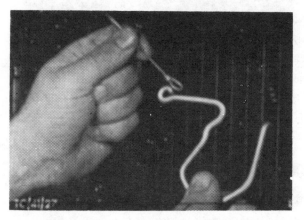

12.14 DETACHING CABLE FROM BONNET LOCK SPRING

18.3B Lifting bonnet away over front of car

This sequence of photographs deals with the repair of the dent and scratch (above rear lamp) shown in this photo. The procedure will be similar for the repair of a hole. It should be noted that the procedures given here are simplified - more explicit instructions will be found in the text

In the case of a dent the first job - after removing surrounding trim - is to hammer out the dent where access is possible. This will minimise filling. Here, the large dent having been hammered out, the damaged area is being made slightly concave

Now all paint must be removed from the damaged area, by rubbing with coarse abrasive paper. Alternatively, a wire brush or abrasive pad can be used in a power drill. Where the repair area meets good paintwork, the edge pf the paintwork should be 'feathered', using a finer grade of abrasive paper

In the case of a hole caused by rusting, all damaged sheet-metal should be cut away before proceeding to this stage. Here, the damaged area is being treated with rust remover and inhibitor before being filled

Mix the body filler according to its manufacturer's instructions. In the case of corrosion damage, it will be necessary to block off any large holes before filling - this can be done with zinc gauze or aluminium tape. Make sure the area is absolutely clean before ...

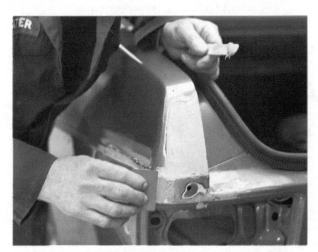

... applying the filler. Filler should be applied with a flexible applicator, as shown, for best results: the wooden spatula being used for confined areas. Apply thin layers of filler at 20-minute intervals, until the surface of the filler is slightly proud of the surrounding bodywork

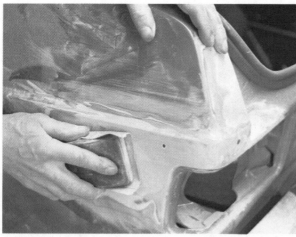

Initial shaping can be done with a Surform plane or Dreadnought file. Then, using progressively finer grades of wet-and-dry paper, wrapped around a sanding block, and copious amounts of clean water, rub-down the filler until really smooth and flat. Again, feather the edges of adjoining paintwork

The whole repair area can now be sprayed or brush-painted with primer. If spraying, ensure adjoining areas are protected from over-spray. Note that at least one-inch of the surrounding sound paintwork should be coated with primer. Primer has a 'thick' consistency, so will fill small imperfections

Again, using plenty of water, rub down the primer with a fine grade of wet-and-dry paper (400 grade is probably best) until it is really smooth and well blended into the surrounding paintwork. Any remaining imperfections can now be filled by carefully applied knifing stopper paste

When the stopper has hardened, rub-down the repair area again before applying the final coat of primer. Before rubbing-down this last coat of primer, ensure the repair area is blemish-free - use more stopper if necessary. To ensure that the surface of the primer is really smooth use some finishing compound

The top coat can now be applied. When working out of doors, pick a dry, warm and wind-free day. Ensure surrounding areas are protected from over-spray. Agitate the aerosol thoroughly, then spray the centre of the repair area, working outwards with a circular motion. Apply the paint as several thin coats.

After a period of about two-weeks, which the paint needs to harden fully, the surface of the repaired area can be 'cut' with a mild cutting compound prior to wax polishing. When carrying out bodywork repairs, remember that the quality of the finished job is proportional to the time and effort expended

12.15 BONNET RELEASE LEVER ASSEMBLY

12.16 BONNET RELEASE CABLE AND GRILLE FITTINGS

12.17 BOOT LID LOCK AND STRIKER PLATE

12.18 LUGGAGE COMPARTMENT AND LID COMPONENTS

12.19 COMPONENT PARTS OF TAILGATE

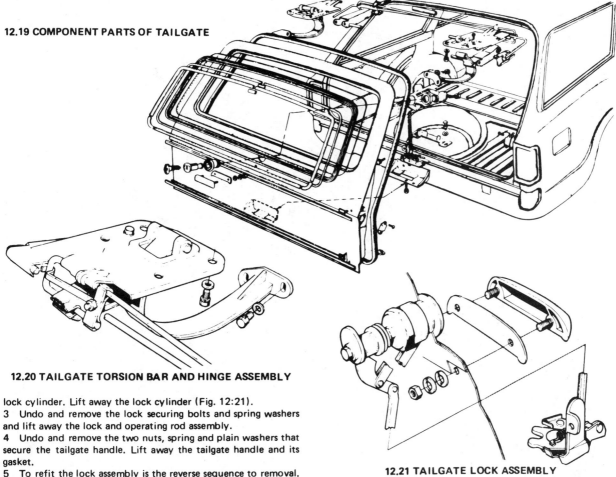

12.20 TAILGATE TORSION BAR AND HINGE ASSEMBLY

lock cylinder. Lift away the lock cylinder (Fig. 12:21).
3   Undo and remove the lock securing bolts and spring washers and lift away the lock and operating rod assembly.
4   Undo and remove the two nuts, spring and plain washers that secure the tailgate handle. Lift away the tailgate handle and its gasket.
5   To refit the lock assembly is the reverse sequence to removal. Do not tighten the lock and operating rod assembly bolts until the lock cylinder has been refitted and the cylinder keyways connected to the operating rod assembly.

26 Tailgate lock striker plate - removal and replacement

1   Open the tailgate and with a pencil mark the outline of the striker plate relative to the luggage compartment floor.
2   Undo and remove the bolts, spring and plain washers that secure the striker plate and lift away the striker plate.
3   Refitting the striker plate is the reverse sequence to removal. Line up the striker plate with the previously made mark and tighten the securing bolts.

27 Tailgate hinge and torsion bar - removal and replacement

1   Refer to Section 24 and remove the tailgate assembly.
2   With a pencil mark the outline of the hinge and torsion bar assembly to the body.
3   Undo and remove the four bolts, spring and plain washers that secure the hinge and torsion bar assembly to the body and lift away the assembly.
4   Refitting the tailgate hinge and torsion bar assembly is the reverse sequence to removal. Line up the hinge with the previously made mark and tighten the securing bolts.

28 Fixed rear quarter window glass - removal and refitting

1   Using a blunt screwdriver carefully ease the moulding from

12.21 TAILGATE LOCK ASSEMBLY

the weatherstrip.
2   An assistant should now be ready to catch the glass as it is released from the body aperture. Working inside the car push on the glass next to the weatherstrip so releasing it from the aperture flange. Lift away the glass and weatherstrip.
3   Remove the weatherstrip and clean off all traces of sealer. Inspect the weatherstrip for signs of splitting or deterioration. If evident, a new weatherstrip must be obtained.
4   To refit the glass assembly, first fit the moulding to its groove in the weatherstrip and apply a little sealer to the groove in which the glass seats. Fit the glass to the weatherstrip.
5   Fit a draw cord in the weatherstrip to body groove and position the glass to the aperture. Working inside the car pull on the draw cord whilst the assistant pushes on the glass so drawing the lip over the flange.
6   Apply a little sealer to the weatherstrip to aperture flange. Clean off surplus sealer with a petrol moistened cloth.

29 Opening rear quarter window glass - removal and replacement

1   Part and remove the window glass moulding halves and then carefully detach the pivot clips from the pivot rubbers in the door pillar (Fig. 12:22). Lift away the glass.
2   Inspect the window aperture weatherstrip for signs of deterioration. If evident the weatherstrip should be removed from the aperture.
3   Before fitting a new weatherstrip apply a little sealer to the weatherstrip to body groove and then carefully fit the weatherstrip to the body flange.
4   Refitting the glass and moulding is the reverse sequence to removal.

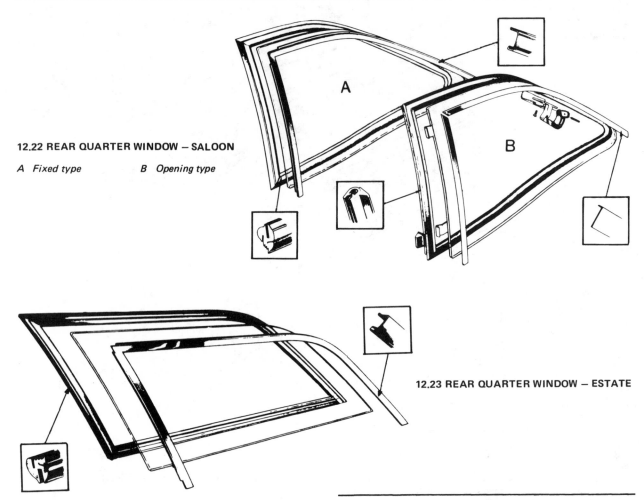

12.22 REAR QUARTER WINDOW – SALOON

A Fixed type   *B Opening type*

12.23 REAR QUARTER WINDOW – ESTATE

30 Rear window glass - removal and replacement

1   Undo and remove the self tapping screws that secure the front edge of the rear seat cushion to the heel plate. Lift out the cushion taking care not to damage the upholstery or headlining.
2   Open the boot lid and undo and remove the screws that secure the top of the rear seat backrest to the body. Carefully lift away the backrest.
3   Remove the retainers and bend back the lock tabs securing the rear parcel shelf. Lift away the parcel shelf.
4   Place a blanket over the boot lid so that it is not accidently scratched and remove the rear window glass using the same procedure as for the front windscreen. Further information will be found in Section 10, paragraphs 3 to 5 inclusive.
5   Refitting the rear window glass is similar to that for the refitting of the front windscreen. Refer to Section 10, paragraphs 8 to 17 inclusive.
6   Beware if a heated rear window is fitted. To avoid damage have a specialist look at this.

31 Tailgate window glass - removal and replacement

The procedure for removal and replacement of the tailgate window glass is basically identical to that for the rear window glass. Refer to Section 30, paragraphs 4 and 5 for full information.

32 Radiator grille - removal and replacement

Open the bonnet and support in the open position. Undo and remove the nine crosshead screws that secure the radiator grille to the front body panels. Lift away the radiator grille. Refitting is the reverse sequence to removal but take care to locate the grille tabs in their respective slots in the front lower panel.

33 Instrument panel crash padding - removal and replacement

1   Refer to Section 36 and remove the heater control knobs and panel.
2   If there is a radio fitted it must be removed before the crash padding can be removed. The method of removing the radio depends on the type fitted.
3   Undo and remove the small screws that secure the heater and radio bezel and lift away the bezel.
4   Undo and remove the nut that secures the crash pad centre stud. Using a thick knife blade carefully ease the crash padding forwards and upwards so releasing its retaining clips, (Fig.12:24).
5   Refitting the crash padding is the reverse sequence to removal.

34 Heater assembly - removal and replacement

1   Refer to Chapter 2/2 and drain the cooling system.
2   Locate the multi pin connector for the heater unit blower motor and detach the plug from the socket.

3 Remove the water drain pipe from the air inlet chamber.

4 Slacken the clips that secure the heater water pipes to the heater unit. Note which way round the pipes are fitted and carefully withdraw the two pipes.

5 Undo and remove the self tapping screws that secure the heater unit to the bulkhead. Their locations are shown in Fig. 12:25. Detach the heater control flap operating lever and draw the heater away from the bulkhead.

6 Note that there are three gaskets located between the heater housing flange and if these are damaged they must be renewed.

7 To refit the heater assembly, stick on three new gaskets to the heater joint face. If the original gaskets are to be retained apply some sealer to the free face of the gasket pack.

8 Move the flap located in the centre of the heater housing and the control lever inside the car to either the 'cold' or 'hot' positions.

9 Fit the heater to the bulkhead and connect the quadrant of the control valve pivot. Secure the heater with the self tapping screws.

10 Refit the water drain pipe and reconnect the multi pin plug to the blower motor.

11 Reconnect the two hoses to the heater unit and secure with the clips.

12 Refill the cooling system as described in Chapter 2/3.

35 Heater assembly - dismantling and reassembly

1 Refer to Section 34 and remove the heater assembly.

2 Undo and remove the self tapping screws that secure the heater radiator lower panel to the main casing. Lift away the lower panel.

3 Carefully slide out the heater radiator together with its foam rubber packing.

4 Undo and remove the three bolts that secure the blower motor base plate and lift away the blower motor assembly.

5 Inspect the heater radiator for signs of leaks. If evident if may be repaired in a similar manner used for the engine cooling system radiator as described in Chapter 2/5. It is a good policy to reverse flush the heater radiator to remove any sediment.

6 Reassembling the heater assembly is the reverse sequence to removal.

7 It is possible to remove the heater radiator and the blower motor whilst the heater assembly is still fitted in the car.

36 Heater controls - removal and replacement

removal

1 Remove the cover plate of the radio recess.

2 Remove the knobs from the control levers (to this effect, tap out the dowel pin of the lower knob).

3 From underneath the dashboard, press out the bezel of the control levers.

4 Remove the bezel of the radio switch.

5 Detach both upper control cables from the control unit and withdraw the wire plug connectors.

6 Remove the screws of the control unit and disconnect the lower cable.

replacement

7 Move the blower control lever to its left-hand stop and lock in this position by pulling the lever out. In this position, connect and adjust the lower control cable.

8 Fit the control switch, reconnect and adjust the upper control cables. Refit the wire plug connectors.

9 Refit the radio switch bezel.

10 Position the control switch bezel and secure.

11 Check operations of heater flaps and blower. Readjust control cables if necessary.

12 Replace the knobs to the levers and press in the dowel pin of the centre knob.

13 Replace the cover plate to the radio recess.

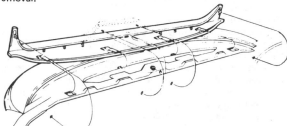

12.24 INSTRUMENT PANEL CRASH PADDING ATTACH—MENTS

12.25 HEATER ATTACHMENT POINTS

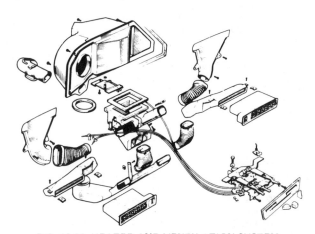

FIG. 12.26. HEATER AND VENTILATION SYSTEM COMPONENTS

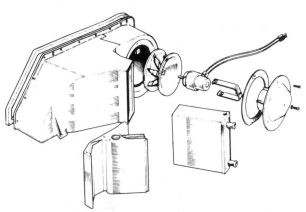

FIG. 12.27. HEATER UNIT BLOWER MOTOR AND RADIATOR

Chapter 13 Supplement for later 1300 models

Contents

1 Introduction

This supplement is to cover any modifications or additions to the Mark III Cortina range of ohv (overhead valve) models from 1973 to their discontinuation in September 1976. The 1600 cc ohv engine was discontinued in September 1973, to be replaced by a 1600 cc ohc unit — which is not covered by this manual. Apart from minor changes to interior and exterior fittings and modified carburation the Mark III Cortina has remained basically unchanged.

2 Specifications

The specifications listed here are revised or supplementary to those given at the beginning of each of the first twelve Chapters of this manual. The original specifications apply unless alternative figures are quoted here.

Engine

Engine code ... ...   JSE 1300 cc HC (Economy)
                                                        J2J 1300 cc HC (Standard)

Firing order ... .   1 - 2 - 4 - 3

Compression ratio ... ...   9.2 : 1

Idling speed ... ...   800 rpm

Maximum engine speed ... ...   5800 rpm

Cylinder block
Number of main bearings   5
Cylinder bore diameter grades:
  Grade A ... ...   3.1868 to 3.1872 in (80.947 to 80.957 mm)
  Grade B ... ...   3.1872 to 3.1876 in (80.957 to 80.967 mm)
  Grade C ... ...   3.1876 to 3.1880 in (80.967 to 80.977 mm)
  Grade D ... ...   3.1880 to 3.1884 in (80.977 to 80.987 mm)
  Grade E ... ...   3.1884 to 3.1888 in (80.987 to 80.997 mm)
  Grade F ... ...   3.1888 to 3.1892 in (80.997 to 81.007 mm)

Camshaft
Cam lift:
  Inlet ... ...   0.235 in (5.984 mm)
  Exhaust ... ...   0.232 in (5.895 mm)

Pistons
Piston diameter grades (standard):
  Grade D ... ...   3.1868 to 3.1871 in (80.944 to 80.954 mm)
  Grade E ... ...   3.1871 to 3.1875 in (80.954 to 80.964 mm)
  Grade F ... ...   3.1875 to 3.1879 in (80.964 to 80.974 mm)

Oversize diameter:
  + 0.0025 in (+ 0.064 mm) ... ...   3.1881 to 3.1904 in (80.978 to 81.038 mm)
  + 0.015 in (+ 0.38 mm) ... ...   3.2005 to 3.2029 in (81.294 to 81.354 mm)
  + 0.030 in (+ 0.76 mm) ... ...   3.2155 to 3.2178 in (81.674 to 81.734 mm)
Piston to bore clearance ... ...   0.0009 to 0.0016 in (0.023 to 0.043 mm)
Ring gap (3 rings) ... ...   0.0090 to 0.014 in (0.23 to 0.36 mm)

Connecting rods
Big end bore diameter ... ...   2.0822 to 2.0831 in (52.89 to 52.91 mm)
Small end bore diameter ... ...   0.8791 to 0.8799 in (22.33 to 22.35 mm)
Internal diameter (standard) ... ...   1.9378 to 1.9392 in (49.221 to 49.256 mm)
Internal diameter (undersize):
  0.0020 in (0.051 mm) ... ...   1.9358 to 1.9371 in (49.170 to 49.204 mm)
  0.0099 in (0.254 mm) ... ...   1.9278 to 1.9291 in (48.967 to 49.001 mm)
  0.0200 in (0.508 mm) ... ...   1.8178 to 1.9191 in (48.713 to 48.747 mm)
  0.0299 in (0.762 mm) ... ...   1.9078 to 1.9091 in (48.459 to 48.493 mm)
  0.0399 in (1.016 mm) ... ...   1.8978 to 1.8991 in (48.205 to 48.239 mm)

Valves
Valve clearance:
  Inlet ... ...   0.008 in (0.20 mm)
  Exhaust ... ...   0.022 in (0.55 mm)
Inlet valve:
  Opens ... ...   21° BTDC
  Closes ... ...   55° ABDC
Exhause valve:
  Opens ... ...   70° BBDC
  Closes ... ...   22° ATDC

Inlet valve
Valve length ... ...   4.3484 to 4.3881 in (110.45 to 111.46 mm)
Valve head diameter ... ...   1.4970 to 1.5070 in (38.024 to 38.278 mm)
Valve stem diameter (standard) ... ...   0.3098 to 0.3105 in (7.869 to 7.887 mm)

Valve stem diameter (oversize):
    0.0029 in (0.076 mm) ... ...   0.3127 to 0.3135 in (7.945 to 7.963 mm)
    0.0149 in (0.381 mm) ... ...   0.3248 to 0.3255 in (8.250 to 8.268 mm)
Valve lift (excluding clearance) ... ...   0.360 in (9.15 mm)

Exhaust valve

Valve length ... ...   4.3366 to 4.3759 in (110.15 to 111.15 mm)
Valve head diameter ... ...   1.2340 to 1.2440 in (31.344 to 31.598 mm)
Valve stem diameter (standard) ... ...   0.3088 to 0.3096 in (7.846 to 7.864 mm)
Valve stem diameter (oversize):
    0.0029 in (0.076 mm) ... ...   0.3118 to 0.3126 in (7.922 to 7.940 mm)
    0.0149 in (0.381 mm) ... ...   0.3238 to 0.3246 in (8.227 to 8.245 mm)
Valve lift (excluding clearance) ... ...   0.354 in (9.00 mm)

Tightening torques

	lbf ft	kgf m
Main bearing cap	54 to 59	7.5 to 8.2
Big end bearing cap	30 to 35	4.2 to 4.8

Carburation

Carburettor

Type ... ...   Motorcraft, single venturi, downdraught
Identification number:
  From May 1975:
    Standard ... ...   76 IF 9510 KBA
    Economy ... ...   76 IF 9510 KTA
  From May 1976 (tamperproof):
    Standard ... ...   77 IF 9510 KBA or 77 IF 9510 KGA
    Economy ... ...   77 IF 9510 KEA

	Throttle barrel diameter	Venturi diameter	Main jet	Idle	CO%	Fast idle
76 IF 9510 KBA ...	1.338 in (34 mm)	0.984 in (25 mm)	122	800 rpm	1.5	1400 rpm
76 IF 9510 KTA ...	1.338 in (34 mm)	0.905 in (23 mm)	115	800 rpm	1.5	1400 rpm
77 IF 9510 KBA ...	1.338 in (34 mm)	0.984 in (25 mm)	122	800 rpm	1.5	1400 rpm
77 IF 9510 KGA ...	1.388 in (34 mm)	0.984 in (25 mm)	122	800 rpm	1.5	1400 rpm
77 IF 9510 KEA ...	1.388 in (34 mm)	0.905 in (23 mm)	115	800 rpm	1.5	1400 rpm

Ignition system

Coil

Type ... ...   Oil filled for use with 1.5 ohm resistor
Primary resistance ... ...   0.95 to 1.60 ohms
Secondary resistance ... ...   5000 to 9300 ohms

Spark plugs

Make (standard) ... ...   Motorcraft
Type ... ...   14 mm AGR 22 (standard) or 14 mm AGR 32 (economy)
Gap ... ...   0.030 in (0.75 mm)

Distributor

Type and make ... ...   Motorcraft, centrifugal/vacuum automatic advance
Identification ... ...   761F 12100 JA (1300 cc HC); 73EB 12100 BB (1300 cc LC)
Dwell angle ... ...   48° to 52°

Distributor advance characteristics (76IF 12100 JA)

	Mechanical	Vacuum	Vacuum
Engine rpm	Degrees advance (crankshaft)	Vacuum, mm of Hg (in of Hg)	Degrees advance (crankshaft)
500 and below	0	75 (3.0) and below	0
600	−1° to + 1°	80 (3.1)	−1° to + 0.5°
1000	−1° to + 1°	100 (3.9)	−1° to + 2°
1100	−1° to + 1°	120 (4.7)	−1° to + 6°
1300	−1° to + 3°	150 (5.9)	5° to 11°
1500	1° to 5°	200 (7.9)	11° to 17°
2000	6° to 10°	250 (9.8) and above	15° to 21°
3000	14.5° to 18.5°		
4000	22.5° to 26.5°		
4500	26° to 30°		
4800 and above	28.5° to 32.5°		

Distributor advance characteristics (73EB 12100 BB)

Engine rpm	Mechanical Degrees advance (crankshaft)	Vacuum, mm of Hg (in of Hg)	Vacuum Degrees advance (crankshaft)
300 and below	0	50.8 (2.0) and below	0
400	-1° to $+1^\circ$	114.3 (4.5)	0° to 2°
925	-1° to $+1^\circ$	127 (5.0)	0° to 4°
1000	-1° to $+2^\circ$	152.4 (6.0)	3° to 8°
1025	-1° to $+2.5^\circ$	203.2 (8.0)	10° to 15°
1500	6° to 10°	236.2 (9.3) and above	14° to 18°
2000	15° to 19°		
3000	19.5° to 23.5°		
4000	24.5° to 28.5°		
4900 and above	28.5° to 32.5°		

Suspension and steering

Front suspension (August 1973 onwards)

Toe-in	0.04 in (1 mm)
Castor	2° 45' $\pm$ 1°
Camber	0° 98' $\pm$ 0° 45'
King pin inclination	3° 35' $\pm$ 0° 30'
Toe out on turns	20° back lock, front lock 18° 40'
	35° back lock, front lock 31° 50'

Steering (1973 onwards)

Minimum turning circle diameter	32 ft 8 in (9.9 m)
Maximum turning angle:	
Outer wheel	35° 28'
Inner wheel	38° 47'

---

3 Engine

General description

The engine specifications given in Section 2 are for the 1300 cc HC Economy and 1300 cc HC Standard engines which are now fitted to the 1300 cc range. Only the figures quoted differ from those in the original engine specifications. Procedures for removal, dismantling and reassembly remain as described in the relevant Sections of Chapter 1.

---

4 Cooling system

Radiator - removal and refitting

1 Later vehicles are fitted with a shroud to protect the fan assembly.
2 Carry out the operations described in Chapter 2, Section 5, paragraphs 1 and 2.
3 Undo and remove the four bolts that secure the radiator shroud to the radiator side panels and move the shroud over the fan blades.

4 Undo and remove the two bolts and washers on each side of the radiator and carefully lift the radiator upwards and out of the vehicle.
5 The fan shroud can now be lifted away from the fan blade assembly.
6 To refit the radiator reverse the removal sequence, remembering to locate the fan shroud over the fan blade assembly before lowering the radiator into position.

---

5 Carburation and fuel system

Accelerator linkage - removal and refitting

1 Prise the accelerator pedal lobes outwards, disengage them from the shaft spigot and remove the spring.
2 If applicable, remove the centre console by first prising out the clock (or blanking plate) and disconnecting the clock leads.
3 Unscrew and remove the two screws accessible through the clock aperture and the two screws located at the rear sides of the console and lift out the centre console (Fig. 13.1).
4 Remove the lower insulator panel which is secured by five screws (Fig. 13.2)

FIG. 13.1 REMOVING CENTRE CONSOLE

FIG. 13.2 LOWER INSULATOR PANEL SECURING SCREWS

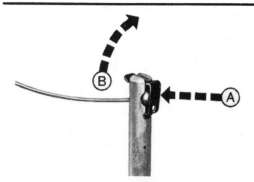

FIG. 13.3   REMOVING ACCELERATOR CABLE
SECURING CLIP

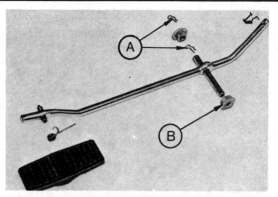

FIG. 13.4   DISMANTLED THROTTLE PEDAL ASSEMBLY
A - Retaining clip   B - Mounting bush

FIG. 13.5   CHOKE CONTROL CONNECTIONS AT THE
CARBURETTOR (Arrowed)

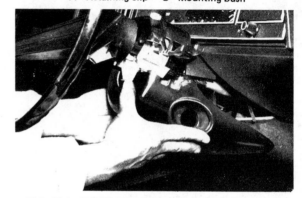

FIG. 13.6   REMOVING STEERING COLUMN LOWER
SHROUD

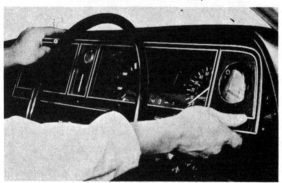

FIG. 13.7   REMOVING THE BEZEL ASSEMBLY

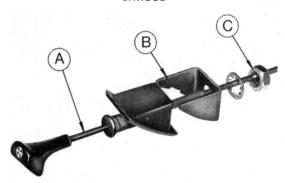

FIG. 13.8   CHOKE CONTROL KNOB ASSEMBLY
A - Inner cable   B - Bracket   C - Securing nut

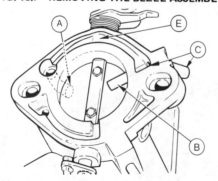

FIG. 13.9   BYPASS IDLE SYSTEM

A - Air entry into by-pass
    system
B - Sonic discharge pipe

C - Idle mixture screw
E - Air distribution
    channel

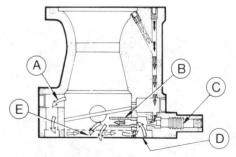

FIG. 13.10   SECTIONAL VIEW OF THE AIR/FUEL FLOW

A - Air entry to by-pass
    system
B - Sonic discharge pipe
C - Idle mixture screw

D - Air/fuel mixing
    chamber
E - Air distribution
    channel

5 Disconnect the accelerator cable from the pedal shaft by removing the retaining clip. Referring to Fig. 13.3, press the retaining clip in the direction of arrow 'A', and at the same time lift the front section of the retaining clip in the direction of arrow 'B'. The accelerator cable can then be pulled slightly forward to clear the nipple location and lifted out.

6 Remove the two locking pins from the left-hand side of the pedal assembly cross-shaft. Turn each cross-shaft bush 45° to disengage it from its bracket location. Remove the bushes from the accelerator pedal bracket. The pedal assembly can now be removed from the bracket.

7 Refitting is the reverse of the removal procedure but ensure that the cable adjustment is as described in Chapter 3, Section 12.

Choke cable - removal and refitting

1 Working under the bonnet, remove the air cleaner assembly as described in Chapter 3, Section 2.

2 Disconnect the inner and outer choke cables at their connections with the carburettor. The inner cable is secured by a pinch screw and the outer cable by a screwed clamp (Fig. 13.5).

3 Where the choke cable passes through the bulkhead, push out the grommet.

4 Remove the instrument cluster and bezel assembly as follows. Unscrew and remove the steering column lower shroud (Fig. 13.6), unclip the upper half of the steering column shroud and remove it. Pull off the instrument panel light switch knob, and where fitted the radio control knobs. Remove the six countersunk screws that retain the instrument cluster and surrounding bezel. Ease the bezel assembly outwards away from the dashpanel (Fig. 13.7). From the rear of the bezel assembly disconnect the two main loom multi-connectors from the back of the instruments. Disconnect three wires from the cigar lighter, and the multi-connector loom plugs from the hazard flasher switch and the heated rear window.

5 Disconnect the speedometer cable and remove the instrument cluster and bezel assembly.

6 Undo and remove the five screws securing the insulator panel, as shown in Fig. 13.2. Pull back the carpet and bend up the securing tangs on the dashpanel and remove the insulator pad.

7 Remove the nut securing the choke cable to the instrument panel. Access is gained from within the aperture made by the removal of the instrument cluster.

8 Before removing the choke cable from the vehicle it is wise to attach a length of string or wire to the choke cable at the carburettor end, then remove the choke cable by pulling it into the car. The string or wire will follow the choke cable through and appear at the dash panel. Untie it from the choke cable and secure it to the steering wheel to avoid accidentally pulling it back into the engine compartment. When refitting the choke cable, attach the piece of string or wire again; this will ensure that the cable follows its original course through the rear of the instrument dashpanel.

9 Refitting is the reverse of the removal procedure but it is important that the choke cable adjustment is correct and as described in Chapter 3, Section 14.

Carburettor - general description

From May 1975, to meet new legislation on atmospheric pollution, the carburettor fitted to the Cortina 1300 cc range has been modified, and is now known as the 'Bypass (Sonic) idle carburettor.' In operation the idle system differs from the conventional type systems in that the majority of the idle airflow, and all of the idle fuel flow passes through the bypass system. The remaining airflow flows past the carburettor butterfly plate, which is held in a slightly open position; this is necessary to prevent the butterfly plate becoming seized in its bore as the carburettor body contracts during the cooling period after the engine has been switched off. During idle, with the butterfly plate almost closed, air is drawn into the bypass system at point 'A' (see Fig. 13.9 and Fig. 13.10). The air travels along the channel 'E' (Fig. 13.9 and Fig. 13.10), mixes with the rich

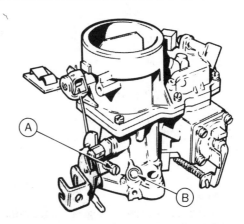

FIG. 13.11 THE 'TAMPERPROOF' CARBURETTOR

A - Idle speed adjusting screw   B - Plastic plug covering mixture screw

air/fuel mixture obtained via the mixture screw 'C' (Fig. 13.9 and Fig. 13.10), and the air/fuel mixture is drawn into the engine through the sonic discharge pipe 'B' (Fig. 13.9 and Fig. 13.10).

The modified carburettor is basically the same as the previous unit but has seven screws retaining the upper body, compared with six screws on the previous unit. The length of the vacuum pick-up tube supplying the distributor advance and retard mechanism is now 1.37 in (35 mm), as opposed to 0.52 in (14 mm) on the previous unit. The idle mixture screw and the vacuum pick-up tube have been repositioned.

From May 1976, to meet increased atmospheric pollution legislation, the bypass carburettor has been made tamperproof, which has resulted in a slightly modified carburettor body to house the recessed idle mixture screw, which is beneath a plastic plug (Fig. 13.11). Apart from changes to specifications (see Section 2) the operations and procedures remain as described in the relevant Sections of Chapter 3. The tamperproof carburettor is so designed that, after the initial running-in period of a new engine, the percentage of carbon monoxide (CO) in the exhaust gas will be in accordance with a predetermined legal requirement. Therefore, for atmospheric pollution legislation to be complied with, adjustment should only be made with an exhaust gas CO analyzer coupled to the car exhaust system. Should adjustment be necessary, the plastic plug can be punctured in its centre with a small screwdriver, and prised out. A replacement plug should be pressed in on completion. Future legislation may (officially) restrict these adjustments, and the supply of replacement plugs may be to authorized dealers only.

6 Ignition system

General description

The ignition system remains basically the same as described in Chapter 4. However, with the introduction of the 'Bypass (Sonic) idle carburettor' in May 1975, and the economy engine in February 1976, slight changes have been made to the distributor specifications (see Section 2), but the distributor design remains unchanged. From May 1975 the spark plug gap is increased to 0.030 in (0.75 mm).

7 Rear axle

Pinion drive angle - adjustment

1 Since January 1972, a modified lower radius arm/rear axle

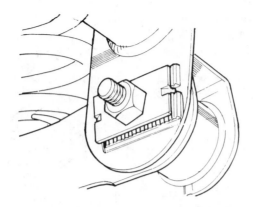

FIG. 13.12   PINION DRIVE ANGLE ADJUSTMENT
WASHER AT LOWER RADIUS ARM PIVOT

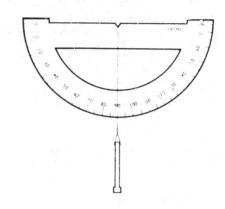

FIG' 13.13   PROTRACTOR AND PLUMB LINE SUITABLE
FOR CHECKING PINION DRIVE ANGLE

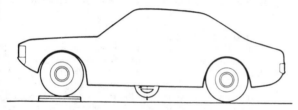

FIG. 13.14   CHECKING BODYFRAME SIDEMEMBER FOR
LEVEL

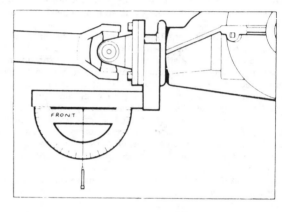

FIG. 13.15   CHECKING PINION DRIVE FLANGE ANGLE

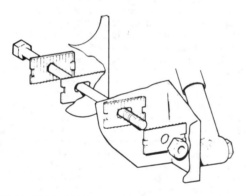

FIG. 13.16   EXPLODED VIEW OF THE LOWER RADIUS ARM
PIVOT AND SERRATED PLATES

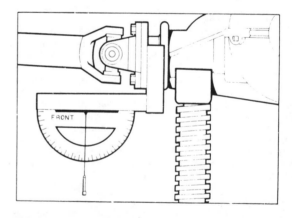

FIG. 13.17   JACKING - UP DIFFERENTIAL CARRIER
TO ADJUST DRIVE PINION ANGLE

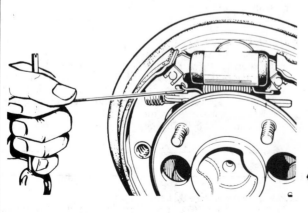

FIG. 13.18   REMOVING
BRAKE SHOE RETURN SPRINGS

mounting is fitted to enable the drive angle to be adjusted. The modified mounting is identified by the serrated washers located behind the radius arm pivot bolts (Fig. 13.12).

2 Position the vehicle on level ground (without any occupants) and using a protractor and plumb line, applied to the centre point of a body frame side-member, raise the front or rear of the vehicle as necessary to ensure that the side-member is perfectly horizontal (Figs. 13.13 and 13.14).

3 Using a right-angled set square located on the rear face of the drive pinion flange, check by means of the protractor and plumb line the inclination of the flange. Where a single piece propeller shaft is installed, the flange should be inclined forward at the top by between 2^O and 3° 30'. For a split type propeller shaft, the inclination should be between 0° and 1^O 30' forward at the top (Fig. 13.15).

4 Where adjustment is called for, slacken the nuts on the lower radius arm pivot bolts at the axle casing sufficiently to permit the serrated washers to slide over each other (Fig. 13.16).

5 Jack-up the differential carrier until (again using the protractor) the specified pinion drive angle is achieved (Fig. 13.17).

6 Engage the serrated washers on both sides of the axle bracket so that identical serrations on the plates with the elongated holes engage with similar ones on the plates with the circular bolt holes.

7 Tighten the pivot bolt nuts finger-tight and then lower the vehicle to the ground and re-check the drive angle. If it is correct, tighten the radius arm pivot bolts to the specified torque with the normal weight of the vehicle on the roadwheels.

8 When the drive angle is correctly adjusted, the distance between the rear end of the propeller shaft and the underside of the floor should be in accordance with the following measurements.

Single piece propeller shaft	*2.7 in (106 mm)*
Split propeller shaft	*3.3 in (130 mm)*

Drive pinion oil seal renewal

9 Cars manufactured from the beginning of 1975 have a collapsible pinion space in place of the selective shim, and consequently there are changes to the procedure for renewal of the drive pinion oil seal.

Note: *Renewal of the drive pinion oil seal requires a great deal of care and the use of some special equipment. Without these, the collapsible spacer can be damaged which will require its renewal, and this operation is outside the scope of the do-it-yourself motorist because a special tool is required for removal of the pinion bearing. Whenever the pinion oil seal is renewed, it is essential that the self-locking pinion nut is also renewed.*

10 Jack up the rear of the vehicle and support it securely under the bodyframe.

11 Remove the rear roadwheels and brake drums.

12 Disconnect the propeller shaft from the rear axle drive pinion after marking them for correct alignment.

13 Using a spring balance and length of cord wound round the drive pinion flange, determine the torque required to turn the drive pinion and record it. Alternatively, a socket wrench fitted to the pinion nut and a suitable torque wrench may be used.

14 Mark the coupling in relation to the pinion splines to ensure that they are refitted in the same position.

15 Hold the pinion coupling flange by placing two 2 inch long bolts through two opposite holes, bolting them up tight; undo the self locking nut whilst holding a large screwdriver or tyre lever between the two bolts for leverage. Using a standard two or three-leg puller, remove the coupling flange from the pinion shaft.

16 Using a hammer and a small chisel or screwdriver, remove the oil seal from the pinion housing. During this operation, great care must be taken to ensure that the pinion shaft is not scored in any way. Note that there will be some spillage of the axle oil as the seal is removed.

17 Carefully clean the contact area inside the pinion housing, then apply a film of general purpose grease to this surface and

between the lips of the new oil seal. Do not remove the existing grease from the replacement seal.

18 Using a tube of suitable diameter, press in the new seal to its full depth in the pinion housing.

19 Refit the coupling in its correct relative position to the pinion shaft.

20 Using a new self-locking nut, prevent the flange from turning then carefully and slowly tighten the nut until the same turning torque is achieved as recorded at paragraph 13. Continue tightening until an additional 2 to 3 lbf in (2 to 4 kgf cm) is achieved, to allow for the friction of the new oil seal. After this torque has been obtained, do not tighten the self-locking nut or the collapsible spacer will be damaged (see note at beginning of Section).

21 Remove the two bolts from the coupling flange then refit the propeller shaft taking note of the alignment marks made when removing.

22 Top up the rear axle with the correct grade of oil, then refit the brake drums and roadwheels.

23 Lower the car to the ground.

---

8 Braking system

General description

Progressively, from August 1974 to December 1974, a new rear brake assembly is introduced to the Cortina 1300cc range of vehicles. After December 1974 all Cortina 1300cc vehicles are fitted with the new rear brake assembly. In operation, the new rear brake is identical to the early type, except that the self-adjustment mechanism is now operated by actuation of the brake foot pedal, instead of handbrake which adjusted the early type brakes.

Rear drum brake shoes - removal and refitting

1 Carry out operations 1 and 2 described in Section 8, Chapter 9.

2 Remove both brake shoe return springs. It is advisable to manufacture a tool from a piece of suitably sized wire; form a small hook at one end, and secure the other end to a suitable handle (Fig. 13.18).

3 Using an old screwdriver with a shank diameter of approximately 0.25 in (6 mm) with the end removed, form a slot in the end of the shank to suit the hold-down springs (Fig. 13.19). Press the hold-down spring towards the carrier plate, then lever the spring hook away from the retainer bracket.

4 Pull the lower end of the front brake shoe towards the front of the vehicle. This will operate the self-adjustment mechanism

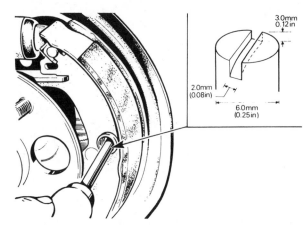

FIG. 13.19 REMOVING THE BRAKE SHOE HOLD - DOWN SPRINGS

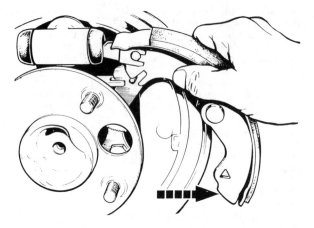

FIG. 13.20 WITHDRAWING THE FRONT BRAKE SHOES

FIG. 13.21 DISCONNECTING THE HANDBRAKE CABLE

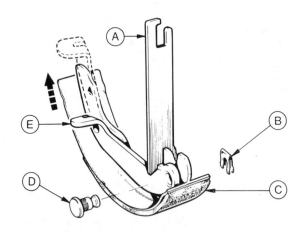

FIG. 13.22 COMPONENTS OF THE REAR BRAKE SHOE ASSEMBLY

A - Handbrake operating lever   D - Pivot pin
B - Spring clip   E - Spacer strut
C - Brake shoe

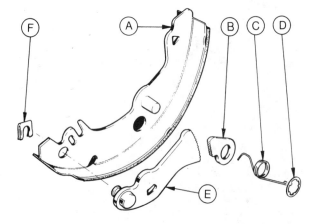

FIG. 13.24 COMPONENTS OF THE FRONT BRAKE SHOE ASSEMBLY

A - Brake shoe   C - Spring   E - Large ratchet
B - Short ratchet   D - Spring retainer

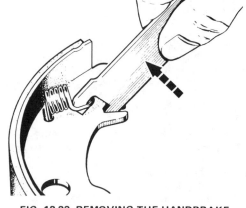

FIG. 13.23 REMOVING THE HANDBRAKE LEVER SPRING

to a point where the two ratchets are out of engagement (Fig. 13.20).

5 Twist the brake shoe to release it from the spacer strut, and remove the brake shoe from the brake assembly.

6 Pull the rear brake shoe assembly away from, and below the carrier plate and disconnect the handbrake operating cable from the lever on the rear brake shoe assembly (Fig. 13.21).

7 To dismantle the rear brake shoe assembly refer to Fig. 13.22. Remove the spring clip 'B' from the pivot pin 'D' and tap the pivot pin from the brake shoe 'C' and the lever assembly. Slide the handbrake operating lever 'A' along the brake shoe and out of the slot in the spacer strut 'E'.

8 Lever the spacer strut from the brake shoe and remove the handbrake lever return springs (Fig. 13.23).

9 To dismantle the front brake shoe assembly refer to Fig. 13.24. Prise off the spring clip 'F' and separate the longer ratchet lever 'E' from the brake shoe 'A'. Remove the spring washer 'D' and separate the second shorter ratchet lever 'B' and the spring 'C' from the brake shoe. **Note**: The spring retaining washer 'D' must be renewed after removal.

10 To reassemble the rear brake shoe, insert the pivot pin into the handbrake operating lever. Fit the handbrake operating lever to the brake shoe and fit the retaining spring clip. Assemble the handbrake lever return spring to the brake shoe. Hook the spacer strut onto the handbrake lever return spring and lever it into position (Fig. 13.25).

11 To assemble the front brake shoe assembly, position the smaller ratchet and spring on the brake shoe pivot pin. Insert two 0.008 in (0.2 mm) feeler gauges between the brake shoe and

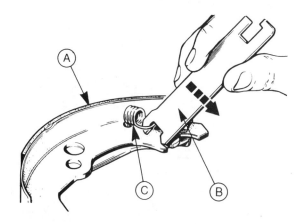

FIG. 13.25 FITTING THE HANDBRAKE LEVER AND RETURN SPRING

A - Rear brake shoe   C - Spring
B - Handbrake lever

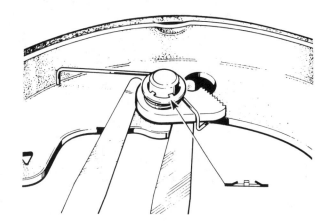

FIG. 13.26 SETTING THE GAP BETWEEN THE BRAKE SHOE AND THE RATCHET

FIG. 13.27 FITTING THE TWO RATCHETS

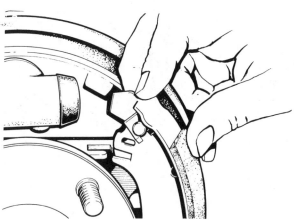

FIG. 13.28 SLIDING THE FRONT SHOE INTO THE SLOT IN THE SPACER STRUT

FIG. 13.29 PULLING THE SPRING LOADED RATCHET LEVER DOWN AGAINST THE SPRING

(The arrow denotes the other ratchet in its minimum adjustment position).

the ratchet, and fit a new spring retaining washer. Ensure that the retaining tabs on the spring retaining washer are correctly positioned (see Fig. 13.26). Remove the feeler gauges and check that the ratchet rotates freely on its pivot pin, and returns with spring pressure. Fit the longer ratchet to the brake shoe and secure it with the spring clip; ensure that there is no clearance between the shoe and the ratchet. Position the two ratchets relative to each other, with an overlap of 4 to 5 teeth (Fig. 13.27).

12 Assemble the rear shoe to the handbrake cable. Locate the brake shoe against the wheel cylinder and the lower pivot position. Check that the handbrake lever is resting on the head of the adjustment plunger.

13 Slide the front shoe into position in the slot of the spacer strut (Fig. 13.28) and then locate the brake shoe against the wheel cylinder and the lower pivot position. Be extremely careful not to damage the wheel cylinder dust covers.

14 Using the tool described in paragraph 2, pull the spring-loaded ratchet lever down and against its spring. Push the other ratchet forward to the minimum adjustment position (Fig. 13.29).

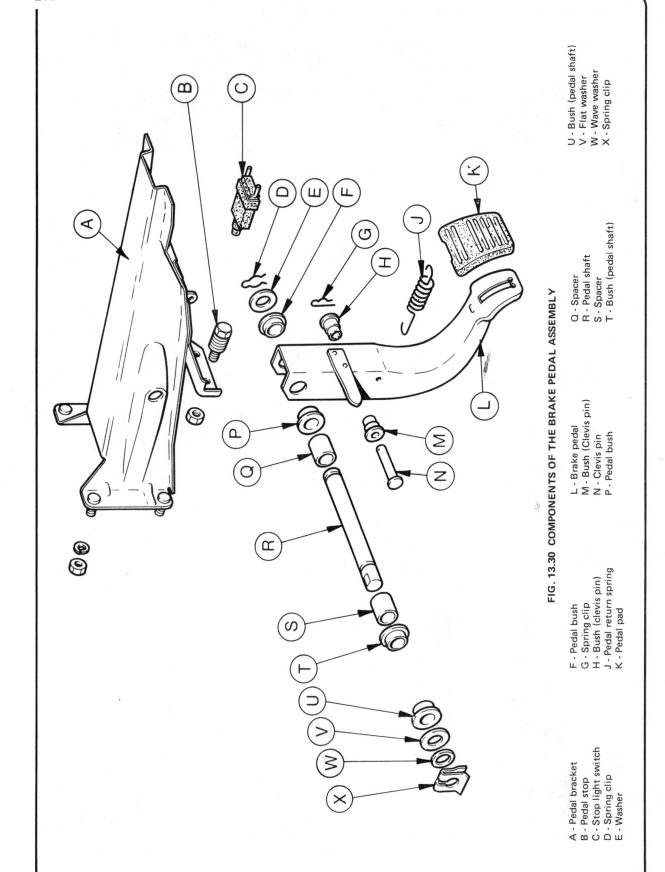

FIG. 13.30 COMPONENTS OF THE BRAKE PEDAL ASSEMBLY

A - Pedal bracket
B - Pedal stop
C - Stop light switch
D - Spring clip
E - Washer

F - Pedal bush
G - Spring clip
H - Bush (clevis pin)
J - Pedal return spring
K - Pedal pad

L - Brake pedal
M - Bush (Clevis pin)
N - Clevis pin
P - Pedal bush

Q - Spacer
R - Pedal shaft
S - Spacer
T - Bush (pedal shaft)

U - Bush (pedal shaft)
V - Flat washer
W - Wave washer
X - Spring clip

FIG. 13.31   REMOVING A RECTANGULAR TYPE
HEADLAMP

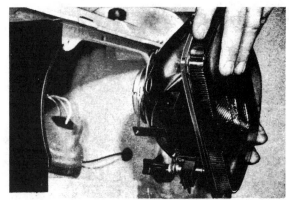

FIG. 13.32   REFITTING A RECTANGULAR TYPE
HEADLAMP

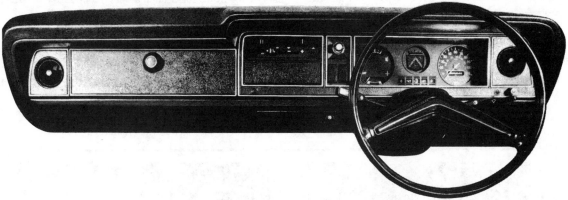

FIG. 13.33   DASHBOARD (BASIC AND L MODELS)

FIG. 13.34   DASHBOARD (XL MODEL)

15 Fit the brake shoe to carrier plate retaining springs, using the tool described in paragraph 3. Ensure that the hook on the hold-down spring is secure in its retaining bracket.

16 Using the wire hook, fit the brake shoe return springs, the larger spring fitting at the top of the brake assembly, adjacent to the wheel cylinder.

17 Refit the brake drums, and adjust the brakes by depressing the brake pedal; the ratchets will be heard 'clicking' as adjustment is taken up. When there is no audible sign of this the brakes will be fully adjusted.

18 Refit the road wheels, lower the vehicle to the ground and finally tighten the wheel nuts.

19 Check the operation of the brakes on a road test.

Brake pedal - removal and refitting

1   Open the bonnet and disconnect the battery.

2   Refer to paragraph 4 of the choke cable removal and refitting sub-Section of Section 2, and remove the instrument panel lower insulation pad. This will give access to the brake pedal bracket.

3   Remove the spring clip 'G' (Fig. 13.30) and push out the clevis pin 'N' from its location. Pull out the two clevis pin bushes from their locations in the pedal end pushrod, and allow the pushrod to fall free from the pedal.

4   Disconnect the pedal return spring from the brake pedal, or the pedal box.

5   Refer to Fig. 13.30 and remove the spring clip 'D' from its groove location adjacent to the 'D' hole in the pedal box

assembly. With the clip removed push the pedal shaft 'R' through the pedal box so that the flat washer 'V', the brake pedal 'L', the spacer 'S' and the wave washer 'W' can be removed from the pedal box location.

6 With the pedal removed the pedal bushes can now be pushed from their locations in the pedal sides.

7 Refitting is the reverse of the removal procedure, but smear a little grease on to the pedal shaft and the clevis pin bushes. If necessary, adjust the stop light switch so that it operates after 0.19 to 0.59 in (5 to 15 mm) of pedal movement.

---

9   Electrical system

Headlight assembly (basic and L models) - removal and refitting

Removal of the circular type headlight assembly is as described in Chapter 10, Section 40, except that the radiator grille is retained by ten screws and flat washers. The headlamp bezel is now retained by four screws and flat washers.

Headlight assembly (XL model 1973 onwards) - removal and refitting

1 Open the bonnet. Disconnect the battery for reasons of safety.
2 Undo and remove the twelve screws and flat washers that retain the radiator grille and carefully lift it away from the vehicle.
3 Remove the crosshead screw securing the headlamp to the body (Fig. 13.31). Pull the headlamp forward from the body and

detach the bulb and holder from the reflector.
4 Refitting is the reverse of the removal procedure. After headlamp removal check, and if necessary, adjust the headlamp alignment, as described in Section 41, Chapter 10.

Glovebox lamp (1973 onwards) - removal and refitting

1 Open the glovebox compartment lid, and with a small screwdriver, carefully prise the lamp lens from its glovebox location (Fig. 13.35).
2 Disconnect the two leads from the lamp lens and pull the bulb holder out of the lens (Fig. 13.36).
3 Remove the bulb from the bulb holder, the bulb is of the bayonet type fixing.
4 Refitting is a reversal of the removal procedure.

Printed circuit (warning lights circuit, basic and L models 1973 onwards) - removal and refitting

1 Open the bonnet and disconnect the battery.
2 Remove the instrument cluster and bezel as described in paragraph 4 of the sub-Section covering choke cable removal and refitting, Section 2.
3 Remove the wiring assembly from the two clip positions; remove the four crosshead screws securing the speedometer unit to the housing and detach the speedometer unit. Likewise, remove the four screws securing the auxiliary gauge housing, and detach it (Fig. 13.37).
4 Unclip and remove the five warning light bulbs and their holders.
5 Lift off the printed circuit board from its three locating pegs (Fig. 13.38).
6 Refitting is the reverse of the removal procedure.

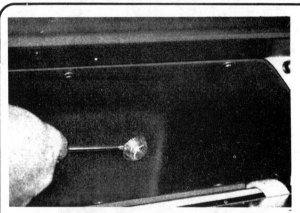

FIG. 13.35 REMOVING THE GLOVE BOX LAMP

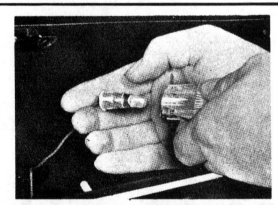

FIG. 13.36 REMOVING BULB HOLDER FROM LENS

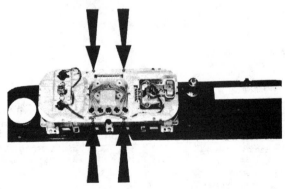

FIG. 13.37   REAR VIEW OF THE INSTRUMENT CLUSTER
(THE FOUR ARROWS DENOTE THE RETAINING SCREWS
FOR THE AUXILIARY GAUGE HOUSING)

FIG. 13.38 PRINTED CIRCUIT LOCATION POINTS.
(WARNING LIGHT CIRCUIT, BASIC AND L MODELS)

FIG. 13.39   REMOVING THE INSTRUMENT VOLTAGE
REGULATOR

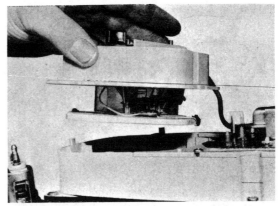

FIG. 13.40   REMOVING THE TACHOMETER

FIG. 13.41   REMOVING THE FOUR NUTS FROM THE
GAUGE RETAINING STRUTS

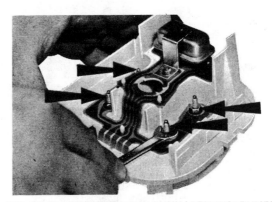

FIG. 13.42   REMOVING THE AUXILIARY INSTRUMENT
HOUSING AND VOLTAGE REGULATOR

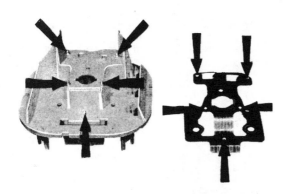

FIG. 13.43   THE AUXILIARY PRINTED CIRCUIT BOARD
REMOVED FROM ITS FIVE LOCATION PEGS

FIG. 13.44   PULLING OUT THE ILLUMINATION BULBS
FROM THE TACHOMETER

*Printed circuit (warning lights and auxiliary gauges, XL
model 1973 onwards) - removal and refitting*
1   Open the bonnet and disconnect the battery.
2   Remove the instrument cluster and bezel as described in
paragraphs 4, 5 and 6 of the second sub-Section of Section 5.
3   Undo and remove the crosshead screw securing the
instrument voltage regulator and remove the regulator (Fig.
13.39).
4   Remove the five warning light bulbs and holders.

5   Unscrew and remove the four screws retaining the
tachometer. Unclip the illumination bulb and holder and remove
the tachometer (Fig. 13.40).
6   Undo the four screws securing the speedometer housing
assembly, disconnect the two illumination bulbs and holders,
unclip the wiring loom and remove the housing assembly.
7   Remove the four screws that retain the centre housing
containing the two auxiliary gauges, and detach the housing
complete.

FIG. 13.45   VIEW SHOWING THE THREE NUTS AND TWO CROSSHEAD SCREWS RETAINING THE TACHOMETER

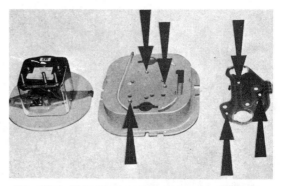

FIG. 13.46   THE THREE LOCATION POINTS OF THE TACHOMETER PRINTED CIRCUIT BOARD

FIG. 13.47   THE TWO CROSSHEAD SCREWS SECURING THE INSTRUMENT LENS

FIG. 13.48   THE TWO SECURING LUGS RETAINING THE INSTRUMENT CLUSTER LENS

8   To avoid soiling or damaging the gauge faces, or distorting the gauge needles in any way, carefully place the centre housing assembly on a clean piece of paper. Remove the four nuts and wave-washers from the gauge retaining studs (Fig. 13.41).
9   Remove the printed circuit board from its locating pegs.
10   Refitting is the reverse of the removal procedure.

Printed circuit (auxiliary instruments circuits, basic and L models 1973 onwards) - removal and refitting
1   Open the bonnet and disconnect the battery.
2   Remove the instrument cluster and bezel as described in paragraphs 4, 5 and 6 of second sub-Section of Section 5.
3   Disconnect the illumination bulb and unclip the associated wiring from the auxiliary instrument housing.
4   Unscrew and remove the four instrument housing retaining screws and remove the housing assembly.
5   To avoid soiling or marking the gauge faces or damaging the gauge needles in any way, carefully place the housing assembly on a clean piece of paper.
6   Remove the four nuts and wave-washers from the gauge retaining studs, remove the instrument voltage regulator screw and remove the regulator (Fig. 13.42).
7   Lift the printed circuit board from its five locating pegs (Fig. 13.43).
8   To reassemble reverse the removal sequence.

Printed circuit (tachometer circuit, XL model 1973 onwards) - removal and refitting
1   Open the bonnet and disconnect the battery.
2   Remove the instrument cluster and bezel as described in paragraphs 4, 5 and 6 of second sub-Section of Section 5.
3   Pull out the two illumination bulbs and holders; one bulb has

attached wiring, the other has not (Fig. 13.44).
4   Unscrew the four tachometer housing screws and detach the housing.
5   Remove the three nuts and wave-washers, and the two crosshead screws that retain the tachometer in the housing (Fig. 13.45).
6   Remove the printed circuit board from its three locating pegs (Fig. 13.46).
7   Refitting is the reverse of the removal procedure.

Instrument cluster lens (1973 onwards) - removal and refitting
1   Open the bonnet and disconnect the battery.
2   Remove the instrument cluster and bezel as described in paragraphs 4, 5 and 6 of the second sub-Section of Section 5.
3   Unscrew and remove the six screws that retain the instrument cluster to the bezel.
4   Remove the two crosshead screws securing the glass to the upper edge of the instrument cluster (Fig. 13.47).
5   At the lower edge of the instrument cluster, prise off two clips from their lugs and lift the lens from the cluster body (Fig. 13.48).
6   Refitting the lens is the reverse of the removal procedure.

Speedometer head (1973 onwards) - removal and refitting
1   Open the bonnet and disconnect the battery.
2   Remove the instrument cluster and bezel as described in paragraphs 4, 5 and 6 of the second sub-Section of Section 5.
3   At the two clip positions, remove the wiring assembly. Unscrew the four crosshead screws securing the speedometer unit and housing to the instrument cluster body.

FIG. 13.49 LIFTING OUT THE SPEEDOMETER UNIT

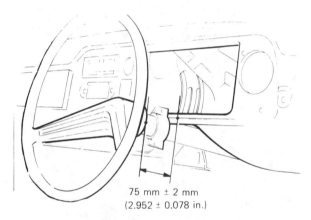

75 mm ± 2 mm
(2.952 ± 0.078 in.)

FIG. 13.50 STEERING COLUMN SETTING DIMENSION

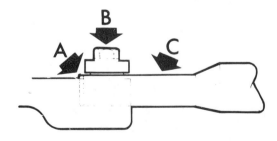

FIG. 13.51 LOCATION OF STEERING COLUMN SHAFT SEALING PLUG IN RELATION TO LOWER CLAMP PLATE

A - Sealing plug   B - Clamp plate   C– Steering column shaft

4 Disconnect the two speedometer illumination bulbs and holders.
5 Unscrew and remove the two slot-headed screws that retain the speedometer unit to the housing. Remove the speedometer unit (Fig. 13.49).
6 Refitting is a reversal of the removal sequence.

Speedometer cable inner and outer (1973 onwards) - removal and refitting
1 Open the bonnet and disconnect the battery.
2 Remove the instrument cluster and bezel as described in paragraphs 4, 5 and 6 of the second sub-Section of Section 5.
3 Refer to Chapter 10, Section 51, and carry out operations 1 to 6, inclusive.
4 Refitting the speedometer cable is the reverse of the removal procedure.

Fuel gauge (basic and L models, 1973 onwards) - removal and refitting
1 Open the bonnet and disconnect the battery.
2 Remove the instrument cluster and bezel, as described in paragraphs 4, 5 and 6 of the second sub-Section of Section 5.
3 Unscrew and remove the four screws that secure the instrument housing to the cluster body.
4 Unplug the illumination bulb and holder and remove the instrument housing.
5 Remove the two nuts and wave-washers from the gauge retaining studs and detach the fuel gauge.
6 Refitting is the reverse of the removal sequence.

Fuel gauge (XL model, 1973 onwards) - removal and refitting
1 Open the bonnet and disconnect the battery.
2 Remove the instrument cluster and bezel as described in paragraphs 4, 5 and 6 of the second sub-Section of Section 5.
3 Unplug the illumination bulb and holder from the tachometer housing.
4 Unscrew and remove the four tachometer housing retaining screws, and remove the tachometer and housing assembly.
5 Unplug the two speedometer illumination bulbs and holders.
6 Unscrew and remove the four speedometer retaining screws and remove the housing and speedometer head complete.
7 Remove the four retaining screws and remove the centre housing from the cluster body.
8 Unscrew and remove the nuts and wave-washers that retain the water temperature gauge and remove it.
9 Remove the two nuts and wave-washers retaining the fuel gauge and remove the gauge.
10 Refitting the fuel gauge is a reverse of the removal procedure.

Water temperature gauge (basic and L models 1973 onwards) - removal and refitting
1 Open the bonnet and disconnect the battery.
2 Remove the instrument cluster and bezel as described in paragraphs 4, 5 and 6 of the second sub-Section of Section 5.
3 Unscrew and remove the four screws that secure the instrument housing to the cluster body.
4 Unplug the illumination bulb and holder and remove the instruments and housing from the cluster body.
5 Remove the two nuts and wave-washers from the gauge retaining studs, and remove the water temperature gauge.
6 Refitting is the reverse of the removal procedure.

Water temperature gauge (XL model, 1973 onwards) - removal and refitting
    To remove the water temperature gauge carry out operations 1 to 8 inclusive, as for removal of the fuel gauge.

Cigar lighter (1973 onwards) - removal and refitting
1 Open the bonnet and disconnect the battery.
2 Remove the instrument cluster and bezel as described in paragraphs 4, 5 and 6 of the second sub-Section of Section 5.

3 From the rear of the instrument panel twist the bulb holder so that the cut-out in the holder aligns with the tab on the cigar lighter body. Remove the holder and spring and withdraw the body from its bezel location.

4 Refitting is a reverse of the removal procedure, but ensure that the illumination ring is correctly positioned on the cigar lighter body before inserting it into its panel location.

Ignition switch and lock (1973 onwards) - removal and refitting

1 Open the bonnet and disconnect the battery.
2 Remove the instrument cluster and bezel, as described in paragraphs 4, 5 and 6 of the second sub-Section of Section 5.
3 Unscrew and remove the dashpanel lower insulation panel.
4 Remove the two bolts which secure the wiper switch and light switch in position. Unplug the multi-connector and detach the switch assembly.
5 Pull off the section of air duct which passes across the steering column.
6 Remove the wiring harness block from the base of the ignition switch (two screws).
7 Unscrew and remove the clamp bolts from the steering column brackets both at the instrument panel and the foot pedal support. Allow the steering column to be lowered until it is supported by the steering wheel resting on the front seat squab.
8 Working within the engine compartment, bend back the locking tabs on the flexible coupling clamp plate. Slacken both bolts and then remove one of them and swing the clamp plate to one side.
9 Withdraw the steering column completely into the vehicle interior and then remove it.
10 Secure the steering column in a vice fitted with jaw protectors and drill out the two shear bolts which retain the two halves of the steering column lock to the column.
11 Commence reassembly by fitting the new lock to the steering column so that the lock tongue engages in the cut-out in the column. Tighten the bolts slightly more than finger-tight and check the operation of the lock by inserting the ignition key. Move the lock assembly fractionally if necessary to ensure smooth and positive engagement when the key is turned.
12 Fully tighten the bolts until the heads shear.
13 Refit the steering column, applying brake fluid to the lower floor pan seal if necessary to ease installation.
14 Before tightening the column clamp securing bolts move the steering column to achieve the dimension illustrated in Fig. 13.50. Tighten the bracket bolts to 15 lb f ft (2.1 kg f m).
15 Position the flexible coupling on the shaft, swing the plate into position and insert the bolt which was removed and then tighten both coupling bolts only finger-tight.
16 Check that the whole of the sealing plug in the end of the steering column shaft is exposed beyond the end of the lower clamp plate. Tighten the flexible coupling bolts and the clamp plate bolts to a torque of 15 lb f ft (2.1 kg f m). Bend up the clamp plate locking tabs (Fig. 13.51).
17 Refit all switches and other components.

Instrument cluster light switch (1973 onwards) - removal and refitting

1 Open the bonnet and disconnect the battery.
2 Remove the instrument cluster and bezel, as described in paragraphs 4, 5 and 6 of the second sub-Section of Section 5.
3 Pull the loom connections off the switch.
4 Unscrew the ring nut securing the switch body to the instrument panel and detach the switch from the panel (Fig. 13.52).
5 Refitting is the reverse of the removal procedure.

Hazard warning lights and heated rear window switches (1973 onwards) - removal and refitting

1 Open the bonnet and disconnect the battery.
2 Both switches are removed from the instrument panel by inserting a screwdriver at their lower edge and then levering them from their locations (Fig. 13.53).

3 Withdraw the switch far enough to permit the multi-plug to be disconnected.

Headlight flasher relay and horn relay (1973 onwards) - removal and refitting

1 Open the bonnet and disconnect the battery.
2 Both the headlight flasher relay and the horn relay are secured to the fender apron (Fig. 13.54) and can be removed by unscrewing the two crosshead screws that retain them.
3 To disconnect the headlight flasher relay pull the multi-plug

FIG. 13.52   UNSCREWING THE INSTRUMENT CLUSTER LIGHT SWITCH RING NUT

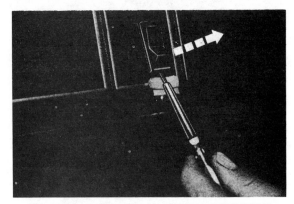

FIG. 13.53   REMOVING HAZARD LIGHT SWITCH

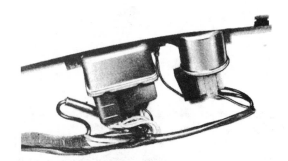

FIG. 13.54   THE HEADLAMP FLASHER RELAY AND THE HORN RELAY

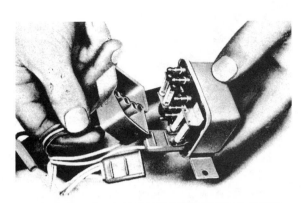

FIG. 13.55   REMOVING THE HEADLAMP FLASHER
RELAY FROM THE LOOM

and two double connectors from their respective terminals (Fig. 13.55).

4   To disconnect the horn relay simply pull it from the loom multi-connector.

5   Refitting of both units is the reverse of the removal procedure.

Heated rear window relay and flasher unit (1973 onwards) - removal and refitting

1   Open the bonnet and disconnect the battery.

2   Where applicable, unscrew and remove the package tray.

3   Unscrew and remove the dashpanel lower insulation panel and remove.

4   Remove the flasher unit assembly from its retaining clip on the bonnet release lever bracket, detach the multi-connector and remove the flasher unit.

5   Detach the relay from the bonnet release lever bracket by removing the two crosshead screws. The relay can then be disconnected from the multi-connector.

6   Refitting the heated rear window relay is the reverse of the removal procedure.

KEY TO WIRING DIAGRAM - BASIC AND L MODELS (1973 ONWARDS' UK MARKET)

1	Direction indicator, LH front
1a	Direction indicator, RH front
2	Headlamp, LH
2a	Headlamp, RH
3	Horn
4	Dipped relay
5	Ignition coil
6	Ballast resistance lead - ignition coil
7	Temperature gauge sender
8	Oil pressure switch
9	Distributor
10	Starter motor
11	Alternator
12	Switch - reversing light
13	Charging current regulator
14	Battery
15	Motor - windscreen wiper

16	Motor - heater blower
17	Fuse box
18	Flasher unit
19	Connection - heated rear window
20	Stop light switch
21	Door switch (LH)
21a	Door switch (RH)
22	Direction indicator switch
23	Light switch
24	Switch - windscreen wiper motor
25	Variable control (instrument illum)
26	Steering - ignition - starter lock
27	Instrument cluster
	1 Flasher pilot lamp (green)
	2 Main beam warning light (blue)
	3 Ignition warning light (red)

4	Oil pressure warning light (orange)
6	Water temperature gauge
7	Fuel gauge
9	Voltage stabilizer
12	Instrument lighting
28	Interior light
29	Headlamp flasher switch
30	Cigar lighter
31	Switch - heater blower
32	Glove compartment lamp
33	Switch - glove compartment lamp
34	Connection - heated rear window
35	Transmitter - fuel gauge
36	Tail lamp cluster (LH)
36a	Tail lamp cluster (RH)
37	Number plate lamp

Fuses

1	Interior lights, emergency flasher cigar lighter, clock, glove compartment lamp
2	Instrument lighting, number plate lamp
3	Side light RH, tail light RH

4	Side light LH, tail light LH
5	Motor-heater blower, horn, heated rear window
6	Windscreen wiper motor, reversing lamps, instrument cluster
7	Direction indicator light, stop light

8	Dipped beam (RH/LH)
9	Dipped beam (RH/LH)
10	Main beam (RH/LH)
11	Main beam (RH/LH)

sw	=	black	rs	=	pink	ge	=	yellow
ws	=	white	gn	=	green	bl	=	blue
rt	=	red						

gr	=	grey
br	=	brown
vi	=	violet

223

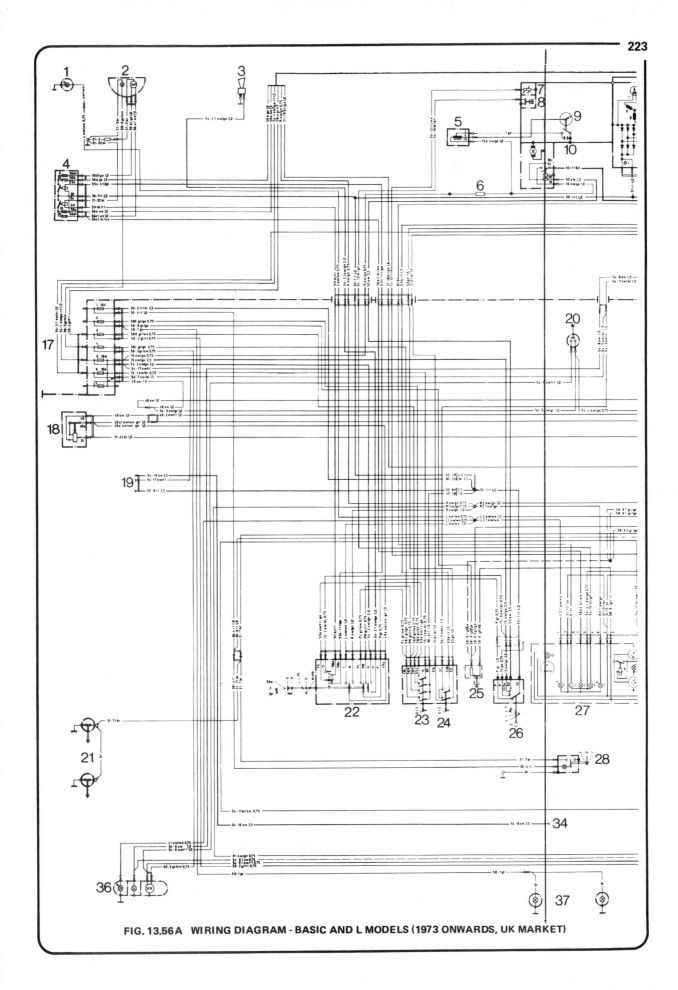

FIG. 13.56A WIRING DIAGRAM - BASIC AND L MODELS (1973 ONWARDS, UK MARKET)

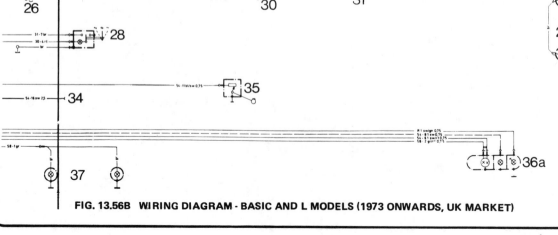

FIG. 13.56B WIRING DIAGRAM - BASIC AND L MODELS (1973 ONWARDS, UK MARKET)

KEY TO WIRING DIAGRAM - BASIC AND L MODELS (1973 ONWARDS EXPORT MODELS)

1 Direction indicator, LH front
1a Direction indicator, RH front
2 Headlamp LH
2a Headlamp RH
3 Direction indicator, LH side
3a Direction indicator, RH side
4 Dipped relay
5 Wiper motor, headlights
6 Windscreen and headlights washer motor

7 Transmitter, water temperature gauge
8 Oil pressure warning light
9 Distributor
10 Starter motor
11 Alternator
12 Fuse link wire
13 Battery
14 Alternator
15 Charging current regulator

16 Inhibitor switch, Auto. trans.
17 Relay, Auto. trans
18 Test switch, dual-circuit brake warning system
19 Fuse box
20 Flasher unit
21 Foot switch, headlights washer system
22 Fuse holder
23 Door switch, luggage compartment lamp
24 Steering- ignition - starter lock

25 Instrument cluster
26 Luggage compartment lamp
27 Selector dial
28 Fuse holder
29 Radio
30 Switch, dual-circuit brake warning system
31 Tail lamp cluster, LH
31a Tail lamp cluster, RH

illumination
3 Tail light, RH rear
4 Tail light, LH rear

7 Flasher unit
8 Main beam (LH/RH)
9 Main beam (LH/RH)

10 Dipped beam (LH/RH)
11 Dipped beam (LH/RH)
12 Headlamp washer system
13 Radio

Fuses

1 Luggage compartment lamp (cluster)
2 Reversing lamps, selector dial

Colour codes - Key

sw = black
ws = white
rt = red

rs = pink
gn = green

ge = yellow
bl = blue

gr = grey
br = brown
vi = violet

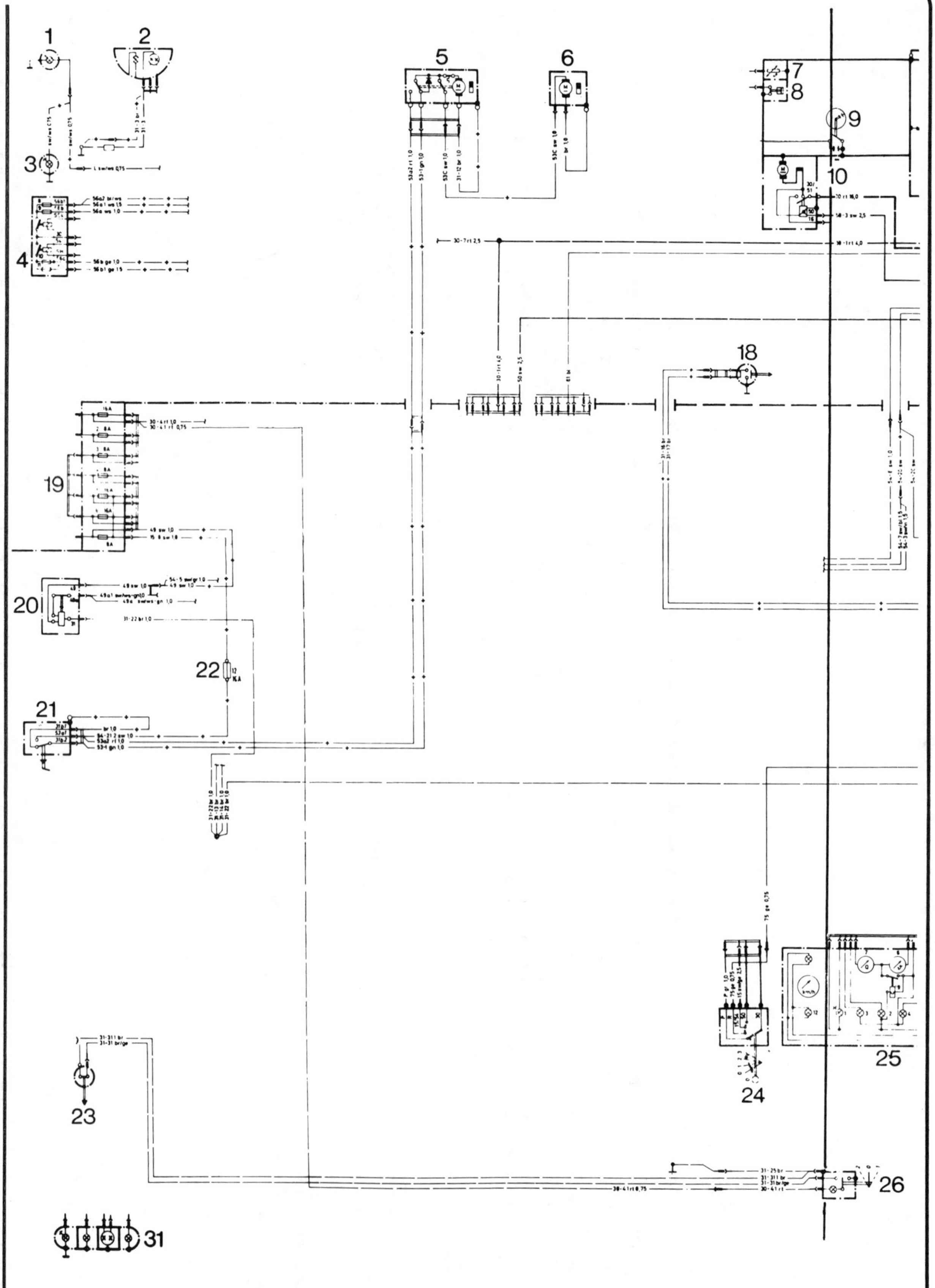

FIG. 13.57A   WIRING DIAGRAM - BASIC AND L MODELS (1973 ONWARDS, EXPORT MODELS)

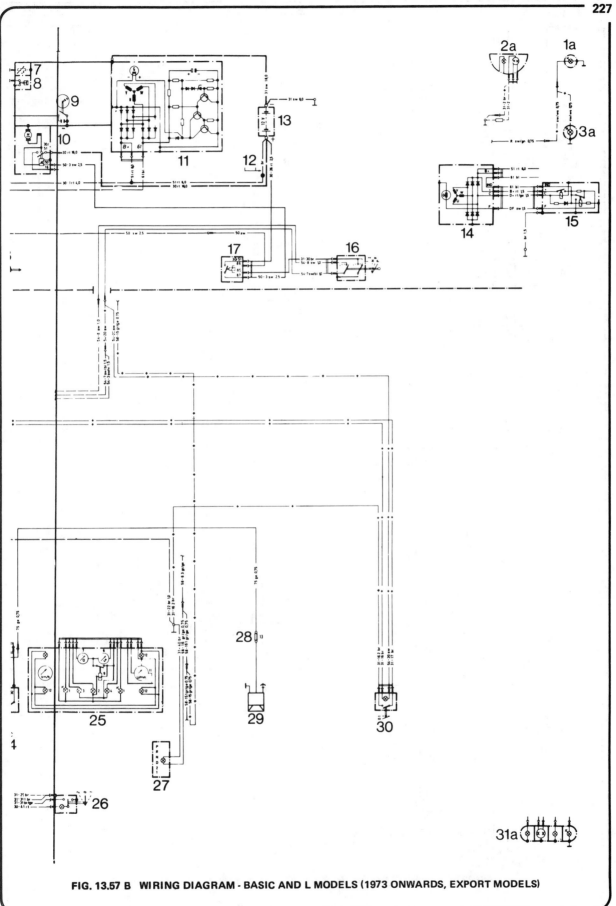

FIG. 13.57 B WIRING DIAGRAM - BASIC AND L MODELS (1973 ONWARDS, EXPORT MODELS)

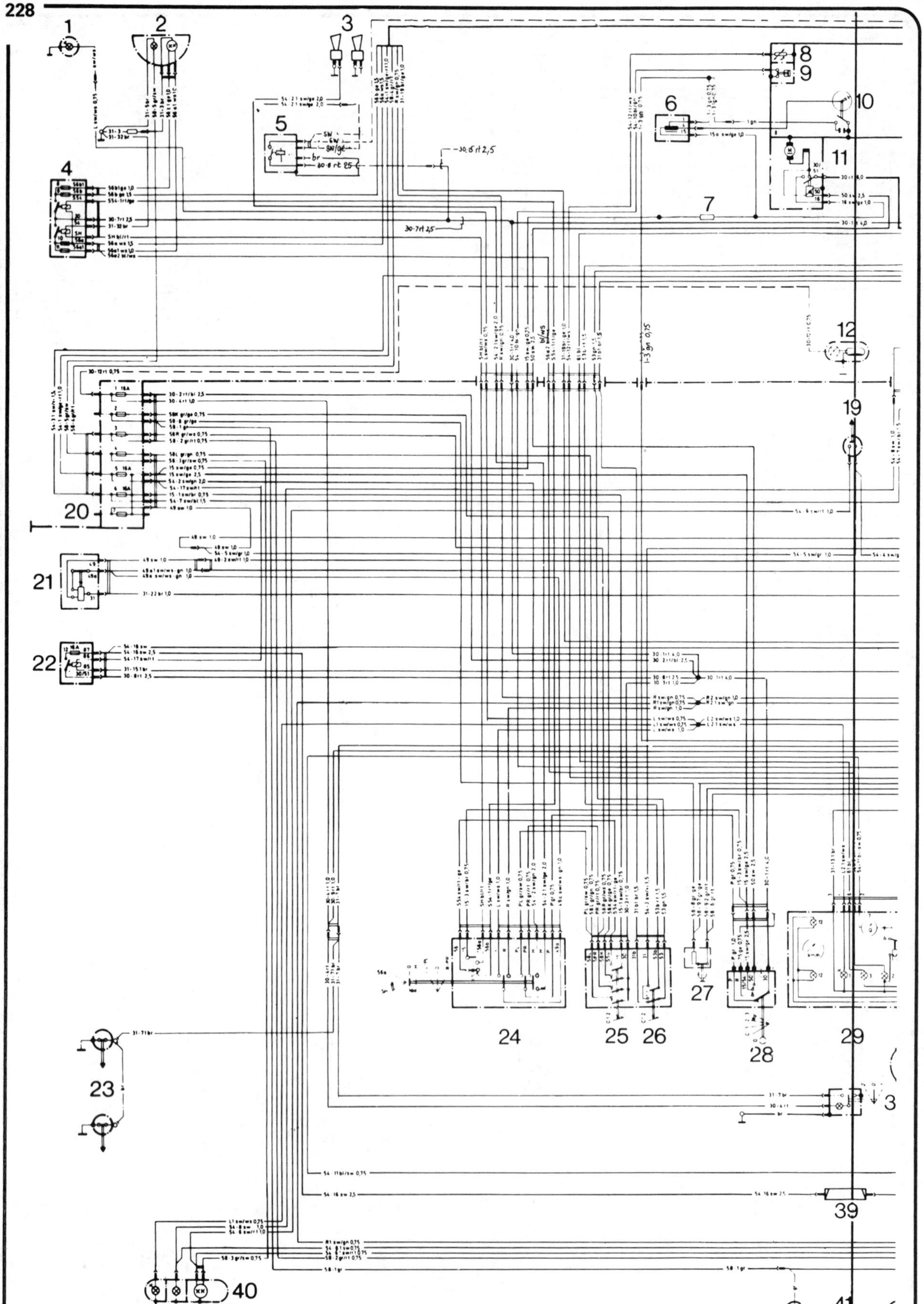

FIG 13.58A WIRING DIAGRAM - XL MODEL (1973 ONWARDS, UK MARKET)

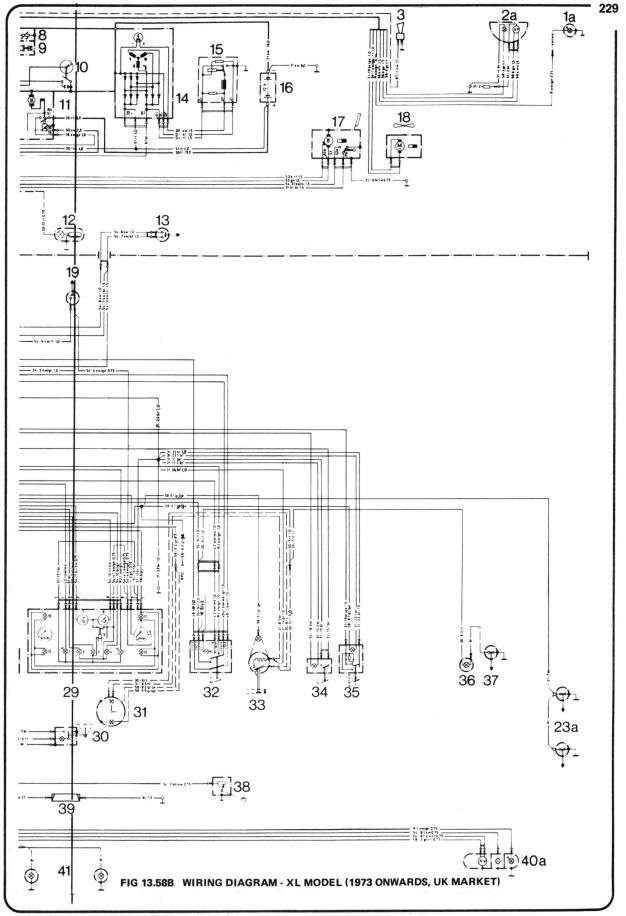

FIG 13.58B WIRING DIAGRAM - XL MODEL (1973 ONWARDS, UK MARKET)

KEY TO WIRING DIAGRAM - XL MODELS (1973 ONWARDS, UK MARKET)

1 Direction indicator, LH front
1a Direction indicator, RH front
2 Headlamp LH
2a Headlamp RH
3 Horn
4 Dipping relay
5 Two-tone horn relay
6 Ignition coil
7 Ballast resistance lead - ignition coil
8 Transmitter - water temperature gauge
9 Oil pressure switch
10 Distributor
11 Starter motor
12 Engine compartment lamp
13 Switch - reversing lamp
14 Alternator
15 Charging current regulator
16 Battery
17 Wiper motor
18 Motor - heater blower
19 Stop light switch
20 Fuse box
21 Flasher unit
22 Relay - heated rear window
23 Door switch (LH)
23a Door switch (RH)
24 Flasher switch
25 Light switch
26 Switch - wiper motor
27 Variable control (instrument illum.)
28 Steering - ignition - starter lock
29 Instrument cluster
1 Instrument pilot light (green)
2 Main beam warning lamp (blue)
3 Ignition warning light (red)
4 Oil pressure warning light (orange)
6 Water temperature gauge
7 Fuel gauge
9 Voltage stabilizer
11 Tachometer
30 Interior lamp
31 Clock
32 Emergency flasher switch
33 Cigar lighter
34 Switch - heated rear window
35 Switch - heater blower
36 Glove compartment lamp
37 Switch - glove compartment
38 Heated rear window
39 Transmitter - fuel gauge
40 Tail lamp cluster (LH)
40a Tail lamp cluster (RH)
41 Number plate lamp
12 Lighting, instruments

Fuses

1 Interior lamp, emergency flasher, cigar lighter, clock, glove compartment lamp
2 Instrument lighting, number plate lamps
3 Side light RH, tail light RH
4 Side light LH, tail light LH
5 Motor-heater blower, horn, heated rear window
6 Wiper motor, reversing lamps, instrument cluster
7 Flasher light, stop light

(Dipping relay)
8 Dipped beam (LH/RH)
9 Dipped beam (LH/RH)
10 Main beam (LH/RH)
11 Main beam (LH/RH)
12 Heated window (live)

Colour codes - Key

sw = black
ws = white
rt = red
rs = pink
gn = green
ge = yellow
bl = blue
gr = grey
br = brown
vi = violet

KEY TO WIRING DIAGRAMS, XL MODELS (1973 ONWARDS, EXPORT MODELS)

1	Direction indicator, LH front
1a	Direction indicator, RH front
2	Headlamp LH
2a	Headlamp RH
3	Direction indicator LH side
3a	Direction indicator RH side
4	Wiper motor, headlights
5	Windscreen and headlights washer pump
6	Charging current regulator
7	Generator
8	Transmitter - water temperature gauge thermometer
9	Oil pressure switch
10	Distributor
11	Starter motor
12	Ignition coil
13	Battery
14	Fuse link wire (for alternator only)
15	Starter solenoid
16	Starter motor
17	Alternator
18	Charging current regulator
19	Inhibitor switch - Auto. trans.
20	Relay - Auto. trans.
21	Test switch - dual-circuit brake warning system
22	Dipping relay
23	Fuse box
24	Flasher unit
25	Fuse holder
26	Relay - heated rear window
27	Foot switch - headlight washer system
28	Door switch - boot lamp
29	Steering - ignition - starter lock
30	Heated rear window
31	Instrument cluster
32	Luggage compartment lamp
33	Selector dial
34	Fuse holder
35	Radio
36	Switch - heated rear window
37	Switch - dual-circuit brake system
38	Tail lamp cluster (LH)
38a	Tail lamp cluster (RH)

Fuses

1	Luggage compartment lamp (cluster)
2	Reversing lamps - selector dial illum.
3	Tail light, RH rear
4	Tail light, LH rear
5	Heated rear window
6	Flasher unit
8	Straight beam (LH/RH)
9	Straight beam (LH/RH)
10	Dipped beam (LH/RH)1
11	Dipped beam (LH/RH)
12	Headlight washer system
13	Radio
14	Heated rear window

Colour codes - Key

sw	=	black	rs	=	pink
ws	=	white	gn	=	green
rt	=	red	ge	=	yellow
			bl	=	blue
gr	=	grey			
br	=	brown			
vi	=	violet			

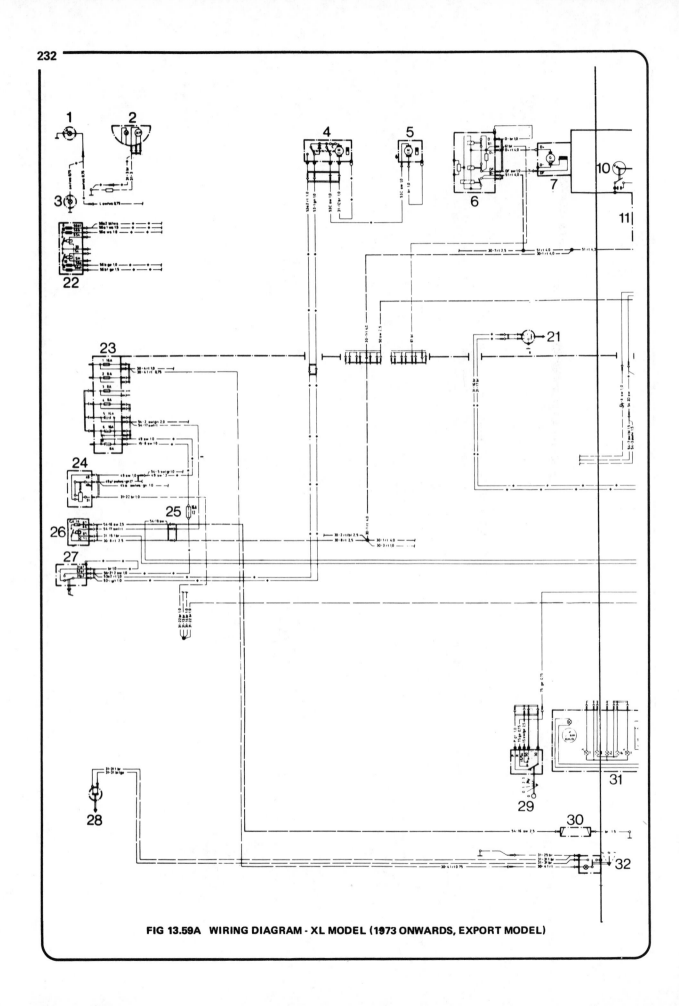

FIG 13.59A WIRING DIAGRAM - XL MODEL (1973 ONWARDS, EXPORT MODEL)

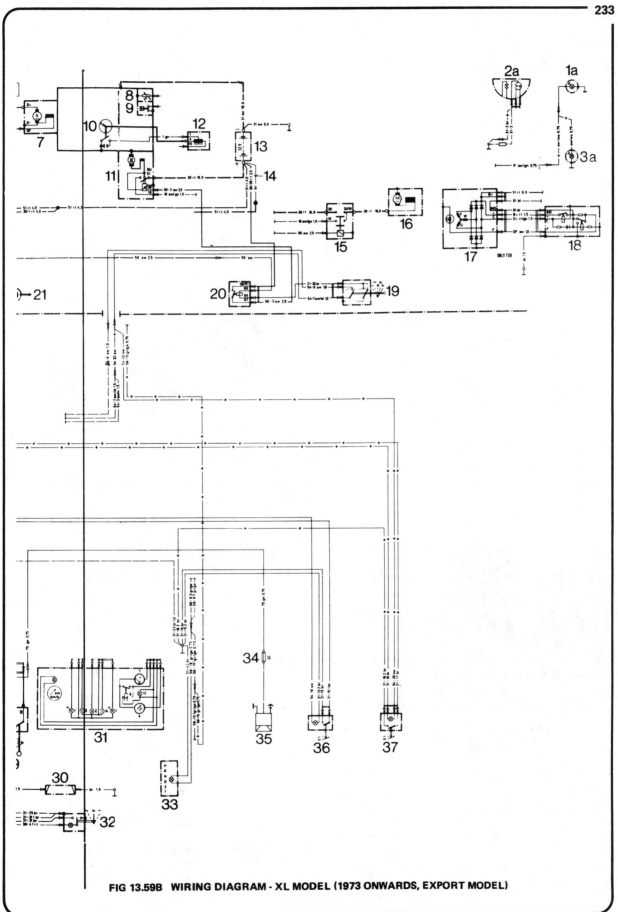

FIG 13.59B WIRING DIAGRAM - XL MODEL (1973 ONWARDS, EXPORT MODEL)

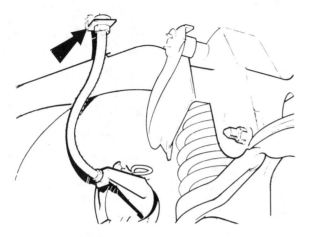

FIG 13.60   A FRONT FLEXIBLE BRAKE HOSE

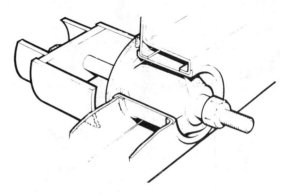

FIG 13.61   REMOVING A FRONT AXLE MOUNTING BUSH

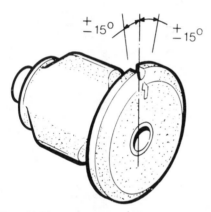

FIG 13.62   FRONT AXLE MOUNTING BUSH ALIGNMENT MARK

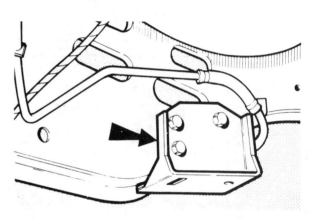

FIG 13.63   FRONT STABILIZER BAR BRACKETS

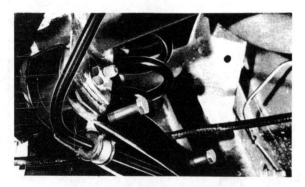

FIG 13.64   REAR STABILIZER BAR TO LOWER RADIUS ARM MOUNTING

10 Suspension and steering

General description

The suspension and steering remains basically similar to that of the early models. From late 1973 there have been changes to components of the front suspension. These include the following:

    (i)   *Front subframe to body insulators of increased diameter.*

    (ii)   *Front brake lines no longer located on crossmember.*
    (iii)   *Re-designed lower arm inner pivot bush and bolt.*
    (iv)   *Re-designed front tie-bar mountings.*
    (v)   *Re-designed stabilizer bar mounting brackets.*
    (vi)   *Bolt-on type bump stop rubber cushions.*

A stabiliser bar is now fitted to the rear suspension. Vehicles built after early 1972 have modified rear axle mountings to permit adjustment of the pinion drive angle (see Section 7, this Chapter).

Front axle assembly - removal and refitting

1   Carry out the operations described in paragraphs 1, 2 and 3, Section 5, Chapter 11.
2   Disconnect the flexible brake hoses at the body support brackets (Fig. 13.60).
3   Carry out the operations described in paragraphs 5, 6, 7, 8 and 9, Section 5, Chapter 11.

Front axle mounting bushes - removal and refitting

Removal and refitting of the front axle mounting bushes is as described in Section 7, Chapter 11. However, new bushes must be fitted so that the arrows are in alignment with the indentation in the bodyframe. The flange position of the bushes must be: *front bush,* flange located *inside* sidemember; *rear bush,* flange located *outside* sidemember (Figs. 13.61 and 13.62).

Stabilizer bar - removal and refitting

Removal and refitting is as described in Section 10, Chapter 11, but modified stabilizer bar brackets are fitted to clear the crossmember (Fig. 13.63).

Rear suspension and rear axle - removal and refitting

Removal of the rear suspension and rear axle is identical to the procedure given in Section 15, Chapter 11, but the pinion drive angle must be checked, and if necessary adjusted, as described in Section 7 of this Chapter.

Rear suspension upper radius arm - removal and refitting

1　Carry out the operations described in paragraphs 1, 2 and 3, Section 16, Chapter 11.
2　Disconnect the stabilizer bar from the radius arm that is to be removed and swing it to one side.
3　Jack-up the rear axle so that the shock absorber can be disconnected from the axle mounting.
4　Lower the jack and press the coil spring from its upper retainer. Now twist the spring from its lower retainer.
5　Again jack-up the rear axle and having relieved the radius arm bolts of any strain, remove the bolts and withdraw the radius arm.
6　Proceed as described in paragraphs 4, 5 and 6, Section 16, Chapter 11.

Rear suspension lower radius arm - removal and refitting

1　Carry out the operations described in paragraphs 1, 2 and 3, in Section 17, Chapter 11.
2　Disconnect the stabilizer bar from the radius arm and swing it to one side.
3　Jack-up the rear axle and disconnect the shock absorber lower mounting.
4　Lower the jack and press the coil spring from the upper retainer. Twist the spring from the lower retainer.
5　Remove the radius arm pivot bolts and withdraw the arm.
6　Proceed as described in paragraphs 4, 5 and 6, Section 17, Chapter 11.

Rear stabilizer bar - removal and refitting

1　Remove the bolts which secure each end of the stabilizer bar to the radius arms (Fig. 13.64).
2　Unscrew the self-locking nuts and withdraw the front and rear mounting brackets together with the insulating bushes (Fig. 13.65).
3　Bushes are renewed in a similar manner to those for the shock absorbers, by first removing the metal spacer. The use of a little brake fluid will facilitate installation of the rubber bush.

Steering column assembly (July 1973 onwards) - removal and refitting

1　Disconnect the battery and then, working within the engine compartment, bend back the locktabs on the flexible coupling clamp plate. Slacken both bolts, extract one and swing the clamp plate to one side.
2　Unscrew and remove the steering column lower shroud and remove it, then unclip the upper shroud.
3　Pull off the instrument panel light switch knob and the radio control knobs.
4　Remove the six screws which retain the instrument cluster and bezel. Pull the bezel far enough forward to enable the multi-pin connectors to be disconnected at the rear of the instruments. Also disconnect the leads from the cigar lighter, the hazard warning switch and the heated rear window switch and the speedometer cable.
5　Unscrew and remove the dash lower insulation panel.
6　Remove the two bolts which secure the wiper and light switch, disconnect the multi-pin connector and remove the switch.
7　Remove the section of air duct which passes over the steering column.
8　Remove the two screws which secure the wiring harness plug to the bottom of the ignition switch.
9　Remove the upper and lower steering column bracket bolts, lower the column and then withdraw it through the vehicle interior.
10　Refitting is a reversal of the removal procedure but great care must be taken to align the column, as described in Section 9 of this Chapter.

Steering column shaft - removal and refitting

It is not recommended that the steering column is dismantled. In the event of wear occurring, a new column assembly should be fitted.

---

11 Bodywork and fittings

Door trim (1973 onwards) - removal and refitting

1　Unscrew and remove the remote lock button.
2　Remove the three crosshead countersunk screws, which retain the wood capping, and detach the capping (Fig. 13.66).

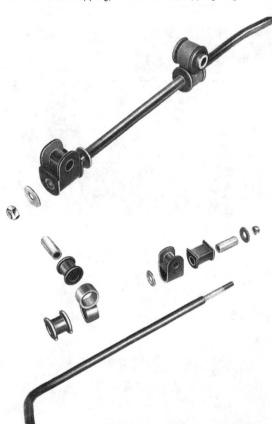

FIG 13.65　REAR STABILIZER BAR MOUNTING COMPONENTS

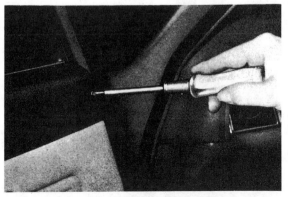

FIG 13.66　REMOVING WOOD CAPPING

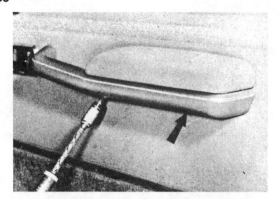

FIG 13.67 REMOVING A DOOR ARMREST

FIG 13.68 UNSCREWING A WINDOW WINDER HANDLE

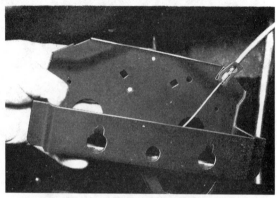

FIG 13.69 BONNET RELEASE LEVER BRACKET

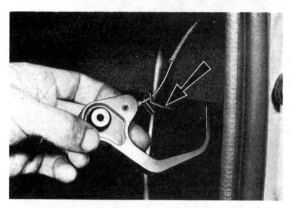

FIG. 13.70 BONNET RELEASE LEVER (RECTANGULAR HEADLAMPS)

FIG 13.71 RADIATOR GRILLE SCREW LOCATIONS (CIRCULAR HEADLAMP)

FIG 13.72 RADIATOR GRILLE SCREW LOCATIONS

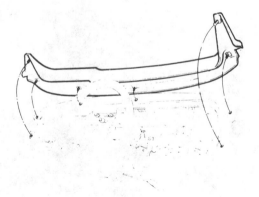

FIG. 13.73 CRASH PAD SECURING POINTS

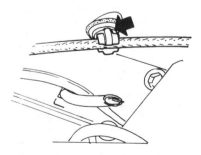

FIG 13.74 SPEEDOMETER CABLE SECURING CLIP

3 To remove the armrest, remove the two crosshead retaining screws. Rotate the armrest through 90° on the forward mounted stud and pull out from the door (Fig. 13.67).

4 Unclip the chrome and black surround of the door catch release lever and detach.

5 Carefully prise out the black plastic insert from the window winder. Unscrew and remove the single retaining crosshead screw and detach the winder handle (Fig. 13.68).

6 Ensure that your hands are clean so as not to soil the door trim, then remove the trim by gripping the outer edge of the panel and carefully pulling it away from the door body. Work round the trim panel edge, unclipping the retaining clips until the trim panel is clear of the door body.

7 Refitting is a straightforward reversal of the removal procedure.

Bonnet release cable (July 1973 onwards) - removal and refitting

1 Remove the parcel tray.

2 Remove the dash lower instrument panel (see Section 5).

3 Detach the direction indicator flasher unit and the heated rear window relay from their mountings (See Section 9).

4 Through the holes in the side of the bonnet release lever bracket, insert a screwdriver and unscrew the bracket securing screws (Fig. 13.69).

5 Remove the bracket and disengage the bonnet release cable.

6 Remove the radiator grille and disconnect the cable from the bonnet lock and extract the cable from its securing clips. Withdraw the cable into the vehicle interior.

7 The bonnet release lever is retained by a pivot pin and circlip and the cable is secured to the lever with a tension pin.

8 Installation is the reverse of the removal procedure.

Radiator grille (circular headlamp) - removal and refitting

1 For safety reasons, disconnect the battery.

2 Radiator grille removal is as described in Section 32, Chapter 12, but the grille is now retained by ten screws and flat washers; the two screws nearest the headlamps secure the headlamp bezel (Fig. 13.71).

Radiator grille (rectangular headlamp) - removal and refitting

1 For safety reasons, disconnect the battery.

2 Remove the screws and flat washers as shown in (Fig. 13.72).

3 Refitting is the reverse of the removal procedure.

Instrument panel crash padding - removal and refitting

1 Disconnect the battery.

2 Remove the steering column shroud and pull off the instrument panel light switch knob (see Section 5).

3 Remove the instrument bezel (six screws) and pull it forward so that all electrical leads, plugs and the speedometer cable can be disconnected. Remove the bezel (see Section 5).

4 Remove the glove compartment lock striker.

5 Remove the glove compartment securing screws, pull the assembly forward, disconnect the lamp leads and remove the assembly.

6 Remove the air vent surround (passenger side) and then remove the two exposed air vent securing screws and pull the vent from the facia so that the hose can be disconnected from it.

7 Access to the crash pad securing nuts can now be obtained through the glove compartment aperture. Installation is the reverse of the removal procedure (Fig. 13.73).

Centre console - removal and refitting

Removal of the centre console is described in paragraphs 2 and 3 of the first sub-Section of Section 5.

Heater assembly - removal and refitting

Removal and refitting is as described in Section 34, of Chapter 12 but on later models the speedometer drive cable

must be disconnected from the clip on the heater assembly (Fig. 13.74).

Heater controls - removal and refitting

1 Disconnect the battery leads.

2 Remove the parcel tray from the transmission tunnel.

3 Remove the cowl trim (five screws) (Fig. 13.75).

4 Remove the steering column shroud (see Section 5).

5 Remove the instrument cluster and bezel (see Section 5).

6 Disconnect the now accessible heater controls from the operating levers of the heater unit and then remove the heater control assembly (three screws) (Fig. 13.76).

7 Should the resistance unit be defective, it can be renewed by drilling out the rivets (Fig. 13.77).

8 Refitting is the reverse of the removal procedure but check for correct operation of the controls before refitting the instrument assembly.

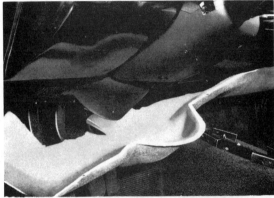

FIG. 13.75 REMOVING THE COWL TRIM

FIG 13.76 HEATER CONTROL CONNECTIONS

FIG 13.77 LOCATION OF RESISTANCE ON HEATER

Conversion factors

Length (distance)
Inches (in)	X 25.4	= Millimetres (mm)	X 0.039	= Inches (in)
Feet (ft)	X 0.305	= Metres (m)	X 3.281	= Feet (ft)
Miles	X 1.609	= Kilometres (km)	X 0.621	= Miles

Volume (capacity)
Cubic inches (cu in; in³)	X 16.387	= Cubic centimetres (cc; cm³)	X 0.061	= Cubic inches (cu in; in³)
Imperial pints (Imp pt)	X 0.568	= Litres (l)	X 1.76	= Imperial pints (Imp pt)
Imperial quarts (Imp qt)	X 1.137	= Litres (l)	X 0.88	= Imperial quarts (Imp qt)
Imperial quarts (Imp qt)	X 1.201	= US quarts (US qt)	X 0.833	= Imperial quarts (Imp qt)
US quarts (US qt)	X 0.946	= Litres (l)	X 1.057	= US quarts (US qt)
Imperial gallons (Imp gal)	X 4.546	= Litres (l)	X 0.22	= Imperial gallons (Imp gal)
Imperial gallons (Imp gal)	X 1.201	= US gallons (US gal)	X 0.833	= Imperial gallons (Imp gal)
US gallons (US gal)	X 3.785	= Litres (l)	X 0.264	= US gallons (US gal)

Mass (weight)
Ounces (oz)	X 28.35	= Grams (g)	X 0.035	= Ounces (oz)
Pounds (lb)	X 0.454	= Kilograms (kg)	X 2.205	= Pounds (lb)

Force
Ounces-force (ozf; oz)	X 0.278	= Newtons (N)	X 3.6	= Ounces-force (ozf; oz)
Pounds-force (lbf; lb)	X 4.448	= Newtons (N)	X 0.225	= Pounds-force (lbf; lb)
Newtons (N)	X 0.1	= Kilograms-force (kgf; kg)	X 9.81	= Newtons (N)

Pressure
Pounds-force per square inch (psi; lbf/in²; lb/in²)	X 0.070	= Kilograms-force per square centimetre (kgf/cm²; kg/cm²)	X 14.223	= Pounds-force per square inch (psi; lbf/in²; lb/in²)
Pounds-force per square inch (psi; lbf/in²; lb/in²)	X 0.068	= Atmospheres (atm)	X 14.696	= Pounds-force per square inch (psi; lbf/in²; lb/in²)
Pounds-force per square inch (psi; lbf/in²; lb/in²)	X 0.069	= Bars	X 14.5	= Pounds-force per square inch (psi; lbf/in²; lb/in²)
Pounds-force per square inch (psi; lbf/in²; lb/in²)	X 6.895	= Kilopascals (kPa)	X 0.145	= Pounds-force per square inch (psi; lbf/in²; lb/in²)
Kilopascals (kPa)	X 0.01	= Kilograms-force per square centimetre (kgf/cm²; kg/cm²)	X 98.1	= Kilopascals (kPa)

Torque (moment of force)
Pounds-force inches (lbf in; lb in)	X 1.152	= Kilograms-force centimetre (kgf cm; kg cm)	X 0.868	= Pounds-force inches (lbf in; lb in)
Pounds-force inches (lbf in; lb in)	X 0.113	= Newton metres (Nm)	X 8.85	= Pounds-force inches (lbf in; lb in)
Pounds-force inches (lbf in; lb in)	X 0.083	= Pounds-force feet (lbf ft; lb ft)	X 12	= Pounds-force inches (lbf in; lb in)
Pounds-force feet (lbf ft; lb ft)	X 0.138	= Kilograms-force metres (kgf m; kg m)	X 7.233	= Pounds-force feet (lbf ft; lb ft)
Pounds-force feet (lbf ft; lb ft)	X 1.356	= Newton metres (Nm)	X 0.738	= Pounds-force feet (lbf ft; lb ft)
Newton metres (Nm)	X 0.102	= Kilograms-force metres (kgf m; kg m)	X 9.804	= Newton metres (Nm)

Power
Horsepower (hp)	X 745.7	= Watts (W)	X 0.0013	= Horsepower (hp)

Velocity (speed)
Miles per hour (miles/hr; mph)	X 1.609	= Kilometres per hour (km/hr; kph)	X 0.621	= Miles per hour (miles/hr; mph)

Fuel consumption*
Miles per gallon, Imperial (mpg)	X 0.354	= Kilometres per litre (km/l)	X 2.825	= Miles per gallon, Imperial (mpg)
Miles per gallon, US (mpg)	X 0.425	= Kilometres per litre (km/l)	X 2.352	= Miles per gallon, US (mpg)

Temperature

Degrees Fahrenheit (°F) $= (°C \times \frac{9}{5}) + 32$

Degrees Celsius (Degrees Centigrade; °C) $= (°F - 32) \times \frac{5}{9}$

*It is common practice to convert from miles per gallon (mpg) to litres/100 kilometres (l/100km), where mpg (Imperial) x l/100 km = 282 and mpg (US) x l/100 km = 235

Index

Printed by
Haynes Publishing Group
Sparkford Yeovil Somerset
England